PRESENT IMPERFECT

Present Imperfect

Contemporary South African Writing

ANDREW VAN DER VLIES

OXFORD
UNIVERSITY PRESS

OXFORD
UNIVERSITY PRESS

Great Clarendon Street, Oxford, OX2 6DP,
United Kingdom

Oxford University Press is a department of the University of Oxford.
It furthers the University's objective of excellence in research, scholarship,
and education by publishing worldwide. Oxford is a registered trade mark of
Oxford University Press in the UK and in certain other countries

First Edition published in 2017
Impression: 4

Published in the United States of America by Oxford University Press
198 Madison Avenue, New York, NY 10016, United States of America

British Library Cataloguing in Publication Data
Data available

Library of Congress Control Number: 2016958127

ISBN 978–0–19–879376–2

Printed and bound by
CPI Group (UK) Ltd, Croydon, CR0 4YY

For my mother and for Patrick,
and in memory of my father.

Preface

Present Imperfect is a study of affect, temporality, and form in writing from postapartheid South Africa. Put another way, this book explores how contemporary literature, for the most part fiction, from one of late-twentieth-century history's most affectively charged locations—stage for the spectacle of dehumanizing racial discrimination, site and occasion for vicarious global investments in the performance of struggle, liberation, and reconciliation—engages with the aftermath of apartheid.

South Africans had much to celebrate on the occasion of the first democratic, universal-suffrage elections in late April 1994, the culmination of a long struggle against centuries of colonial and subsequently white-minority rule that had made apartheid a byword for racism. There were great expectations for the multi-racial democracy that Desmond Tutu memorably named the 'Rainbow Nation'. Hopes were high that this decolonization would be different, that it would not devolve, as it had done elsewhere in Africa, into a version of what had come before, that (as Neil Lazarus put it) '*our* national liberation front would not serve, once it became the party in power after decolonization, to cover over its traces and disavow both its heritage and its historic responsibility; *our* leaders, our "men of the people" (and "women of the people") would not become, as elsewhere on the continent, the puppets of international capital'.[1]

And yet, perhaps inevitably, much of the hopefulness of the early post-transition years has faded. South Africans now find themselves, in Achille Mbembe's diagnosis, mired in 'the bloody miasma of the Zuma years, these years of stagnation, rent-seeking and mediocrity parading as leadership, [. . .] as institutions after institutions crumble under the weight of corruption, a predatory new black élite and the cynicism of former oppressors'.[2] If the poor hoped that the Age of Zuma might yield more than had accrued to them through the Mandela and Mbeki (and Motlanthe) administrations' accommodations with neoliberal economics, they were to be further disappointed. Indeed, it might be said that life in the postapartheid nation has come to be characterized, for many, by a profound experience of disappointment—disappointment that the liberation struggle failed to deliver the equality of opportunity and shared access to the country's wealth that was promised, that the price paid by many for reconciliation, a guiding principle of Nelson Mandela's presidency, may have been too high.

Similar bad feelings can of course be read into South African history and in the literature that explores its lived experience from the moment of first contact—in relation to promises to autochthonous peoples betrayed by European settlers, through proto-Afrikaner reactions to British hegemony (the end of slaveholding, the annexation of the Dutch Republics, the Boer War), to the despair, grief, and outrage of black South Africans, denied their land in the wake of the Natives Land Act in 1913 and their dignity under the dehumanizing apartheid laws enacted after 1948. Varieties of disappointment and the dysphoric feelings associated therewith thus have a past in South Africa; all involve feeling trapped in an imperfect present that is not as the future was imagined, a present beyond which it might be a struggle to see.

This book develops from my sense that disappointment is a significant structure of feeling in contemporary South Africa. This is an observation neither new nor singular (disappointment is in the air), but there is something a little different this time around, I believe. If disappointment is a structuring affect, I argue, it should also be understood as a temporal condition. As feeling, in the sense of the term that is most familiar, disappointment connotes the frustration of the expectation of—and desire for—something different.[3] In this sense, South Africans are disappointed because their leaders are corrupt, inequalities persist, and the gap between rich and poor grows each year. However, in a meaning now obsolete, but close to that of undoing or frustrating something determined or appointed, to disappoint once also meant 'to fail to keep or comply with (an engagement); to fail to fulfil an appointment'.[4] South Africans exist in this *temporal* state of disappointment—or dis-appointment—because they have missed the appointment they were promised with a better future, with democracy and the promise of equality, the putative fruits of revolution. That they were led to believe that the appointment had been kept, the claim implicit in the presentation of the country as wholly 'New', as an unprecedented 'Rainbow Nation', makes postapartheid disappointment (and all of its associated bad feelings) distinctive.

Present Imperfect does not track the representation of a uniformly expressed or understood affect or experience, nor are the works about which I write representative of the same shared sense of disappointment, either as bad feeling or missed appointment. Disappointment serves instead to focus and direct my engagement with a range of negative feelings that are also experiences of temporal disjuncture, including stasis, impasse, boredom, disaffection, and nostalgia. I use disappointment as a category description, emphasizing variously its suggestions of affective or temporal dislocation as the works in question, and their cultural contexts, demand. As such, what the chapters that follow offer is a cohesive approach rather than a single argument.

Attuned to the sometimes elusive workings of the writerly, *Present Imperfect* asks what thinking about affect and temporality together might unlock for the reader, the scholar, and the student of present-day South African writing, and of postcolonial and contemporary world literature more broadly. It addresses key questions in South African studies about the evolving character of the historical period in which the country now finds itself: the long transition that has followed the end of apartheid. It also looks outward, making a case for the key place of South African writing in global conversations. It does this both by following intertextual conversations that the works under discussion themselves frequently pursue, and by testing the usefulness of conceptual frames not frequently considered in the study of South African writing. I am interested in what the payoffs might be when we follow these already global conversations and read 'local' literary works with (or alongside) such global frames. One payoff is that mobilizing the energies of a turn to affect in recent literary and cultural-studies scholarship allows us to understand as political those feelings—and especially *bad* feelings—that might otherwise seem merely personal or private. Rather than a sign of its evacuation, these feelings index a potential to *reinvigorate* the political. Another payoff is to understand how literature, and especially the novel, might provide spaces in which imaginative openings out of the present uncertain aftermath of the end of apartheid are made visible.

This book traces such openings in work by key fiction writers of the contemporary moment, specifically J.M. Coetzee, Marlene van Niekerk, Ivan Vladislavić, Zoë Wicomb, and Ingrid Winterbach, as well as in the last work of the late Nadine Gordimer and in debut novels by younger writers Songeziwe Mahlangu and Masande Ntshanga. Several of these authors (Coetzee, Gordimer) have established international reputations; some (Wicomb, Vladislavić, Van Niekerk) have rising profiles; others (Winterbach, Mahlangu, Ntshanga) are still relatively unknown outside of South Africa. Van Niekerk and Winterbach both write in Afrikaans, and in discussing their work I hope to aid the expansion of the canon of contemporary South African writing visible to international anglophone readers. I mobilize readings of writing marked in various ways as 'South African' but which also contest such labels in order to complicate the contours of 'World Literature' as it is developing in the present moment—as category, discipline, and pedagogy. What South African writers have to say continues to reverberate in a world that becomes, perversely, more like the country every year: more unequal, but also concerned with the legacies—and in some cases the resurgence—of restrictive and exclusionary ideologies, and at the whim of non-state actors and speculative capital. This is, in consequence, also a book about the discontents of neoliberalism, about the political energies of reading, and about the fates of literature in our troubled present.

Acknowledgements

I have incurred many debts during the period it has taken for this book to find its shape. I am grateful to audiences at events at which I presented versions of a number of chapters, or indeed material that has not found a way into the book but informed its general direction: in South Africa, at the Universities of Cape Town, Rhodes, Stellenbosch, the Western Cape, and the Witwatersrand; at Stockholm University in Sweden; in the United Kingdom, at Postcolonial Seminars at Cambridge and Oxford Universities and at events at King's College London, Queen Margaret University in Edinburgh, and University College London; in the United States, at Ithaca College, the Latitudes seminar group and a colloquium at the University of Pennsylvania, ACLA convention gatherings at Brown, New York, and Harvard Universities, and several MLA panels. My thanks to facilitators, especially Aaron Bartels-Swindells, Elleke Boehmer, Sarah Brouillette, Patricia Hayes, Stefan Helgesson, Christopher Holmes, Ankhi Mukherjee, Sarah Nuttall, Ruvani Ranasinha, Graham Riach, Deborah Seddon, Pieter Vermeulen, Chris Warnes, and Sandy Young. For especially productive responses at these events, I am grateful to Patrick Hayes, Pramesh Lalu, Suvir Kaul, Lily Saint, Paul Saint-Amour, Ross Truscott, Hedley Twidle, Michael Wessels, and Hermann Wittenberg.

My mentors and interlocutors have been many, but amongst them Peter D. McDonald and Rita Barnard deserve special thanks. Peter, my erstwhile doctoral supervisor, has continued in the years since as staunch supporter and wise counsel; I thank him for useful feedback on Chapter 2. Rita's work has been a model of insightful reading and elegant writing and her collegiality as a co-convenor of ACLA seminars and co-editor of *Safundi* has taught me much about scholarly generosity. I am grateful to her for reading the manuscript in its near-final state. Other readers who deserve thanks include Brenna Munro, who made suggestions about some of my queer framings, Rebecca Walkowitz, whose ear for argument proved helpful at a critical juncture, and Derek Attridge and Stephen Clingman, for very welcome advice. The Press's two readers helped to make this a better book; its deficiencies remain my own. Thanks also to David Attwell, Neville Hoad, Mark Sanders, and Jennifer Wenzel, for scholarship that has been enabling.

I am indebted to the authors whose work I discuss in this book for their assistance or tolerance of my interest: John Coetzee, Songeziwe Mahlangu,

Masande Ntshanga, Marlene van Niekerk, Ivan Vladislavić, Zoë Wicomb, and Ingrid Winterbach. Thanks, too, to Isobel Dixon, Jacob Dlamini, Mark Gevisser, Fanie Naudé, Henrietta Rose-Innes, and Fourie Botha. I acknowledge Kylie Thomas, Rowan Roux, and staff at the National English Literary Museum in Grahamstown and the African Studies Library at the University of Cape Town for assistance with research. At OUP, thanks to Jacqueline Norton, Eleanor Collins, Aimee Wright, Anthea Davey, Monica Kendall, and Vaishnavi Venkatesan.

For the funding that enabled the most sustained period of writing, I am grateful to the Leverhulme Trust for the award of a Fellowship during the 2013–14 academic year, and the Faculty of Humanities and Social Sciences at Queen Mary University of London for a sabbatical in the spring of 2013. Funding from Queen Mary's Department of English has allowed several research visits to South Africa since 2010, while Rhodes's English Department extended a Research Associate position that facilitated visits in 2012 and 2013 (part-funded by a Mellon Visiting Fellowship). The British Academy awarded a research grant that allowed trips in 2009 and 2010, during which some defining questions in this study first took shape; their award of a Newton Advanced Research Fellowship for another project facilitated visits in 2015 and 2016. These research trips and frequent sojourns with my South African family and friends have helped mitigate the difficulties of expatriation and allowed me to keep my ear to the ground. I am grateful, too, to the Harry Ransom Center, University of Texas at Austin, for a Research Fellowship in the Humanities, supported by the Andrew W. Mellon Foundation Endowment, which made possible a very pleasant month in the Coetzee archives, in July 2015.

Queen Mary has provided a stimulating environment for the germination and completion of this project. Successive Heads of the School of English and Drama—Julia Boffey, Michèle Barrett, and Markman Ellis—have proffered sound advice and fostered a humane and productive research culture. Thanks, too, to Morag Schiach in the Faculty. Several colleagues have been more than fellow travellers: my particular thanks to Nadia Valman, Bill Schwarz, kitt price, Sam McBean, David James, Rachael Gilmour, Mark Currie, Shahidha Bari, Nadia Atia, and Rehana Ahmed. Thanks also to Andrea Brady, Jerry Brotton, David Colclough, Charlotta Salmi, David Schalkwyk, and (in the School of History) Saul Dubow. Would that all my academic friends could credit the superb administrative support offered variously and at different times by Jenny Gault, Beverley Stewart, Patricia Hamilton, Daphne Rayment, Huw Marsh, Faisal Abul, Jonathan Boffey, Richard Coulton, Rob Ellis, Suzi Lewis, Matthew Mauger, and Kate Russell.

I have had occasion to teach, advise, or simply be around some remarkable students over several years. Thanks in particular to Phoenix Alexander, Lara Atkin, Roger Blanton, Alexandra Effe, Xiaoran Hu, Andrea Thorpe, Asha Rogers (from Sheffield days, latterly a much appreciated colleague), and all those in my South African literature modules at Sheffield and Queen Mary since 2005.

My colleagues on the editorial team of *Safundi*, especially Shane Graham, Alex Lichtenstein, and Karin Shapiro, have helped keep the field of contemporary South African (and transnational) humanities scholarship in focus.

Two extended periods away from London (and South Africa) proved more productive than I could have imagined: six weeks at the School of Criticism and Theory at Cornell University in the summer of 2012; and a month, as partner of a Fellow, at the Rockefeller Foundation's Bellagio Study Center on Lake Como in the spring of 2014. During the former, I benefited beyond measure from the Queer Technics seminar, particularly from the hopeful pedagogy and courageous engagement with theory modelled by Amy Villarejo, and from six weeks of conversation with attendees and others, amongst whom thanks in particular to Ben Bascom, Jax Bialostozky, Tony D'Agostino, Alexander Eastwood, Terri Geller (bar-quiz partner) and David Maynard, Erin Gray, Hailey Haffey, Kai Horstmannshoff, Gabrielle Jung, Sarah O'Brien, Bill Martin, Kate Morris, Jonathan Mullins, Patti Nelson, Ivan Ortiz, Annalise Pippard, Jen Spitzer, Anna Terwiel (tennis partner), Nancy Wadsworth, and Nick Webber. I am grateful, too, for having had occasion in Ithaca to talk about hope and disappointment with Lauren Berlant and Ania Loomba, and to have begun to learn from Amanda Anderson how to hear the hole in almost any argument. At Bellagio, where Pilar Palaciá facilitates the most elegant intellectual salon I have yet encountered, I learned from conversations with public health advocates, research scientists, artists, writers, social anthropologists, child psychologists, art historians, lawyers, and economists, often relating directly to some of the themes of this book—temporality, revolution, impasse, and the imagination—at an important stage in the writing process. Thanks to Gigo and Alyssa Alampay, Jankhi Andharia, Simon Chapman, Susan Crawford, Signe Howell, David Hunter, Anna Lora-Wainright, Desmond McNeill, Anne Nelson, Soroush Parsa, Leona Sampson, NFN Scout, Wu Tsang, Leon Wainwright, and Cecilia Wainryb.

Heartfelt thanks to friends, far and near, who have helped me see beyond a troublesome paragraph and appreciate the importance of relationality. For hospitality, encouragement, and solidarity, thanks to Adrianne Rubin-Arlow and Noah Arlow, Rita Barnard and Dana Phillips,

Nadia Davids and John Gutierrez, Michael Holtmann and Abby Norris, Katie and Chris Holmes, Bronwyn and Ben Law-Viljoen, Sarah Linville, Ania Loomba and Suvir Kaul, Mike Ludewig, Peter McCullough and Thomas Knollys, Nosipho Mngomezulu, Neel Mukherjee, Kimberly Ochs and Malte Herwig, Roger Palmer and Zoë Wicomb, Angela Rae and Justin Cornish, Aimee Stoffel, Sandi Willows and Cam du Plessis. Very special thanks to Carli Coetzee, Lucy Graham, Deborah Seddon, Undine Weber, my nieces Kirsty, Catriona, and Annabel MacLeod, sister and brother-in-law Marti and Alasdair MacLeod, and parents-in-law Gail Flanery, Glenn Breuer, and Jim Flanery. Thanks also to Buddy, terrier extraordinaire, proof that the most engaging souls are not always human.

I am grateful beyond words to my mother, Nan van der Vlies, who borrows from her local public library any book I mention and who knits for those in need, and to my father, Eddie van der Vlies, who talked to me about wildlife and the weather. Each, in sometimes surprising ways, has been a model for dealing with many of the negative affects with which I engage in this book. My father passed away as it was nearing completion, and I offer it to the world in his memory.

I am constantly surprised that I have the good fortune to share my days with my partner, the novelist Patrick Flanery, my first reader and most honest critic. This book, and much else besides, would not have been possible without him. We may suffer disappointments together, but we hope together too, always.

*

A portion of the final section of Chapter 3 appeared in different form in '"MÊME DYING STOP CONFIRM ARRIVAL STOP": Provincial Literatures in Global Time: The Case of Marlene van Niekerk's *Agaat*', in *Institutions of World Literature: Writing, Translation, Markets*, ed. Pieter Vermeulen and Stefan Helgesson (London & New York: Routledge, 2015), 191–208.

Fragments of the following are repurposed in a portion of Chapter 5: 'Zoë Wicomb's Queer Cosmopolitanisms', *Safundi: The Journal of South African and American Studies* 12.3-4 (July–October 2011), 425–44. This material (©2015, ©2011) is reproduced by permission of Taylor and Francis Group, LLC, a division of Informa plc.

I acknowledge permission for the use of material as epigraphs as follows:

In the Introduction, the extract from Joan Bybee, Revere Perkins, and William Pagliuca's *The Evolution of Grammar* (1994), is used by courtesy of University of Chicago Press.

In Chapter 1, lines from Wopko Jensma's 'Spanner in the What? Works', published in *I Must Show You My Clippings* (1977), are quoted with the permission of Ravan Press and Pan Macmillan South Africa.

In Chapter 2, the extract from J.M. Coetzee's 'Erasmus: Madness and Rivalry', from *Giving Offense: Essays on Censorship* (1996), first appeared in print in *Neophilologus*, volume 76, no. 1 (1992), 1–18, and is cited with permission of Springer.

In Chapter 3, lines from the 'Introduction', in *The Queen of America Goes to Washington City*, by Lauren Berlant, pp. 1–24, ©1997, Duke University Press. All rights reserved. Republished by permission of the copyright holder. www.dukeupress.edu.

In Chapter 4, lines from Walter Benjamin, 'Excavation and Memory' (c. 1932), p. 576, translated by Rodney Livingstone, from *Walter Benjamin: Selected Writings, Volume 2: Part 2, 1931–1934*, translated by Rodney Livingstone and Others, edited by Michael W. Jennings, Howard Eiland, and Gary Smith, Cambridge, Mass.: The Belknap Press of Harvard University Press, Copyright © 1999 by the President and Fellows of Harvard College. Cited with permission of Harvard University Press.

In Chapter 5, the excerpt from Njabulo Ndebele's *The Cry of Winnie Mandela* is quoted with kind permission from Ayebia Clarke Publishing Limited.

In Chapter 6, lines from Sindiwe Magona's 'The More Things Change', published in *Letter to South Africa: Poets Calling the State to Order* (2011), is published with kind permission from Umuzi, Penguin Random House South Africa.

The extract, quoted in Chapter 2, from John Ashbery's poem 'Grand Galop', published in *Self-Portrait in a Convex Mirror* (New York: Viking, 1975), is copyright and reprinted by kind permission of Carcanet Press Limited, Manchester, UK, the rights holder in the UK and Commonwealth excluding Canada, and with the approval of Penguin Random House US.

Quotations in Chapter 2 from J.M. Coetzee's handwritten notes for a reading in Reykjavik on 12 September 2007 ('Iceland' folder, box 62.4, Coetzee papers) is made with the kind permission of John Coetzee and of the Harry Ransom Center, The University of Texas at Austin.

I am grateful to South African artist Kate Gottgens for permission to reproduce one of her extraordinary paintings on the cover: 'Higher Ground' © Kate Gottgens. The image facing the first page of Chapter 6, 'Unsupported. Stuck. Frustrated. Private security guards outside the Department of Student Affairs after students were evicted from the building during the #FeesMustFall, #FreeDecolonisedEducation #BringBackOurCadres #EndOutsourcing movement. Steve Biko Students Union Building, University of Cape Town, 4 October 2016', is from the Instagram feed @therealcityofcapetown by its contributor @tships (Leanne Brady), and is reproduced with permission.

Contents

Introduction

No Time Like the Present

> An imperfective restricted to the present is simply a present, since a present situation cannot be perfective.
>
> —Joan Bybee, Revere Perkins, William Pagliuca, *The Evolution of Grammar* (1994)[1]

Jabulile Gumede and Steven Reed, the protagonists of Nadine Gordimer's final published novel, *No Time Like the Present* (2012), begin the first years of postapartheid South Africa with great hopes. A black woman and a white man, Jabu and Steve are raising biracial children to be citizens of a country no longer ruled on the basis of a hierarchy of racial privilege. This is 'nothing less than a New Age', they believe, one in which 'the law is not promulgated on pigment', in which 'anyone may live and move and work anywhere in a country commonly theirs'.[2] Jabu and Steve's experience of the present is necessarily structured by what has come before: 'everything is after', *after* the Struggle (both are veterans of the liberation movement), *after* the traumas of apartheid's brutalization of communities and its criminalization of cross-racial relationships like theirs.[3] With fellow comrade-veterans they 'follow the beginning of what is apparently an era in the aftermath of revolution attained',[4] moving from an inner-city apartment in which they had managed to live clandestinely as a couple to a suburb once the preserve of working-class white Afrikaners. They become progressively middle-class: Jabu, a teacher, retrains to become a paralegal and then a lawyer; Steve, a chemist whose employment in a paint factory had given him cover as a bomb-making saboteur, reinvents himself as a university lecturer. They buy their house, take holidays, send their children to good fee-paying schools, and give a home to an elderly relative from Jabu's home village in Zululand. But their expectations of a brave new future are slowly eroded.

Gordimer charts Steve and Jabu's experience of the postapartheid nation's decline from hopeful postcolonial state to run-of-the-mill developing country beset by the poisonous legacies of decades of strategic under-development and blighted by corruption and shortsightedness.

No Time Like the Present offers a catalogue of the disappointments of the new era, between 1994 and 2009, from Nelson Mandela's inability to satisfy the expectations of the masses, his setting of reconciliation ahead of revolution (his critics would claim), through the years of Thabo Mbeki's culpable AIDS-denialism and signal failures to engage with crises in Zimbabwe, to the spectacle of Jacob Zuma's rape trial, his alleged role in a crooked arms deal, and his elevation, despite these scandals, to the office of President.[5] After the momentous party conference, held in Polokwane in December 2007, at which Mbeki was ousted as African National Congress (ANC) leader, William Gumede observed presciently: 'For all the doubts that hang over Zuma's character, many argue that he offers a critical conduit for the poor's grievances. These people are going to be disappointed.'[6] Jabu and Steve are two of these. Blow by blow, the reader experiences these characters' alienation from optimism. We live with them their outrage and confusion at the shocking xenophobic violence perpetrated against migrants from elsewhere in Africa, at car hijackings and house invasions, at ongoing incidents of racism—including an infamous case of white university students making black workers, old enough to be their parents, participate in humiliating initiation practices at a university whose new name becomes unintentionally ironic: the University of the Free State.[7] Gordimer links this case with incidents of bullying at Jabu and Steve's son's school. Steve dismisses the headmaster's excuses for the older boys' actions (that it is merely adolescent play-acting and rebellion), suggesting instead that the bullies are 'young fascists in the making, Mussolini-style, Nazi-style, Apartheid-style'. History, Steve warns chillingly, is 'always ready to make a comeback'.[8] In one particularly bitter interrogation of the disappointments of the postapartheid situation, Steve asks himself angrily, invoking slogans of the struggle (the rationale 'Better Life' and the war-cry '*the struggle continues!*'), what the difference might be 'between not doing anything' and arriving, 'while desperately opposing' it, at an understanding that

> what had been believed, fought for hasn't begun to be followed—granted, couldn't be realised—in fifteen years—and right now, every day degenerates. Oh that fucking litany, Better Life, how often to face the dead with it, the comrades, who died for the latest executive model Mercedes, the mansions for winter or summer residence, the millionaire kickbacks from arms deals and tenders for housing whose brand-new walls crack like an old face. Who would have had a prescient nightmare of ending up sickened, unmanned of anything there is for you to take on, *a luta continua*.[9]

The prospect of disappointing the dead, those who died for this future, is a particularly upsetting one for Steve. His disaffection is palpable, and it is arguably the author's, too.

Over a long career, Gordimer consistently and fiercely opposed apartheid, exploring its contradictions and injustices in essays, short stories, and novels (several of them banned) that evidence an unwavering advocacy 'on behalf of literature and free speech in a police state, where censorship and persecution of books and people exist' (to quote the Swedish Academy's citation on the award to her of the 1991 Nobel Prize for Literature).[10] But while Gordimer always maintained she was proud to vote for the ANC, in her final years she became one of the ruling party's fiercest critics, turning her ire in particular on its proposed Protection of State Information Bill, worded to allow unprecedented censorship on the grounds of state security. At what had been billed a reading from *No Time Like the Present* at London's Southbank Centre in March 2012, the visibly frail Gordimer instead insisted on reading a statement critiquing the proposed legislation and turned each question into an occasion to lament the course to which South Africa's leaders were committing the country. The ANC paid tribute to Gordimer on her death, aged 90, on 13 July 2014. 'Our country has lost an unmatched literary giant whose life's work was our mirror and an unending quest for humanity', the official statement read. Meanwhile, as Justice Malala observed, the very bill against which Gordimer had fulminated subsequently passed through parliament and sat, awaiting signature, on President Zuma's desk.[11]

Steve and Jabu hope that the transition to democracy will usher in a 'different time', but find—and these lines from *No Time Like the Present* read like Gordimer's own credo—that '[t]here is only one time, all time, for principles you live by'.[12] What Gordimer means here, of course, is that one should always live by one's principles, and specifically that the ANC government should be held to the standards that guided the anti-apartheid movement, though the formulation—that there is 'one time, all time'—also plays on the idea of present now-time being the only time in which we are conscious, in which we account for the past and hope for the future.[13] In an op-ed in South Africa's *Mail & Guardian* newspaper in October 2013, Gordimer had insisted that no-one should have the right to foreclose on the '"culture" of freedom in our country'; the task of defining the 'borders of "public interest"' should be entrusted, she insisted, only to the country's Constitutional Court, to 'the ears of those who hear and have the mouths to speak for the justice still to fulfil in peace, entrenched in our Constitution, the suspended revolution'.[14] It is this state of suspension, and the concomitant sense of disappointment experienced affectively *and* temporally, that *No Time Like the Present* charts, indeed that it has the reader experience so powerfully.

Gordimer had long been the preeminent chronicler of the experience of life in a country whose public discourse was riven with competing narratives of history, with contests not only over space but also over interpretations of the future. She famously observed in one of her best-known essays, 'Living in the Interregnum' (first delivered as a speech in New York in 1982), that with the independence of Mozambique and Angola (in 1974; bases for the South African liberation movements were soon set up in those countries), the student uprising that began in Soweto in July 1976, and the growing isolation of the white South African government, the past had begun to 'drop out of sight, even for those who would have liked to go on living in it': the old 'coordinates' did not 'fit life any longer'. Gramsci's well-known diagnosis of capitalism's discontents—'The old is dying and the new cannot be born; in this interregnum there arises a great diversity of morbid symptoms'—seemed to Gordimer to describe well this new South African temporality. It gave her essay its title, and she used the statement as the epigraph for *July's People*, her dystopian 1981 novel, with its famously ambiguous ending, in which the character Maureen Smales runs towards a helicopter that might bear either soldiers of the new regime, or of the old.[15] The interregnum was retrospectively adopted as a useful shorthand term for describing the long transition to democracy, from the late 1970s—when it became clear that apartheid had entered its endgame—through the early 1990s. But if, despite its suggestion of entrapment in intractability, Gordimer's description of in-between time emphasized its unpredictability, the description is predicated on a conviction that change would come, that another regime, however postponed, had to follow. At 'the back of our minds', Gordimer told Stephen Clingman in 1992 (the interregnum still in place, though political prisoners had been released and the Congress for a Democratic South Africa convened to discuss the path to free elections), 'there was this kind of apocalyptic feeling'. This was 'perhaps [. . .] always self-fulfilling', she conceded (possibly also meaning self-exculpatory): 'we wanted there to be a kind of big-bang ending, because we didn't want to tackle it ourselves. But now it's so incredible and fascinating to see there's no end to the process.'[16] By the end of her life, in her final battle against the government's secrecy and surveillance legislation, Gordimer seems to have felt that the country still lingered in a state of interregnum, still faced the threat of apocalypse. Steve Reed's warning in *No Time Like the Present* that history is always about to repeat itself clearly voiced a personally felt danger on the author's own part.

South Africa's revolution did not result in apocalypse, but in a process of negotiation in which few would lose any real privilege. The liberation movement needed 'now to deal with the crisis of expectation', Gordimer told Clingman in 1992.[17] Novels about the crisis of conscience of white characters needing to take sides, or indeed facing the consequences of understanding the side they were already on (by virtue of the privilege accruing to them because of skin colour), novels that had concluded in open-ended fashion but nonetheless in expectation of revolution—one thinks again of *July's People*, but also the earlier *The Late Bourgeois World* (1966), with its invocations of Gramsci and Lukács—made way at this time, Clingman observed the same year, to works like *A Sport of Nature* (1987) and *My Son's Story* (1990). In these Gordimer began, in Clingman's words, to voice 'doubts' just at the moment that 'black South Africans are about to achieve what they have struggled for for so long'.[18] As freedom seemed within reach, Gordimer diagnosed 'a division within that moment itself', Clingman noted.[19] The present was the end-point of a narrative of progress, but that narrative might not end up mapping onto the lived experiences that would follow; the present was but a moment in a narrative whose end would always be unpredictable, was perhaps now unpredictable in ways that could not have been foreseen by the narratives that sustained the Struggle. Gordimer's *The House Gun* (1998), published four years into the new dispensation, figures its central character in relation to the idea of a loose or jagged end. Here this character's bisexuality is at issue in the subversion he offers to determinate ends, a narrative of progress imagined in relation to a genealogical line, but the idea of a loose end serves, too, to describe Gordimer's growing sense of the fate of the narrative of progress that had structured the liberation movement but that could only issue in a present that was no time like that which it had imagined.

No Time Like the Present takes as its title a phrase beloved of Jabu's father, Elias Gumede, a stern but principled school principal in rural KwaZulu-Natal. He had used it 'often as a reproach for tardiness among pupils and his children'.[20] He used it as a maxim, too, to justify grasping the promise of freedom when agreeing to send Jabu over the border to be educated in Swaziland (where she would be recruited into the liberation movement). Yet when Elias refuses to believe that the charges against Jacob Zuma, especially of rape, can be anything other than slander, perpetrated by an 'impertinent' woman and promoted by white-run media, he confirms other interpretations of the maxim: that the present is a time in which even he, hitherto paragon of fair-mindedness and optimism (in Jabu's estimation), might be entranced by discourses of ethnic pride and misogyny. It is no time imagined by the liberation movement for which his daughter fought; it is not the future once imagined in the Struggle's narrative of freedom and progress. Rather, it is the stalling of such a narrative, the utopian promise devolved to impasse. If the revolution has run out of time, has been suspended, then characters in *No Time Like the Present* find themselves in a present also somehow outside of time, caught in a temporality that is a *no*-time—but more than in the sense that the present is not able to be understood (yet) as past. It is, instead, a present that did not feature in the past's privileged narrative of time's future unfolding. In his study of aspect, Bernard Comrie observed that a defining characteristic of the imperfective is its reference to the 'internal temporal structure of a situation, viewing a situation from within'.[21] Joan Bybee and colleagues, citing Comrie in their assessment of comparative scholarship on the evolution of grammar, affirm his spatial metaphor for grasping the imperfective: the imperfect denotes speaking from within a situation, understood either as being in progress at the time from which one speaks (the reference time) or as habitual; the imperfect sets up the background situation, rather than narrating a sequence of events that has a definite end. Thus while the imperfective situation might be past or present, when relating to the present it is 'simply a present, since a present situation cannot be perfective'. The present tense, they observe, might in fact be regarded as 'the present imperfective, since most situations that are contemporaneous with the moment of speech are imperfective'.[22] It is from and of such an ongoing imperfect present that Gordimer's characters speak, of which they (and she) speak, in an attempt to imagine another temporality in which such stasis might be overcome.

NO-TIME AND NOW-TIME

There is something about this no-time that is not only *any* present, neither past nor future, but a very specific *kind* of present, one experienced as impasse and that follows the frustration of a revolutionary endeavour that is strongly reminiscent of Walter Benjamin's ideas about revolutionary potential and historiography. Benjamin's scepticism about progress narratives has proved useful to several recent theoretical engagements with projects of social and aesthetic revolution, and most especially with their aftermaths. (I cite some of these in due course.) And if his context—Europe in the 1920s and 1930s, overwhelmed by fascism—is different from contemporary South Africa in crucial respects, his ideas seem nonetheless unusually productive in contemplating present-day South Africa, something its writers have in fact long recognized. Benjamin's imagination of what he calls the angel of history, evoked for him by a small Paul Klee watercolour sketch, is invoked in several works of the long transition from the late-apartheid period to the present, from Coetzee's *Age of Iron* (1990) through Jeremy Cronin's *More than a Casual Contact* (2006), to Ivan Vladislavić's *Double Negative* (2010), serving variously as shorthand for helpless observation of the chaos of human action and the unknowability of its consequences.[23] I discuss several of these references more fully in Chapter 4 of this study, but Benjamin's general reflections on history and time are suggestive here because they offer a way of engaging the affective and temporal energies of disappointment understood as umbrella term for states of affective dysphoria and temporal disjuncture. Disappointment is central to understanding Benjamin's own attempt to bring together Jewish mysticism and a revisionist Marxism to address the fact that Marx's dialectical interpretation of history, committed to a narrative of progress, seemed palpably to have stalled in Benjamin's own day.

Benjamin posits in his enigmatic 'Theses on the Philosophy of History' that the universal historicist, whose project he derided, and the proponent of a historical materialism, who is closer to his own radical and recuperative imperatives, both thought about the present as a point of stasis, although with important differences. For the historian whose commitment is to a narrative of progress, the temporal location of the 'construction' of history is 'homogeneous empty time'—empty because it has not yet been given shape by the narrative the historian sets out to construct. By contrast, for the historical materialist, the kind of historian Benjamin valorized (and modelled in his unfinished *Arcades Project*), the present was 'time filled up by now-time'.[24] The word Benjamin uses is '*Jeztzeit*', by which he does not mean simply 'an equivalent to *Gegenwart,* that is, present', Harry Zohn observes (in a note to the translation in *Illuminations* that first brought the theses to a wide anglophone public); Benjamin seems rather to mean something like 'the mystical *nunc stans*'.[25] Now-time, 'time filled by the presence of the now',[26] is for Benjamin consequently *not* the present. It is no time like the present—at least not any present imagined in relation to a narrative in which past remains past, accounted for as a 'sequence of events like the beads of a rosary', consigned to the proverbial dustbin of history (not to mix metaphors!), which is to say universalist historical narrative.[27]

Benjamin's use of the image of a rosary to describe the work of the universal historicist method that he derided suggests a sequential, consecutive ordering, but it also implicitly sets a Catholic sense of a messiah having come (and gone, and who is expected again—though in a coming of a different order) against the sense of 'redemption' that informs Benjamin's ideas about the task of the historical materialist. This is informed by a Jewish sense of a messiah still expected, and is structured by what Benjamin calls '*weak* messianism'—weak because not dependent on outside (divine) intervention but achievable by human agency and imagination.[28] The historical materialist 'stops telling' the sequence of events like a rosary and is committed instead to revivifying the utopian possibilities of the past from a point in the present structured by disappointment and anticipation.[29] This resuscitation is achieved by reaching into the past, the image used is that of a *leap*, to bring past events into what Benjamin calls a 'constellation' with the present.[30] In this speculative methodology, thought is brought to a standstill in what the *Illuminations* translation calls 'a configuration pregnant with tensions' of the unfulfilled promises of earlier moments,[31] and it results in a 'messianic arrest of happening, or (to put it differently) a revolutionary chance in the fight for the oppressed past'.[32]

The disjunction between an experience of temporality in the present and a relationship to the idea of history cast as narrative is one to which I will return. Consider first the remarkable suggestiveness of Benjamin's observation, offered in a supplement to his theses, that '[o]nce the classless society has been defined as an infinite task, the empty and homogeneous time was transformed into an anteroom, so to speak, in which one could wait for the emergence of the revolutionary situation with more or less equanimity'.[33] The diagnosis serves uncommonly well to describe the condition of present impasse experienced by South Africans—like Jabu and Steve, and indeed Gordimer herself—as the suspension of South Africa's National Democratic Revolution, which is how the ANC and its partners characterize that which followed liberation in 1994.[34] The revolution has yielded to an accommodation with globalization and neoliberalism and the rise of a new authoritarianism that correlates to global responses to post-Fordist precarity. The word *precarious*, we might remind ourselves, describes, in legal terms, the situation of living on land that is owned by another, but it—and the neologism *precarity*—has come to be used as shorthand for conditions of contingent labour (the under-employed, the working poor) that characterize the post-Fordist present, which is to say the era of flexible capital accumulation and the withdrawal of investment from labour-intensive (Fordist or assembly-line) production. South Africa, observes anthropologist Hylton White, 'could hardly fit the paradigm' of an 'authoritarian post-Fordism' more completely.[35] The consequences of accommodations with neoliberalism, most observers would concede, have contributed to horrors like the massacre of striking mineworkers at Marikana in August 2012—an event that, more than any other in recent memory, recalled for postapartheid South Africans the spectre of apartheid brutality, and certainly contributed to the rise of Julius Malema, expelled President of the ANC-Youth League and now leader of the Economic Freedom Fighters (EFF), who cites Marikana as a prime instance of the consequences of the ANC government's accommodations with capital.[36] The EFF, which sent its first MPs to Parliament after the May 2014 elections, has been at the forefront of moves to hold the presidency to account in a number of cases of over-spend or over-reach, both in Parliament and before the Constitutional Court.

I am not suggesting that Benjamin offers a template for reading South Africa's present, but his meditations on the role of the historical materialist in moments of such impasse are useful if we read 'historical materialist' imaginatively to designate a range of creative engagements with the past from a position of stasis in the present—and indeed if we go so far as to imagine the work of fiction as offering a constellation with the past in the present unfolding of the reader's experience. Benjamin allows us to read stasis and impasse less as waiting-room than operations-room. It is no surprise that his enabling metaphorics have been much invoked in accounts of the aftermath of failed revolutionary projects as well as in queer theoretical meditations on affect—especially bad feelings (feeling stuck, bored, ashamed, disappointed)—and temporality (whether concerned with looking backwards, or with futurity).[37] Works from both loose groupings of disparate studies, which I am suggesting share broadly similar orientations, have proved generative for my own project, and I canvass some of their most useful insights in the following sections of this introduction.

BAD FEELINGS AND HOPEFUL ORIENTATIONS

Present Imperfect is not expressly a study of queer politics or poetics, though the reader will notice that queer characters are to be found in many of the texts discussed in the chapters that follow; this was not a criterion for selection (I reflect on some of the reasons for queer figures recurring in contemporary South African writing in Chapter 5).[38] What such characters make more visible, however, is the usefulness of much recent queer theory and literary and cultural studies with investments in the legacies of gay and lesbian activism, for this project. Such work, and that interested in understanding bad feelings more generally (many of them attending to queer figures, too, and influential in queer studies), provides useful theoretical and methodological models for thinking affect and temporality together—and for taking literary texts as archive and promise. Heather Love's interests in *Feeling Backward* (2007), for example, are—like mine—in readings that focus on awkward feelings. In Love's case, these are those of queer subjects in the past who refuse heteronormative sociality (she repurposes *backward*, heard as pejorative description of intimate attachments, in order to look back). In my case, these are varieties of disappointment and experiences of impasse. Love endorses what she understands as the lesson of the antisocial turn in queer theory, a refusal to accept that advances towards equality necessarily mean that the revolutionary energies of past queer struggles are spent.[39] It is no surprise then that the enigmatic but endlessly suggestive figure of Benjamin's angel of history serves well as representative of Love's queer historian, poised on the cusp of a supposedly better future yet looking back in the hope of resuscitating past—and truly utopian—promise. The backward glance, shared with Orpheus at the point he loses Eurydice (and which leads to his abjuring women) and with Lot's wife, who looks back at the destruction of Sodom and Gomorrah (both figures are associated, then, with queer life), serves both as description of the (queer) historical materialist's task *and* as metaphoric marker of negative affect, of feeling otherwise.[40] It is to such feelings in work from an earlier era—by Walter Pater, Radclyffe Hall, Willa Cather, and Sylvia Townsend Warner—that Love attends most closely, modelling a literary analysis alive to the political potential in the present of attending to a historical archive in relation to which backward describes the direction of the critic's glance. While Love's project appears to bear little resemblance to my own concerns with postapartheid fiction, it models a similar refusal to construe backwardness as negative, a refusal to interpret concern with past hopes as disinclination to engage with the *now*. It embraces instead the critical potential of such orientation—in Love's case 'backwardness' serves 'both as a queer historical structure of feeling and as a model for queer historiography'.[41] Something similar can be said for the sense in which I have deployed disappointment as a critical catch-all term: characters frequently look back and model forms of refusal that might be construed as backward in comparable ways.

For Elizabeth Freeman, looking back describes a similar desire to attend to what trails rather than what is in advance of social formations. She argues in *Time Binds: Queer Temporalities, Queer Histories* (2010) that if a dominant strand of queer theory, playing on the energies of queer as a verb meaning to unsettle, dissolve, or otherwise disregard the social text, has privileged the avant-garde, such work seems disarmingly close to what Eve Sedgwick calls paranoid criticism: 'having the problem solved ahead of time, [...] feeling more evolved than one's context'. Freeman suggests instead that a queer historiography should pay attention to what she calls 'the tail end of things', should be 'willing to be bathed in the fading light of whatever has been declared useless', and that such attention is closer to Sedgwick's idea of reparative criticism, a mode of reading that is eclectic, interested in 'cultural debris', concerned to construe provisional constellations '"*not necessarily like any preexisting whole*," though composed of what preexists'.[42] As I have indicated, I am similarly interested in loose ends in this study. In *Cruising Utopia* (2007), José Muñoz likewise invokes Sedgwick's notion of reparative criticism, labelling the anti-utopian trend in queer theory that is exemplified for him in Lee Edelman's polemical *No Future* (2004) as prime example of paranoid criticism. For

Muñoz, such focus has occasioned a critical impasse in which futurity is obscure. Readings attuned to the utopian instead evidence a reparative hermeneutics.[43]

Many works of postapartheid writing invoke queer figures' complicated relationships to genealogy and futurity, but I choose not to take sides in debates about some of queer theory's antisocial and anti-utopian interests; arguments are too often caricatured in the process. It does, however, seem to me that, as Sara Ahmed has noted in her attempt to take seriously the politically progressive determination to be ambivalent about those things which we are told we *should* desire in order to be happy (and as Ann Cvetkovich has observed in response to Michael Snediker's critique of Edelman), to affirm the utopian energies of non-normative difference necessarily revalues the negative. It seeks 'the utopian in perversion, abjection, failure, depression, and struggle', in Cvetkovich's words, and so refuses 'binary distinctions between positive and negative affects'.[44] Gay men, lesbians, and bisexuals serve frequently in postapartheid writing as markers of the new social possibilities of freedom, but often also trouble narratives of the new national family's futurity.[45] They do both in Gordimer's *No Time Like the Present.* A former Dutch Reformed Church in Steve and Jabu's new suburb has been turned into what passes for a gay commune ('one of our gay families'), the neighbourhood comrades who show them around explain. Steve and Jabu's response is 'laughter—this is the final blasphemy, housed'.[46] In this new dispensation '[t]he gays could enjoy their holy pool', in which Jabu and Steve first see them swimming, and from which they take their affectionate collective name, the Dolphins.[47] It is no longer Steve's gay brother Alan who is 'what's queer in the family', but rather 'sibling Jonathan who's for some reason deviated'—in his case from the family's non-observance of religion through his embrace of orthodox Judaism (their mother is culturally Jewish, their father an agnostic raised as a Presbyterian).[48] Yet there is still unease in Gordimer's novel with the non-reproductive nature of gay sexuality. At one party at the Dolphins' house, the straight comrade-women, noting how 'old conventions in allocation of domestic roles have been discarded in Constitutional normalcy of gay households more completely than in heterosexual ones', still find time (rather Gordimer still requires them) to blame the queers for political correctness—'Oh, by the way, I resent, that's one thing I hold against them, they've hijacked the word. You can't say you had a gay time, you like gay colours, and what about "gaily", you can't walk gaily along feeling happy'—and to speculate, with some disgust, at the mechanics of gay sex: 'How can they do it to each other?— An abrupt gesture—stayed—in the direction of the swimming pool.—And we have the clean soft smooth place specially for them. To take them in.'[49]

I will have more to say about Gordimer's engagement with queer figures later in this book; there are loose ends aplenty to gather here.

Perhaps what the straight women in Gordimer's fiction struggle to accommodate is the resistance posed by queer figures to what Elizabeth Freeman calls *chronobiopolitics*, the synchronization of normative measurements of time with the time of *bios*, the harnessing of bodily cycles, including reproductive ones, in oversight of the policed body and body politic. Freeman is interested in other modes of engaging with time than what she calls the chrononormative, those institutional modes of policing temporality—time zones, timetables, working hours—that 'come to seem like somatic facts'.[50] Consequently, she turns her attention to an array of artists and writers of the 1970s and 1980s who worked in minor media, artists and activists who came after the mass political movements of the late 1960s and whose radical hopes had most often given way, or been 'detoured into individualistic projects', commodified by mainstream artistic practice and the media.[51] Freeman's interest in engagements with the dead-ends of social revolutionary movements—class revolt, second-wave feminism, the still under-developed links between black and queer liberation—indicates a broad area of shared theoretical and political interest with projects like Jane Elliott's on the aftermath of second-wave feminism registered in writing by women in the present, and Jennifer Wenzel's on the afterlives of anti-colonial prophecy (on both of which more shortly), and indeed also with my own.[52] The chrononormative and the harnessing of chronobiopolitics are at issue in many works of South African fiction that engage with the duration of apartheid and with its aftermath, perhaps none more so than Marlene van Niekerk's *Agaat*, a reading of which occupies the bulk of Chapter 3 of this study.

José Muñoz shared Freeman's interest in times that are otherwise, more particularly in the potential for alternative futures just discernible in everyday queer aesthetic practices—whether camply ornamented, or those celebrating banality. *Cruising Utopia* focuses most engagingly on such varieties of queer performance art, in which Muñoz finds what he calls 'schemata of a forward-dawning futurity', here invoking Ernst Bloch rather than Benjamin as his touchstone thinker, though Bloch and Benjamin influenced each other and there are clear links between their attitudes to the utopian potential of present stasis.[53] Bloch's complex and often idiosyncratic blend of idealism and materialism, classicism and expressionism, Aristotelian ideas of entelechy and Hegelian ideas of process, held that studying everyday practice might reveal, like sedimented layers, the surplus of past utopian aspirations remaining in the present.[54] Of particular use to Muñoz is that this approach allows a corrective to the anti-utopian impulses he decries in some queer theory, endorsing instead a focus on the quotidian. The everyday features in my project, too, though for current purposes Bloch's close attention to literary texts (alongside ephemera, daydreams, habit and so on) as records of utopian surplus from the past is particularly useful. Not all literary works might serve thus, Bloch makes clear in a discussion of historical fiction, but his admiring reading of Thomas Mann's *Doctor Faustus*, which includes astute observations about its modernist treatment of time, could apply equally to Gordimer's *No Time Like the Present*—in fact, to many of Gordimer's earlier works, when compared with more obviously instrumental protest writing. Mann was always conscious of 'the reader coming later', Bloch notes, and thus attentive to

> how much [...] it takes to advance to understand expressions of the now-time [...]. Although there is no social rising forced in this late amazing work [...], the homelessness of the transitional period is portrayed more precisely in an indirect way than in those contemporary novels attempting a direct approach and doing justice to the social ascending forces [...].[55]

Belatedness and indirection are ideas to which I will return during the course of this book.

In an inaugural address at the University of Tübingen in 1961, the title of which, 'Can Hope Be Disappointed?', poses a question everywhere implied by *No Time Like the Present*, Bloch made the following observation, which seems germane to all critiques of South Africa's transition to democracy:

> [I]s it not the case that a thing, once it has become realized, tends—as something still standing in its own darkness—to obscure whatever has been attained by its realization, so that it does not resemble what was previously hoped for, even though its content has passed, wholly undiminished, from the possible into the actual? And yet, a residue remains, in this instance only because of the still undiscovered (with respect to its content) 'true and perfect being.' But even such disappointment over realization's 'minus' finally counts toward the credit of well-founded hope, and advances its existential as well as its essential demands.[56]

Bloch's observation might be read to suggest, in the South African context, that the postapartheid state *is* an achievement; a hope for freedom *was* realized, even if a 'residue' remains (and particularly because a 'true and perfect' society has not yet been achieved). There is more to be positive about than not and yet hope, in another of Bloch's memorable turns of phrase, is 'unconditionally disappointable' precisely because its orientation is futural, it can have no guarantee of success, it must incorporate chance. Bloch averred that there can only inevitably be disappointment ('hope holds *eo ipso* the condition of defeat precariously within itself'), hence what is to be cultivated is a species of hope that is informed—crucially—by *past* disappointments, a hopefulness that Bloch called *educated*. '[N]ot only hope's affect (with its pendant, fear) but, even more so, hope's methodology (with its pendant, memory) dwells in the region of the not-yet', he notes, 'a place where entrance and, above all, final content are marked by an enduring indeterminacy'.[57] Something like this educated hope, alongside a desire to endorse the potential of desiring otherwise than the status quo, a desire like that I have suggested is shared with recent queer theory, informs both my method *and* the engagements with the form of the novel offered by the authors I discuss in the body of this book. It is a variety of hope that might guide South Africans genuinely grateful for political change, but critical of those moments in which decisions were taken that have forestalled on the delivery of even greater freedom and equality. Hoping with the past in mind, this is to be cultivated. And this might be taken, too, to describe a form of reading with which I engage, and which I hope to model. In his study of the politics of land restitution in Fiji, Cornell anthropologist Hirokazu Miyazaki expands on Bloch's idea of hope as methodology. Looking to Bloch, but also to Benjamin and Rorty, Miyazaki argues that hope serves these thinkers 'as a method of radical temporal reorientation of knowledge'; it is, he contends, nothing less than 'a *method* of knowledge'.[58] In a helpful gloss on both Bloch and Benjamin's methods, Miyazaki comments that, for both thinkers, 'moments of hope can only be apprehended as other moments of hope'. In consequence, 'attempts to objectify these moments and turn them into outcomes of some process, as both philosophy and history tend to do, are destined to fail to capture the temporality of these moments'. Bloch and Benjamin aim instead to recapture the temporal structure of such hopeful moments 'by reproducing another hopeful moment, the moment of hope *in their own writing*'.[59] I am hoping—and how can I but use the term advisedly—that the same might be said both of the writing I consider in this book, and about *Present Imperfect* itself.

HISTORY, TRAGEDY, AND BLOCKED FUTURITY

As Bloch understood, however, it is sometimes difficult to discern the utopian in the present. The present feels for many like a state of impasse—in South Africa as in other states of disappointed postcolonial promise. This and similar terms register both affective and temporal displacement, a feeling otherwise, an enduring of something (some condition) other than that for which one has hoped. Impasse has concerned recent theorists of the postcolonial condition, of whom David Scott, anthropologist of the Caribbean, has perhaps written most engagingly about its implications for subjectivity and narrative. In *Omens of Adversity*, his 2014 account of the failures and aftermath of the Grenada Revolution, Scott considers the New Jewel Movement's internal fissuring and its overthrow (sponsored by the Reagan administration), the murder of Prime Minister Maurice Bishop and his associates, and the compromised process of transitional justice that has marked Grenadian political life since. The account does not map exactly onto South African conditions (there was no actual revolution in South Africa, although a revolutionary movement came to and has stayed in power), but there are striking similarities with the ways in which those who hoped for real revolutionary change in South Africa have been disappointed, and in the condition of stasis that marks the present in both places.

Scott's analysis, in fact, suggests a general disjunctive experience of time, what he calls a 'contemporary aporia of the crisis of political time', amongst those who live on in the wake of failed or partial revolutionary projects.[60] His hypothesis is no less bold than that time itself has come, in the wake of Marxism's apparent failures, to seem to stand apart from history. Once more or less interchangeable, time and history 'seem no longer synchronized', as if 'time had found itself *betrayed* by history'[61]—at least history imagined as dialectical process. If, as Hannah Arendt suggests in *On Revolution*, 'the idea of revolution has been a founding paradigm for the modern organization of political time, for connecting old endings to new beginnings',[62] Scott observes, then in the wake of failed revolutionary projects in our own times, and compounded by the end-of-history narratives current at the close of the Cold War, the teleological imperative driving revolutionary movements (indeed encoded in that term *movement*) seems increasingly weak, even absent. 'The present as time, as a temporal frame of meaningful experiential reference, no longer appears—as it was once prominently pictured as appearing—as the tidy dialectical negation of an oppressive or otherwise unwanted past', Scott contends.[63] Another way of saying this is that classical Marxism has been disappointing, affectively and temporally. One response is nostalgia, another melancholia—particularly of the leftist variety.[64] I return to melancholia at various points in the chapters that follow.

Tragedy is the genre to which subjects in such contexts seem most attuned, Scott argues, reprising an argument of his earlier monograph, *Conscripts of Modernity*. A tragic sensibility animates and encourages 'contingency, chance, *peripeteia*, and catastrophe', he suggests, pointing to Raymond Williams's *Modern Tragedy* (1966) as precursor for his observation.[65] Here Williams had sought to put an expressly political and historical engagement with his own time into conversation with his sense of the ways in which tragedy might be understood to function, arguing that twentieth-century political change had altered our understanding of the tragic, making it more ordinary and more social in its resonances. Williams offered the very useful observation that to understand revolution in a longer frame, as entire and protracted action, is to realize its pitfalls, its tragic tendency; he understood that revolts against human alienation sometimes result merely in different kinds of alienation, and that these must be confronted and overcome if revolution is to continue and not end in stasis or reaction.[66] In characterizing postcolonial temporality as most often or inherently tragic, Scott draws from Williams the suggestion that freedom—or its promise, glimpsed in revolution—invites the possibility of tragedy precisely because of the unpredictability of human behaviour. Tragedy may in fact be 'the price of freedom' because 'to act in freedom is to initiate a pursuit of ends that, however reasoned, willed, or well-intentioned, are always in significant part *incalculable*' and hence subject to unintended consequences.[67]

Gordimer's *No Time Like the Present* features something like this understanding of the tragic too. The novel's lesson, if it has one, is that everyday life after apartheid is (as voiced by Jabu Gumede) 'a normal life, not a miracle. It was made by human struggle'.[68] It is thus liable to the consequences of the frailties and shortcomings of human behaviour, that which attends normal life everywhere. South Africans learned this only too well as they watched Winnie Madikizela-Mandela, who had waited for so many years for her incarcerated husband and was transformed into a maternal and heroic figure for the nation-to-come, turned tragic, hiring thugs to guard her, allegedly condoning acts of violence (even murder), being unfaithful to Nelson—being undone by flaws, ambushed by circumstance, making bad choices.[69] Gordimer invokes tragedy directly: Jabu and Steve's daughter, Sindi, acts in a school production of *Antigone*, a tragedy thoroughly appropriate for a novel in which a pivotal moment involves a daughter's disappointment at her father's proud refusal to recognize wrong or empathize with the wronged. Steve responds to this encounter with the classics by borrowing 'a translation and interpretation of Epicurus from the philosophy department'; as far as Steve is concerned, Epicurus validates 'human freedom to pursue aspirations, live better, increase pleasure, a condition that can be created only by self-constraint in dealing with others, respecting the principles of justice which ensure that condition's very existence'.[70] This, he thinks sardonically, invoking what I have suggested we might read as Jabu's recognition of the inevitability of tragedy in postapartheid politics, should constitute 'a normal life. After the Struggle.'[71] Steve wants to refuse the tragic and embrace the ethical; he wishes not to foreclose on Struggle aspirations to utopia.[72] Gradually, however, Steve thinks an approximation might instead be found elsewhere, and the family's plans to emigrate to Australia occupy much of the novel, though they appear on the final page—in a move reminiscent of so many of Gordimer's open endings—to be shelved.

Just as Scott's analysis has application more broadly than in Grenada, it is not only in postcolonial contexts that a sense of disconnection from history and narratives of progress manifest, nor is it necessarily the case only in relation to revolutions widely taken to have failed. In the novels of some American women writing in the wake of the apparent success of the feminist movement in the West, for instance, Jane Elliott notes a paradoxical 'sense of failed futurity' too, suggesting by way of explanation that this 'perception of blocked futurity' was shared by progressive movements in the United States after the 1960s precisely because connections amongst temporality, agency, and narrative had been strained.[73] If 'history comes to be defined as a narrative whose goal is freedom', Elliott observes, narrative has nowhere to go when the goal is achieved.[74] Elliott posits that such logic is built into teleological narratives of revolution: what comes after is no time like the future promised in the narrative of revolutionary promise. Works of fiction that try to engage with this apparent after-time of history, she argues, 'appear to place us on a metanarrative path in which our own drive to produce freedom appears eventually and inexorably to render us unfree, trapped in a homogeneous world at odds with both change and human agency', such that '[t]he road to freedom [. . .] arrives inevitably at static time'.[75] Such a pessimistic vision might be thought to deny the possibility of revolution yielding a more free, more equal society. It is difficult, however, to think otherwise given the apparent success of the neoliberal project, or the rise of new fundamentalisms and nationalisms.

Several scholars turn to literary texts for what these might register about such temporal and affective orientations, these conditions of blocked futurity. Lauren Berlant, for one, considers how subjects adjust to the loss of fantasies of the good life promised by liberal democracy—economic wellbeing, rewarding intimate attachments, political representation—that seem forestalled by the neoliberal consensus. Deploying the phrase that is the title of her 2011 book, *Cruel Optimism*, as 'an analytic lever' to account for continuing attachments to these aspirations, even as they wear out their subjects, she reads texts and films from late-twentieth-century Western Europe and the United States for examples of—or to offer analogies for—the means of coping with contingency in which she is interested.[76] Her work shares with that of others in various Public Feelings projects across the United States an interest in the becoming political of everyday experience. In a similar vein, Ann Cvetkovich makes the case—in *Depression: A Public Feeling* (2012)—that instead of construing negative affects 'as getting in the way of politics or needing to be converted to something more active in order to become politics', we should recalibrate our sense of 'what counts as political'.[77] Both Berlant and Cvetkovich subscribe to the idea that representations of impasse ('I start where things are stuck', Berlant observes) can enable something other.[78] For Cvetkovich, assessments of what she calls 'political depression' develop from a need to find ways 'to survive disappointment' and revivify radical vision. The link between depression—the experience of stasis, of being mortgaged to a sense of hopefulness that proves time and again to be disappointable—is of relevance not only to queer theory, Cvetkovich reminds us: it also pertains 'to the politics of race in the wake of the incomplete projects of civil rights and decolonization'.[79] It certainly pertains to conditions in contemporary South Africa.

Neither Berlant nor Cvetkovich is ultimately interested in the aesthetic object per se, however. For both, novels, films, performance art, and everyday habits provide occasions for observing the unfolding of forms of cruel optimism (or of political depression), or offer analogies for its operation, or provide evidence for (or promise of) the operation of a means to rework or counter such bad feelings. This is not a critique (indeed, Berlant's observations on the emergence of new genres appropriate to contemporary 'stuckness' prove useful to me in Chapters 1 and 6[80]). Nor is it to quibble about methodology. Sianne Ngai, by contrast, while no less interested in the 'politically ambiguous work' of what she calls 'ugly feelings' (the title of her 2005 book), attends closely to how they manifest in the aesthetic object, specifically in the tone or mood legible in forms of narrative in the Western tradition, from fiction to film.[81] She is unapologetic about privileging 'the circumscribed standpoint of the literary to examine problems whose greatest import arguably lies beyond the sphere of the aesthetic per se', suggesting in fact that literature might be the perfect form in which to read negative affects. The 'situation of restricted agency from which all of them ensue is one that describes art's own position in a highly differentiated and totally commodified society', she observes.[82]

In the chapters that follow, each offering readings with the aim of addressing a range of affective and temporal versions of (or cousins to) disappointment, I focus on literary texts from a more restricted—but coherent—field than any of these critics: work by authors from one place, South Africa, focusing on writing produced after 1994. And I am interested in the works as literary artefacts at least as much as for what they might tell us about the moment in which they were written and about the ongoing moment in which I have been reading and rereading them. Thus, while—like both affect-studies and queer-studies scholars—I am drawn to Raymond Williams's argument for the usefulness of artistic production, not least literature, in discerning societal 'structures of feeling' in the present,[83] I am mindful too that (as Heather Love puts it so well) 'the public sphere and affect are different kinds of objects', requiring different responses and modes of analysis.[84] I try not to make generalizations about feelings held universally in common by South Africans; to claim such insight or presume such a collective would be folly. I read individual works for what they suggest about structures of feeling that might be said to be abroad in the land, but more importantly for the manner in which these are registered *in fiction*, for what we might say about the formal and thematic capacities of fiction—and of the novel in particular—in the present, in and in relation to this particular geographical and historical context.

OPEN ENDINGS, CLOSE READINGS

Literary fiction can tell us a great many things, but it does not serve as narrative might do in an anthropological investigation. It is different, too, from history regarded as narrative. Jennifer Wenzel makes a similar point in relation to her discussion of narratives of promise and failure in South Africa: fiction offers 'alternatives to the foreclosures inherent in reading *history* as narrative', she avers, 'particularly in reading the South African democratic transition in terms of a narrative closure that assumes a single, inevitable trajectory to the postapartheid present'.[85] Fiction keeps things open. Because it encodes what Susan Stewart calls a 'structure of desire', and because the location of that desire 'is always a future-past' (by which Stewart means both a closure imagined in a moment that necessarily passes, and a closure that necessarily implies a beginning; reading constitutes a 'deferment of experience in the direction of origin and thus eschaton, the point where narrative begins/ends', in Stewart's words), fiction both engenders and transcends 'the relation between materiality and meaning'—or lived experience and its representation.[86]

Narrative, both fictional *and* historical, serves for Paul Ricoeur as the most adequate response, in distinction to philosophy and speculative thinking, to the seeming aporias of our time-bound lives. As David Scott observes, Ricoeur posits a '*reciprocal* tension between time and narrative' whereby human time is organized as narrative, and one in turn rendered meaningful through its representation of the experience of temporality. 'Human action, then, unfolds in time, and the linguistic form best suited to the intelligibility of the temporality of action is narrative.'[87] But if readers anticipate an ending to a narrative, a degree of anxiety is inevitable if it does not come or arrives precipitously or in uncertain fashion.[88] If it is 'the structuring presence of the end to come' that directs our experience of narrative, in Peter Brooks's account (in *Reading for the Plot*), if 'we read in a spirit of confidence, and also a state of dependence, that what remains to be read will restructure the provisional meanings of the already read' ('the *anticipation of retrospection*' serving as 'our chief tool in making sense of narrative'),[89] then it is the disappointment of such anticipation that so often characterizes the experience of reading many of the works of fiction discussed in this book. It is also the case that disappointment, which is to say the frustration of expectation of closure or completeness, might be regarded as being at the heart of the novel as form. For Bakhtin, it was the novel's 'failure to maintain the monologic and authoritative voice of epic' that enables its representation of everyday life's heteroglossia, that allows it (in John Su's formulation) 'to perceive the world in terms of its multiplicity, not homogeneity'.[90] For Lukács, it was a 'strange and melancholy paradox' that the novel's moment of value is precisely its moment of failure, in contradistinction to life: what the novel depicts is 'the total absence of any fulfilment of meaning' (it ends, but it is not an end), 'yet the work contains the rich and rounded fullness of a true totality of life'.[91] Both Lukács and Bakhtin, then, regard disappointment as a defining generic feature of the novel, central to apprehending 'its potential contribution to politics'.[92]

It is a central premise of this study that it is largely in contemporary fiction, and particularly the exemplary works (representative and sui generis) that I discuss in detail in the chapters that follow, that we see examples of the treatment of now-time (in tension with backward glances and backward feelings) that do what historical narrative cannot: turn missed appointments and bad feelings into new appointments with the unfolding experience of alternative lives and possible futures. These, for the most part, offer plots without an ending, however—just as the temporality of South Africa's long interregnum has been the suspension of the plot of revolutionary overcoming. Wenzel's study of the means by which 'apocalyptic visions'—her focus is subsequent invocations of the infamous 1856–57 Cattle Killing episode in what is now South Africa's Eastern Cape province—'survive an apocalypse', which is to say the failure of that which they promised, proposes that moments of the failure or frustration of hope serve strongly in the South African imaginary as prompts to future transformation. She identifies what she calls a widespread 'recursive but ultimately future-oriented critical melancholia' in postapartheid writing, a diagnosis that will haunt many of the chapters that follow, as will Wenzel's exhortation for scholars to attend to the ways in which narrative fiction is equipped, in a way that historical description is not, to grasp 'heterotemporality and nonrationalist [...] pasts'.[93] Working in this spirit, my study will think about multiple simultaneous imperfect *presents*.

South African writing, of course, is replete with examples of disappointment in works that, frustrated with the constraints of colonial and apartheid-era social and political conditions, dwell thematically on expectation and enact formally the frustration of readerly expectation. Scholars have long observed on the occurrence of open endings in this literature, which might be recast as the disappointment of closure, figured variously as despairing *or* hopeful. Elleke Boehmer, for example, in a 1998 essay, contextualized the many open endings in works from Olive Schreiner's *Story of an African Farm* (1883) through Solomon T. Plaatje's *Mhudi* (1930), and beyond.[94] Then there is the open-endedness of any number of Coetzee's novels from the 1980s: the Magistrate lives on in his frontier settlement in *Waiting for the Barbarians* (1980); the eponymous protagonist—if that is what he is—is left wandering the slopes of Signal Hill at the close of *Life & Times of Michael K* (1983); characters' words surround the implied author in the curiously submerged now-time of the final chapter of *Foe* (1986); David Lurie promises to give up his favourite dog at the end of *Disgrace* (1999), but has not yet done so. More recently, in writing about trauma and what she figures as the country's state of 'Permanent Risk', Boehmer draws attention to instances in fiction—by Achmat Dangor, K. Sello Duiker, Damon Galgut, and others—and creative non-fiction (as in the collection *At Risk*) of 'hiatus, abrupt halt, suspended action', what she calls 'the often recurring moment of fade-out, the final glancing and seemingly meaningful impression that lacks follow-through', 'instances of irresolution, or of a dogged but undirected, even unwilled movement forwards'.[95] For Boehmer, these are signs of sublimation or repression of a traumatic past and evidence of a collective national repetition compulsion.[96]

The analyses in this book, while informed by Freud's discussion of melancholia, do not commit to such a psychoanalytic assessment of a putative shared national literary response to the past. Nor are my invocations of affect committed to either psychoanalytic or Deleuzian models. In Freud's early writings on emotional experience, affect is something like undifferentiated feeling, while in recent affect- and queer-studies work indebted to Deleuze, affect serves (Cvetkovich notes in a useful gloss) as 'force, intensity, or the capacity to move and be moved'.[97] Like Cvetkovich, I deploy affect 'in a generic sense' instead, 'as a category that encompasses affect, emotion, and feeling, and that includes impulses, desires, and feelings that get historically constructed in a range of ways'.[98]

I am committed to maximum pragmatism and the sensible use of analytical levers, rather than new theoretical orthodoxies, while remaining cognizant of Eugenie Brinkema's injunction against the generalities that some (particularly Deleuzian) turns to affect have produced. In *The Forms of the Affects* (2014), Brinkema warns against 'the vagueness of purely negative definitional endeavors' that risk ceding 'specificity—generic, emotional, historical—to cognitivists [. . .] who have taken Aristotelian taxonomizing to heart in their ever-narrowing treatment of, say, startle in horror films, or empathetic weeping in melodramas' (or, indeed, disappointment in novels).[99] '*The turning to affect in the humanities does not obliterate the problem of form and representation. Affect is not where reading is no longer needed*', she notes.[100] Hence paying attention to how particular kinds of affect are bound to particular forms is required: 'Treating affect as a problematic of structure, form, and aesthetics is an attempt to reintroduce particularity to any consideration of affects. It is also an attempt to seize the passions of affect studies for textual interpretation and close reading.'[101]

While many critics have debated the open-endedness of apartheid-era writing or attended to questions of temporality and form in—for example—black South African negotiations of modernity,[102] none has offered an engagement with issues of temporality and affect *together* in writing, and especially fiction, from or about South Africa *since* 1994, and furthermore not in a way that has in view the wider relevance of such analyses for understanding the ways in which literatures from (for want of a better term, and with due cognizance of the operation of local and global institutions of publishing) non-metropolitan locations, literatures that are produced in or because of their subject matter associated with the Global South (nuanced in this case to take account of the layering of first- and third-world in a country like South Africa), function in configurations of World Literature—pedagogically, institutionally, and (yes) affectively. *Present Imperfect* aims to do all of this. It explores the capacities of fiction for thinking through impasse, for rendering the everyday political, for inviting a phenomenological encounter with feeling otherwise and with looking backwards, but also with educated hopefulness. The chapters that follow explore these capabilities and performances as evidenced in the work of several of the most significant novelists of the postapartheid period, authors with expansive oeuvres of considerable depth and sophistication. It concludes by testing some of these modes of reading on debut novels by two young South African novelists. I could well have offered a broader survey of work by a wider range of writers, but I make no excuse for focusing on the particular authors and texts that I treat in detail; my analyses can be augmented by the reader with reference to the work of many more, whether Dangor, Duiker, and Galgut (invoked by Boehmer), Lauren Beukes, Zakes Mda, Thando Mgqolozana, S.J. Naudé, Henrietta Rose-Innes, Etienne van Heerden, or Eben Venter, amongst others.

Chapter 1 considers the representation of impasse, of waiting, in three of Winterbach's novels. I am interested in the forms of precarious life at issue in these texts, in what is at stake in how they speak to the present-ness of contemporary South African experience. I test the usefulness of Berlant's idea of cruel optimism, and of the 'situation tragedy' as the genre in which we see its consequences formally engaged, putting Berlant's affect-studies analysis in conversation with David Scott's notion of postcolonial, post-emancipation temporalities as tragic. Chapter 2 asks what representations of various kinds of what I call disaffection—and most especially boredom, a mood associated with waiting in which the unfolding of the present is not as one might have thought it could or should be—have to tell us about genre, form, and the politics of writing in the present. My focus is primarily on Coetzee's fictionalized memoirs, the *Scenes from Provincial Life*, through which I read his staging of disaffection in places regarded as marginal, somehow at a tangent to metropolitan engagements with temporality, in which disappointments, temporal and affective, proliferate productively. Here, as elsewhere where a discussion of intertextuality is a key function of my analysis (in Chapters 1 and 5, for example), the conversations that South African writers conduct with texts that are frequently *not* South African in origin or subject serve as key formal (and ethical) instances of an insistence on engaging with broader, global themes and concerns—mine, but crucially also the authors'. Intertextuality, viewed in this way, appears as a form of what Bloch calls educated hopefulness, a refusal to cede the revolutionary potential of the transition to monolithic constructions of nation or family, or national family. (Indeed, my use of a wide range of theoretical perspectives serves a similar function, offering an analogous refusal to expectations about what might be expected in a study of South African literature.) I do not make this case in a focused way again, but rely on my readings to illustrate the potential of these frequently surprising and inventive conversations.

Chapter 3 considers the question of the forced adoption of the temporality of another—a different episteme, political order, cultural or racial performed identity—and the multiple disappointments (missed appointments as well as frustrated desires) that result, principally in relation to Van Niekerk's magisterial Afrikaans-language novel *Agaat* (2004). This chapter also considers the usefulness for thinking through questions of the locatedness of memory, cultural competency, and the archive, and of regarding translation as metaphorical appointment promised with the text to speakers of a different language, elsewhere. Chapter 4 examines the nature of the critical form of nostalgia offered in Vladislavić's varied oeuvre (I focus on short fiction, two novels, and a work of creative non-fiction) as response to the dangers of selective memory—and memorialization—that characterizes some engagements with the disappointments of postapartheid South Africa. Wicomb's subtle and complex fictions respond in part to similarly pernicious, selective renderings of the new nation's national imaginaries. In Chapter 5, I consider her particular engagement with the promises of new social formations by focusing on a number of loose ends—chiefly on queer figures, who offer new ways of thinking about the structure of the national family, and on what I cast as formally queer strategies, including Wicomb's exploration of the subversive, ethical possibilities of meta- and intertextuality.

Finally, in Chapter 6, I turn to consider writing by a new generation of writers, represented by two young black novelists. I focus on two debuts: Mahlangu's *Penumbra* (2013) and Ntshanga's *The Reactive* (2014). Recent as these works may be, however, we might well be witnessing what appears to be a turn in legible structures of feeling in South Africa in the wake of the #RhodesMustFall and #FeesMustFall campaigns of 2015 and 2016, and in tandem with ongoing activism against the failures of the ANC government (though also for broader transformation of all kinds), away from a disappointment registered as impasse towards an anger whose future effects are entirely unpredictable. Changing conditions will produce new responses. It is my hope that this book will point towards ways in which we may read these, too.

1

On Being Stuck

Stasis and Situation Tragedy

i was born 26 july 1939 in ventersdorp
i found myself in a situation
i was born 26 july 1939 in sophiatown
i found myself in a situation
i was born 26 july 1939 in district six
i found myself in a situation
[....]
i still find myself in a situation
[....]

—Wopko Jensma, 'Spanner in the What? Works' (1977)[1]

Unexplained things happen to apparently ordinary characters in recent novels by Afrikaans-language author Ingrid Winterbach.[2] They wake suddenly conscious of an emptiness that cannot be explained. A burglary or a phone call, or an anticipated phone call that does not come, precipitates profound existential ennui. Personal and professional networks begin to unravel—family members make unanticipated demands, relationships collapse, employment ceases. In short, they find plans thwarted and expectations of happiness postponed. Having thought of themselves as agents, subjects of their own life stories, men and women in Winterbach's fictions find themselves subject to events, trapped in situations beyond their control, in unfolding plots that answer to an unfathomable logic. This happens, for example, to the character Maria Volschenk in Winterbach's 2012 novel, *Die aanspraak van lewende wesens*, published in 2015 in Michiel Heyns's English translation as *It Might Get Loud* (the title could have been rendered 'the address'—or claim—'of living things'). Maria, a divorced woman of late-middle age resident in Durban, in a more-or-less stable relationship with one grown son living away from home, suddenly feels one day as if something—'*iets*' in Afrikaans—has descended upon her:

> Something, one day, starts closing in on Maria Volschenk. It manifests itself first of all in her body as a sensation of emptiness, exactly at the juncture of

> her last two floating ribs, approximately at the lowest point of the sternum [. . .]. Right there is what feels like an ice-cold, hollow spot—something closely akin to pain—gradually permeating the rest of her organs. [. . .] Eventually the sensation of a percolating void, a vacuum, settles in her head as well.[3]

Maria is a 'systematic woman'—by profession an accountant—and so sets about taking stock of her life in search of an explanation for the 'sudden beleaguered sensation' she experiences physically and emotionally.[4] She fills her time with evening classes (on the naked figure in Western art; on Bronze Age China) and games with neighbours (cards with one, chess with another). She tries therapy. Nothing helps. Perhaps, she muses, 'she needs an alternative vocabulary', one that features '[f]orgiveness, purity, remorse'.[5] Where to find this new lexicon becomes the puzzle she must solve. The limits of language frequently concern Winterbach characters, though we should note here that much is inevitably lost in translation.

Meanwhile, across town, small-businessman Karl Hofmeyr receives a summons from mysterious artist-figure Josias Brandt, a modern-day magus who presides over a hillside city farm in Cape Town, here offering shelter to a motley crew of the down-at-heel and dispossessed of all races. Brandt demands Karl retrieve his artist brother, Ignatius (Iggy), who has suffered some kind of breakdown. Karl's cross-country car journey is not easy, however, for he is both absent-minded and obsessive-compulsive: he cannot abide oil, bad smells, 'rats, excreta or open wounds'; he washes his hands repeatedly; he is incapacitated by anxiety when encountering numbers he considers unlucky.[6] Karl forgets a bundle of Iggy's letters at a guesthouse, has car trouble, and is distracted by fellow travellers encountered along the way: right-wingers, who mistake him for one of their own; heavy-metal fans, with whom he exchanges stories of memorable concerts (this, too, being an obsession). Lured to a graveyard in a dusty town (Beaufort West) midway through his journey, he is shot in the leg in a farcical melee, and by the time he arrives in Cape Town finds that Iggy has been hospitalized and lies sedated in a mental ward.

Maria and Karl's situations are broadly representative of the predicaments of characters in most of Winterbach's novels, including the two immediately preceding *Die aanspraak van lewende wesens—Die boek van toeval en toeverlaat* (2006), translated as *The Book of Happenstance* (2008), and *Die benederyk* (2010), translated as *The Road of Excess* (2014).[7] Each features characters caught in states of listlessness, if not of despair, as well as representatives of mystical or esoteric experience who challenge protagonists' scepticism or cynicism, prompting physical or metaphorical journeys in search of redress, resolution, or change. In all three, the quests remain unfinished—are in fact unresolvable. Characters may be jolted from complacency into action they barely comprehend, but they find themselves simply in a different variety of being stuck. In *The Road of Excess*, for example, crippling ennui strikes Aaron Adendorff, a visual artist struggling with cancer (it is in remission), with the loss of his late wife, and with the waning of his career. When the owner of the gallery that represents him chooses younger, edgier artists for an exhibition and refuses to take his calls, he is seized by a 'mood of infinite desolation' until a new neighbour named Bubbles Bothma appears on the scene.[8] One of the most memorable minor characters in recent Afrikaans fiction, she is 'decked out in a Donald Duck sweatshirt, back-to-front cap, brightly-striped exercise pants, plus silver running shoes' when Aaron first encounters her. 'Be careful, he thinks. This one looks like a tricky customer.'[9] A messenger in winged Nike trainers, prospective Virgil to his Dante or Sancho Panza to his Quixote, Bubbles tries to take a reluctant Aaron under her wing, lending him self-help tapes and offering to assassinate his gallerist (he is not sure whether she is serious). Then there are Aaron's brothers: Benjamin, who is 'in the grip of an unidentifiable, incapacitating psychic malaise',[10] and Stefaans, once a promising criminologist, now a recovering Phensedyl addict who sends Aaron regular mobile phone messages as he tries to unpick aspects of their shared past. These characters' names, we might notice, are shared with biblical figures who face temptations and judgment but emerge sanctified by their trials: Aaron and Benjamin, notable Old Testament brothers (to Moses and Joseph, respectively); Stephen, the first martyr of the Christian church; and Mary Magdalene (Bubbles's birth name is Magdalena), the prostitute whose feet Jesus bathes before the Last Supper. But names are often ironic in Winterbach's work: Volschenk suggests *volgeskenk*, to have filled up (a glass, for example), though Maria's current situation is one of overwhelming emptiness.

The Book of Happenstance features a first-person narrator, Helena Verbloem (her name suggests a blooming, a flowering, long past), who describes a short period spent in Durban, between March and October 2005, as a lexicographer on a project cataloguing Afrikaans words that have fallen into disuse. Three months into her contract, her rented garden flat is burgled and thirty-two seashells from her collection are stolen; only nine are later recovered. Soon afterwards, Helena's employer, Theo Verwey, is murdered (his death is announced proleptically on the opening page) and she is left on the verge of great uncertainty. Not only does Helena feel unmoored in subtropical Durban, far from her upcountry hometown of Johannesburg, she is plagued by self-recriminations over her treatment of family members and disturbed by late-night phone calls from a mysterious man who claims they met twenty-seven years previously. It is the loss of her shells, however, that concentrates her sense of dispossession and displacement most acutely. They have been objects of contemplation and a source of solace, and her narrative is marked by an obsessive, endlessly frustrated quest for clues that might lead to their recovery.

If I have made Winterbach's novels sound like peculiar mixes of elegy and farce, comic metaphysical—and metafictional—detective fiction and works of mourning, they partake of all those genres. More to the point, there is something about the overwrought and the bathetic in each text that approximates a variety of affective responses to the textures of daily life for some in postapartheid South Africa. They chart the becoming-historical, the political valences, of the everyday ordinary. That they also frequently engage the mythical or allegorical suggests their appeal beyond the local conditions depicted, however. Characters are self-consciously concerned with testing alternative structures of meaning, forms of faith, the explanatory potential of grand narratives and metadiscourses, all precisely what people who seem stuck—who are waiting for something—do. These novels might depict 'South African' characters (most, it should be said, are middle-class white Afrikaners) suffering from a range of bad feelings, from ennui, frustration, boredom, and disappointment, but these same disorders befall many modern subjects elsewhere. Stasis, banality, disappointment: these keywords, and my formulations above, evoke the engagement of affect-studies scholars, and Lauren Berlant in particular, with conditions of being stuck as it registers in contemporary Western culture.

In interventions over two decades, Berlant has extended her concern with sentiment and sexuality in the discourses of American national fantasies and 'counterfantasies' to make a strong case for paying attention to what representations of affect, and especially feeling stuck, reveal about our psycho-social modes of coping with uncertainty.[11] The uncertainty that particularly interests her is characterized by the deferral of those longings for the good life, for the politics and polities that might enable it, that have been inherited (to paraphrase and simplify) from the Baby Boomers, longings that are increasingly unsustainable—even naïve—under conditions of globalization, post-Fordism, and neoliberal governance in contemporary post-Cold War Europe and North America, the sites of Berlant's principal interests. Yet the implications of such an analysis run wider: if the 'fantasies that are fraying' (in Berlant's reading of the situation) range from 'upward mobility, job security, political and social equality' to 'lively, durable intimacy', South Africans long for these things, too.[12] And if continuing to long for such things is, in Berlant's suggestive phrasing, cruel (we continue to invest in them even as we understand that it is bad for us to do so, precisely because they are no longer realistic; we feel compelled to 'repeat a toxic optimism' '*just in case* it will be different' next time around), many South Africans, including many who could not—or would not have been able to—vote before 1994, might think the same thing with every five-year national and provincial election cycle: perhaps the promises of the 'New' South Africa will yet become tangible.[13]

The novels discussed in this chapter demonstrate uncommonly well a series of cruel optimisms and conditions of impasse very like those described by Berlant. Characters in Winterbach's fictions frequently hope for better, even as they know that such expectation might be wishful thinking. Repeated commitment to such thought can, however, be productive. Our 'vague expectations of normative optimism' might offer 'an opening and a defense', Berlant suggests, which might generate what she calls 'small self-interruptions' that point to 'heterotopias of sovereignty amid structural inequality, political depression, and other intimate disappointments'.[14] Hope, in other words, provides the opening for alternatively imagined futures, even as subjects feel stuck. In Berlant's suggestive formulation, affect's usefulness lies in its potential to register 'conditions of life that move across persons and worlds, play out in lived time, and energize attachments'.[15] It is attachments—familial, aesthetic, psychological, and societal—that Winterbach investigates repeatedly, and all are obliquely but pervasively *political*. If 'the aesthetic or formal rendition of affective experience provides evidence of *historical processes*', in Berlant's assessment, we might reasonably ask what Winterbach's novels have to say about South Africa now, and about the particular capacity of the kind of novel she writes to engage with the affective landscape of the present.[16] What responses are registered in the fiction, and with what implications for understanding the present, and the work of fiction *in* the present?

In this book's introduction I implied reservation about the status of exemplary texts in Berlant's work. Where I see her analysis in *Cruel Optimism* as being of particular use for my project is in what she suggests about texts themselves rather than in how they signify in her argument. In particular, what she observes about generic improvisation in the midst of uncertainty is instructive. 'Genres provide an affective expectation of the experience of watching something unfold', Berlant observes; what she calls the 'waning of genre' thus offers a glimpse of 'potential openings within and beyond the impasse of adjustment that constant crisis creates'.[17] Of particular interest to Berlant is what she calls the *situation*—in the sense that police procedurals involve a police officer conventionally saying something like: 'We have a situation here'.[18] A situation, in other words, is something that is not or is not only (or yet) an event, whose state of 'animated suspension—not suspended animation' anticipates an end that those within the situation cannot foresee or predict. A situation is something in which subjects try to maintain equilibrium while figuring out 'how to adjust'.[19] It is in what Berlant calls the 'situation tragedy', a 'new generic hybrid' in cultural production in the United States and Western Europe since 1990, that such animated suspension plays out most clearly. The situation tragedy blends situation comedy with tragedy: 'people are fated to express their flaws episodically, over and over, without learning, changing, being relieved, becoming better, or dying'.[20]

The idea of situation tragedy as genre is suggestive for reading Winterbach's novels, with their questing characters, conditions of stasis, and frustrations of the expectation of narrative closure. It also re-energizes the traces of an older engagement with political stasis indexed by the word *situation* in the South African context. Consider its ironic use by Lewis Nkosi, Bloke Modisane, and other black writer-intellectuals of the 1960s, who called themselves *situations*, invoking the label used by township gangsters to deride the aspirations of black workers applying to 'situations vacant' advertisements in the newspapers to describe their own sense of being caught between white culture and the conditions of black life under apartheid.[21] Or consider the iconic poem 'Spanner in the What? Works', by the apartheid era's perhaps most enigmatic anti-poet, Wopko Jensma, who imagines the situation into which he was born, white, in Middelburg in 1939, one differently inflected but no less fraught than had he been born black in Sophiatown, or coloured[22] in District Six, a condition of stasis and alienation shared across race, one in which he is trapped apparently interminably. Jensma's own end is the open ending to end all others: he disappeared without trace from a boarding house in Johannesburg in 1993, aged fifty-four, on the eve of the new era, rendering the hopes expressed in the poem—'to live to the age of sixty / [. . .] to leave some evidence / [. . . .] / that i created something / out of my situation'—especially poignant, even tragic. He is presumed dead.[23]

Thinking about Winterbach's work in relation to the idea of some version of what Berlant calls the situation tragedy offers a way to read them socio-politically—something Afrikaans-language critics of the work have largely failed to do. We could pause here to speculate about the novels' popularity amongst Afrikaans-language intellectuals, for Winterbach has been one of the most garlanded with prizes of recent Afrikaans-language authors.[24] We might ask what it is about these novels, concerned as they are with language, with ageing white Afrikaners, and with the waning of varieties of faith, that speaks so powerfully to those who continue to wield the power to validate fiction as literary and prizeworthy in South Africa. I will not seek to answer this question directly in what follows: those qualities that are attractive to particular awarding bodies are not necessarily the same as those that, in my view, make Winterbach's amongst the most moving and perceptive works of fiction published in South Africa in any language in the last three decades.

I am interested in the forms of material and metaphorical precarity at issue in the three texts described above, which I treat as something like a trilogy. What is at stake in understanding how they speak to the present-ness—how do they represent the now-time—of contemporary South African experience? These novels fit the following criteria: published since 1994; set in postapartheid South Africa; available in English translation. *The Elusive Moth*, first published as *Karolina Ferreira* in 1993, deals with many of the same issues. *To Hell With Cronjé*, which appeared in Afrikaans in 2002, does so too, but is set at the close of the Anglo-Boer War (in 1902). *Vlakwater*, published in 2015, was not translated at the time of writing, neither were *Landskap met vroue en slang* or *Buller se plan*. Much of what I observe in what follows might have been written in relation to these texts, too, and I encourage the reader who is so able to engage with them in the light of what I have to say about *The Book of Happenstance*, *The Road of Excess*, and *It Might Get Loud*. Thinking about Winterbach's work in relation to the idea of some version of what Berlant labels the situation tragedy opens the way, too, to suggest grounds for comparison with an emergent literature of stasis featuring *black* South African subjects—particularly township, inner-city, and new-elite youth characters. I turn to these works in this book's final chapter.

ACCIDENTAL ATTACHMENTS

The Book of Happenstance could be described—Helize van Vuuren suggests—as a novel that explores the tensions between the discourses of religion and evolution, a detective novel, an urban novel treating 'cosmopolitan life in Durban', and as 'a contemporary postcolonial novel with strong socio-critical commentary'.[25] While Van Vuuren does not specify what the socio-critical commentary might be, like many Afrikaans-language critics she refers to the novel's engagement with the supposed threats facing the Afrikaans language and Afrikaner culture in the post-apartheid dispensation, citing as evidence Helena's dictionary work and the city library's thinning out of its Afrikaans-language literary holdings. While such threats might be in Winterbach's sights, and while it is true that white Afrikaner characters tend to be most acutely beset by ennui or despair in her novels (by contrast, black characters tend to be optimistic), such instrumentalized readings do not account for the way white anxieties are often rendered ironic or bathetic, and are contextualized—as in *The Book of Happenstance*, in relation to natural processes of evolution.[26] It is the novel's engagement with the everydayness of life in postapartheid society, with its small despairs and the ongoing injustices to which *all* are now prone, that makes *Happenstance*'s oblique 'commentary' very much more than a variety of white nostalgia or despair. Indeed, the text's testing of the tensions between discourses of science and faith suggests that Winterbach's focus is in part altogether more global, which is to say ambitious for what postapartheid fiction might do.

Throughout her period of displacement in Durban, Helena becomes fascinated with extinction and evolution, extending to an existential plane the processes charted in her lexicographical work. Her office is suggestively located in a building also housing the city library and the natural history museum, bringing together language, literature, evolutionary science, and shells (there is a collection in the museum's basement). One of the museum's employees, the palaeontologist Hugo Hattingh, tells Helena that coincidence ('*toeval*') has driven species development, that evolution is about happenstance, not progress.[27] '*Toeverlaat*'—in the novel's original title—gestures towards expectation, but also refuge, a settled place of safety amidst chaos.[28] These twin poles, accident and security, are reflected in the novel's competing discourses of science and belief. Helena seeks comfort in the structure of scientific explanation ('On the internet I look up the geological periods. [...] These periods will form the framework for my new knowledge, for everything that I hope to learn from Hugo Hattingh'), yet she is simultaneously troubled by the insignificance ascribed to humans by evolutionary science and astrophysics.[29] The perceived indifference of the universe is exemplified for her by the stark, unsympathetic, lens-less eye of the nautilus (thus it comes back to shells, or the creatures who used to inhabit them), which strikes her as a Platonic 'blueprint of an eye', 'wholly eye: intrepid, inexorable' and 'primeval', 'created after the image of God'.[30] Even if the eye allows for an apprehension of intelligent design (although the formulation does not wholly endorse this), it appears entirely unintelligible.

Sof Benade, Helena's closest friend in Durban, is important in respect of the tensions between accident and order: her first name, for *Sofia*, suggests wisdom; she was raised in a *pastorie*, the daughter of a Dutch Reformed minister, but is foul-mouthed and opinionated, holding all received verities up to examination. Sof represents disillusioned religious belief, yet she maintains the merest *possibility* of faith. 'Eternity is God's time', she answers Helena's query about eternity's nature; 'It is when our time has run out.'[31] She is also, appropriately enough for a translator (her day job), Helena's metaphorical guide to the underworld and her guardian during their visits, to pursue leads in their search for the shells, to Ladybrand, a real Free State town named for the wife of a peer with the surname Brand that also—because *brand* means fire (or 'to burn') in Afrikaans—references the danger of Helena herself being consumed by her quest. The novel repeatedly casts searches for stability and authority as invariably fruitless, even dangerous. Yet just as it stages the valorization of coincidence, it also refuses resolution: there are no neat tie-ups, only loose ends and, just as a reader begins to expect profundity, bathos. 'On the one hand', Helena explains, 'I feel myself moved by the drama of evolution, and on the other by the drama of my stolen shells.'[32] In a misguided attempt to speak in terms she thinks will be understood by a black man she assumes adheres to the cultural practice of ancestor veneration, she tells police detective Modisane that the missing shells are like her 'ancestors', though she knows at the same time that the comparison is ludicrous: 'the shells are invertebrates, mollusks, and this young man with the smooth, dark-brown skin and I share a vertebrate primal ancestor'.[33] What the shells represent remains in doubt. In that they are an aid to meditation, they serve as prompts for Helena to think about how her responses to *things* are more emotionally charged than her responses to *people*. Her overwhelming emotional investment in the hope of their recovery suggests something like what Berlant describes as a cruel optimism: hope likely to be endlessly frustrated, hope that might in fact damage our attachments to others.

Berlant's injunction that we 'attend to the convolutions of attachment that involve a desire to stay proximate, no matter what, to the potential openings marked out by fantasies of the good life, self-continuity, or conflictedness' is germane here.[34] By *conflictedness* I think Berlant means a kind of self-knowledge of our own implication—our being implicated—in perpetuating structures of investment that are self-defeating. These include investment in optimism, but also in that which subtends the status quo, which generates the *need* for optimism. Hegemony, Berlant reminds us, is 'not merely domination dressed more becomingly', it is rather—or it is also—'a metastructure of consent'.[35] Consent is central to our complicity in hegemony because we have consented implicitly to a structure of collective agreement about the desirability of the fantasy of a good life, or what Sara Ahmed might describe as the promise of happiness. 'As citizens of the promise of hegemonic sociability', 'we have consented to consent to a story about the potentialities of the good life around which people execute all sorts of collateral agreements', Berlant suggests.[36] Unpicking what these collateral agreements might be—or assessing the chances of a good-life pay-off for such consent—is never easy, but such agreements are at the very centre of sociality, of attachment.

The operation of power at multiple levels, including the power to divest subjects of any good-life aspirations (let alone of life itself), is entirely opaque in *The Book of Happenstance*. It is clear neither who kills Theo Verwey, nor who steals Helena's shells (Patrick Steinmeier, the man from whom some are recovered, is found hanged).[37] Power, hegemony, and consent are all rendered mysterious, and power is mysteriously *absent*, indeed in a manner not unlike the absent-but-everywhere-implicated agents of apartheid in Alex La Guma's *A Walk in the Night* (1962), whose structure and obsessional detail J.M. Coetzee compared in a 1971 essay with the naturalist novel, with which it shared implicit social critique, and the American detective noir, with which it shared a propensity for moral judgment.[38] Both models are at play here, evident in Winterbach's obsessive detail and in the structure of the frustrated detective plot, complemented in a complex manner by exploration of the language of guilt and predetermination (that runs parallel—rather than counter—to the novel's engagement with evolutionary discourse). Helena, for example, meditating on the utopian and thinking about her ex-husband's difficult life, remarks: 'Utopian fantasies? All his life he paid for sins he had not committed. Hereditary sin. The sins of the fathers visited upon the children.'[39]

As for attachment, the theft of her shells forces Helena to take stock of her own, in particular her relations with her family: her late sister, an older brother who died before she was born, a younger brother who has removed himself from the family, her maternal grandfather (who abandoned his family for two decades), and her adult daughter, who now has a life of her own.[40] Helena thinks, too, about her messy divorce, the unsatisfactory relationship with her long-distance lover, Frans de Waard, and about claims made upon her—as in those late-night phone calls from the mysterious Freek van As—to which she has no recollection of consenting. This (non-) relationship with Frans is representative of many of the novel's dead-end encounters, which are neither fulfilling nor generative for Helena. She recalls a number of failed relationships and at least one instance of attempted sexual abuse (she was fourteen and it was at the hands of an older man; later she chooses Dolly Haze, in allusion to Nabokov's *Lolita*, as a pseudonym).[41] Johannes 'Sailor' Taljaard, the natural history museum's dashing 'curator of exhibits', might have been having an affair with Theo. Helena comes across Sailor and Hugo Hattingh having sex in a storeroom and thinks of them in relation to the word '*Doodjakker*—to gambol, frisk, cavort, and caper *to death*'.[42] Note, too, that the stranger who calls at night bears a name encoding the threat (or promise) of death: 'Freek' is not far from '*vreet*', meaning 'to eat' (especially like an animal), nor from '*vrek*' (to die), while 'van As' might be translated as 'of or from ash'. The invocation of death echoes a current preoccupation of Helena's dictionary work: words formed with the stem '*dood*'—death, dead.[43] Subjection to an indifferent universe, to the inevitability of death, to everyday crime, and to the deterioration of relationships, are all placed on a continuum, all frustrate narratives of (endless) progress. Another word on which Helena muses is '*Doolhof*', maze, a place in which (she elaborates) 'one cannot find one's way', used figuratively to refer to 'a complex situation or set of circumstances in which it is difficult to follow the right way; a situation that makes no sense'.[44] Where a labyrinth might be understood as a ritual space of metamorphosis, indeed which even houses a monster (there are allusions to the minotaur), a maze is merely a place in which one is likely to get lost, to become stuck. Helena wonders about whether her shells have entered a metaphorical labyrinth, as if the association with ritual or magical transformation might offer an explanation where there appears to be none.[45]

In related vein, *The Book of Happenstance* is concerned with questions of affiliation in other ways, through its dense allusiveness. Helena is a writer (she published a novel in her thirties and is busy writing another), and she and Sof reference a range of texts and writers, from canonical Afrikaans authors Johannes van Melle, Jochem van Bruggen, C.M. van den Heever, D.F. Malherbe, Eugène Marais, and C. Louis Leipoldt, to Europeans and Americans like Kafka (Sof quotes from *Der Schloss* as they make their first journey to Ladybrand), Joyce (whose exile in Trieste and relationship with his daughter is discussed), Wallace Stevens (an influence on a poet in Helena's past), Nabokov (references to *Lolita*), Beckett (Malone and Molloy), and Stoppard (*Rosencrantz and Guildenstern Are Dead*).[46] This is catholic taste for a South African text, but allusiveness and intertextuality signal more than a magpie habit or a desire for markers of cultural cosmopolitanism. Two particular intertexts bear this out. Understanding the implications of Winterbach's choice of these particular texts is crucial to teasing out the implications of her work's representation of stasis more broadly, hinging as it does on two key—and related—issues: an engagement with death, loss and mourning; and an investment in the aesthetic, the work of art, in its face.

A STILL LIFE, STILL ALIVE

The first intertext is J.M. Coetzee's *Age of Iron* (1990). Set in Cape Town in mid 1986, against the backdrop of the State of Emergency declared by President P.W. Botha a year earlier and of the state-sponsored vigilante violence that rendered many black shack-dwellers homeless in the middle of the Cape winter that year, this novel constituted a break from the author's previous work—the more overtly allegorical *Waiting for the*

Barbarians (1980), the future dystopia of *Life & Times of Michael K* (1983), the intertextual historical fantasy of *Foe* (1986).[47] But if *Age of Iron* examines the demands made on people of conscience in a *particular* time and place, those who, like the novel's narrator Mrs Curren, have not thought of themselves as political and who wish to hold the aesthetic separate from protest, it is simultaneously concerned with broad and potentially universal enquiries: liminality, provisionality, contingency, crises of attachment, and engagements with alterity, all personified in the novel in Mrs Curren's encounter with the enigmatic Vercueil, a vagrant who takes up residence in the dying woman's home.

The Book of Happenstance shares this impulse to balance the local and universal. What is more, Helena Verbloem discusses Coetzee's novel directly, commenting that she and Sof Benade had once sat in a car overlooking a Durban beach 'in the manner of Mrs. C and Vercueil' (the allusion is to a scene in which Coetzee's characters are parked on Boyes Drive, above Muizenberg Beach, in Cape Town).[48] Helena is struck by Mrs Curren's humanism, by her expressions of sadness, and by the fact that she compares herself to a shell ('"I am hollow," she says, "I am a shell"'), yet she is also aware of the differences between her experience and that depicted in Coetzee's novel: unlike Mrs Curren, Helena concedes, she is 'not there yet', is 'not yet a shell'. Sof is also not really like Vercueil, nor is Helena 'as old as Mrs. C' or terminally ill. 'As a character, I am not as sorely tried as she is', Helena thinks. 'My *shells* have been stolen, but this is hardly anything compared to the losses she has to endure in the course of that novel.'[49] The comparisons are suggestive, but so is Helena's disavowal of their congruence. *This* time is not precisely like *that* time, and yet the quality of 'limbo' that Mrs Curren frequently observes in her experience of the death-throes of apartheid (the period called by Gordimer, after Gramsci, the interregnum, beset by morbid symptoms) seems entirely appropriate to the country as depicted in *The Book of Happenstance*, nearly two decades later.[50]

Through these allusions, *The Book of Happenstance* confirms that it is self-consciously concerned with the space of literature as one in which a certain kind of life, however fragile, might persist. Yet such a space is also under threat. *Age of Iron* takes the form of a narrative addressed by Mrs Curren to her expatriate daughter in North America, possibly in the form of letters, entrusted to Vercueil, which may or may not reach their intended reader. Towards the end of her own narrative, Helena muses that:

> Mrs. C dies at the close of *that* book. Vercueil folds his arms around her like the angel of death, but it brings her no comfort, no consolation. The writer does not see it as his writerly task or duty to console either Mrs. C or the

> reader. Resolution, yes, there is resolution at the end of that novel, but not consolation.[51]

Later, Helena thinks about 'Mrs. C's visit to the young black boy in hospital, the child with whom she spoke of Thucydides' and how for Mrs Curren 'there was no more hope of consolation—that was the author's conclusion'.[52] One might in fact read the ending in precisely opposite terms, and it is certainly consolation despite an absence of resolution (perhaps consolation in the very fact of uncertainty) that Helena's own narrative seems to will at its close. Her sister Joets is dead, as are her mother and father, but her own daughter lives, as does her younger brother (who 'is somewhere', though she has 'no idea where'); most importantly, she reflects, 'I am alive', even if 'my shells I shall never find again'.[53] *The Book of Happenstance* ends with Helena expecting to see the prodigal brother whose return has been promised, about which she is optimistic, but which may not come to pass.

Death, uncertainty, the tension between specific local conditions and power diffused globally, and the role of art in the face of annihilation—all these issues are central, too, to the second of the key intertexts with which Helena engages. She has recently read Don DeLillo's *Cosmopolis* (2003) and discusses it on a number of occasions with Theo Verwey, telling him about the young billionaire Eric Packer's desire to buy the Rothko Chapel, how he loses his and his estranged wife's money in risky financial trading, and about the funeral procession of a rap singer that Packer's limousine encounters as it makes its way westward across Midtown Manhattan.[54] DeLillo's novel is set in April 2000, the month key indices on Wall Street reached record highs—but also wobbled, in a precursor to the downturn later in the decade.[55] At a moment that speaks powerfully to the decay of a narrative of the universal accessibility of the good life fantasy, in other words, *Cosmopolis* sets extreme wealth, exemplified in Packer, against extreme precarity, in the person of his disgruntled former employee, who shoots Packer at the end of the novel. When the limousine encounters anti-globalization protesters, Packer loses no time in critiquing their tactics: they have lost the battle; it is he who represents the future—in fact he employs a full-time futurologist, Vija Kinski (who bears a resemblance to the sidekicks in Winterbach's novels).[56] In an echo conflating the funeral procession and the anti-globalization protests in *Cosmopolis*, Winterbach has Theo's funeral cortege encounter a protest march by trade unions and the AIDS Treatment Action Campaign, groups insisting on the rights of people subject to precarious working conditions *and* precarious conditions of life (*The Book of Happenstance* is set at the height of the South African government's culpable questioning of AIDS anti-retroviral treatment regimes[57]).

There are many other formal and thematic points of affinity between Winterbach's work and DeLillo's. These include their reworking of the detective plot (which DeLillo offers in *Libra* and *Mao II*, for instance), critiques of often-occluded structures of power, and fondness for ambiguous endings. DeLillo's fascination with the inexplicable, the tension between modernity's valorization of the rational and the continuing attractions of older explanatory models—the supernatural, ritual, knowledge promised by secret societies—is shared by Winterbach.[58] These aspects of her work also evidence a debt to the work of Etienne Leroux, the avant-garde Afrikaans-language novelist and a leading member of the '*Sestiger*' (Sixtier/60s) group with whom a young Winterbach, aged eighteen, had engaged in a correspondence that formed the basis for Leroux's 1967 novel, *18–44* (forty-four being his age at the time). One might think especially of Leroux's most famous novels, the *Silberstein* trilogy, metaphysical and allegorical works that blend postmodern experiment with the deconstructed detective novel, classically indebted allegory, Jungian theory, and the *plaasroman* (farm novel).[59] Winterbach, however, expands on Leroux's reworking of the *plaasroman*, a genre central to white Afrikaner self-mythologizing (in the 1930s in particular: Van den Heever's 1939 *Laat vrugte* is paradigmatic, and doubtless on the shelf of library books being de-accessioned in the Durban public library in *The Book of Happenstance*), to focus on Afrikaners long cut adrift from the land, on the urban experience that predominates in the present and that is, crucially, shared across race and ethnic divisions, one in which all characters—white and black—are alike ultimately prone to chance and precarity. Winterbach's allusions to *Cosmopolis* thus serve to situate everyday South African experience on a continuum with that depicted by DeLillo. Helena tells us that she and Theo did not speak about how Packer died, but she infers that Theo's death is just as mysterious—and likely as banal—as the young billionaire's. Whether chance or revenge is the cause of Theo's death, whether or not he occupies a position of relative privilege (however much less affluent he is than the super-rich Packer), death comes to all.

This is how one interpretation of the parallel might run. But here we should consider the broader import of the engagement with death, of the broader threat of annihilation, and what both authors suggest about the role of art in the face of death. *Cosmopolis* was published in 2003, in other words *after* the terror attacks against the United States on 11 September 2001. Although the novel was substantially complete before the event, the timing of publication makes its engagement with narratives of futurity all the more striking. In an essay entitled 'In the Ruins of the Future', published in *Harper's* in December 2001, DeLillo mused on the implications of the attacks for the seemingly infinite faith in what he calls 'the utopian glow of cyber-capital'.[60] 'The dramatic climb of the Dow and the speed of the Internet' had, he argued, 'summoned us all to live permanently in the future, [. . .] because there is no memory there and this is where markets are uncontrolled and investment potential has no limit.' This changed utterly after the September 11 attacks, DeLillo suggests—now 'the world narrative belongs to terrorists'.[61] But if those narratives of faith in progress, in the market, in technology (exemplified in Packer's unbounded faith in the future) had been usurped, and if the narrative of the terrorist ends in annihilation, 'the old slow furies of cutthroat religion', it is up to 'us' (it seems from the tenor of the remainder of DeLillo's essay that he is referring, at least in part, to writers) 'to create the counter-narrative'.[62]

It is art that serves in DeLillo's fiction, as Adam Thurschwell argues, to 'represent—perhaps we should say, memorialize—the continuing vitality of present lived experience' in the face of this threat of annihilation.[63] Any number of instances from DeLillo's oeuvre might be cited as evidence, but perhaps none is as powerful as the body-as-living-still-life in *The Body Artist* (2001), or the performance artist's evanescent, time-bound enactments of the aesthetic in *Falling Man* (2007). *Falling Man* also dwells on Giorgio Morandi's tellingly muted (inanimate) still life paintings, which also refuse definitive interpretation, containing a multitude of 'latent meanings [. . .] free from authoritative comment'.[64] The Italian for still life, the title of nearly every painting Morandi produced, is *natura morta*, dead nature. We might say that death hangs over every act of representation because it replaces life with an approximation, or because it is always in danger of being commodified, of entering into the machinery of capitalist consumption (in *Cosmopolis*, Packer refuses to believe that the Rothko Chapel cannot be bought). The counternarrative that DeLillo imagines in his *Harper's* essay, 'to give memory, tenderness, and meaning to all that howling space' after 9/11, might thus be thought similarly susceptible—to being overwhelmed by death, to rendering life lifeless.[65] The novel's virtue, however, lies in the fact that its memorializing function is saved by its ambiguity from the danger of being seen as a replacement for the thing that is memorialized.[66] It is this function, and this formal open-endedness, that serves DeLillo well, and which we witness in all of Winterbach's novels too—perhaps nowhere offered with greater suggestiveness about its political import than in *Die benederyk*, whose Afrikaans title would, in direct translation into English, echo almost precisely that of DeLillo's 1997 novel *Underworld*.[67]

'NEW ERA' WAITING

The Road of Excess and *It Might Get Loud* both recapitulate key motifs of *The Book of Happenstance*, including its concern with being stuck, and especially with the role of the aesthetic in the face of death. In place of

Helena's shells, *The Road of Excess* offers Aaron Adendorff's canvasses, and *It Might Get Loud* a range of art and music—including Karl Hofmeyr's obsession with heavy metal and its deathly metaphorics. There is a shared concern with the freight and the fate of language, particularly in the latter novel's original Afrikaans text, *Die aanspraak van lewende wesens*, less easily conveyed in the English translation, in which the representation of Afrikaans no longer in pure form is pervasive. Maria's wayward adult son, Benjy, has severely challenged communication skills, which drives his mother to distraction. Like one of the upstart younger artists, Jimmy, in *The Road of Excess*, and not coincidentally also an aspirant performance artist, Benjy makes recourse to English jargon that obfuscates rather than clarifies, as in the following exchange with his mother:

> I'm like busy with research, he says. Research of what kind? she asks. Research like into the origin of everything, he says. The origin of everything, she says. Yes, he says, like in the big picture. That sounds very big, she says. Yes, he says, it's like *vast*. And with a view to what are you engaged in this research? she asks. Oh, he says, with a view to like an installation I'm working on.[68]

The contamination of standard Afrikaans, the *Algemene Beskaafde* (generally cultivated or civilized) form associated with the Dutch Reformed Church and the apartheid government, by English (in terms of sentence structure and vocabulary), is clearer in the original text:

> Ek is soos in besig met research, sê hy. Navorsing van watter aard? vra sy. Research soos in die oorsprong van alles, sê hy. Die oorsprong van alles, sê sy. Ja, sê hy, soos in die breë picture. Dit klink baie breed, sê sy. Ja, sê hy, dis soos in *vast*. En met die oog waarop doen jy hierdie navorsing? vra sy. O, sê hy, met die oog op soos in 'n installation waaraan ek werk.[69]

But here, too, is another Winterbach character seeking to make sense of the present in relation to vast metanarrative structures.

In both *The Road of Excess* and *It Might Get Loud*, as in *The Book of Happenstance*, protagonists encounter characters whose worldviews represent opposites in the tension between science and faith, reason and fundamentalism. In *It Might Get Loud*, for instance, Karl encounters right-wingers who cite prophets of apocalypse, 'Siener' or Seer 'van Rensburg' and 'Siener Serfontein', some of whose predictions, we learn, 'have already come to pass':

> worldwide recession, the destruction of the Twin Towers, the irresistible rise of a young black despot (Malema), the fall of the Berlin Wall, the gradual demoralization of the Afrikaner [. . .] the growing imperialism of the English language [. . .] and its devastating effect on Afrikaans.[70]

A range of conservative fantasies, informed by right-wing panic in a post-Cold War, war-on-terror moment (and sounding DeLillo-esque), here feeds a willing of the end-times, a chiliastic, eschatological narrative energy that appeals widely to people who feel stuck. (I will pick this thread up later in this chapter, and again in Chapter 6.)

Protagonists in both novels also make metaphorical descents into hell (like Helena's trips to Ladybrand, and her reflections on past trauma) to confront illness and loss, journeys for which they also have trusty sidekicks—indeed Aaron not only has Bubbles, the Disney-sweatshirt-and-silver-Nike-wearing neighbour, but also his domestic worker, Gloria Sekete, who shares with *Happenstance*'s Sof Benade a familiarity with religion, though where Sof is sceptical, Gloria is devout, 'a firm believer, she attends church enthusiastically'.[71] In *It Might Get Loud*, Maria Volschenk is accosted in a Stellenbosch cemetery by two down-and-out characters, a couple, who offer to show her 'the way' and warn against expecting answers from the dead.[72] Maria, like other of Winterbach's characters an adopted Durbanite, has journeyed to the Western Cape to visit her parents' graves and to try to understand why her sister, Sofie, a promising poet, has committed suicide. All she finds are notebooks crammed with cryptic scribbles about Thucydides, Gnosticism, Blake, Dickinson, and Plath, references that place reason and mysticism in tension in characteristic Winterbach fashion. Here political realism and scientific historicism are associated with Thucydides, while Gnosticism, which developed a particular theology of *Sophia*, wisdom, alongside *gnosis*, knowledge, stands for the mystical.[73] The juxtaposition of Sofie's name with Maria's is clearly deliberate: it is mysticism, not organized religion, that is cast as attractive; Maria wants answers (and to act as an intercessor), while Sofie presents herself as a 'disciple, in a state of readiness and sharpened, purified receptiveness'.[74] Blake, Dickinson, and Plath, all suitably aphoristic and obsessed with prophecy, apocalypse, and death, are similarly suited to the juxtaposition.

In *The Road of Excess*, death and art (death-focused art, art as counter to death) are also overwhelming concerns. Here characters' textual and artistic points of reference—the parallels, if you will, to *The Book of Happenstance*'s citation of *Age of Iron* and *Cosmopolis*, or *It Might Get Loud*'s of poets and singers of prophecy and apocalypse—are similarly suggestively freighted. Bubbles reads Gogol's *Dead Souls*, while Stefaans is given to discussing—in the work of Yeats, Eliot, and St John of the Cross—engagements with transformation, Sumerian fertility myths, and representations of metamorphosis and resurrection. He also discusses books by Karl Barth, Dostoyevsky, Kierkegaard, Niebuhr, Niemöller and others that a Svengali-like preacher called Reinecke (who once had Aaron, Stefaans, and Benjamin's mother, among other bourgeois Afrikaners, in thrall during the 1970s and 1980s) made his acolytes read, all apparently in service of opening their eyes to the claims of otherness—an awareness of relationality—and to a critique of apartheid.[75] Reinecke's politics may be admirable in theory, but his interpersonal ethics leaves much to be desired: he turns out to be abusive, adulterous, and manipulative. His range of theological and literary reference, however, and the general interest of Winterbach's characters in narratives of death and transformation, would doubtless not have surprised anthropologist Vincent Crapanzano, whose *Waiting: The Whites of South Africa* (1985), a seminal fieldwork-based study of a community of white South Africans in the winelands north of Cape Town, noted the attraction of the end-of-the-world discourse offered by revivalism and Pentecostal Christianity for white South Africans, whom Crapanzano regarded as being trapped in a condition of waiting—of hoping for something, anything, to happen, and of being paralysed by such hope.[76]

Crapanzano's cast of characters reads like the dramatis personae of an Etienne Leroux novel, or indeed of the sections of Winterbach's novels that feature protagonists' experiences of young adulthood or reflections on their parents. His informants included pastors, preachers, and educated professionals, who cite many of the same theologians and philosophers as Winterbach's characters, who are similarly interested in mysticism and narratives of metamorphosis. Crapanzano's organizing trope came, he said, from a conversation with a South African friend, whom he calls 'Carl', who had left the country to teach in the United States and happened to be visiting South Africa during one of the anthropologist's fieldwork trips. During a conversation in a steakhouse in Cape Town, Carl told Crapanzano that he had emigrated because he 'couldn't stand the waiting any longer for something, anything, to happen', and Crapanzano understood all at once what was at stake for the whole community.[77] Looking back a quarter-century later, he observed that his subjects had 'found refuge' in a 'sustained and indefinable waiting'; 'they were not responsible. This was important. They had given themselves up to a fate that was, so it seemed to me (perhaps like all visions of fate *in situ*) empty.'[78] We might think here about empty now-time, and the helplessness of Benjamin's angel of history, blown backwards into the future (on which I expanded in the introduction). Benjamin's historical materialist would know how to stir her- or himself to action, to make something of this empty now-time; not so the white South Africans of Crapanzano's study. How are Winterbach's characters any different, one might ask, from these antecedents? Perhaps they are not; they are certainly attracted to similar mystical explanatory systems of thought that promise ways out of present impasse. But as DeLillo does with his figures of ambivalent artistic mutation and mourning, Winterbach also offers us images of artists who try, despite their cynicism and scepticism (both ways of justifying an acceptance of waiting, Crapanzano notes[79]), to effect a transformation.

In *The Road of Excess*, Aaron is immersed in artistic representations of death and metamorphosis: his touchstones are works by Piero della Francesca, Masaccio, Mantegna, Botticelli (the illustrations to the *Divine Comedy*), Bosch, Goya, and Louise Bourgeois. His struggle to find a visual language equal to his sense of being stuck, or to find a way through grief and disappointment, is at the heart of a novel that is also a biting and very perceptive satire on contemporary artistic production in South Africa.[80] (Winterbach is herself an accomplished visual artist.) Sparked by the snub he feels he has suffered at the hands of his gallery and the implied judgment of younger artists that he is now decidedly a member of the old guard, Aaron is prompted to think more generally about his affective condition. He finds that it encompasses more than merely professional resentment, that it is directly related to his sense of not being equal to the new age in which he finds himself. Specifically, he feels that he lacks 'the optimism required by the NEW ERA'.[81] His work and his actions *had* been political in the past; he had evaded conscription into the apartheid army by spending time in Germany in the 1970s, there falling under the influence of Joseph Beuys, another artist obsessed with death, rites of passage, and forms of transformation—all of them deeply political in the context of post-war Germany.[82] On his return to South Africa, we learn, Aaron had 'made politically relevant' work during a period of crisis, the 1980s, marked by 'unrest and turmoil inside the country'.[83] Yet it is not clear what visual language might be equal to the new era. Having found relief in abstraction, which had suggested 'a way of escaping the tyranny of the specific while still offering a means to express emotion', Aaron discovers that his 'renunciation of the recognisable' has come to be experienced as loss: 'Even in his most abstract—his most nonfigurative—work, there would be a wound, like internal bleeding, just below the skin, a seepage in the tissue of the paint'.[84] Figuration thus reappears in the work, but in service of affective expression—'[w]arm clusters of emotion, longing, memory'[85]—and suggestive of the claims of the other, emblematized in the face that emerges in many of Aaron's canvasses, as described here in an aside to himself that speaks to the novel's engagement with the place of the aesthetic in spite of death:

> His subject matter has been stripped down to a few elements: a disembodied head (rolling down a hill with a staring eye); bloodied fists; shields; a wall; the sea; a table; an upside-down ladder (Jacob's struggle with the angel); the hand of God that doubles as the hand of the painter; the naked light bulb

> (another comic-strip motif). Apocalyptic imagery. A flood with drifting heads: a self-portrait and the faces of his parents and brothers, the heads frequently stylised, reduced to little more than a staring eye. [. . .] The works form part of a series of paintings he calls 'End of the World'. Large canvases. [. . .] A piled-up heap of human debris [. . .]. Comic, chaotic, *raw* [. . .].[86]

Here, as in other passages in the novel, we see Aaron seeking a way of representing his own vulnerability (his intimations of death), but also his own attachments as brother, son, husband, and father, and those he has as an artist in relation to artistic progenitors. His models are Renaissance artists (Uccello, Signorelli, Piero della Francesca) who similarly sought modes of representation equal to turbulent times, were self-effacing and dependent on patronage, and negotiated competing discourses of politics and religion.[87]

The face, the head, and the eye can be read in relation to Levinas's sense of the otherness of the Other, expressed for Levinas in the idea of the face.[88] The recognition of an attachment to others is intrinsic to this metaphorics; '[t]o be in relation with the other face to face is to be unable to kill', Levinas writes.[89] But the imagining of his own head alongside the heads of his siblings, all subject to death, also marks Aaron's representations as elegiac, as part of the work of mourning. He had previously, after his wife Naomi's death, sought consolation in the presence of Goya's work in the Prado in Madrid, we learn, although because many were not on display he had still needed to find another way to deal with 'unprocessed grief'. Later, during his own illness, he realizes that he had never enacted a ritual of mourning for any of those close to him who had died. 'He should have been less concerned with his own emotional distress and more focused on the needs of the dead: a prayer, a kaddish, anything to strengthen and accompany the soul, only just escaped from its bodily confinement', he thinks.[90] Though cast in relation to ritual and metaphysics, what is really at issue in *The Road of Excess*, as well, I would argue, as in Winterbach's other novels, is an engagement with the tension between mourning and melancholia, one that invites comparison with the affective experience of life after apartheid in all of its racially inflected complexity.

Mourning, Freud tells us, involves the severing of bonds from a lost beloved object, which may be a person or an ideal. Such withdrawal of feelings is crucial if we are to be able to invest once more in external objects of devotion. A failure so to 'decathect' results in melancholia, a refusal to let go of the object loved that is characterized (Freud suggests) by severe depression, withdrawal from the world, and self-recrimination—the latter because the loved object has been metaphorically absorbed into the self.[91] In *The Road of Excess*, such manifestations of unworked-through emotions are tellingly also ascribed to the previous generation: Aaron's father is twice described as 'melancholic', and Aaron thinks of his mother's cancer as having been caused by 'unprocessed emotions and trauma'.[92] Wilhelm Reich ascribed Freud's own cancer to 'emotional resignation', calling it 'a bio-energetic shrinking, a giving up of hope', and Susan Sontag reminds us that the 'mythology of cancer' suggests that its cause is 'a steady repression of feeling'.[93] But here, too, Winterbach may have *Age of Iron* in mind: Mrs Curren ascribes her cancer to 'bitterness'—following Galen's contention that an excess of black bile caused the disease—and 'an accumulation of shame'.[94] In a reading that is careful to avoid reducing the novel to allegory it might be possible to construe the older generation's failure to recognize the pathological narcissism of apartheid, to admit the humanity of the racial other, or to acknowledge their concomitant trauma, with melancholia. Likewise, Aaron's attempt to mourn, which finds form, despite his speculation about rituals unperformed, in his art *and* in his reconnection with others, might be understood as suggesting something like a desire to escape the melancholia that comes from not having worked through the sense of loss associated with his identity—not only as a son and husband who has lost loved ones, but as a white South African whose privileged identity (however unwanted) has been lost.

Meditating on what constitutes the act of mourning, Judith Butler suggests that to lose something is not to know what it is *absolutely* that has been lost, what defining characteristic in the person or abstraction in question. To mourn is to know that one has been changed by loss, but crucially also to understand that everyone exists in relation to all that might be lost without necessarily being able to grasp absolutely its distinctiveness in any single moment. Butler goes further: our relation to others is constituted by our sense of vulnerability, our ability to suffer loss, because we simultaneously and necessarily recognize others as similarly vulnerable. This recognition might offer the basis for an ethics that does not return us 'to a solitary situation' (a solitariness that serves to depoliticize affect), she argues, but that instead points the way to 'a sense of political community of a complex order' based on a mutual acknowledgement of vulnerability to loss.[95] Grief thus has the potential to be turned into 'a resource for politics' insofar as it offers a view of the possibilities for what Butler calls relationality. Grief 'can be a point of departure for a new understanding if the narcissistic preoccupation of melancholia can be moved into a consideration of the vulnerability of others.'[96] This describes well the positive turn we can ascribe to Winterbach's protagonists—Helena Verbloem, Aaron Adendorff, Maria Volschenk, Karl Hofmeyr—as we leave them on the brink of hoped-for reunions or resolutions, apparently newly aware of their own vulnerability and relationality, their need to mourn and to recognize a community through loss. Both Butler's sense of grief as a resource for politics and Berlant's suggestion that we pay attention to the widespread tendency for people to remain attached to fantasies of the good life that are known to be just that, recognize the political energies of acknowledging vulnerability in common. Berlant warns, however, against imagining too easily that such an apprehension can have real political consequences. The subject envisaged by Butler, Berlant charges, is too quick to ignore—or misguided in thinking she can do so—those more restrictive and often insidious ties Berlant identifies. Berlant is particularly suspicious of Butler's contention that we might easily throw off our 'sense of defensive sovereignty' in order to identify with others, with those who need inclusion in 'communities of compassion', and that in so doing they might be granted access to justice. Attending to others without speaking for them is difficult, and 'projects of compassionate recognition' can enable 'a habit of political obfuscation of the differences between emotional and material (legal, economic, institutional) kinds of social reciprocity'.[97]

What we see in Winterbach's novels, I suggest, are compelling (engaging, entertaining, beautifully realized) surveys of the time being, of those affective states in which individuals traffic and subsist in the present. Winterbach's are neither fictions of diagnosis nor restitution. They do not identify categorically why it is that characters feel bad, or feel trapped, in the present, nor do they represent the righting of injustice—for such one might look to the growing piles of crime, hard-bitten detective, and noir titles (by the likes of Deon Meyer, Mike Nicol, and Margie Orford); some formulaic, many inventive and engaging, these have much to say about vulnerability, precarity, and disappointment, but their models are more John Grisham than Don DeLillo, the resolutions that are frequently their end-points are often merely 'experiential end[s]' in themselves (to quote Berlant).[98] By contrast, Winterbach takes the measure of a discontent that is less focused on political actors, of agents of political or legal transformation, in the strict sense, while recognizing the political in the everyday. And there *is* critique of current socio-political conditions. In *The Road of Excess*, such critique is voiced by Aaron's domestic worker Gloria Sekete, who offers an indictment of all politicians: 'Lies, it's all lies these people speak. [. . .] All of it to make them rich, and we, the poor—we stay poor.' She is particularly scathing of President Jacob Zuma, whose lack of empathy with the poor she sees as the chief problem of the new era: 'If she were to arrive at one of his rallies, she says, and say to him: Hi, I'm Gloria, and Zuma were to ask her what she wanted, and she said: I'm poor, I want work, he'd just say to her: Ag, suka': *oh, go away, get lost.*[99]

SITUATION VACANT: ON TRAGEDY

I alluded earlier to the suggestiveness of Berlant's contention that the situation tragedy is the genre par excellence of the precarious present. Berlant draws on the situation comedy and police procedural, adding the idea of tragedy: actors in the situation tragedy 'are fated to express their flaws episodically, over and over, without learning, changing, being relieved, becoming better, or dying'.[100] In concluding this—and looking ahead to *Present Imperfect*'s final—chapter, I want to put into conversation with Berlant's perhaps tongue-in-cheek, but nonetheless productive, generic description (which suits very well, it seems to me, each of the novels by Winterbach I have discussed), David Scott's understanding of postcolonial, postemancipation temporalities as inherently tragic, to which I referred in this book's introduction. To do so is to energize the descriptive quality of the label situation tragedy in a slightly different manner.

Scott first developed his analysis of a shift in the experience of temporality in the present, specifically in relation to investments in dreams of alternative futures such as those that have driven anti-colonial movements, in response to C.L.R. James's reading—and rereading—of the example of Toussaint Louverture, leader of the Haitian Revolution in the 1790s, in *The Black Jacobins*. James's important account of the rise and fall of Louverture made possible a reinterpretation of the Caribbean's brutal history of slavery as the narrative of a journey to emancipation and national self-determination, but its composition also serves, Scott observes, as a document of its own time and its conception of future-directed politics. First published in 1938, James's study was informed by the Spanish Civil War and the decline of the Communist dream in the Soviet Union after Stalin's turn to paranoid dictatorship, but retained an investment in a narrative of dialectical progress. By the time the study was revised and reissued in 1963, however, during the early years of postindependence disillusionment in the Caribbean, Africa, and elsewhere, tragedy had become the animating—or 'conceptually generative'—driver for James's analysis, and Toussaint Louverture had become a tragic hero, '*paradigmatic* of a certain kind of encounter with the modern'.[101] Such encounters meant that one could neither return to the past nor engage with the future without vocabularies inherited from the enlightenment and mediated by colonialism. This, Scott argues, is the legacy of '*all* conscripts of modernity'.[102]

Yet if this is a tragic fate, it is so not merely in a metaphorically descriptive way—in the vein of regarding as tragic the fact that Toussaint died a captive in Napoleon's France with no certainty that the Haitian

Revolution would succeed. Rather, tragedy unsettles the certainty implicit in future-oriented action; it urges that '[e]mbodied intention' can never be 'invulnerable to the unforeseeable and unexpected in time's unfolding'; it holds that political action 'is therefore potentially always exposed to forces and factors beyond human choice' and control. In short, tragedy calls into question a 'familiar (enlightenment) view of historical time as moving teleologically and transparently from sovereign agency to determinate end'. Toussaint thus becomes representative—according to James—of a more universal post-independence subjectivity, and this early Caribbean independence movement becomes a precursor for the fates of many subsequent anti-colonial struggles. Furthermore, in Scott's analysis, tragedy is the key to understanding our own experience of temporality. He writes as an expatriate Grenadian, but by 'our' in the previous sentence I invoke a similarity of experience in compromised revolutionary projects in Southern Africa, too. Scott comments that he reads James as suggesting that a 'tragic sensibility [...] is one more attuned to the varied ways in which we, like Toussaint, carry the time of our pasts within ourselves as the not-always-legible scripts of our *habitus*'.[103] Thus to be attuned to the tragic, indeed to the situation tragedy, is to be attentive to the hubris at the heart of narratives of progress, to the complex relationship between temporality and action, or indeed inaction and impasse.[104] One might look in vain for a more appropriate vocabulary to describe the affective and temporal engagements in Winterbach's recent fiction, their interest in chance, frustration of teleology, and invocation of multiple genres—perhaps especially the *tragic* understood in relation to Berlant's description of a situation tragedy that mixes sit-com with the seeming intractability of political impasse. Scott's formulations—or rather his exegesis of James's reformulation of his own earlier account of Toussaint Louverture—seem useful, too, in understanding the kinds of conditions that Winterbach's protagonists endure.

Crapanzano noted in a new preface to *Waiting* (in 1986) that while waiting or 'entrapment' had the potential for a 'tragic dimension', the term was not entirely appropriate to his subjects' circumstances. This was because tragedy demanded 'a kind of consciousness that is generally lacking in white South Africa', he wrote, a community in which 'what could have been tragedy is often little more than a tale of self-indulgence, cowardice, and bad faith'.[105] Apartheid's endgame had not yet been played out when Crapanzano published his work, of course, though it was clearly in the offing: P.W. Botha's State of Emergency had recently come into force; disinvestment was in full swing; meetings with ANC leaders in exile were taking place. We might, however, wish now to contest Crapanzano's refusal of the tragic label. Whites like his informant Carl certainly seemed conscious of the condition of waiting, but it is in conjunction with the much-vaunted end of history that attended the conclusion of the Cold War, in which South Africa provided a minor theatre, that the tragic self-consciousness of white and black alike—waiting for something to happen, anything like that promised by the narratives of revolution (whether construed as bloodbath or land of milk and honey), and knowing that it would not—makes the description of the *present* as situation tragedy, after Berlant *and* Scott, much less gainsayable.

2

Bad Feelings in the Provinces of History

> At a personal level he found conflict uncongenial (which is not to say that his reluctance to take sides was merely a matter of temperament: in a deep sense it was political too).
>
> —J.M. Coetzee, 'Erasmus: Madness and Rivalry', *Giving Offense* (1996)[1]

In a folder of notes in the Coetzee papers, archived at the University of Texas in Austin, are several pages photocopied from John Ashbery's 1975 collection, *Self-Portrait in a Convex Mirror.* The title is suggestive for a chapter whose principal focus is Coetzee's fictionalized memoirs, *Boyhood* (1997), *Youth* (2002), and *Summertime* (2009), but so too are the three lines that Coetzee highlighted (with a neat vertical line in the left-hand margin) on a copy of the poem 'Grand Galop'. They read: 'And now it is time to wait again. / Only waiting, the waiting: what fills up the time between? / It is another kind of wait, waiting for the wait to be ended.'[2] There is much one could say about Ashbery's attraction for Coetzee, but let me note here simply the appeal of a poetic description of a condition of stasis very like that which, according to Vincent Crapanzano, marked white life in South Africa in the 1980s (Coetzee's notes date from this period).[3] Waiting describes the experience of a great number of characters in J.M. Coetzee's early fiction, too, from Magda, waiting it out in a no-time in the middle of nowhere in *In the Heart of the Country* (1977) to the Magistrate, who, as the title suggests, is *Waiting for the Barbarians* (1980), stuck in a temporality in which empire thrives, one predicated on an eschatological vision of an externally induced end-time that only empire's superior bureaucratic and military forces can forestall. Consider, too, the enigmatic eponymous protagonist of *Life & Times of Michael K* (1983), who appears to want to escape the temporality of a dystopian authoritarian state very like late-apartheid South Africa for a condition that is not construed as waiting—although, in the event, he can only wait for the forces of history to catch up with him. The medical officer, the first-person narrative voice in the novel's second part, thinks about the eponymous K as stubbornly resisting the temporality of 'history', seeking 'to live in the old way, drifting through time, observing the seasons'.[4] In *Age of Iron* (1990), perhaps Coetzee's most potent exploration of the impasses of the interregnum, Mrs Curren complains about white South Africans' ongoing state of 'limbo', of being as yet unredeemed, comparing her condition to waiting on the banks of the Styx: 'All the days you have known me'—she addresses the enigmatic vagrant Vercueil, her visitor from the future—'I have been standing on the river-bank awaiting my turn. I am waiting for someone to show me the way across. Every minute of every day I am here, waiting.'[5]

The old order's death throes, the morbid symptoms of the interregnum (again invoking Gordimer's borrowing of Gramsci's phrasing), manifest in *Age of Iron* as Mrs Curren's cancer, a disease she regards as a consequence of an 'accumulation of shame'.[6] Shame is a bad feeling that recurs for characters in the states of waiting Coetzee so often represents: it is embodied, self-reflexive, and assumed as a burden (or an excuse) rather than being adjudicated externally—as would arguably be the case with disgrace. According to Timothy Bewes, who deploys dual notions of shame as instantiation and as event, as 'place' and as a 'taking-place' (after Badiou), it attaches understandably to white characters in late-apartheid South Africa, but its frequent invocation in Coetzee's oeuvre also reflects the quandary of the writer if writing itself might be thought complicit with—or a disingenuous attempt to escape complicity with—that which it challenges. Coetzee's characters' shame is potentially the author's too. To be in a position to feel shame, shame being 'a marker of privilege', is in this context itself shameful, thus shame in Coetzee's work marks (Bewes argues) the structural impossibility of a good-faith literary response to apartheid, one that cannot not represent shame, while the writing itself is an event of shame, its taking-place rather than merely its representational instantiation. Such shame exceeds representation, and Coetzee's oeuvre is therefore most usefully considered as a 'struggle *on behalf of shame* in opposition to the propensity of writing towards conceptualization, naming, and disembodiment'.[7] We might cast this a little differently, as a struggle to avoid the categorical, an insistence on the right to dwell instead with uncertainty and difficulty, a refusal of rivalrous positions, even if such refusal appears to be something like disaffection, or indeed is marked by or results in a variety of negative affects. Such feelings—like frustration or disappointment—might appear less extreme than shame, but shame is never far away, and insofar as they mark (or mask) a desire to escape charges of complicity, to escape the political, they are associated with shame.

I suggested in Chapter 1 that waiting is still useful as a description of the condition in which characters persevere in the present in South Africa, although it might be differently inflected—as tragedy (after David Scott), or as situation tragedy (after Lauren Berlant). I think in this chapter about dysphoric affects that characterize the condition of waiting. These are necessarily structurally conditioned by our negotiation of time-bound relationships, our orientation to a hoped-for future that has become a present without fulfilling certain desires and to the past in relation to which one is not (or is not much) better off. Gathering such affects under the usefully suggestive umbrella term *disaffection* captures their disjunctive capacity, the way they interrupt the straightforward unspooling of narratives of fulfilment or progress. Forms of disaffection are structurally integral to conditions of waiting in which we might feel trapped, or in which we might choose to persist, which potentially extend the no-time of now-time into a temporality that does not necessarily foreclose on possible futures, but in which we might seek not to precipitate consequences that could be adverse for our hopes and desires. Weighing the political work of such (dis)affect(ion)s is the primary concern in what follows. I do not of course argue that the work is somehow an instantiation of any variety of disaffection (principally, as we will see, boredom), whatever might be said by those critics who have found Coetzee's late style taxing. We cannot say in any straightforward way that the works reflect the disaffection of the author himself; we can—and I *will*—say that Coetzee's determined occupation of a position that refuses absolutely to disavow what might appear to be a variety of disaffection, a kind of studied anti-politics, is precisely political. In this sense it is, perhaps, an event, a *taking-place* (as Bewes would have it), with important ramifications for how we consider Coetzee's memoir-project in relation to South Africa now. We will get to this in due course.

With Coetzee there is always slippage between instantiation and event, representation and performance, and it is precisely the slippage that is the challenge. It is clearest, or most tantalizing, in the three volumes of fictionalized memoir now collectively known as *Scenes from Provincial Life*, in which we encounter a John Coetzee, Coetzee's own staging of a version of himself.[8] The portrait that emerges is of the artist as a young man trying to escape varieties of disaffection, including boredom, alienation and disappointment, all bad feelings associated not only with life in places at a remove from what is perceived to be the centre of the cosmopolitan life he craves—places like the South Africa Coetzee described in 1981 as being 'in the provinces of history too', but also endured by many memorable protagonists of the modernist narratives of aesthetic and moral education, from Conrad to Musil, Joyce to Beckett, that serve at various points as models for John and J.M. Coetzee alike.[9] I want to ask what implications an engagement with the enduring of such feelings by a narrative voice associated with a fictional version of the author himself has for this book's reflection on representations of stasis in contemporary South Africa. The discussion that follows proceeds on the assumption that to be disaffected—disappointed, alienated, bored—is to be in a mood in which one's engagement with the unfolding of the present is not as one might have thought it could or should be (such moments can be revisited retrospectively, of course, in memoir). These are species of temporal disjuncture, in other words. They are also ways of discovering oneself in the world, of discovering both one's limits and potential.

'"IN NO MOOD" TO TAKE POSITIONS': *AUTRE*BIOGRAPHY, AFFECTLESSNESS, *APATHEIA*, *ACEDIA*

The three volumes of *Scenes from Provincial Life* are frequently described as *autre*biographical, using a term coined by Coetzee himself to suggest that any autobiographical project necessarily engages with the other (*autre*) that one was in one's own past, consequently that '[a]ll autobiography is storytelling'.[10] In his inaugural professorial address at the University of Cape Town in 1984, tellingly titled 'Truth in Autobiography', Coetzee suggests that '[a]n autobiographer is not only a man who once upon a time lived a life [. . .] he is also a man engaged in writing a story'.[11] He has offered many versions of this formulation. Autobiography cannot be 'a kind of self-writing in which you are constrained to respect the facts of your history', he observes in an exchange in *Doubling the Point* (1992): 'All the facts are too many facts. You choose the facts insofar as they fit in with your evolving purpose.'[12] To hold to the notion that there is an 'autobiographical pact between writer and reader' that entails an expectation that the reader is offered 'no outright, deliberate lies', he noted in a later interview with David Attwell (in 2002), would not allow for the writer who 'wants to trouble the boundaries of the genre'.[13] The exchanges with psychotherapist Arabella Kurtz published as *The Good Story* (2015), are driven by his question, early in their correspondence, about the stories we tell ourselves: 'Are all autobiographies, all life-narratives, not fictions, at least in the sense that they are constructions (fictions from Latin *fingere*, to shape or mould or form)?'[14]

In an exchange omitted from the volume, Coetzee suggests that such necessary fictions (he is talking about therapy, but we can extrapolate to autobiography, I would argue) have the capacity to ameliorate feelings of being stuck (a term that will resonate from the Introduction and Chapter 1): 'I think one can help people who are stuck (as a record is stuck) by telling them (or getting them to tell) a story about themselves that they can believe and tell to other people with a fair chance of other people believing it too.'[15] I am not suggesting that we consider the *autre*biographical fictions as self-therapy, though we might interrogate what purpose the story about his life that John tells himself—or is reported to have told himself—serves in relation to the stuckness he so clearly feels, and that manifests in varieties of disaffection.

It is clear, too, that *Scenes* troubles the generic boundaries that Coetzee finds restrictive. *Boyhood* and *Youth* are third-person accounts, largely in free-indirect discourse, of episodes in the mostly unhappy childhood and young adulthood of John Coetzee, who shares significant biographical details with the writer we know as J.M. Coetzee.[16] *Summertime* is a collection of fragments collated by an ambitious English academic (Mr Vincent) working on a somewhat unpromising biography of the recently deceased novelist 'J.M. Coetzee': notebook entries from the early 1970s, ostensibly by this Coetzee, bracket transcripts of the biographer's interviews with four women and one man who knew the late author in South Africa between 1971, when he returned from studying and teaching in the United States, and 1977. It is worth noting here that Coetzee offers a corollary to his claim that all autobiography is *autre*biography, is storytelling, namely that 'all writing is autobiography', a claim he later revisits to observe the possibility of infinite regress: if this is true, 'then the statement that all writing is autobiography is itself autobiography, a moment in the autobiographical enterprise'.[17] David Attwell argues that this is true in Coetzee's case, too, such that 'the texts marked as autobiography are continuous with those marked as fiction—only the degree of fictionalisation varies'. He makes the useful point, too, that the final volume, *Summertime*, ends as John Coetzee has become an author, having published *Dusklands*.[18] *Summertime* departs more obviously from the autobiographical pact than do *Boyhood* and *Youth*. For one thing, the author whose work is gathered under the sign 'J.M. Coetzee' has killed off a character with substantially the same biography. For another, the historical John Coetzee's wife and children, who returned from America with him, are written out of existence in *Summertime*, whose partly fictionalized John Coetzee is unmarried and childless.[19] *Summertime* is thus the impossible end-point of an *auto*biographical project, but not an *autre*biographical one. (Also: Coetzee has responded to the inevitable interest in the biography of a Nobel Laureate with a painful—and painfully funny—refusal to comply. Julia Frankl, one of the interviewees, observes, without making clear whether she laughed with or at him: 'John Coetzee was actually quite funny. A figure of comedy. Dour comedy.' In some respects then the performance is an extended joke.[20])

All three volumes dwell on the character John's frustrated disaffection and longing in a manner that makes of boredom, amongst other negative affects, a defining tone. In *Ugly Feelings*, Sianne Ngai observes that tone designates 'a cultural object's affective bearing, orientation, or "set toward" the world'; it is a kind of collective mood, but one that seems aesthetically immanent, that attaches itself to an artwork.[21] Ngai's definition—an 'orientation, or "set toward" the world'—owes much to Heidegger's deployment of the idea of mood. For Heidegger, what is central to human existence is a self-conscious relation to and reflexivity about existence. We are self-interpreting beings, and it is specifically by attending to moods that we 'uncover the fundamental affectedness (*Befindlichkeit*) of human existence', 'of *how* it is to *be* in the world'.[22] We find ourselves *in* a mood, but mood arguably comes to us from outside, as a consequence of our exposure to the world. 'The mood'—Heidegger writes in his book on Nietzsche—'is precisely the fundamental way in which *we are outside of our self*.'[23] This opens a fascinating way of thinking about the use of the third-person narrative voice in *Scenes from Provincial Life*. Furthermore, the mood that we discern so often in John's engagement with the world, the mood in and through which he is *in* the world of *Boyhood* and *Youth*, is a profound form of disaffection that registers most often as boredom—and boredom (although Ngai privileges anxiety in her discussion) was Heidegger's privileged mood, 'an attunement highly conducive to self-knowledge'.[24] An approach to such self-knowledge is suggested, at least, in the ironic gap between *J.M.* and *John* Coetzee, I suggest.

We might note in passing that Coetzee is well versed in philosophical engagements with boredom. His working notes, from 1981–82, for the essay that became 'Idleness in South Africa', later the first chapter of *White Writing: On the Culture of Letters in South Africa* (1988), include quotations from Kierkegaard, Heidegger, and Nietzsche (under the heading 'The problem of boredom').[25] None of these thinkers is ultimately cited in *White Writing*, however; for that the reader might turn to one of J.C.'s diary entries in *Diary of a Bad Year* (2007), 'On boredom', which proposes a revision to Nietzsche's dictum that only 'the higher animals are capable of being bored': this might be so, J.C. (a character at a further remove from J.M. Coetzee than the John of the *Scenes*, even as he shares some of his biography) decides, but they only cope with boredom 'by learning to sit through things', 'by domesticating boredom, giving it a home'.[26]

Ngai does not address boredom at length in *Ugly Feelings*, though her category of 'stuplimity', suggested by the conflation of the stupefying and the sublime, engages with a version of boredom and of shock that she situates in relation to Kant's idea of the sublime, and especially of *apatheia*. She notes—after Paul de Man—that while Kant's 1764 *Observations on the Sentiment of the Beautiful and Sublime* argues that affectlessness ('*Affektlosigkeit*'), the lack of affect (something not unlike disaffection), has no relation to the sublime, in his third *Critique*, published nearly three decades later, Kant performs something of a *volte face* in arguing that the absence of emotion—the opposite of enthusiasm—*is* aesthetically sublime, perhaps even 'in a far preferable way, because it has also on its side the satisfaction of pure reason'. If boredom's lack of affect registers reflexively as 'dysphoric', Ngai explains, *apatheia* as posited by Kant is 'a more neutral state, reflexively yielding neither pleasure nor discomfort, that "frees" the subject for other mental activities and thus finds an ally in reason'.[27] While the *autre*biographical John's boredom might well be a species of *apatheia* (he strives to separate emotion from reason), his state of boredom is not wholly validated—as one might expect in a Coetzee text. Insofar as *Scenes from Provincial Life* is a sentimental education, John has a lot to learn; there is a great deal that separates him from J.M. Coetzee (that makes him an *autre*), and his propensity to take positions valorizing art over life, Europe over Africa, is one of the most significant.[28]

Coetzee himself, on the other hand, studiously contextualizes every position that might be ascribed to him, and in another exchange with Kurtz not included in *The Good Story* invokes 'mood' in a sense that might remind us of Heidegger, despite the language of medieval humours (after Galen) in which Coetzee dresses it up (doubtless in service of disavowing any position—or opinion—that might be ascribed to him):

> I will venture one opinion, a mild and hopeful one in the form of a footnote or sidenote, on the subject of a psychology for our time (whatever 'our time' means in a world of multiple times): that such a psychology will pay more serious attention to mood, the loose name I give to one's total disposition toward the world at any given moment. Tonight, for example, I am in a melancholy mood, and that is reflected in my responses to you. My rudimentary psychology of moods divides them into four classes, corresponding to the four elements earth, water, fire and air. Melancholy is a watery mood. Because water provides no footing, it is hard to 'take a position' in a melancholic mood (more accurately, one is 'in no mood' to take positions).[29]

Let me venture a final question in this section: might disaffection in any of the varieties we encounter in Coetzee's work (boredom, melancholia) be thought to share traits with the state of *acedia*, a condition that preoccupied the early Christian church? Fourth-century John Cassian's guide to monastic life warned against *acedia* as one of monasticism's chief perils.

Although in the later codification of the seven deadly sins *acedia* would be absorbed into the sin of sloth and, with *tristia,* into the sin of despair, it was marked less by affective lack than by strong feelings of disgust and disdain, while also occasioning a desire for spatial and temporal escape.[30] We certainly observe such impulses to flee in Coetzee's *Youth*, in particular. For Roland Barthes, who turns to *acedia* early in his 1977 Collège de France lecture course *Comment vivre ensemble*, translated as *How to Live Together*, it took the form of 'a loss of investment' that occasions a '[d]epressive state: melancholy, lassitude, sadness, boredom, loss of heart'. The Greek word denoted negligence or indifference, Barthes observed, although it might be thought of now as 'boredom or anxiety of heart'. With *acedia*, he continues, 'I'm both the subject and the object of abandonment: whence the feeling of being blocked, trapped, at an impasse'.[31] This conflation of active and passive, of abandoning and being abandoned, is significant, and the acedic's negotiation of the tension between being an isolate and being a member of society, one who acknowledges ties that might be considered *political*, of the polity, is central to the particular form of disaffection visible in the case of John Coetzee in *Scenes from Provincial Life*.

PORTRAITS OF THE ALIENATED ARTIST MANQUÉ

Boyhood follows John between ages nine and eleven, from 1949 through 1951, during which time the Coetzees live first in Worcester, a provincial town some 70 miles from Cape Town, in a dusty suburb in which John, the elder son, is almost as defeated as his mother, whom he associates with a narrowing of opportunities he is determined to resist. John 'will not accept the vision that she wants to force upon him: sober, disappointed, disillusioned'.[32] He hates Worcester, wondering whether it is 'a purgatory one must pass through', but when the family returns to Cape Town, life turns out to be little better.[33] Coetzee *père* sets up practice as an attorney, but it ends in fraud and disgrace. John fails to gain a place at an elite Cape Town school, and is faced with the realities of his family's class position. A picture of stasis emerges: South Africa is provincial, a place unworthy of a protagonist who feels keenly his own election. It is 'a country without heroes', or rather with *inadequate*, dead or foreign ones, indeed here one may not even read superhero comics—among the first acts of the National Party government in 1948 was to ban 'all Captain Marvel and Superman comics, allowing only comics with animal characters, comics intended to keep one a baby, to pass through the Customs'.[34]

It is precisely this provincialism that the older protagonist of *Youth* tries to escape; we follow this John Coetzee from 1959 through 1964. Late in the text, having resigned the employment that granted him a right to remain in Britain and facing the prospect of deportation, he imagines being asked, were he to claim asylum (as he briefly contemplates doing), 'From what are you fleeing?', to which he imagines he would answer: 'From boredom [. . .]. From atrophy of the moral life. From shame.'[35] Aged nineteen, John has freed himself from his parents, paying his way through university, yet he yearns to be elsewhere, convinced that there are perhaps only 'three places in the world where life can be lived at its fullest intensity: London, Paris, [. . .] Vienna'.[36] South Africa, after a decade of National Party rule, is governed by fear and racial tension. When a march by the radical Pan Africanist Congress takes place along the road in front of the university, causing disruption to a class he is supervising, John is appalled ('What is the country coming to when one cannot run a mathematics tutorial in peace?')[37]. He notes that it is his vocation to be an artist and that this is not a political calling—it is intensely personal, even narcissistic. He may be bored, after a fashion, but being an artist and a great lover (his parallel quest) will save him, he hopes, from being 'boring'.[38] He leaves for the United Kingdom.

In London, John turns down a number of posts that seem either too time consuming or which would take him outside London, before settling for a post as trainee programmer at IBM. Predictably, he is miserable; the work makes him feel 'like a bored clerk in Dickens',[39] but the regular hours allow time for reading, as he searches for models for his own writing, to transform misery into art. Through Pound's letters he discovers Flaubert, and out of Flaubert develops an interest in James, Conrad, and Ford Madox Ford. He does not get along with D.H. Lawrence, is astonished when he stumbles on Beckett.[40] 'Misery', he tells himself, 'is a school for the soul'; this is the lesson of many of his models. 'If Eliot chooses to seem dull, chooses to wear a suit and work in a bank and call himself J. Alfred Prufrock, it must be as a disguise,' he reasons, 'as part of the necessary cunning of the artist in the modern age.'[41] We might comment here on the kinds of modernist antecedents John chooses, on their performance of a posture in relation to the autonomy of the artwork, and on his assumption that Eliot *is* Prufrock. In a lecture entitled 'Homage', delivered at Berkeley in 1991, Coetzee had recalled the overweening influence of Eliot in his South African education. Eliot 'had, by the 1950s,' he wrote, 'laid down standards that my academic mentors followed and passed on to me. I did not question these standards. On the contrary, I found Eliot's example highly seductive.'[42] Attwell observes that if Eliot's example urged a striving after impersonality, an escape from emotion, the overlooked corollary in the essay in which that imperative is framed observes that 'only those who have personality and emotions know what it means to want to escape from these things'.[43] We are firmly in the realm of the performative.

What John discovers to his chagrin, however, when he finally begins to write—more accurately to write prose—is that he is drawn precisely to that from which he sought an escape, to provincial subject matter. *Youth* ends memorably with John sitting in the domed reading room of the British Museum, engrossed in accounts of eighteenth- and nineteenth-century travellers to South Africa, books to which he turns, significantly, when 'bored' with his own writing,[44] determined that he will do what he must to 'write a book as convincing as Burchell's', to 'lodge it in this library that defines all libraries', even if this requires that he offer gritty realism to effect 'the aura that will get it onto the shelves and thus into the history of the world: the aura of truth'.[45] *Youth*'s epigraph from Goethe, 'Wer den Dichter will verstehen / muß in Dichters Lande gehen' ('Whoever wishes to understand the poet, must go into the land of the poet'), is therefore suggestive on multiple levels. Having travelled to England, home of Lawrence and Ford, adopted home of Eliot, John understands that it is to his *own* country that he must travel—imaginatively—to understand his calling.[46] Furthermore, it is to this episode in his life, this past-as-another (and an-other's)-country that readers are returned in order to understand *J.M.* Coetzee. Paul Sheehan also reads this turn as a staging by Coetzee of a 'kind of modernist showdown' that pits the likes of Pound, Eliot, and Ford, metropolitan modernists and 'the totemic names of his youth', against not only his own provincial background, but also those modernists sharing similar backgrounds, 'Conrad, Kafka, Beckett and Dostoevsky—the figures of his maturity, the standard-bearers that will shape the writing life to come'.[47] We might also add Musil, Svevo, Joseph Roth, and others, on whom more shortly.

If boredom is associated first with South Africa's distance from the centre of anglophone culture (which John, in *Youth*, first imagines London to represent), it soon appears that this boredom may also have a positive valence. In one of the third-person notebook fragments that begin *Summertime*, we read the following musing by John about his project to lay an apron of concrete around the small bungalow he shares with his father in one of Cape Town's southern suburbs (Vincent, the biographer, suspects that it is an early attempt to write in the mode that characterizes *Boyhood* and *Youth*):

> Above all the labour bores him. Yet he is not unhappy. What he finds himself doing is what people like him should have been doing ever since 1652,

namely, his own dirty work. In fact, once one forgets about the time he is giving up, the work begins to take on its own pleasure.[48]

The idea that John is giving up time that might otherwise be spent on leisure or his academic pursuits is presented here as something like a sacrifice that sets him apart. Embracing boredom—the boredom of labour—constitutes a refusal of the posture of superiority that white South Africans have performed since the settlement by the Dutch East India Company in the mid seventeenth century, by regarding such work as beneath them. Julia Frankl, John's erstwhile lover, tells Vincent that 'it was not customary in those days for a white man' to perform such tasks.[49] In the interview with John's cousin, Margot, rewritten by Vincent as a narrative, John's indictment of white South Africans' 'long history of making other people do our work for us while we sit in the shade and watch' is similarly invoked.[50] But academic labour is cast as boring, too, as a fate to which John has, some interviewees imagine, resigned himself. A former colleague, Martin, asked why he thinks John did not write more about his working life, responds that one explanation 'is that it might have seemed too complex a topic to be explored in a memoir or diary'; another 'is simpler: that the story of his adventures in the academy was too boring to go on with'.[51]

What is this artist to do if being in the margins is boring, if it is here that the apprentice artist with metropolitan sensibilities fears being stifled, but here that he is compelled to be? (We should remember here that the historical Coetzee was compelled to return to South Africa from the United States, that he did not choose to do so.) *Scenes from Provincial Life* represents this dilemma, and is its own answer, which is to say it stages the dilemma thematically and formally, and refuses expectations (just as it represents the disappointment of the protagonist's own). Coetzee very early addressed the problem of his own expectation, and the expectation of those who would regard his work as South African. In remarks made on the occasion of receiving South Africa's CNA (Central News Agency) prize for *Waiting for the Barbarians* in 1981, he commented that it was 'not easy to be a provincial artist', especially not 'at times when the humanist-internationalist values that the artist derives from his metropolitan heritage and orientation and affiliations put him in conflict with provincial mores (something we are familiar with in South Africa)'. Under such circumstances, Coetzee continued, South African writers should 'learn to dismiss the cries from metropolitan critics for, let us say, an "authentically South African" art which does not "ape European or American models" but "finds its own roots". Demands of this kind come out of a naïve, idle, and typically metropolitan yearning for the exotic.'[52] In other words, they should not be afraid to write in a way that refused metropolitan expectations. (One might hear here an echo of Olive Schreiner's famous refusal of metropolitan expectations of imperial romance in the preface to *The Story of an African Farm*, and note that Coetzee regarded Schreiner highly.) Later, in what was something of an aesthetic (and political) credo, he would argue that he had the right if not the duty as a writer to refuse not only metropolitan but also politically inflected local expectations, to resist the 'powerful tendency, perhaps even a dominant tendency' in South Africa in the mid 1980s 'to subsume the novel under', to make it merely a supplement to, 'history'.[53]

The scholar-magistrate in *Waiting for the Barbarians*, reading the runes and wanting to abjure the time of empire, offers one example of what such a response might resemble. And yet, of course, the imperial outpost in that novel is not South Africa, nor the Magistrate Coetzee, in the way that the John Coetzee of *Boyhood*, *Youth*, and *Summertime* finds himself in South Africa and becomes a novelist. What Coetzee is asserting more straightforwardly in these interventions is the right to embrace the relationship of distance from, and indebtedness to, metropolitan models (and provincial-metropolitan models, if you will—like Kafka, Musil, even Joyce). Being in the provinces might be boring, but that boredom is fit matter for a literature that embraces amongst other things the resources of modernism in order to explore that affect's aesthetic, not to mention political, energies. 'A provincial literature is not necessarily minor.'[54] Coetzee is also asserting the right to a non-position, to a disposition that might appear disaffected, but is deeply political.

THE FORESTALLED *BILDUNGSROMAN*

The deployment of disaffection, and in particular of the boring, that I have been sketching is similar to the banality that Saikat Majumdar suggests writers like Amit Chaudhuri and Zoë Wicomb take up in their work, staging the tedium, dwelling on everydayness of life in the long shadow of empire for strategic political ends. In such work, Majumdar writes, while banality is 'linked to the sociopsychological consequences of imperialism', it also becomes 'a locus of cultural resistance to the spectacular narratives of colonialism and its nationalist heirs'.[55] Its supposed rediscovery is thus ambivalent, 'politically irresponsible' because it counters normative constructions of politics that animate anti-colonial movements and persist in what Majumdar calls 'the imaginary of postliberation progress', yet also subversive and empowering.[56] The banal and the boring are 'radically noncathartic' affects, he notes (the debt to Ngai is clear), but also traditionally 'aesthetically oppositional tropes' that can be transformed into markers of innovation as well as into resources for critique.[57] Majumdar links contemporary engagements with the banal with earlier modernist ones, reading Wicomb and Chaudhuri's work alongside Joyce and Mansfield's with the unequal distribution of modernity between periphery (Dublin, New Zealand) and centre. This tracing of political and aesthetic links between canonical modernist and contemporary postcolonial writing, and his foregrounding of the centrality of colonial conditions and affects associated with it in high modernism itself, speaks to a broader phenomenon of the new modernist studies, reconsiderations of the locations of work we group under that label, its institutions and implications, as well as of work on the resources of modernism deployed by contemporary writers like Coetzee.

A consequence of recent reconceptualizations of modernism is that the term has come to describe 'a mode of being rather than a time-bound phenomenon', 'a flexible posture rather than a fixed period'.[58] There have been countermoves, too, as modernism's reach has extended forward (and the postcolonial's backward). David James and Urmila Seshagiri, for instance, propose a return to periodization that would restrict aesthetic modernism ('experimental fiction shaped by an aesthetics of discontinuity, nonlinearity, interiority, and chronological play', in their definition) to the period 1890 to 1940, with other terms (they propose '*meta*modernist') qualifying contemporary writing for which modernism serves as 'an aesthetic, and an archive'.[59] Coetzee's *Youth* certainly engages with modernist models in many of the ways James and Seshagiri list. It repeats modernist challenges to liberal expectation (and aesthetics).[60] It stages the evaluation of an archive: aside from the authors I have mentioned, writers named include Anouilh, Sartre, Ionesco, Brecht, Enzensberger, Brodsky, Ingeborg Bachmann, and Zbigniew Herbert. References to other art forms inheriting the formal energies of high modernism include films by Antonioni and Bergman.[61] The extent to which we might regard Coetzee's *autre*biographies, and *Youth* in particular, as *meta*modernist—or indeed, following Fredric Jameson, perhaps *late* modernist—is not the province of this discussion.[62] I do want to suggest, however, that there is a genre of modernist writing that provides a key to some of the valencies of disaffection in *Scenes from Provincial Life*.

The *Bildungsroman*, as Franco Moretti and others have suggested, is the *locus classicus* of the elaboration of modern historical temporality in post-Enlightenment Europe, animated by the figure of youth and the sense of guaranteed futurity.[63] Bakhtin defined it as presenting 'an image of *man growing* in *national-historical time*', though Jed Esty observes that modernist revisions of the genre frequently 'explore the contradictions inherent in mainstream developmental discourses of self, nation, and empire'.[64] Esty charts the manner in which the trope of frustrated or curtailed development ('frozen youth') recurs in such fiction, from Woolf's Rachel Vinrace, to

Conrad's Lord Jim, Joyce's Stephen Dedalus to Kafka's Gregor Samsa (there are many others, each different from the next). These protagonists do not grow up conclusively, or not in the way inherited conventions of bourgeois sociality dictate. 'Arrested development' is an important trope, he suggests, because it recurs in multiple discourses in the late Victorian and Edwardian periods, 'from psychological theories of industrial stagnation to anthropological theories of structuralized difference to geoeconomic theories of colonial immiseration'. All are imbricated with crises of faith and political legitimacy, debates about progress in contemporary historiography, and tensions between 'the open-ended temporality of capitalism and the bounded, countertemporality of the nation', in Esty's useful phrasing.[65]

The *Bildungsroman*, in other words, is a specialized version of the 'biologico-literary experiment' that is the novel—the words are Paul Rayment's in Coetzee's novel *Slow Man* (or at least are his thoughts, or perhaps Elizabeth Costello's behind his).[66] The novel, as Arne de Boever reminds us, developing as it did at the moment at which the shift in power relations in which Foucault is most interested took place (from sovereignty to governmentality), might be considered one of the apparatuses (*dispositifs*) of the new era, 'a form of government over oneself and over others'.[67] It is a form in which characters are made to behave (or misbehave) at the behest of the author, though the development of the novel, like that of the *Bildungsroman* in its forestalled instantiation, attests to a questioning of the biopolitical impulse buried in its form. Joseph Slaughter ties the rise of the genre to the development of human-rights discourse, and in discussing the contemporary postcolonial version emphasizes its continuity from the ideal vision of the free self-development of the individual that is at the heart of its nineteenth-century iteration. In Slaughter's analysis, the individual subject of the European *Bildungsroman* has become 'part of the freight of globalization as the West has prosecuted it through colonialism, (neo)imperialisms, international humanitarianism, and multinational consumer capitalism'.[68]

As forestalled *Bildungsroman*, Coetzee's *autre*biographical project shares the disjunctive energies of its modernist antecedents. *Boyhood*, *Youth*, and *Summertime* all stage breaks rather than progress. *Boyhood* notes of John's time at school in Cape Town that '[w]hoever he truly is, whoever the true "I" is that ought to be rising out of the ashes of his childhood, is not being allowed to be born, is being kept puny and stunted'.[69] Disruption of expectation marks John's exceptionalism, manifest most clearly in his belief that he has been 'chosen', is 'special' and 'waiting to be called' to something greater, or has been 'given a second life', a conviction reinforced when he is saved from drowning at a Scout camp.[70] There are numerous instances of his feeling himself not what society expects a boy of his age and location to be: unlike the Afrikaner boys at school, he has soft feet (he wears shoes); he *thinks*, and 'thinking' is not normal, he comes to realize.[71] This sense of difference marks his divided relationship to his own sense of self; he shows one face to the world ('at school, meek and mild'), another to his family ('an irascible despot'), and through 'this double life he has created for himself a burden of imposture' that comes to be associated with the possibility of fiction itself, as when his lies in a homework essay (his mother polishes his shoes so he has no idea how it is done, which is clear to his teacher in his fanciful fiction) seem to him crucial to his mode of self-understanding.[72] His propensity for lying prepares us for the act of *autre*biography itself. In one memorable moment, John sees himself momentarily as if from above ('[t]he sky opens, he sees the world as it is, then the sky closes and he is himself again'); this registers as awareness that 'the story of himself' is necessarily a fiction, that he is 'living the only story he will admit'.[73]

All three volumes of the *Scenes* challenge the *Bildungsroman*'s logic of conformity and development, but with the added twist that the artist manqué who models himself on modernist forebears (and whose development is halting, or frozen) is not a disruptive creation of a self-effacing modernist writer-creator, but a version of the author's own self whose rendering as other, as an *autre*, dramatizes the forestalled growth of the traditional subject of *Bildung* in categorical fashion. There has been a break, and in *Summertime* that break is even more radical: the younger-self-as-other is dead. The very form of this volume—its fragments, frustrated biographer's futile search for edifying information about the author, implicitly unreliable interviewees (each refusing to endorse a narrative of development)—offers only stasis and disappointment. Julia Frankl is perhaps the exemplary underminer of the biographical project, offering the following challenges to Vincent: 'let me be candid: as far as the dialogue is concerned, I am making it up as I go along'; 'I *really* was the main character. John *really* was a minor character.'[74] Margot Jonker, John's cousin, is deeply uncomfortable throughout with the biographer's narrative presumptions, interrupting his paraphrases and dramatizations. Meanwhile, Adriana Nascimento refuses to believe John was special, insisting that to her he 'is nothing, was nothing, just an irritation, an embarrassment'.[75]

POLITICS IN THE PROVINCES (I): THE *NON*POSITION

Adriana, however, has more to say on the matter, insisting that John 'was nothing and his words were nothing. [. . .] [T]o me he really was a fool'.[76] Folly has long been associated with a position from which certain truths might be told with impunity: think of Shakespeare's wise fools, or indeed Desiderius Erasmus's *The Praise of Folly* (1509), about which Coetzee writes with great insight in a 1992 essay, later included in the collection *Giving Offense* (1996). Erasmus's essay is an attack on clerical excess, and in its rhetorical validation of a kind of madness steers between the Papacy and the Lutheran radicals then ranging against it. Though in sympathy with many of Luther's ideas, Coetzee suggests, Erasmus was also 'disturbed by the intolerance and inflexibility of the actual reform movement' and sought to maintain his distance from it. As the epigraph to this chapter indicates, Erasmus found rivalry uncongenial, though Coetzee is quick to observe that this is not to say that a 'reluctance to take sides' might not be deeply political.[77] In fact, *The Praise of Folly* 'sketches the possibility of a position for the critic of the scene of political rivalry, a position not simply impartial between the rivals but also, by self-definition, off the stage of rivalry altogether, a *non*position'. We would not be wrong to hear in these careful formulations something like a revalidation of Coetzee's own position in 'The Novel Today'; cast there as an insistence that fiction not be read as supplement to history, here it is nuanced to admit that such a refusal would likely fail ('In the realm of political action, maneuvers such as this, too clever by half, are rarely allowed to prosper', Coetzee comments of Erasmus's *non*position), but that it is essential all the same.[78]

Rather than insist that the fictions operate according to a different logic, must not be co-opted by political orthodoxies on left or right, many of Coetzee's works show us characters whose studied attempts at holding *non*positions themselves become positional—and thus compromised. In his essay on Erasmus, Coetzee argues that putting any authority's position (even Erasmus's *non*position) to work as a position (as he thinks Stefan Zweig did, for instance, in making of *The Praise of Folly* a critique of interwar politics), is to force it to occupy a position, which is precisely what it critiques. The 'power' of Erasmus's text lies instead, Coetzee suggests, 'in its weaknesses—its jocoserious abnegation of big-phallus status, its evasive (non)position inside/outside the play'.[79] *Summertime*, I contend, does this particularly well (Adriana finds John an 'embarrassment', 'a fool'; all interviewees find him somehow disappointing; we might see the elision of the historical Coetzee's wife and children from the book as itself an 'abnegation of big-phallus status'). We see a slightly different version of this critique in the book that appeared just before *Summertime*, *Diary of a Bad Year*. Here J.C.'s series of 'Strong Opinions', the line of narrative offered in the top third of those pages making up the first section of the text, includes direct commentary on domestic (in this case, Australian) and international politics. J.C.'s confidence in his positions on events of the day is deflated, however, by his typist-amanuensis Anya's impatience for pretence and hilarious typos. 'What has begun to change since I moved into the orbit of Anya is not my opinions themselves so much as my opinions of my opinions', J.C. observes. 'I should thoroughly revise my opinions, that is what I should do.'[80]

In strong opinion 30, 'On authority in fiction', J.C. wonders whether one might, as Kierkegaard directs, as a way of acquiring a kind of divine authority, '*Learn to speak without authority*', in a manner perhaps not unlike that of the mad fool. But 'copying Kierkegaard's words', J.C. realizes, turns 'Kierkegaard into an authority', which is precisely the opposite of what was desired.[81] Here is an example of the paradox attending the Erasmian nonposition. It is exemplified for J.C. by Harold Pinter, who used his Nobel Prize acceptance speech to denounce Tony Blair and the war in Iraq. Because he spoke as himself rather than 'through [. . .] art', because he used 'the rhetoric of the agora', Pinter engaged in 'a battle he was unlikely to win', J.C. contends.[82] As David Attwell observes, the strong opinions of the first part of *Diary* are also incapable of delivering the kind of nonposition Coetzee associates with Erasmus.[83] Yet *Diary* as a whole—because it offers J.C.'s opinions on the same page as two more recognizably fictional strands (narratives of J.C.'s encounters with Anya, and commentary by Anya and her partner Alan), because of the distance between J.C. and the author J.M. Coetzee (biographical details, while similar, are not the same), and because of Anya's repeated interruptions, questions, and ultimately because of her care—cumulatively and compositely approximates an Erasmian text, and 'attempts to carve out a position off the stage of political rivalry'.[84]

Speaking in his own person, Coetzee has tried to replicate this striving for a nonposition, but acknowledges the danger of infinite regress (also in a way that suggests the strong opinions in the *Diary* are in fact his). Prefacing a reading from *Diary* in Reykjavik in September 2007, for example, he offered comments that reflected on his many years lecturing at American and South African universities:

> Though I was a conscientious teacher, I was not a successful lecturer. Part of the reason was that I did not believe in the lecture as a form. Why did I not believe in the lecture? Because, as I conceive of it, the lecture requires that you have a subject and take a position on that subject. The trouble was, I was mistrustful of myself when I took the position of taking a position. I had opinions, as many opinions as any other person, but I did not have a very high opinion of people who had opinions. I did not have a high opinion of opinions, including the opinion that ~~one~~ I should not have a high opinion of opinions.[85]

POLITICS IN THE PROVINCES (II): ON IRONY

I want to approach the question of the political nature of provincial bad feelings obliquely in this final section, which might be thought to offer its own approximation of an Erasmian nonposition—by offering a nonposition on *Scenes* precisely by talking about another text altogether, but one that I believe is almost certainly a hitherto unnoticed intertext for Coetzee's *autre*biographical project. Whether or not it was an influence is ultimately less interesting than the project of reading it *alongside* Coetzee's volumes to ask what the similarities might tell us about bad feelings as markers of a particular kind of self-conscious and situated engagement with genre, temporality, and pre-eminently with politics in the provinces. Numerous possible influences on the *Scenes* have already been mooted, from Caesar's accounts of the Gallic and Civil Wars (for their third-person narrative voice) to Joyce's *A Portrait of the Artist as a Young Man*. Some point to similarities in title with work by George Eliot (*Middlemarch*'s subtitle is *A Study of Provincial Life*), William Cooper, Balzac, and Tolstoy (whose fictionalized autobiographical trilogy includes *Boyhood* and *Youth*).[86] The text I have in mind is none of these. Its narrator—and its author—was born in the twilight years of the Austro-Hungarian empire, and to establish the basis for some of the echoes I want to unpick, I need to observe how fascinated Coetzee has long been by this context.

Derek Attridge notes in his introduction to Coetzee's 2007 nonfiction collection, *Inner Workings*, that the first seven essays, on writers born in central Europe at the close of the nineteenth century, form a related group: all experienced Europe in painful transition.[87] What is really remarkable about these seven, however, is that no fewer than five—Sándor Márai, Robert Musil, Joseph Roth, Bruno Schulz, and Italo Svevo—were born in Austro-Hungary.[88] *Inner Workings* also includes an essay on Paul Celan, born Paul Antschel in Czernowitz in the Bukovina, once a peripheral province of the Austro-Hungarian Empire but by the time of Celan's birth a part of Romania, while Coetzee's earlier collection, *Stranger Shores*, includes essays on Kafka, Rilke (both born in Prague), Musil, and Aharon Appelfeld, in whose *Iron Tracks* a character has a grandfather, Coetzee tells us, who was a rabbi in the Bukovina.[89] Once one begins to look for them, in fact, one finds references to Austro-Hungary (or modern states once under its rule) throughout Coetzee's oeuvre. In *Youth*, John briefly contemplates escape to Vienna before discounting it: it is 'for Jews coming back to reclaim their birthright: logical positivism, twelve-tone music, psychoanalysis'. One of his most awkward relationships is with a pasty Austrian au pair, Astrid, from Klagenfurt, Musil's hometown.[90] In *Summertime*, John lives in Tokai, a suburb named for Hungary's Tokaj wine-region. Julia Frankl recalls his insistence that they make love to the Schubert string quintet in order to feel 'what it had been like to make love in post-Bonaparte Austria'.[91] Julia is the daughter of a Hungarian Jew born during the period of the Dual Monarchy, who hallucinates that he is in a Kafkaesque German *Strafkolonie* on Madagascar; she tells Vincent that her family name (Kiš) comes from Szombathely, one of the oldest cities in Hungary—also, we know from Joyce's *Ulysses*, the birthplace of Leopold Bloom's father, Rudolf Virág.[92] (Having made the argument for an interest in Austro-Hungary, I should note here too that Coetzee's broader interest in central Europe has a genealogical connection to his own family history. In *Boyhood* we learn of John's great-aunt Annie, whose father, Balthazar du Biel, had been a missionary. Coetzee's mother's maternal grandmother was indeed the daughter of this Rhenish missionary, who used a German-sounding version of his Polish birth-name, Balcer Dubyl, and whose family came from Odolanów in Poland, at the time Aldenau in Prussia.[93])

Quite apart from its extraordinary literary heritage, we can but speculate on Coetzee's interest in Austro-Hungary's historical peculiarities: its attempt to bind heterogeneous populations with the fiction of equality, even as one culture (of German-speaking Austrians) dominated.[94] Does this suggest a parallel with anglophone, anglophile South Africa at mid-century? It, too, could not regard itself as its own centre. Musil, Coetzee tells us, 'did not take seriously the idea of an autonomous Austrian culture'; writers like him looked to Berlin, as John, at the *start* of *Youth* at least, looks to London.[95] There is also something of the nostalgia for a home imagined lost after empire's demise, a capacious supra-national identity, that is powerfully suggestive for—even attractive to—the writer who chafes at being categorized as citizen of a single country rather than of a more expansive republic of letters. In his essay on Roth, Coetzee discusses the widespread dismay amongst Jewish intellectuals, including Freud, at Austro-Hungary's devolution into nation states in which they had no ethnic claim.[96] Here we have another key connection: the (supposedly) racial other. For central Europe's interwar Jewish question, substitute the so-called native question in early twentieth-century South Africa—though there are Jews, too, in South Africa, and in the pages of Coetzee's books, and thus the long shadow of anti-Semitism.[97]

The (inter)text I have in mind is Gregor von Rezzori's *Memoirs of an Anti-Semite*, published in English in 1981 and in German two years previously. Its fourth section, originally composed in English, was published in the *New Yorker* in 1969.[98] We can only wonder whether Coetzee, then teaching at SUNY Buffalo, might have encountered this fragment in print, just as we can only speculate that it influenced *Scenes*. Coetzee's interests—in the effects of the decline of a repressive state, of race and complicity with racism, and of the difficulties of locating a stable, narratable self in such circumstances—are certainly strikingly analogous in the South African context to Rezzori's in the Eastern European one. Rezzori (1914–98), like Celan, was born to German-speaking parents in Czernowitz just before the Bukovina was absorbed into Romania. He would spend his adolescence and young manhood navigating the competing claims of a cultural commitment to Austria (like most of the minor nobility, he was educated in Vienna), linguistic and literary affiliations to Greater Germany, and citizenship of Romania (he would live in Bucharest and serve in the Romanian army). He lived in Berlin during the Second World War, then, after being rendered stateless, in West Germany, and for the remainder of his life in Italy.

Memoirs of an Anti-Semite is fictionalized autobiography. Rezzori had tentatively called an earlier novel, *The Death of My Brother Abel*, a 'hypothetical autobiography'.[99] There is much in common, then, with Coetzee's position that all autobiography is storytelling, all writing autobiographical. Narrated in the first person, unlike Coetzee's *Scenes*, Rezzori's *Memoirs* is also a fragmentary set of fictions whose protagonists appear to be versions of the author, though chronological inconsistencies add to the sense of narrative unreliability amongst the fragments, as well as across the composite account. Like *Scenes*, it details the claims of metropolitan culture on an artist who feels himself marginal and desires an artistic vocation. What I have called John's boredom in *Boyhood* is very close to the affect experienced by the narrator of Rezzori's first chapter, a sketch of provincial torpor and dawning awareness of the racial prejudice that defines his extended family's sense of ethnicity. Sent to country relatives in a 'remote spot in the eastern borderland' of erstwhile Austro-Hungary, Rezzori's protagonist suffers from an affect best described in Russian as '*Skushno*' (also the title of the chapter), a word 'difficult to translate', we are told, that signifies 'more than dreary boredom', 'a spiritual void that sucks you in like a vague but intensely urgent longing'.[100] One might well be put in mind of the medieval *acedia*. Slightly older than John (thirteen during the summer described), Rezzori's narrator is both trapped in this backwater, far from Vienna (like John in Worcester, seeming light years from Cape Town), but also delights in its freedoms (like John on the Karoo farm). He is aware, however, that others have a keener claim on the land here: Jews, especially scruffy children speaking Yiddish, and the Romanian and Ruthenian (or Ukrainian) majority. These are groups analogous, in different ways, to Worcester's scruffy coloured children, and to the Karoo farmworkers in *Boyhood*. There is something of the same ironic judgment on youthful blindness, then, as there is on John's romantic attachment to his family's farms, 'places of freedom, of life'.[101] John is himself aware of the contradictions at the heart of his family's identification with land that they do not work (rather, they are overseers), land on which others have a prior claim.[102] '*Skushno*' features a cast of relatives spouting unsavoury anti-Semitic prejudice with the same ease as John's mother and maternal uncles in *Boyhood*.[103] It culminates in a scene in which the narrator, whom we know only as Bubi, inflicts an injury on his new Jewish friend, Wolf Goldmann, son of the local doctor. They play with an 'electrostatic machine' in the doctor's study and Bubi, too cowardly to hold the rods, has Wolf do so before pressing the buttons for too long, badly burning Wolf's hands. It is difficult not to compare this episode with that in *Boyhood* in which John makes his younger brother insert his hand into an old maize grinder before turning the handle.[104] This machine is later linked to a printing press in John's great-aunt's dusty apartment, bringing together betrayal, the machine and text (with echoes, too, of Kafka's *Strafkolonie*).

The analogous explorations of comparable affects are clearer still in Rezzori's second chapter, entitled 'Youth'. Also a story of provincial boredom and metropolitan flight, its protagonist, like *Youth*'s John (and also aged nineteen), is an aspirant artist (in Rezzori's case, painter rather than a poet, although in the third chapter he begins his transformation into a prose memoirist). Rezzori's character has disowned his parents, as John feels he has outgrown his, and moves from 'provincial confinement' (the Bukovina) to 'national metropolis' (Bucharest).[105] Here, like John in London, he feels like 'a refugee or even an exile'.[106] There are similarly awful sexual encounters, a relationship with an older woman, the desire no longer to be treated like a child, and compromises between artistic aspiration and dead-end job.[107] Much more could be said about the feelings the characters share about their parents (especially their fathers), and about the similarities between the emotional attachments to the language and culture associated with the provinces: Yiddish in Rezzori's text; Afrikaans in Coetzee's.[108] Interestingly it is a Yiddish term, *Schlemiel*, that comes to Julia's mind in *Summertime* to describe her first impression of John, who had inadvertently prodded her in the breasts with a roll of wrapping paper in a supermarket.[109] There is also Julia's fascinating observation to Vincent that 'white South Africans in those days liked to think of themselves as the Jews of Africa, or at least the Israelis of Africa: cunning, unscrupulous, resilient, running close to the ground, hated and envied by the tribes they ruled over'. None of this is appropriate, she contends: 'Those people were not tough, they were not even cunning, or cunning enough. And they were certainly not Jews. In fact they were babes in the wood. That is how I think of them now: a tribe of babies looked after by slaves.'[110] Jewish characters appear in each of the volumes of Coetzee's *Scenes*: in *Boyhood*, Wolf Heller (notice the first name), John's father's employer in Worcester, and Goldstein and Greenberg, John's favourite Worcester playmates, at whom John's Afrikaans-speaking schoolmates, whipped into a frenzy of prejudice by the Dutch Reformed *dominee* during school assembly, hiss the insult '*Jood*'.[111] In *Youth*, there is the uncomfortably stereotyped money-counting property agent on the first page. In *Summertime*, Julia and the Silverman brothers (who employ John's father in their auto-parts store) are Jewish.

The most promising point of comparison for my purposes, however, is Rezzori's and Coetzee's ironizing of their respective protagonists' apparently *anti*-political stances, an irony bound up in the distance implied between narrating or focalizing consciousness and narrated, experiencing selves—or proxy-for-the-self, or proxy-for-the-(other-)self-that-one-was. In *Memoirs of an Anti-Semite*, it is the feckless narrator's willingness to turn a blind eye to the consequences of his culture's anti-Semitism that the reader is invited to judge. 'It was an ancient, traditional, and deep-rooted hatred, [. . .] any motivation, no matter how absurd, would justify it. [. . .] We just didn't like them, or at least liked them less than other fellow human beings.'[112] The narrator has Jewish acquaintances and (in all but the first chapter) lovers, and yet can still respond to Jewish friends' dismay at the rising tide of hatred by exclaiming in the episode set in Vienna at the moment of *Anschluss* that they are merely exaggerating: 'You Jews are always making a fuss about something.'[113] Rezzori's final chapter, '*Pravda*' (Russian for truth, of course, here dripping with irony), a series of reminiscences about the narrator's marriages and a meditation on mortality (sharing much in spirit with *Summertime*), addresses the otherness of one's past self. 'Yesterday's "I" is mythical, a mere possibility of today's "I"', the narrator observes, exhorting the reader to consider 'at random this or that possibility of yourself: you always come across someone you would be embarrassed (or even outright ashamed) to identify with, someone you'd refuse to frequent if you weren't forced to live with, because he happens to be yourself'.[114]

This seems to me precisely the species of embarrassment, even shame, performed by Coetzee: the judgment is implied in *Boyhood* and *Youth* and it is performed by a series of deeply critical interviewees in *Summertime*, in which the anti-political stance, the desire for aesthetic autonomy on the part of the artist John, is most expressly and uncomfortably described—but always contextualized, questioned, rendered naïve, even comic. *Summertime*'s final interviewee, Sophie Denoël, John's erstwhile university colleague and lover, calls him 'not political at all', claims that '[h]e looked down on politics', 'looked forward to the day when politics and the state would wither away'.[115] Notice, too, that in *Summertime*'s first (framing) notebook entry, John thinks about Jesus as anti-political. Christ might have been 'a key man in Roman Judaea, a big operator' had he 'stooped to play politics', he notes, but it was his indifference to politics that led to his being 'liquidated'. The example of Jesus, John muses, poses a challenge: 'How to live one's life outside politics, and one's death too: that was the example he set for his followers.'[116] In the interview with Sophie, Vincent presses her on '*What would have been Utopian enough for him?*' and Sophie answers: 'The closing down of the mines. The ploughing under of the vineyards. The disbanding of the armed forces. The abolition of the automobile. Universal vegetarianism. Poetry in the streets. That sort of thing.'[117] And yet while entertaining utopian impulses, she insists, he was 'too much of a Calvinist' to invest too heavily in them.[118] In fact, his utopianism appears reactionary; Vincent asks Sophie whether she thinks of John Coetzee '*as a conservative, an anti-radical*' and she answers that he was, just as were 'many of the [. . .] modernist writers from Europe who were his models', though he was also 'deeply attached to the South Africa of his youth', as evidenced in '*Boyhood*, where you find a palpable nostalgia for the old feudal relations between white and Coloured'.[119] However much irony we allow (are these positions the historical Coetzee's?), John's position is itself ironized; judgment is passed about pretence to autonomy, to an *a-* or *anti-*political stance.

Rezzori's text—and my reading of it—offers a powerful analogy for the operation of irony in the redirection of dysphoria that is (also) crucial to Coetzee's work. In other words, the dysphoria associated with the politics of prejudice with which Rezzori's protagonist grapples, and the ironic distancing implied between these bad feelings (anti Semitism) and the larger project of the work as a whole (an examination of privilege, complicity, and trauma), is analogous to the operation of similar bad feelings encountered, with similar attendant irony, in a strikingly analogous provincial location, and with similar ethical and political investments, in Coetzee's *Scenes*.

*

Coetzee's *autre*biographical work, along with the staging of figures with whom he shares the vocation of authorship (Elizabeth Costello in *Elizabeth Costello* and *Slow Man*; J.C. in *Diary of a Bad Year*), are legible as late manifestations of a long-running attempt to write characters who exhibit the desire both to escape the margins of history and to make peace with the fact of being there, but whose positions are rendered untenable, are ironized, shown to be riven with contradiction and bad faith—or misplaced good faith invariably corrupted by circumstance. Think of the Magistrate in *Waiting for the Barbarians*, *Age of Iron*'s Mrs Curren, and *Disgrace*'s David Lurie, whose responses are to stand up for liberal but not radical values in a time of emergency, the value of humanistic education and metropolitan aesthetic models. These positions are shared by the John(s) of *Scenes* and they are revealed by the ironic distance between author and his *autre*biographical self to be deeply political. In these works, Coetzee has dramatized an-other self's desire for the posture of the anti-political, by staging a form of boredom that refuses metropolitan expectation at the same time that it models itself on metropolitan explorations of the desire for artistic autonomy. Its genius is that it renders ironic a desire for the autonomous aesthetic artefact: the judgment on these desires is that *this* artist-isolate Coetzee is, after all, dead. There is a critique here, too, of the position of liberalism in South Africa; anxiety about the seeming impossibility of escape from the position informs Coetzee's work from the very first. I began with a glimpse from Coetzee's research notes, and end with another. On photocopied pages from the opening of a chapter titled 'Twentieth-Century Liberalism: The Mood of Withdrawal' in Anthony Arblaster's *The Rise and Decline of Western Liberalism* (1984), Coetzee has highlighted the following:

> The liberal outlook, as Russell conceived it, did indeed generate scepticism about all but the most negative and limited kinds of politics. As Forster put it in 1941: 'Each time Mr Wells and my other architectural friends anticipate a great outburst of post-war activity and world-planning my heart contracts. To me the best chance for future society lies through apathy, uninventiveness and inertia.'[120]

Richard Rorty calls the person with 'Socratic doubts about the final vocabulary he inherited', about 'his own moral identity, and perhaps his own sanity', an ironist.[121] Mark Sanders reminds us in his discussion of post-apartheid literature and the Truth and Reconciliation Commission that irony, in particular Socratic irony (*Eirōneia*), is the staging of a position of ignorance, 'a feigning of ignorance'.[122] Literature holds verifiability in abeyance, as a court does when hearing testimony in advance of determining the juridically accepted facts, Sanders notes. The peculiar now-time of this abeyance of judgment is a space given to the operation of desire for alternative futures, as well as reimagined relations with the past. It is something like an Erasmian *non*position, always alert to paradox. In the *Scenes from Provincial Life*, Coetzee performs this for us with exquisite skill, and as a challenge to all contexts—like contemporary South Africa, still—in which there are pretences to final vocabularies, to categorical positions.

3

Temporal Adoption, Novelistic Prosthesis

> [T]he dominant idea marketed by patriotic traditionalists is of a core nation whose survival depends on personal acts and identities performed in the intimate domains of the quotidian.
>
> —Lauren Berlant, *The Queen of America Goes to Washington City* (1997)[1]

The prospects for 'a great, authentic South African novel' were slim, J.M. Coetzee declared in an essay in 1983. While it stood 'a better chance of coming into being in Afrikaans than in English' (Afrikaans had a closer relation to the land, Coetzee reasoned, although it stood in 'a peculiarly compromised relation to the soil [. . .] of South Africa'), such a novel would have to effect 'a clean break' with tradition, since Afrikaans literature remained 'haunted, even into our day, by the idea of the *plaas* (*farm*) [. . .] that stands somewhere in the not too distant past of every Afrikaner'.[2] This hypothetical 'Great South African Novel' might have its start in that context, certainly, but it would have to do something radically different. This chapter argues that the novels of Marlene van Niekerk (b. 1954)—two to date, published a decade apart—rise to Coetzee's challenge, making the most significant attempt at formal and thematic overhaul of the possibilities of the novel as genre in Afrikaans. They also constitute one of the most significant bodies of work of a contemporary novelist in *any* language in present-day South Africa, combining concern with personal disappointments set in their socio-political contexts with a metaphorics of disappointment (as missed appointment) as it relates to the temporal predicaments of language and culture, literary form and genre, race and gender. Van Niekerk's fictions feature characters whose sense of their own place in history has been overwhelmed, whether by political events beyond their immediate control, or through their own bad decisions. Their appointments with the future, with what they believed would lie in store for them, have not been met. In that Van Niekerk's works have been translated into English (amongst other languages) in ways that foreground—and challenge—the claims of a link between place and language that Coetzee posits, they raise significant questions, too, for the relation of South African literatures *not* written in English to the idea of World Literature.

The first novel, *Triomf* (1994), a dark tragi-comedy, takes on the narrative of the poor-white family at the heart of Afrikaner-nationalist mythmaking since at least the 1920s. The Benades—Pop, Mol, Treppie (all siblings), and Lambert (Mol's mentally handicapped son by one of her brothers)—are making do, marking time during the months before the first democratic elections of April 1994, scrounging a living, alienating their neighbours, and beating up one another. Two generations back, the Benades were small-scale farmers in the erstwhile Western Transvaal, bankrupted by the depression of the 1930s, their children forced into the city.[3] The present generation has lost all connection to the land—however problematic the family's claim on it may have been in the first place. *Triomf* is Afrikaans for *triumph*, and the novel plays out in the eponymous and hubristically named central Johannesburg suburb built directly atop the ruins of Sophiatown, a freehold black settlement synonymous with early and mid-twentieth-century black cultural production destroyed by the apartheid government. Van Niekerk's first novel is an indictment of the ideologues who exploited people like the Benades, in whose name the whole apartheid edifice was constructed. It presents the family as both pathetic and repulsive, their characterization as inbred 'white trash'—an insult hurled at Lambert by the prostitute procured by his family for his birthday—itself an indictment of apartheid's master-race mythology.[4]

Triomf might feature characters for whom the farm is a distant memory, but in *Agaat* (2004), Van Niekerk sets out to reimagine the *plaasroman* (farm novel) to explore the limits of—and the possibilities that might be repurposed in—modes of representation central to the literary self-imagining of the language community that is its subject, one that is implicitly understood to be racially white. At the heart of this novel is the relationship between two women on a farm somewhere in the Overberg region of the Western Cape: Milla de Wet, white, widowed, nearly eighty in the novel's present (December 1996), terminally ill with Amyotrophic lateral sclerosis (Charcot's or Lou Gehrig's disease) and restricted to communicating through blinking or rolling her eyes; and Agaat Lourier, Milla's coloured servant, nurse, and companion.[5] Through slow accretion of detail, the reader learns that Agaat was removed as a child from a family working on Milla's mother's farm and, despite the hostile judgment of the white farming community, adopted into Milla's family. When Milla falls pregnant, however, she moves Agaat, aged twelve or thirteen, into an outside servant's room, telling her that she will henceforth be a housemaid. Agaat spends the next thirty-six years nursing the pain of her betrayal, managing the household, raising Milla and husband Jak's son, Jakkie, and turning herself—or indeed being turned—into a subject both deracinated and Other, barred from white Afrikaner culture and yet more accomplished than Milla (and Jak) in those skills and competencies that, the book suggests, are taken by a self-defining community to be significant markers of membership.[6]

It is the combination of temporal disjunction, disappointment as sense of missed appointment *and* as frustrated desire, and the question of what it means to be forced to adopt the temporality of another—the means of marking time and of regarding oneself as defined thereby (another episteme, a new dispensation, a differently raced subjectivity) with which this chapter is principally concerned. The primary focus is on *Agaat*, though a preliminary return to *Triomf* will set the scene for my discussion of cultural conceptions of temporality, of memory and the archive, and of the trope of forced adoption that takes centre-stage in the later novel. In conclusion, I will pose the question of translation—of the appointment with readers elsewhere that is promised to a translation—to ask what challenge determinedly provincial texts like *Agaat* might pose for conceptions of World Literature.

PROLOGUE: IDEOLOGY AND THE ARCHIVE

Sophiatown, the storied home of a vibrant urban black culture at mid-century, home of jazz, hard-nosed anti-apartheid journalism, and fiction that looked outward to the world, was regarded by apartheid town planners as a so-called 'black spot' in the white city and bulldozed (after 1955), its residents moved to far-flung townships—the no-place of the absurdly euphemistic 'location'—to make space for what are described in *Triomf* as '[d]ecent houses for white people'.[7] It is in this highly charged space that the Benades 'just muddle along through the rubble', according to Mol, while reminders of the destruction wrought in their name resurface from the very first page of the novel: the simple-minded Lambert digs about in the yard and the family's dogs sniff at shards and fragments from the past. Mol thinks: 'it's not like they're exactly on top of things', although this is quite literally where they are.[8] In the present, the Benades' only visitors are representatives of two groups attempting to sell visions of a better life: Jehovah's Witnesses and canvassers for the National Party (NP), the party of apartheid, now trying desperately to mobilize its historic supporters ahead of the elections. The Witnesses read passages from Exodus about another trek to a land of milk and honey, land appropriately enough also already occupied. The NP volunteers, aspiring academics who parrot a garbled definition of the culture they promise to defend in the new dispensation, regard the Benades both opportunistically as 'our foot-soldiers in the election' and contemptuously as backward country people ('at the bottom of the ladder') who will 'buy anything we tell them'.[9]

Significant episodes in Afrikaner-nationalist mythmaking surface in the Benades' reminiscing. Pop and Mol's romantic narrative of selling corsages at the Voortrekker Monument on Republic Day, 31 May 1961, for example, is revealed at a key moment to be a fabrication: the epileptic Lambert had vomited on the roses, rendering them unsellable. Treppie, the novel's key voice of political critique, punctures his siblings' illusions, and recognizes the canvassers' propaganda for what it is: 'the same old rubbish recycled under a new name'. The NP is trying to peddle just another 'wagonload of shit', he claims, just like the story for which an earlier generation 'fell, hook, line and sinker' in 1948.[10] All politicians are susceptible to critique in Treppie's—and indeed the novel's—angrily disappointed analysis. The full spectrum appears on the Benades' television screens, from left-wing firebrands Peter Mokaba and Winnie Madikizela-Mandela, to right-wing demagogue Eugène Terre'Blanche, who falls off his horse during a parade.[11] In Treppie's analysis they are all liars, all deny life's realities in a manner likened to 'wallpaper' (his favourite metaphor).[12] Wallpaper represents false consciousness and ideological cant; it covers over cracks. The romantic novels Mol borrows from the library, like Afrikaner folksongs and stories of Voortrekker heroes, are forms of wallpaper. So too is a preacher's promotion of forgiveness as the answer to political discord. At one poignant moment, after the family has inadvertently become caught up in a political march in central Johannesburg and retires to a park for a picnic, Treppie composes an ode to nature entitled '*THIS IS NOT WALLPAPER*'.[13] When they get home, Mol sticks the poem up on the wall: everything is liable to ideological appropriation, to become wallpaper.

The walls of the Benades' house are but one site of inscription and archiving in the novel, to which metaphors and technologies of memory and futurity that record versions of the past and fantasies about the future are central. Treppie, we learn, has a 'photographic memory'. The men think of Mol as an 'echo machine', and what she repeats reveals her central role as voice of abused and misdirected moral purpose.[14] The personal drama that animates the novel (whether Lambert will discover his incestuous origins) hinges on information hidden in a locked sideboard, a scene of the storage of crucial records repeated in *Agaat*.[15] Lambert expends considerable energy on a 'never-ending' wall painting that imagines an alternative history, one in which early Dutch governor Jan van Riebeeck shares a drink (brandy and coke, a favourite of working-class Afrikaners) with a representative autochthon, 'Harry the Strandloper' (beachcomber), and in which white Afrikaners might escape to a mythical north—a dream that is abandoned in the novel's final lines.[16]

Questions about what it is necessary to remember and how this might be effected (through what technologies and in what locations), indictments of the bankruptcy of nationalist ideologies, and the political potential of the suffering body—all these recur in *Agaat*, a novel in which, like *Triomf*, the role of language itself in past traumas (and more specifically the role of Afrikaans, the language that bears the heaviest burden of the last century's history in South Africa and the language in which Van Niekerk writes) is interrogated. This observation forms part of a broader engagement in what follows with ideas of adoption and translation, both also understood metaphorically, and with the idea of text as enabler of a repetition necessary for the transmission of culture.

ADOPTION AND CULTURAL COMPETENCY

Agaat animates the experience of epistemic shifts in political dispensations; it spans the period from the NP's election victory in 1948 through the first year of the new postapartheid dispensation. At the same time, it both examines and, in terms of its own afterlives in languages other than that in which it was written (for example), is the subject of the experience of what I want to describe as the *adoption of*, or adoption *into*, what I call a differentiated temporality, more specifically that of another culture or way of life. Such temporality is evidenced most obviously in spoken and written language, but also understood as those specific vocabularies it deploys, its arcane terminology and cultural references. *Agaat* offers itself as its own kind of reckoning with these vocabularies, epitomized in the language of its folksongs, craft activities, and—as novelist Sonja Loots notes, 'with what Van Niekerk jokingly describes as "purple prose full of noble labour terminology, overly lyrical . . . and loaded with the farming-is-burdensome-topos"'.[17] It is an act of archiving, marked both by affection for a language of childhood (Van Niekerk grew up on a farm) and by disavowal, disgust at the violence enacted in and through this language. The novel is also conscious to undermine the lie that Afrikaans is first and foremost a *white* language: its central character, Agaat, who would have been classified Coloured by the apartheid state,[18] owns the language with greater force and competence than her white mistress. I will return to these competencies (and to how we might read the implication of her mastery of them), as well as to the challenges posed by the language in which the novel was written, in due course.

Agaat's initial adoption is metaphorically a translation that requires her to take on the culture of her parents-turned-employers, but one whose domesticating impulses are ultimately undone by the insistence on ethnic otherness as an impermeable boundary in 1960s South Africa. In the present moment of the novel's narration we encounter the women, having endured a working life on the farm Grootmoedersdrift ('grandmother's ford') marked by constant battle between hope and disappointment, still bound by this interrupted, imperfect entanglement, and embittered by their multiple temporal disjunctions, missed or curtailed opportunities. The adoption or synchronizing of unfamiliar or unexpected temporalities is also a demand made on the reader by the novel's organization. This is to say that *Agaat*, a novel concerned with life on a farm, with the differentiation among seasons, with the contrast between periods of relative inactivity and moments of frenetic hyperactivity (not to mention with great changes in cultural-historical epochs, which are always off-stage), teaches us how to read it in the process of our reading.[19] We learn how to piece together the four narrative strands that alternate, not always in the same order, in each chapter: Milla's thoughts on her deathbed in the novel's present; an account of past events, addressed apparently by Milla to herself in the second person;[20] italicized passages of free-indirect discourse in part appearing to reflect on the winter of 1993, when Milla first realized she was ill; and finally extracts from Milla's diaries, largely from the 1950s and 60s, which, we are given to understand, are read to Milla in the novel's present by Agaat as an act of reckoning.[21] A Prologue and an Epilogue are offered in the voice of Jakkie, now an expatriate living in Canada, who has been summoned by Agaat to his mother's deathbed.

In respect of its representations of what I am calling adoption, the taking as one's own the child of another, *Agaat* is in a line of descent, in the South African context, of texts like Olive Schreiner's *From Man to Man* (1926), at the end of which we glimpse Rebekah adopting (or taking in as quasi-indentured servant) the mixed-race child of her estranged husband, and of Dalene Matthee's *Fiela se Kind* (1985; *Fiela's Child*, 1986), in which the characters occupy very different positions of relative racial privilege: the adoptive parents are coloured, the child is white, although, like Agaat, he too is cast out of an accustomed way of life into an alien one during his adolescence.[22] Novels in which adopted children feature alongside and within 'disrupted and reformed families' offer intriguing perspectives on evolving notions of nationhood, suggests Carol Singley, whose study of American—especially Northern antebellum—texts (whose contexts might be thought not dissimilar in terms of hierarchies of racial privilege from apartheid-era South Africa) reveals two major representational and ideological strands. Adoption either saves a child from desperate conditions, allowing the adoptee to participate in the national narrative of new beginnings and unbounded opportunity, or it delivers unequal benefits: the child remains dependent on account of gender, class, or race, and in extreme cases is shown to be 'unworthy of adoption or unlikely to benefit from its support'.[23]

Singley discusses Harriet Wilson's *Our Nig: Sketches from the Life of a Free Black* (1859), in which the mixed-race Frado Smith is abandoned as a child and adopted by a white family that abuses and exploits her, making her an indentured worker very like Agaat becomes in the De Wet household.[24] Both texts deny the adopted child a happy ending, subverting along the way genres that might have framed very different outcomes—in *Our Nig*, slave and conversion narratives; in *Agaat*, the farm novel (in farming terms Agaat is a *hanslam*, an orphaned or rejected lamb[25]). Several genres are in fact tested throughout Van Niekerk's novel for their appropriateness. There are references to tragedy as a form befitting Agaat's story, and also to soap opera, which Milla notes is the mode through which Afrikaners are often portrayed.[26] In her overheated and simultaneously defensive acknowledgement of the cruelty she has inflicted on Agaat, Milla reaches for biblical comparisons: Milla and Jak are the childless Abraham and Sarah; Milla forgets Agaat's assigned birthday three times, like Peter thrice denying Christ—though Agaat is like Peter, too, bearing the household (standing in for the apostolic) key. Agaat is also like Joseph, removed from family, the overseer of the ruler's lands, and bearer of a multi-coloured—in her case, embroidered—coat.[27] In Jak's eyes, Milla and Agaat's relationship seems more like a 'magazine story', however, a 'trashy novel, ladies' fiction for the airport', or like a 'Bedtime story'.[28] There are frequent references to embroidery as metaphor, made to stand for a particular genre, the tall tale, while also referencing Agaat's skill as craftsperson: 'Só, Agaat, Jak said, thát's the story. Can you think us up a conclusion? After all, you're used to embroidering!'[29] Jak also renders Agaat's role in the De Wet family as parodic and racist telegram.

In the multiple versions of Agaat's origins offered in the novel, however, the predominating generic touchstone is the fairy-tale, especially in its darker, gothic form: 'Grimm meets Goth in the Overberg', the adult Jakkie thinks about the female household (Jak is long dead at this point).[30] Agaat begins life as 'Asgat', literally *ash-arse*, because she crouches in the dirty fireplace of her parents' hovel, the name and the site of her magical rescue recalling Cinderella (Aspoestertjie in Afrikaans).[31] As an evil stepmother might do, Milla renames the child, changing cinder to semi-precious stone: not white enough to be precious, Agaat (agate) can nonetheless be polished. Agaat also sounds pleasingly close to *Agatha*, whose etymology—from the Greek *agathos*, meaning good—serves '[l]ike a holy brand [...], like an immanent destiny, the name on the brow, to do good, to want to be good, goodness itself', explains the local minister, Dominee van der Lught (who suggests the name for this reason).[32] The hubris of Milla renaming Asgat, of her adoption of the child as her own (Jak disparagingly calls this Milla's 'project'[33]), is signalled for the reader by the date on which it takes place, 16 December, the Day of the Covenant, a day in Afrikaner nationalist mythology celebrating divine intervention, manifest destiny, and a narrative of election.

In the novel's epilogue, we read a version of this adoption-as-(re-)creation story, offered as if Jakkie remembers the fairy-tale-like version of her origins that Agaat would whisper in his ear when, as a child, he would fall asleep in her arms:

> *And from that day the little girl was good and sweet and a child like every other child and she was baptised with the name Good.*
>
> *And the woman taught her to bake and cook and wash and iron and sweep and polish and knit and sew with needle and thread. And she taught her to read and to write. And she tied a ribbon in her hair and showed her a mirror and she said:*
>
> *See, now you are a human being.* [...]
>
> *And then one day after seven years something happened that changed everything.*
>
> *The woman was expecting her own baby.*
>
> *Óut she said to Good. Óut of my house, from now on you live in a little room outside in the backyard.* [...]
>
> *From now on you're my slave. You'll work for a wage.* [...]
>
> *Now, Good, you are dead.*[34]

Several things can be said about this passage. The published English translation does not convey as forcefully as the Afrikaans text the play on the word 'Goed', which also means 'thing' or 'property' (as in 'goods and chattels': the singular noun is now classed as obsolete or archaic in English).[35] When Jak chides Milla for pandering to Agaat, creating expectations amongst the staff in general, he refers to them as 'goed' in Afrikaans, though the English translation by Michiel Heyns renders this 'creatures'.[36] The passage indicts Milla's presumption, in renaming Agaat, to attempt to create her anew. Jak jokes that she has 'broken' the child 'in', that Agaat is like clay in Milla's hands or a 'blank page' on which she 'can impress anything'. When he warns Milla that she had better 'know [her] story', her version of events, and that it had 'better be a good one', the irony of the pun on good is chilling.[37]

Finally, the passage serves to draw attention to those skills that Agaat indicates she acquired from Milla: '*to bake and cook and wash and iron and sweep and polish and knit and sew with needle and thread* [. . .] *to read and to write*'. It is precisely these skills that might—for the white farming community, for Milla, and Milla hopes in vain for Jak, too—mark Agaat as member of a particular group, as one of Milla's family and racial community. Yet they are also markers of what is expected of a servant, and so we observe how investment in a child raises anxieties about assimilation that are never far from the surface in Afrikaner policing of the discursive and performative boundaries of whiteness.[38] Asking what it means for Agaat to have been adopted and then trained as a servant requires us to ask what the signs are that she has been made to adopt those competencies that are the sign of sameness, and what it means when these become a sign of difference.

Milla gives Agaat three guidebooks to particular skills when she moves her into the backyard room: *Hulpboek vir boere in Suid-Afrika*, a handbook for South African farmers published by the government in 1929; the *FAK-Volksangbundel*, an anthology of folksongs published by the Federation of Afrikaans Cultural Organizations; and *Borduur só*, a guidebook to embroidery by Hetsie van Wyk, with an introduction by Betsy Verwoerd, wife of Prime Minister H.F. Verwoerd, the leading architect of legal apartheid.[39] These three texts also provide the novel's epigraphs. Agaat masters the competencies described in each: she becomes an accomplished embroiderer; she sings Afrikaans hymns and alludes frequently to the culture's folksong and poetry (at least in the Afrikaans-language original: I will return to the question of how the translation accounts for these references in due course); and she is adept as a farmer. Indeed, many of the novel's set-piece moments of high drama involve her saving the day through an understanding of local conditions in the face of Jak's ineffectual agricultural husbandry. In short, Agaat's skills involve her adoption into ways of behaviour and (crucially) ways of spending time, of having her time organized by the demands of the house and the farm and accompanied by the performance of song (temporal objects that encode and reinforce such demands and such means of passing time), in a way that accords remarkably well with Elizabeth Freeman's notion of the chrononormative and the chronobiopolitical: 'Chrononormativity is a mode of implantation, a technique by which institutional forces come to seem like somatic facts'; '[c]hronobiopolitics harnesses not only sequence but also cycle, the dialectical companion to sequence, for the idea of time as cyclical stabilizes its forward movement, promising renewal rather than rupture'.[40]

Each of the texts that impart the skills Agaat acquires seems intended perversely to complete the education of an adoptee at the precise moment that she is made to understand that she is no longer a member of the family, but rather a servant required to adopt the culture of master and mistress (not father and mother). Even so, Agaat becomes in many ways *more* Afrikaans—and more of an Afrikaner—than Milla and Jak, if these identities are predicated on a facility with language and confirmed by familiarity with skills linked to cultural stereotypes of farmer and craftsperson. Agaat's dedication to labour, to craft and handwork, to taking on and taking over that which is supposed to be a mark of Afrikaner aptitude and celebration of its pastoral origins and heritage, also ironically foregrounds the black labour occluded by this pastoral myth.[41] It is juxtaposed, too, with Jak's dedication to modernity, his advocacy of new modes of farming that are shown to be profoundly short-sighted and ecologically damaging.[42]

These skills raise questions about the arbitrary nature of the community predicated on their mastery. Here the *FAK-Volksangbundel* serves as prime example, as it offers a largely fabricated 'tradition' in order precisely to cement very fragile notions of community: its introduction emphasizes that the anthologized folksongs are intended to facilitate discovery of the 'force and flavour of this Southland' such that 'the nation' would 'press it to their hearts and *adopt* it as their own'.[43] Rather than collect material a priori in existence, the assemblage required being adopted precisely because many of the melodies were appropriated from German and other northern European songs, using new lyrics and settings of poetry associated with the language movements that had given an instant canon to Afrikaans, only latterly acknowledged (at the time of the *Volksangbundel*'s publication) to be a language in its own right, rather than a debased Dutch dialect. Agaat's mastery of multiple competencies draws attention to a range of questions about supplementarity, memory, and performance in the novel: *Agaat* is replete with metaphors tying the eponymous character to the reflecting and the retentional—by which I mean that which serves memory and in turn facilitates repetition. But what does it mean to invoke the idea of reflection and retention, and with what ramifications for thinking through the challenges posed by *Agaat* for the novel in contemporary South Africa?

APARTHEID CYBORGS AND RETENTIONAL PROSTHESES

'She was a whole compilation of you', Milla thinks to herself about Agaat: 'Your archive. Without her you and Jak would have known nothing of yourselves. She was your parliament, your hall of mirrors.'[44] Central to this concentration of images tying Agaat to the archival is the question of survival, which is to say repeatability. By virtue of the cruel intimacy that marked domestic service under the conditions of apartheid South Africa, Agaat has been witness to everything that has transpired in the De Wet household. But there is more to it than this: the child (first Agaat, then Jakkie) embodies for Milla the promise of the continuation of the parent through knowledge of the parent's competencies, through transmission of knowledge of praxis (hence the invocation of 'compilation' and 'archive'): how to embroider; how to sing folksongs; how to farm. Knowledge of this sort is a kind of remembering forwards, the cultivation of habit. Brian Massumi reminds us that Kierkegaard distinguished between forms or regimes of memory on account of the direction of repetition: 'What is recollected has been, is repeated backward, whereas repetition is recollected forward.' Massumi glosses this as follows:

> Whereas memory is normally understood as a recollection of what has been, repetition is a recollection of what has not yet come—a memory of the future. This is not so hard to grasp if we think of repetition as self-contracting, the model of habit. [. . .] We say we have a habit, but we all know that it is really the habit that has us. It is an automatism that has taken hold and *in*habits us.[45]

In the child Jakkie, we see a similar concern with these regimes of memory. As a boy, Jakkie is made to sing for visitors to the farm, though not to embroider: some competencies are gendered (although Agaat transcends such divisions by her mastery of both feminine and masculine competencies, embroidery and farming). But if it is hoped his skills will allow repetition of learned competencies (as a culturally adept Afrikaner farmer), Jakkie instead becomes an ethnomusicologist, recording First Nations Canadian and Native American songs to make them available as memorializations of genocide. And he regards Afrikaans folksong as culturally and context-specific, in other words not as expressing or enacting or allowing the adoption of affect that pretends to be natural or truthful.[46] Jakkie and Agaat each frustrate the expectations of the child as agent of repetition: Jakkie, by choice; Agaat on account of the deformation of intimate relations that turn an adopted child into a forced adopter whose retentional potential (one that makes possible a repetition) is redirected for ideological reasons from the quasi-genealogical to the utilitarian.

In contrast to Jakkie, Agaat is expected to cultivate habit without inferring a relationship of inheritance or belonging, because *Afrikaner* implicitly means *white* according to the understanding of the community in which she finds herself. Indeed, this means she is expected to reflect without repeating (in the sense of *becoming* the next generation), hence the invocation of mirrors in the text—though mirrors also gesture to the novel's formal subversion of realism.[47] There is something about the change forced on Agaat that we might compare to the kind of mimicry about which Bhabha writes: Agaat is expected to mimic, but the mimicry always also produces a difference, so offering a point of potential resistance.[48] Yet Agaat does not seem able to return to a state anterior to the learned mimicry: there is something about the force and expansiveness of the competencies that she must adopt that transforms her, indeed, into something else, which the text suggests is part archive, part machine. Agaat performs a kind of prosthetic memory function for Milla, recording or making the storage of knowledge and memory possible, but in a way that is not generative (or in a line of genetic descent); instead, Agaat becomes simultaneously *technical* and *monstrous*. Agaat indeed appears to be a monster of Milla's own making, standing to Milla as the monster does to Dr Frankenstein. Several descriptions reinforce this suggestion. Jakkie recalls Agaat as 'poker-faced', with a 'pop-eyed glare' that suggests a '[w]ooden eye'. She has a 'little hand on [a] wrong-way-round arm', as if the pieces were not put together properly.[49] When Jakkie, returning to Canada, thinks about how Agaat seemed to him a 'Cyborg' at his mother's funeral, we begin to see how fruitful and allusive this metaphorics might be. He recalls that Agaat

> didn't twitch a muscle. Her cap was higher, more densely embroidered than I remembered it, spectacles on her nose. For the rest she was as always, perhaps a bit stouter, her chin pushed far out, her steps energetic, her soles squelching on the wooden floor. Apartheid Cyborg. Assembled from loose components plus audiotape.[50]

Van Niekerk is here almost certainly referencing Donna Haraway's positing—in her 'Manifesto for Cyborgs' (1985)—of a radical, boundary-breaking socialist feminism that departs from the essentialisms of feminist theory and the metanarratives of psychoanalysis and Marxism. 'What kind of politics could embrace partial, contradictory, permanently unclosed constructions of personal and collective selves and still be faithful, effective—and, ironically, socialist feminist?', Haraway asks.[51] She proposes a kind of 'Cyborg writing' that deploys 'retold stories' as tools, 'versions that reverse and displace the hierarchical dualisms of naturalized identities', subverting the 'central myths of origin of Western culture' that have 'colonized' us all 'with their longing for fulfillment in apocalypse'. We have for too long valorized both 'victimhood as the only ground for insight', and 'the constructed revolutionary subject' awaiting a liberatory apocalypse, she asserts; each of these subject positions is inadequate and it is in 'the fraying of identities and in the reflexive strategies for constructing them' that 'the possibility opens up for weaving something other than a shroud for the day after the apocalypse that so prophetically ends salvation history'.[52] How can we not think of Agaat when rereading this utopian manifesto? Agaat weaves (strictly, she embroiders) a shroud, using linen from Milla's trousseau, on which she records her alternative narrative of life on the farm to counterpose Milla's diaries.[53] But Agaat's eschewal of victimhood, her mastery of the tools of the dominating discourses of the time and place in which she survives, marks her as an aspiring cyborg in Haraway's terms, a *bricoleuse* bent on subversion and displacement, at least in theory. Van Niekerk comments in interview, and only half-jokingly, that she 'would not like to be a member of Agaat's future kibbutz on Grootmoedersdrift' once the farm has passed into her ownership, as it does at the close of the novel: 'Survival and good order, good bookkeeping, would be her first priorities. As "boss-girl" she has learnt all the worst lessons of coercion and oppression and corrupting of the poor from her former masters.'[54]

None of this is to suggest either that we read Agaat straightforwardly as an allegory for Haraway's cyborg, or that we discount Haraway's essay as a seminal examination of human-animal and organic-machine boundaries (that pre-empted all manner of cybernetic and post-human theorizing, none of which is germane here).[55] However, a great deal in Haraway's manifesto is useful for thinking about repetition and memory in relation to character (Agaat) and novel (*Agaat*). 'The main problem with cyborgs'—writes Haraway—'is that they are the illegitimate offspring of militarism and patriarchal capitalism, not to mention state socialism. But illegitimate offspring are often exceedingly unfaithful to their origins. Their fathers, after all, are inessential'.[56] Her 'cyborg myth', she continues, 'is about transgressed boundaries, potent fusions, and dangerous possibilities which progressive people might explore as one part of needed political work'.[57] Both Agaat and *Agaat* answer these descriptions uncommonly well; both challenge the idea that those competencies a character is made to adopt might belong to one culture (marked linguistically or racially). Agaat's biological father has faded from memory, and her quasi-adopted father, Jak, is long dead in the novel's present (and had been eclipsed in his life by the formidable Milla). The novel thus renders the male-dominated *plaasroman* genre but a pale and inessential model. *Agaat*, I am suggesting, is itself a kind of storehouse of lore, that which Agaat has to adopt, in a way that makes of it metaphorically cyborg too. In other words, the novel, a *tour-de-force* performance of genre transgressions that posits the 'dangerous' possibility that Afrikaners' cultural products, competencies, and language might belong to all, is 'Cyborg writing'.

Another way of describing this approach to the novel is to assert that both character and novel are machines, Agaat metaphorically and *Agaat* formally and generically. More specifically, they are both retentional prostheses. Here I use a term offered by Bernard Stiegler in *Technics and Time*, an ambitious revisionist philosophical project (three of a projected five volumes have been published to date) in which Stiegler proposes that at the heart of ontology is the question of the human as *technical* being, something misunderstood or suppressed since Plato. In simplified terms, Stiegler argues that because we live with the knowledge of death, knowledge in other words that we are neither immortal nor, like most animals, unselfconscious about mortality, the question of how we come to know what we know (and need to know) in every generation is fundamental to our being human.[58] The technical, what Stiegler calls technics, is that which facilitates such knowledge; it *is* such knowledge. Much of the finer detail of Stiegler's argument is developed through disagreement with Heidegger, whose idea of *Dasein* as something that is a priori there to be accessed or inherited Stiegler challenges for failing to engage with precisely where this there might be: 'access to this already-there is only possible to the extent to which the fact of its exteriorization'—in other words, its being already *outside* the self—'guarantees its preservation'.[59] It follows that of primary importance to humans (as technical beings, in this sense) are what Stiegler calls retentional prostheses (etymologically, *pros-thesis* names that which is set in front of, is already there, exists in anticipation).[60] These prostheses make memory possible, and thus enable repetition, inheritance, and (crucially) 'heritage', through forms of signification that encompass everything from cave art to writing, from the codex to the internet.

Stiegler speaks in interview of a process of 'grammatization' being at the heart of 'discretization and repetition', the rendering discrete in order to enable preservation and inheritance.[61] He calls this kind of memory that is dependent on prostheses *epiphylogenetic*, as opposed to the *epigenetic* (somatic memory), or *genetic* (germinal memory), that which is inherent (embodied) or biologically inherited. By contrast, epiphylogenetic memory is exteriorized, 'inscribed in the non-living body'.[62] Stiegler also discusses what he calls tertiary retention, that which is enabled by forms of recording. He later includes under this heading those spaces and forms of technology that retain or make possible the memory of a temporal experience, implying that this category might be expanded to include all forms of recording of the expectation of an affective response.[63] 'No matter the technical object', he explains, 'it is a memory aid', and to this extent 'enables a repetition, and this is what accounts for technicity—it stabilizes a repetition'.[64] Repetition is central to human survival and to the transmission of culture through generations. 'The question of repetition *is* the question of *tekhne*, of prostheses', Stiegler concludes, and the '*unheimlich* character of all prostheses'—the uncanny, perhaps also the monstrous—'derives from the fact that to look at a prosthesis', as Stiegler defines it, 'amounts to staring at the fact of one's own mortality'.[65]

Stiegler has come to the attention of anglophone film scholars because of his elaboration, in particular in the third volume of *Technics and Time*, of a Frankfurt-School-like critique of the industrialized technologies of cinema and broadcast media, in particular of Hollywood.[66] For my purposes, I want to gesture to the usefulness of Stiegler's ideas about the synchronization of consciousness with the temporality of an artwork (which forms the basis of his critique), and of an artwork thought of as an example of retentional prosthesis—in this case one in which a character (Agaat) is presented as analogous to, or the occasion for, a set of reflections on this idea. The suggestive connection is with the way Stiegler uses adoption to name the process through which such synchronization, the 'synthesis of apprehension', takes place.[67] In short, adoption is a kind of prosthesticity: through it the past that I did not live becomes mine and I am co-opted into the projection of a future made common, in Stiegler's formulation (in translation), 'under the eschatological authority of a final judgment' (for example that offered by ideas like progress, civilization, or race) that forces the 'construction of a *We*'.[68] Here Stiegler elaborates the ideas of André Leroi-Gourhan, especially in *Milieu et techniques* (1945) to observe that '[c]onnection to the *future* [. . .] requires them to share a common past, but this past can only be common through adoption, concretized only through projection'. This past, Leroi-Gourhan contends, is 'the sum total of primary, secondary, and tertiary retentionality constituting, *through projection*, the protentional mechanism that is, finally, the identificatory flux of an *I and* the adoption of a common *temporal* navigational mechanism'.[69] We might think back to the *FAK-Volksangbundel* editors' desire, quoted in one of the epigraphs to *Agaat*, that the notional (white) Afrikaner nation might 'adopt' the songs 'as their own'.

The stakes, for Stiegler, of trying to unpick this question of *who* and *what* in relation to memory, retentionality, and identity, are high. In his conception of the technicity of our being, 'natural' memory cannot exist: it is always 'produced by programs that are largely memory's prostheses'.[70] Consequently, he is led to ask whether it is 'the reader, the spectator, or the listener' who is being 'auto-programmed, prosthetically[,] when reading a book, watching a film, or listening to a CD, a DVD, or an iPod', or whether it is in fact the person reading, watching, or listening who is the program doing the processing of data stored in those devices. He considers a third possibility: 'do these programs consisting of mnemo-technical data permit the "processing" of data in the receiver's "own" memory, which then program their execution?' In other words, '[i]s a book a translation (and production) interface between reader and Literature, as a vast collective memory?'[71]

If the three books that Milla gives Agaat are intended as 'translation (and production) interface[s]', in Stiegler's formulation, *Agaat* serves both as retentional prosthesis, a storehouse and model, and, through the figure of Agaat within it, as critique of the suggestion that such prostheses (as well as the prosthesis that is the novel itself, perhaps) might be the preserve of a community produced as a 'race' through its performance, the metaphorical translation of competencies that it enables, and indeed in *Agaat*'s case subverts. Stiegler's final question above restates what I have been suggesting is at stake in asking questions about the operations that are facilitated by, made possible through, and that we might think of as being at stake in, the reading of works like Marlene van Niekerk's *Agaat*. However, here another question hovers, that of the language in which a reader encounters the novel, with whose representation of temporality the novel requires the reader to grapple. What if we take the question of translation in Stiegler's positing of a book as 'a translation (and production) interface' literally?

PROVINCIAL LITERATURES AND THE TEMPORALITY OF 'WORLD LITERATURE' IN ENGLISH

Agaat summons Jakkie to Milla's deathbed with a telegram that reads, in English, 'MÊME DYING STOP CONFIRM ARRIVAL STOP'.[72] 'Même' here replicates Agaat's accented pronunciation of an honorific, Ma'am, a term of endearment and of grudging deference to Milla. Without the accent, it becomes simply 'meme', an element of culture passed by non-genetic means, which is to say by imitation.[73] In common usage, a meme is also something passed from one internet user to another without care of originating context or local meaning. Non-genetic relations, those of adoption, I have suggested, are at the heart of Van Niekerk's novel, as are imitation—in relation to recurring images of mirrors and Agaat's ever-present performance of mimicry. Both might also be taken as metaphors for the operation of translation. Another way of framing the issue is to ask how literatures lose their accent(s) in translation, and how or why this might matter. What is at stake in asking such a question in relation to a text so deeply immersed in its locality at the same time that it is aware of the restrictions of such locatedness (the tendency to exclude; the difficulties of communicating across language barriers)?

Agaat stages the question of linguistic losses and gains directly when Milla writes in her diary on 6 September 1960, during her post-natal depression: 'Perhaps I should try to write in English. Perhaps domesticities will sound better to me in a world language.'[74] Here we participate in a fiction within the translation: Milla is expressing the possibility of writing in English, but is not doing so in the world of the text in the language in which we read her expression. This is something like an invitation to what Derrida calls 'suicide by translation'—it dramatizes a failure to write in English as it insists that the enunciation of such failure be understood *not* to be in English, even if the reader encounters the words in English.[75] Milla's speculation—about how English might render domesticities—therefore ironically refuses the possibility of a completely domesticating translation, one that does not remind the reader that what is being read is a translated text.[76] It accrues pathos because it reflects on her feeling that she is trapped in a 'provincial' language at the same time that it offers a metafictional foregrounding of the novel's insistent concern with the legacies of that same language. The novel indeed sets out to be encyclopaedic in relation to words that have fallen out of current Afrikaans usage; it is already performing a kind of translation in the very language in which it is written. It offers itself as an archive, though whether as repository for future recuperation and transmission or as a kind of drawing of the line, a respectful but resigned packing away, is left open.

What happens, however, when none of this is offered in the language that is the subject of direct (as well as meta-) reflection? The English-language text is obviously not a purely semantic translation, nor could it be, though it is a considerable and admirable feat to have rendered the original's 718 pages of often very difficult Afrikaans in a translation that continues to convince anglophone readers of Van Niekerk's extraordinary talent.[77] It is, however, a substantially different *version*—an observation made by Leon de Kock, who translated *Triomf* into English. Though full of praise for Michiel Heyns's work (elsewhere he calls it a 'value-enhancing English translation'[78]), De Kock suggests that 'the best way to read *Agaat* is to read it twice, because it's been written twice'—both in Afrikaans, and 'then in its extended English version'.[79] I do not mean to find fault in pedantic fashion with Heyns's translation, but considering some implications of the choices made raises a question with wider ramifications: what does it mean for a text—and, by extension, a linguistic community's cultural products—to adopt (to be adopted by or into) another linguistic or cultural tradition?[80] This, after all, is one way to understand translation. More specifically (and with all the usual caveats about not essentializing linguistic traditions, being cautious about the label *tradition,* and so on), what does it mean if the target language is not a geographically specific one?

The translator's note to the English version of *Agaat* gives a sense of the interventions Heyns deemed necessary in the project of conveying the complexity of Van Niekerk's original. He attempted to make his 'own translations', insofar as that was possible, of what he calls the many 'traces of Afrikaans cultural goods' in the novel ('songs, children's games, [. . .] idiomatic expressions, farming lore'), but always with an ear to retaining 'something of the sound, rhythm, register and cultural specificity of the original'. Where Van Niekerk quotes from 'mainstream Afrikaans poetry', Heyns explains, however, he looked for 'equivalents from English poetry'.[81] An example is the substitution for a broken quotation from G.A. Watermeyer's 'Ballade op die Dronkparty' (Ballad of the Drunken Party). The Afrikaans text of *Agaat* reads:

> Kom Milla, het hy gesê, dink jy nie dis tyd vir 'n gediggie nie? Wat is daardie een wat jy altyd so graag vir my aangehaal het? Die liefde is die leë glas. En dan? Donker? Bitter? Wat in die hart se holte pas? Hoe gaan dit nou weer?[82]

This passage, with its halting quotations from Watermeyer, might be rendered (in my own translation) something like: 'Come Milla, he said, don't you think it's time for a little poem? What is that one that you used always to quote so eagerly for me? Love is an empty glass. And then? Dark? Bitter? That fits in the heart's hollow? How does it go again?' The lines Jak is searching for from Watermeyer's poem are in fact the following:

> Die liefde is die bitter glas,
> die droë glas, die donker glas;
> die liefde is die naverdriet
> wat in die hart se holte pas.[83]

In the Afrikaans text, Jak goads Milla to recite a poem he only vaguely recalls (love is, respectively, the bitter, empty, dark glass, the regret that fills a void in the heart). In the English translation, Jak remembers a different poem entirely: Auden's 'As I Walked Out One Evening' (1937; published, revised in 1940):

> Come Milla, he said, don't you think it's time for a little poem? What's that one that you were always so fond of quoting to me? O stand, stand at the window. And then? As the tears scald and start? How does it go again? You shall love your crooked neighbour with your crooked heart?[84]

Auden's poem carries very different symbolic freight: it allows Jak to chide Milla for her gloomy worldview rather than suggest an engagement with intense personal regret at love turned sour. Jak quotes Auden's lines in full in the English translation; this Jak recalls poetry without flaw, despite inebriation, making him even more coldly calculating than in the Afrikaans text.

Heyns explains that he took what he calls 'the liberty of *extending* the range of poetic allusion' such that readers would 'thus find scraps of

English poetry interspersed, generally without acknowledgement, in the text', as with this Auden ballad.[85] The assumption is that these are poems and poets the anglophone reader might recognize. Heyns mentions four poets by name: Hopkins, Donne, Auden, Eliot. Wordsworth, Pound, and Tennyson are also cited (still others appear in the acknowledgements). A line from Tennyson's 'Tears, idle tears' (1847), for example, is added to the end of the entry in Milla's diary for 4 July 1960.[86] Intriguingly, the Swedish translation renders this additional line in Swedish—which is to say without marking the fact that it is a quotation from English poetry, and even though it does not appear in the Afrikaans text.[87] Niclas Hval indicates in his Swedish translator's note that although he made reference to the original text, particularly for help translating 'songs, rhymes and chants', his is 'essentially [. . .] a translation of the English Edition'.[88] The Dutch translation, by contrast, uses the Afrikaans original as its source text.[89] The versions of Van Niekerk's novel circulating in Europe are thus, and will continue to be, more varied than merely the same text directly rendered in different languages.

As if to explain these extended allusions, the English version places different books on the novel's characters' bookshelves. In chapter 2, Milla recalls unpacking books from her parents' house into her own shelves in 1947, to join those books she had 'read at university'.[90] The English text adds T.S. Eliot, Donne, Hopkins, Shakespeare, and the *Oxford Collected Poems* (referred to at another point in the Afrikaans text[91]). Heyns retains Afrikaans titles, real and fictitious, but has Milla read an English translation of Eugene Marais ('*The Soul of the White Ant*') where we might expect her, given that other Afrikaans works in this list are not translated into English, to own it in the Afrikaans (*Die siel van die mier*).[92] In the opening chapter, Agaat repacks books that have fallen from the bookcase in Milla's sickroom: in some cases, published English translations of Afrikaans titles are used in the English version, in others (including for fictitious books) the titles are translated loosely. Henry James's *The Portrait of a Lady* is added to the bookshelf, and Eben Venter's 1996 novel *Ek stamel ek sterwe* ('I stammer I die') is replaced with Faulkner's (equally appropriately titled) *As I Lay Dying*. Venter's novel was published in English translation as *My Beautiful Death* in 2006, so the translation could not be in Milla's bookshelf in 1996, the novel's present, and yet the fact that Venter's Afrikaans text was published in the same year that Agaat handles it in the Afrikaans text suggests that it is she—Agaat—who has kept up with new local fiction, Milla having been incapacitated for nearly three years at this point, an inference that is lost through the substitution with Faulkner. Furthermore, the Milla in the English translation and in those other translations that follow the English text, becomes something *other* than the Afrikaner woman she is in the original text: a much more bilingual reader, more au fait with canonical anglophone texts, her bookshelf rather less domestic—in the sense of being local—than in the original, in which we see her simply *imagine* herself *possibly* rendering her locatedness less domestic through access to a world language.[93]

Moments of potential confusion about the language Milla is presumed to be using (whether spoken aloud or not) recur, as do the importation of quotations that have evidently been judged *equivalent* to items of Afrikaans cultural production. One might consider, for example, Heyns's attempts to render the quotations from the *FAK-Volksangbundel*, Afrikaans psalms and hymns, as well as place names, although merely enumerating the changes would risk an instrumental critique too reliant on expectations of fidelity. Nonetheless, and not only in relation to the question of responsibility for a translation that becomes a bridge text for further translations, one must be allowed to interrogate some decisions because of the ways in which they facilitate the production of a particular kind of text in global circulation. Here the range of imported references to T.S. Eliot in the English translation is especially germane. Frank England has discussed the many extended or wholly imported allusions to *The Waste Land* and *Four Quartets* (in addition to the epigraph Heyns adds, from 'Little Gidding') in the English *Agaat*, and I will not rehearse them here. England faults Heyns for assuming that references to Eliot would be familiar to the target audience, which he assumes Heyns regarded as English-speaking South Africans rather than readers in a global anglosphere.[94] England finds it 'difficult to resist at least questioning whether' allusions to Eliot increase the 'distance between the source text and the target reader' for English-speaking South African readers. Van Niekerk's 'local allusive intertext may well be more familiar to them than the [...] less proximate one', which is to say that imported by Heyns, England argues.[95]

Writing in 2009 about the process of translating *Agaat*, Heyns recalls telling Van Niekerk that her text seemed to him frequently to evoke *The Waste Land* and *Four Quartets*, and her confirmation that these had been in her mind 'licensed' him 'to interpolate from time to time references to Eliot that underlined *Agaat*'s place in a different tradition, of what one might call "formal culture"'.[96] This phrase, like 'cultural goods', 'mainstream poetry', 'formal culture', suggests an attitude to canonicity indicative of a deference to the notion of a metropolitan standard. Eliot's work serves as a global modernist standard of literariness, a kind of north-Atlantic English Literature (with a capital L) that is—ironically, as a consequence of being thought transnational and cosmopolitan (and thus, if you will, unmarked)—heavily ideologically marked, valorizing a very circumscribed, conservative, and anglocentric sense of a world literature. Heyns comments that '[b]y almost subliminally citing Eliot (and also, elsewhere, Shakespeare and Donne)', he 'could establish links between *Agaat* and an English cultural context enriching to both'.[97] In a discussion of the translation with Van Niekerk and De Kock, he added that what made *Agaat* 'not unique, but exceptional, is that it's *not just a South African book* in the sense that, if you go back to T.S. Eliot's "Tradition and the Individual Talent", you get the idea that every work draws on tradition, changes the tradition, while it is also added on to it'. It both 'subsumes good European tradition' and 'has the best of the novel that is from this country', it 'recognises that it's not just an African tradition that we're working in'; this was why the novel 'should have a worldwide appeal'.[98]

If Van Niekerk's novel is a masterpiece on its own terms, we might ask whether it is necessary that such status be endorsed, as it were, through allusion to canonical figures from a quite different tradition. But this is perhaps also the place to note Van Niekerk's active collaboration with Heyns (in approving the translation) complicates any reading of the English version as a translation that plays fast and loose with an 'original' to which a translation ought to be 'faithful'. The collaboration does not render any less compelling or significant questions about the fate of minority—or provincial—literatures transposed into a world language, however. When he translated *Triomf*, an equally demanding novel, De Kock had taken the decision to render what he called Van Niekerk's 'calculated bastardisation of Afrikaans' in the kind of English he grew up speaking himself in the lower-middle-class white suburb of Mayfair, in Johannesburg, just over the hill from Triomf. As he explained, 'if the original *Triomf* was a hybrid of Afrikaans with English', his translation attempted to approximate a recognizable 'hybrid of English with Afrikaans'.[99] 'Many if not most of my fellow [South African English]-speakers would have heard the kind of language I intended to use, or they would be able to get the drift', he argued.[100] However, when the English rights outside of South Africa were sold to multinational publisher Little, Brown, De Kock was forced to produce a second version of his translation, omitting most of the remaining Afrikaans words and finding equivalences for idiomatic expressions; in some cases, Van Niekerk wrote new sections. There is here evidence of a two-way feed for writing *not* in a global language, writing that must perhaps transcend—in translation—both a provincial language (Afrikaans) and the provincial version of that global language (South African English)—in order for its potential global attractiveness to be realized, for it to be synchronized with a putative global readerly expectation that requires works of World Literature to be immediately accessible, their codes and cultural contexts legible in a kind of global now-time, because they have travelled across linguistic borders, because they are able to have been translated—linguistically, metaphorically, and materially.

I am not arguing that Heyns's translation *should* have been different. Rather, I raise the question of the inevitable loss that occurs in translation, and in particular when the novel in question is self-consciously linguistically encyclopaedic, when such loss is imagined within the world of the novel itself, in relation to Afrikaans. The loss involved in translation from Afrikaans necessarily also replicates structurally the unquantifiable loss that results from the enforced adoption of Agaat into the De Wet household, which stands for a language community that polices its boundaries in such a way that someone rendered an outsider can never be entirely at home. How might we consider the implications of translation for thinking about conceptualizations of World Literature as works that travel 'beyond their culture of origin' (to invoke David Damrosch), or literature that is written with its own translatability in mind (to invoke Rebecca Walkowitz)?[101] Might *Agaat*—as Afrikaans novel—be considered a work of provincial literature in the sense elaborated by Coetzee in 1981 when he argued that writers in South Africa might rehabilitate the notion of the provincial rather than regard themselves as 'building a new national literature'?[102] If a South African novel is to be something other, must it be accessible in what Milla de Wet calls a 'world language'?

The main target of Emily Apter's *Against World Literature* (2013) is the imperialism she sees in the research methodologies and pedagogies that characterize an emerging consensus about the contours of World Literature as a discipline, its 'expansionism and gargantuan scale'.[103] The discipline, she charges, 'increasingly resembles the global museum in its practice of curatorial salvage' or 'possessive collectivism': it 'gathers up swaths of literary culture deemed vulnerable to extinction and performs preservational intervention'.[104] The student of World Literature (*in the West*, we should add as qualifier to Apter's description) has unfettered access to the world's riches through a flattening out, a levelling of complexity to easily consumable units, disbursed in courses saleable as a kind of vocational one-world-citizenship training in the increasingly corporatized university. Apter's analysis is notably grounded almost entirely in relation to curricula for United States-based (American and Comparative literature) programmes, and in an understanding of *world* that reflects US and Western European foreign policy priorities (Israel/Palestine, the North Atlantic rim, and so on), thus her argument might be understood simply to propose new rhetorics easily subsumed under the existing rubric. Indeed, Apter suggests that to hold open the category of the 'Untranslatable' is not to endorse 'pure difference in opposition to the always translatable' (the 'always translatable' remains 'suspect', she notes, as simply 'another non-coeval form of the romantic Absolute, or fetish of the Other, or myth of hermeneutic inaccessibility'); rather, it constitutes 'a linguistic form of creative failure with homeopathic uses'.[105] This is a striking metaphor, but it is not clear whether Apter means to suggest it is World Literature as discipline that is the patient to whom are administered drugs that would produce symptoms in a healthy body similar to those of the disease being treated (homeopathy's original definition: the practice by which 'likes are cured by likes'[106]), nor indeed whether the drug in this analogy is the imperfect translation (the creative failure; this would seem to be the tenor). Taken as description of the argument of *Against World Literature* as a whole, it seems to suggest that the always-imperfect translation, falling midway between the absolutes of perfect accessibility and complete opacity is to be welcomed insofar as it troubles what Apter posits as World Literature's metaphorical illness, its acquisitive designs and presumption of complete accessibility.

'If the contemporary novel is increasingly an object to be translated and translatable', Chris Holmes asks provocatively, 'will there be a remainder from this process?'[107] Foregrounding the remainder pays homage to the idea of the Untranslatable, even as (even if) there is a translation. I do not believe there is much to be gained from maintaining a position that holds that certain works are intrinsically untranslatable—unless, in fact, such a claim is largely rhetorical (as it seems to be in Apter's case). Loss is inevitable when translation enters a (so-called) world language, but the remainder in this case raises an ethical dimension. Musing on his translation of *Triomf*, De Kock suggests that the ethics of translation matter in South Africa, as they do in any multi-lingual, multi-ethnic society with a history of colonialism, trauma, and inequality, because these ethics are metaphorically at the very core of writing—or representation—more broadly: 'in a setting of unresolved heterogeneity, the translation of experience, the mediation of perception, and the static-ridden transfer of intercultural communication become the matter of a bigger, more problematic mode of translation', he argues.[108] If reading literature in translation is something of which we ought to do more in order to encounter that which is not like us, it seems a paradox that the otherness we encounter in literature that travels *across* borders is so often rendered familiar, serving something like a 'possessive individualism' also posited by Apter as an animating drive in the consumption of World Literature.[109]

Agaat's disappointments are translated into missed appointments of a different order in the case of translation. Viewed as Afrikaans-language retentional prosthesis, *Agaat* is separated from one of the key competencies whose acquisition and transmission it represents mimetically *and* synecdochically, a particular temporally and geographically specific version of Afrikaans, and one that in hindsight can be seen to have missed its own anticipated appointment with history: mimetically, insofar as it represents the process of language acquisition, as well as the acquisition more broadly of the competencies I have discussed, by Agaat; synecdochically, insofar as the novel itself is a means of the transmission (or archiving) of language forms and idioms. That global anglophone readers of the novel's translation, and readers of the work in translations into other languages that use the English translation as bridge text, read about Agaat's disappointments—temporal and affective—in such a text, might also be thought ironically appropriate, failure to translate the specificity claimed by this kind of Afrikaans taken as comment on its community's presumptions, and constituting a temporal disappointment that conveys more about affective disappointment than it knows. In this way, *Agaat*—and I should here write *Agaat* in Afrikaans read with *Agaat* in English (and perhaps, in time, at least hypothetically, in isiXhosa, isiZulu, Sesotho, and other South African languages, too)—in its very always-already compromised encyclopaedic form and in the losses its utterances *and* translations represent, reflect, and encode, is the great *New* South African Novel bar none.

4

Towards a Critical Nostalgia

> Epic and rhapsodic in the strictest sense, genuine memory must therefore yield an image of the person who remembers, in the same way a good archaeological report not only informs us about the strata from which its findings originate, but also gives an account of the strata which first had to be broken through.
>
> —Walter Benjamin, 'Excavation and Memory' (*c.*1932)[1]

Nostalgia—whether understood as shorthand for various projects of memory work, or as naming a preoccupation with the past—is much abroad in contemporary South Africa.[2] David Medalie calls 'the majority' of postapartheid writing of nostalgia 'glib, unambitious and utterly lacking in self-consciousness', comparing as evidence Jo-Anne Richards's *The Innocence of Roast Chicken* (1996) unfavourably with Anne Landsman's more sophisticated *The Rowing Lesson* (2007).[3] We might substitute many other titles for these, for instance Trevor Roman's *Random Kak I Remember about Growing Up in South Africa* (2013) and Denis Hirson's *I Remember King Kong (the Boxer)* (2004): the former is an illustrated digest of memories of South Africans of all races (though arguably catering chiefly to white readers); the latter takes inspiration from George Perec's *Je me souviens* (and behind that, Joe Brainard's *I Remember*) to produce an incantatory litany of recollected fragments from Hirson's 1950s and 60s childhood in Johannesburg. This sophisticated, self-reflexive project suggests that nostalgia—a longing (*algia*) for a time and place in the past (literally a lost home, *nostos*)—can be both empowering and debilitating, politically reactionary or progressively utopian.[4] Romain's compilation, by contrast, capitalizes on an ongoing postapartheid vogue for accounts of what things used to be like, most often simpler, or presented as such, even if simplistic divisions between people, especially on the basis of race, are flagged as *regrettable.*[5]

Many other works that have gained popular attention in South Africa and abroad in recent decades occupy positions in a similar dichotomy—of critical reflection and memorialization, or of a potentially reactionary turning away from present conditions in the country. The most ethically and aesthetically engaging examples of a contemporary South African literature of nostalgia, in fiction and creative non-fiction, are those that look back in service of understanding the present, whose emphasis on futurity means that they seem close to what Svetlana Boym describes as 'reflective' nostalgia, one that embraces the pain of temporal longing and acknowledges—indeed embraces—the imperfections of memory. Against reflective nostalgia, Boym contrasts what she calls 'restorative' nostalgia: this is not self-conscious, holding instead that to remember the past is in effect to propose its recuperation.[6] Here nostalgia becomes pathological, a kind of melancholia resulting from a reactionary disappointment in a present in which (in the words of Mark Gevisser, whose *Lost and Found in Johannesburg* is an exemplary work that *avoids* such pathology) 'one loses oneself in the past, looking for a route home—a route to oblivion, to death, really—through one's childhood, in which one becomes so preoccupied with this search that one loses sight of the present'.[7]

There are many non-fiction examples of profoundly thoughtful and engaging reflective nostalgia (including Gevisser's 2014 text, and Jacob Dlamini's provocative *Native Nostalgia*, 2009). The work of Ivan Vladislavić (b. 1957), however, offers the most sustained multi-generic engagement with nostalgia as critical and self-reflective project in recent South African writing, bridging fiction and creative non-fiction. Vladislavić had at the time of writing published several collections of short stories (including a volume of suggestively unfinished ones) and three—or four—novels (depending on one's working definition[8]), in addition to a creative work of memoir and essays on art and architecture. All the work is marked by a fascination with states of transition, with the provisional, with that which supersedes the only ever apparently stable status quo, with varieties of disappointment left in the wake of political change. In a 2006 interview with journalist and translator Fred de Vries, he offers a striking account of the stakes of his project. Acknowledging that *Portrait with Keys*, a work of psycho-geography-cum-memoir then recently published, engaged strongly with nostalgia, Vladislavić observes: 'I've looked up the meaning of nostalgia. It comes from the Greek word *nostos*, meaning to return home. I think that my book is about that question.' Nostalgia, he continues, is necessarily 'part of any attempt to affirm the sense of belonging to place that home implies', and yet the process of 'finding a place for the past in the present' benefits from being mindful of 'the individual consciousness's neighbours in public exchange'. The injunction here is an ethical one to make any reminiscence 'a self-conscious, critical kind of nostalgia, one that understands the limitations under which it operates', of 'the conditions that make our access to consoling histories so unequal' in a country like South Africa.[9] Writing about Willem Boshoff, one of South Africa's first concrete poets and among its first conceptual artists, in a short monograph published in 2005, Vladislavić observed that South Africa had entered 'a second interregnum, a parenthetical era, in which a provisional country asserts itself, but drags its history behind it in brackets, like a skin it has not properly sloughed'. He would put a similar observation into the mouth of the photographer-protagonist of his 2010 novel, *Double Negative.*[10] It is the tensions and ambivalences of the emotional landscape of this long period of uncertain aftermath, of ongoing interregnum, of the never-ending process of looking back, that concern Vladislavić in the representative works with which I engage in this chapter.

MONUMENTALISM, MEMORIALIZATION, AND NOSTALGIA

It was difficult to 'ignore' history during the late 1980s and early 1990s, Vladislavić notes in *The Loss Library and Other Unfinished Stories* (2012), a collection of his fragments and notes for work never brought to completion. 'Within months of one another, two apparently indestructible systems, the Soviet empire and the apartheid state, broke apart like badly made monuments, leaving their subjects to scavenge for building materials in the ruins.'[11] Their simultaneous decline occasioned, in one strand of public discourse, triumphalist assertions of the victory of anti-communist forces with which the apartheid government had aligned itself; recall Francis Fukuyama's speculation that we had reached the 'end of history', the 'end point of mankind's ideological evolution', with the victory of market capitalism and 'remarkable consensus' about the 'legitimacy of liberal democracy'.[12] Many of Vladislavić's fictions feature attempts to negotiate competing versions of past events measured against the uncertainty of the present, interrogations of the folly of the monumental—whether of ideologies, systems of government, projects of social engineering or of memorialization—that seeks to pre-empt future (re)interpretation. Such negotiations mark Vladislavić's published work from the beginning, including his first novel, aptly titled *The Folly* (1993), and early collections of stories, *Missing Persons*, which appeared on the cusp of change (in 1989), and *Propaganda by Monuments*, published in 1996, just after the first elections.

In 'Propaganda by Monuments', the title story of this latter collection, social and political analysis meets absurdist comedy in a story that brings together an interest in nostalgia, catastrophe, boundaries and interstices (temporal and geographic), in compelling ways. Boniface Khumalo, the enterprising owner of an informal bar (or shebeen) in Atteridgeville, a township outside Pretoria, hoping to purchase a decommissioned statue of Lenin from a 'square at the dead end' of a street in suburban Moscow, corresponds in early 1992 with an official in the post-Soviet Russian civil service.[13] A monument of an ideology that has apparently run into its own dead-end is here imagined as being able to serve a quite different (commercial) purpose in another society in the midst of its own transition from defunct ideology to uncertain future. Monica Popescu reads in the 'imaginary voyage' the statue might undertake (it does not, in the end) 'a communist artifact's movement through new symbolic markets and globalized economies'.[14] But the story features an engagement with futurity, disappointment, and form, that transcends the specific context—which is to say the coincidence of the collapse of the Soviet Union and the ending of apartheid.

The story consists of a series of numbered sections that include focalized omniscient third-person narration, the text of letters exchanged, and, most intriguingly, four pages of text (beginning and ending in mid-sentence), from a book entitled *Lunacharski and Lenin*. This text, which may be Vladislavić's fabrication, draws on the historical Anatoly Lunacharski's 'Lenin and Art' to meditate on the Soviet leader's scheme to promote the construction of monumental public artworks that would instruct the Soviet people after the Bolshevik Revolution. Apparently inspired by Renaissance frescoes depicting a 'utopian state' that had been 'used to educate the young', Lenin proposed commissions involving 'concise, trenchant inscriptions showing the more lasting, fundamental principles and slogans of Marxism'.[15] The project soon descended into trouble, however. Lunacharski complains (in the fragment included in Vladislavić's text) that 'modernists and futurists ran amok', producing a statue of Bakunin 'so hideous that the horses shied when they passed it'; one sculptor proposed 'a statue of Marx standing somewhat acrobatically on four elephants' (which was of course deemed 'inappropriate').[16] Projects seeking to consolidate the heroic stature of the guiding spirits of an ideology are always, in Vladislavić's work, liable to ridicule.

In the story's present, not only are Lenin statues superfluous in post-Soviet Russia, but Khumalo, adult subject of a regime that was still in place in early 1992 (*before* the whites-only referendum that in March of that year gave support to F.W. de Klerk's decision to engage with the newly unbanned liberation organizations) and that had erected monuments to its own ideologues, seems never properly to have connected such objects with their historical subjects. He realizes that he has miscalculated the size of the Lenin statue, that it is three times larger than the monumental head of Prime Minister J.G. Strijdom ('one of the great builders of apartheid') in central Pretoria. Yet Khumalo has little idea who the historical Strijdom was, recognizing the name on the plinth only dimly from a struggle-era song, 'Sutha sutha wena Strijdom! [. . .] Give way, Strijdom!'; '*This* Strijdom is *that* Strijdom', Khumalo realizes with surprise.[17] Vladislavić deflates the former Afrikaner nationalist leader's place in public consciousness in an uncanny metaphorical foreshadowing of a real event so strange one might expect to find it fabricated in a Vladislavić fiction: the collapse of Strijdom's bust through the ceiling of the underground car park beneath it on 31 May 2001, years after the publication of this story and, ironically, on the fortieth anniversary of the Union of South Africa becoming a white-ruled republic.[18]

The fragment from *Lunacharksi and Lenin* claims that, a decade after Lenin's scheme was abandoned, Lunacharski proposed that a 'second wave of propaganda by monuments' be embarked upon (the found text ends here), and that his attempted recuperation of this utopian hopefulness was prompted by 'nostalgia' for the 'immediate post-revolutionary years'.[19] Lunacharski's nostalgia is for the early days of revolutionary governance, not for Tsarist Russia, but the introduction of the word is crucial here because nostalgia is always on the edges of the mental worlds of Vladislavić's protagonists, and is central to the author's negotiation of the politics of hope and disappointment in postapartheid South Africa. Nostalgia is central to Khumalo's plan to rename his tavern the 'V.I. Lenin Bar & Grill'; the opening is planned (in an ironic deflation of the socialist May Day holiday) for '1st May for publicity stunts'.[20] Affixing a socialist hero's name to a capitalist enterprise repurposes nostalgia for the ideal of a workers' utopia, a dream that informed at least one important strand of liberation rhetoric in South Africa. It is easy to read this as a prescient gloss on the accommodations with neoliberal economic policies that would soon be made by the ruling alliance of African National Congress, South African Communist Party, and Congress of South African Trade Unions, groups that had advocated socialism during the liberation struggle.

Khumalo's correspondence with the Russian civil servant addresses him not only 'in the name of the struggling masses of South Africa, comrades, freedom fighters, former journeymen to Moscow' (historical links between the Soviet Union and banned South African liberation movements are clearly in view), but also on behalf of his 'boergious [sic] countrymen'.[21] *Boergious* for *bourgeois* alerts us not only to Khumalo's misspelling, but to the fact that we are to imagine reading his letter at a remove from the language in which Khumalo has written it: it is translated and annoted by one Pavel Grekov, a 'junior translator in the Administration for Everyday Services', and we read a version in English that approximates the uncertain translation offered in Russian to Grekov's superiors.[22] Grekov's notes record his puzzlement: does *boergious* signify 'business "contacts"' or 'class alliances'? They might be either, the neologism conflating the pejorative *boer*—for Afrikaner (originally meaning simply *farmer*)—with bourgeois, and the dream of becoming bourgeois with the complicities of a metaphorical whiteness to which a liberation-era comrade might harshly suggest Khumalo aspires (his letter offers a genealogy of his own advancement from gardener, garage attendant, and taxi-owner, to tavern proprietor). Grekov's translations are also clearly inflected by his nostalgia for a Soviet past, evoked for him (ironically) by images on the South African postage stamps accompanying Khumalo's letter: a pastoral scene evokes a socialist-realist image of 'fertile steppes'; a 'collage of cooling towers, dynamos and pylons' suggests 'energy and industrial progress'.[23]

As in so many of Vladislavić's fictions, points of origin are rendered suspect. *Lunacharski and Lenin* is a fake. Grekov's translations of his superiors' responses to Khumalo are 'so ruthlessly invaded and occupied' by sometimes startling asides in broken English that Khumalo has to wonder who possesses the authority to negotiate, the translator or his superiors.[24] Any longing for that which a monument from the past might once have been assumed to signify is inevitably 'a romance with one's own fantasy' (in Boym's formulation), but such nostalgia is therefore also future-directed insofar as it negotiates, in the present, a relationship with the past that will have an affective consequence for how one might experience the future.[25] 'Propaganda by Monuments' offers not only a critical interrogation of nostalgia on Vladislavić's part, but itself constitutes an act of critical nostalgia that leavens recollections of those early days of the transition, when everything seemed both unlikely and possible, with a note of the surreal and absurd such that the reader cannot but be conscious of nostalgia's costs, complicities, and qualifications.

ANGELS OF HISTORY

The end of 'Propaganda by Monuments' finds Boniface Khumalo on a warm summer's day, standing 'upwind of the stinking Freedom Symbol', a stagnant fountain that formed part of Strijdom Square's monumental array, 'his eyes half-closed, squinting', musing on 'how, but not necessarily why', in the narrator's enigmatic formulation, 'the impossible came to pass'.[26] Moments before, Khumalo has contemplated how, given that his acquaintance with Strijdom had hitherto been with the imagined subject of a Struggle song, the monumental bust before him—with its 'serene, far-sighted expression'—seems utterly unlike his imagination of the politician's face. The face that he had imagined had borne 'a look of stupefied terror', had been 'the face of a slow-footed pedestrian, a moment away from impact and extinction, gaping at the juggernaut of history bearing down on him'.[27] It is not fanciful to detect in these descriptions of Strijdom—or in Khumalo's own position as he daydreams ('upwind' of something in decay)—allusions to Walter Benjamin's thoughts on the angel of history, transfixed by chaos and blown backwards into the future. These are not the only such allusions in Vladislavić's fiction, nor are they unusual in South African literature during the long transition and its aftermath, as I indicated in this book's Introduction.

Catherine Taylor's *Apart*, a narrative poem by an American poet about a return to South Africa, the country of her birth, in her middle age, cites the angel to emphasize the redemptive possibilities of 'wreckage' ('O angel-wreckage, turn around').[28] In J.M. Coetzee's *Age of Iron*, which is haunted by intimations of the angelic, Mrs Curren, having read Tolstoy's story about an angel moving in with a shoemaker ('What Men Live By'), contemplates the chances of locating her 'own angel to bring home and succor' and wonders whether the enigmatic, homeless drifter Vercueil might be 'an angel come to' guide her. She feels trapped in a purgatory imagined in chilling chiliastic terms as a '*time being*, a suspension, before the return of the time in which the door bursts open and we face the great white glare'.[29] Sam Durrant argues that Mrs Curren's inability to name the horror she witnesses amidst the burning shacks on the Cape Flats approximates the author's own desire—as an artist rendered 'overwhelmed' and 'helpless' (in Coetzee's words) 'by the fact of suffering in the world'—to remain 'speechless before history', a position of helplessness that is, Durrant implies, *like* that of Benjamin's angel.[30]

I discussed Benjamin's engagement with now-time in the Introduction; it is useful to reprise in slightly greater detail his imagining of this angel. Here is the passage in question (quoted in Harry Zohn's *Illuminations* translation):

> His eyes are wide, his mouth is open, his wings are spread. This is how the angel of history must look. His face is turned toward the past. Where a chain of events appears before *us*, *he* sees one single catastrophe, which keeps piling wreckage upon wreckage and hurls it at his feet. The angel would like to stay, awaken the dead, and make whole what has been smashed. But a storm is blowing from Paradise and has got caught in his wings; it is so strong that the angel can no longer close them. The storm drives him irresistibly into the future, to which his back is turned, while the pile of debris before him grows toward the sky. What we call progress is *this* storm.[31]

Vladislavić himself has suggested that, in his understanding, the angel 'represents an ahistorical view; looking back on history the angel sees a catastrophe, whereas the materialist looking back sees a dialectical process of events'.[32] We might share this interpretation of the angel as deluded historicist against whom Benjamin inveighs in other of the Theses, one whose desire for historiography that constitutes the past as a narrative of inevitable progress has led to—or simply reveals—nothing more than a pile of wreckage. But we could also view the angel as Benjamin's historical materialist him- or herself, here 'stripped [. . .] of all illusions about human history' (in Rolf Tiedemann's words).[33] Regardless of interpretation, Vladislavić's practice resonates unusually powerfully with Benjamin's sense that an engagement with the past that is content merely to establish 'a causal nexus among various moments in history', or indeed is simply in service of an unreflective nostalgia, should be resisted in favour of setting diverse past moments in 'constellation' with the present.[34] Rather than 'ideal scenes of nostalgia', what Benjamin's materialist appears to seek to create are moments of relational understanding in which past potential is re-energized in the present. Such work constitutes the '*weak* messianic power' Benjamin describes, power to revivify lost utopian impulses, but weak because not occasioned by the messiah's return (and so outside the eschatological narratives of faith communities).[35]

Vladislavić notes that his engagement with Benjamin dates to his time at university and forms part of an ongoing attempt to understand attitudes to the past in South Africa, 'to understand our movement away from that intense focus on history in the 1970s and 1980s, to a point where many people resist the idea of looking back'.[36] This sounds very like remarks he made in the later 1990s about the pressures—'institutional' and 'public'—that faced writers in immediate post-transition South Africa. He cast these in terms of tensions between the need to provide positive representations of the present, 'to be part of a proposed Renaissance' (the idea that would animate Thabo Mbeki's presidency after 1999), and the duty to recall the traumas of the past: 'one of the things writers can do is keep the past alive'.[37] Both imperatives held dangers: 'if you lose sight of apartheid, then people say you've forgotten about the past, and you're part of the trend towards "amnesia"'; 'if you go too deeply into apartheid, they say you're holding onto the past, and it's negative, you should be writing about the future'. Future and past were opposites in this conceptualization, Vladislavić continued, 'poles of optimism and pessimism', which was altogether too simplistic.[38]

Allusions to Benjamin serve for Vladislavić to highlight an empathetic understanding at the heart of which is a responsibility to the past, a critical nostalgia that is always directed to the future and not beholden to the narratives of inevitable progress that seek to monopolize interpretation, and which are always flawed by their own (monumental) blind spots.

Vladislavić's fascination with Benjamin's ideas has not, thus far, been much noted by scholars, except to assert obvious similarities between his protagonists—most especially the autobiographical narrator of *Portrait with Keys*—and the figure of the *flâneur* that so intrigued Benjamin. Thinking more loosely and expansively with Benjamin's ideas about historical materialism, however, and paying attention both to invocations of Benjamin's angel and to the methodological resonances between Vladislavić's and Benjamin's interest in the fragment and the found object (I have in mind Benjamin's *Das Passagen-Werk*, the Arcades Project, which Vladislavić cites briefly in notes to *Portrait with Keys*[39]), allows for insights into his particular attempts to balance the poles of disappointment and hope, to explore a version of nostalgia that is responsible to the present and mindful of the future.

In *The Loss Library*, Vladislavić describes an abandoned story whose preoccupations resonate with all of these commitments. 'Frieze' was to take as its starting point a sculptor planning a series of monumental panels conceived during the last decades of apartheid and abandoned at the artist's death on the eve of the transition to democracy.[40] An art historian, having collected oral narratives that had circulated in the family of the granddaughter of the artist's assistant (the only person to survive the sculptor with a sense of his original scheme), has to take account of a journalist's uncovering—in the story's projected present, 2040—of interviews in which the sculptor himself sought, before his death, to answer claims that his work had served the purposes of the apartheid regime. The frieze recedes as the relation among a series of frozen moments is established and questions of complicity and interestedness raised. 'Five versions of the absent artworks collide', Vladislavić explains in his unfinished sketch: 'the Journalist's *skeptical* interpretation, the Artist's *self-serving* defense, the Assistant's *businesslike* descriptions, mediated across three generations by the Poet's *lyrical* recollections and the Historian's *clinical* analysis' (although these adjectives are, he remarks, 'tentative').[41] At the heart of the projected story, then, is an interrogation of the politics of memorialization and of competing truth claims by differing accounts of the past. All are concerns evident in 'Propaganda by Monuments' and central too to Benjamin's exploration of alternatives to universal historicism. In fact, in explaining how his (narrative) relation to the proliferating number of focalized perspectives in the story became increasingly difficult to keep clear ('Where do "I" stand in all this?'), Vladislavić compares *himself* to Benjamin's angel: 'I saw myself walking backwards into the future, stumbling through thickets of interpretation, like an earthbound angel of history, erasing his tracks with the feathers of one costume-hire wing, footsore and fed up.'[42]

WALKING BACKWARDS INTO THE FUTURE

If Vladislavić feels that the writer in South Africa has to navigate the demands of investments in future and past, Aubrey Tearle, the cantankerous anti-hero protagonist of the 2001 novel *The Restless Supermarket,* believes that his profession, proofreading, equips him supremely well to deal with equally demanding polarities. A proofreader, Tearle declares, 'is a tightrope artist, managing the difficult tension between momentum and inertia, story and stock, sentence and word'; he is also a 'trailblazer and minesweeper', clearing the reader's path.[43] In the first and third parts of *The Restless Supermarket,* Tearle finds this particular skill challenged by a world that, in the dying days of 1993, the novel's present, is changing too fast for his comfort. Accused of thinking himself better than those with whom he mixes at his beloved Café Europa, in Hillbrow, in inner-city Johannesburg, Tearle protests that he is simply holding himself—and others—to what he regards as the standard of the 'European way of life'. It is because he is 'an incorrigible "European"' that the Café Europa suits him so well, he claims without irony; he relishes the establishment's 'European ambience' even as he admits that he has 'never been abroad'.[44] With its columns and representations of the Eiffel Tower in its cast-iron balcony rail, it fits—or at least used to fit—his idea of a cosmopolitan European coffeehouse.

When Tearle learns that the café is due to close, he feels even more acutely that an entire era is coming to an end. Mimicking an Afrikaans-speaking acquaintance's pronunciation, he renders this the 'end of an error', inadvertently drawing the reader's attention to the larger 'error' in question, apartheid, though Tearle's discomfort with the 'unstable epoch' being ushered in around him blinds him to the ways in which others are accommodating themselves to the country's new realities, raising the ongoing cultural error of unassimilated European models of spatial and temporal engagement with Africa as one of the novel's key concerns.[45] What most unsettles Tearle is the demographic change he notices in Hillbrow. Although theoretically the preserve of white residents under the Group Areas Act until that law's repeal in 1991, this area of high-rise apartments, residential hotels and fading commercial buildings had long since ceased to be white, housing many people classified Coloured or Indian since the 1970s. In the early 1990s, the arrival of black migrants from peripheral townships and rural areas across the country increased apace until, by mid 1993, black residents formed around 85 per cent of Hillbrow's population.[46] Tearle's proofreading of telephone directories for the greater Johannesburg area has allowed him, over several years, to chart this movement. He goes so far as to check one address to confirm that the family's name (Merope) denotes what he thinks it does (that they are black), confirming for him that 'they'—that capacious yet precise euphemism in white speech—'were living in our midst'. Why did the authorities do nothing, he wonders, his attitudes marking him as reactionary and racist. 'Silently, while we slept,' he notes ominously, 'the tide was darkening.'[47] Thus while Tearle claims that his primary concern is with the parlous state of proofreading (standards 'have been declining steadily since the nineteen-sixties'), he sees a correlation between textual standards and the state of being 'civilized', awkwardly identified in his understanding with the racial order that has persisted under apartheid.[48] Here it is difficult to escape the weight of the legacy of the use of the term European to denote a state-policed idea of whiteness in apartheid-era South Africa.

Despite attempts to sublimate his sense of race panic, it is clear that Tearle believes the proximate cause of the decline he discerns around him to be the political transformation being negotiated—'The new order?' he scoffs: 'The new *disorder* is more like it'—by the all-party talks, the Congress for a Democratic South Africa (CODESA), then taking place across town in Kempton Park.[49] In this charged context, proofreading, setting 'error' to rights, assumes a chilling association with reactionary social engineering, made clear in a metaphor that links the textual with the biopolitical. A proofreading error, Tearle asserts, might become 'exuberant and prolific' if left unchecked, it might 'settle down in respectable company and become naturalized as a citizen of good standing'.[50] In an attempt to stay the tide, Tearle collects all manner of 'corrigenda' (items 'to be corrected') from newspapers and advertising leaflets, and notes them down from street signs and overheard conversations, before compiling into a fanciful narrative, 'The Proofreader's Derby', which he intends offering as a challenge to those assembled at the Café Europa's farewell party.[51] This narrative, featuring proofreader extraordinaire Aubrey Fluxman, a proxy for Tearle, constitutes the middle section of the novel.[52] It expresses most clearly Tearle's desire to administer a cure, to reverse the decline that threatens his world.

Fluxman must, as his name suggests, overcome change, marshalling his colleagues to reverse the proofreading errors that have unsettled the very geography of his city, Alibia. Indiscriminate mixing is the most threatening aspect of this disorder, and it is evidenced by the trope of the Restless Supermarket itself. In Tearle's present, this 24-hour convenience store's name, its Greek manager explains, denotes that it never closes, although Tearle believes the name 'creates the wrong impression', suggesting 'groceries jumbling *themselves* together, of wilful chaos'.[53] The supermarket returns in 'The Proofreader's Derby' as Fluxman's most challenging project, its produce a 'seething', 'indiscriminate, indefatigable jumble' of items, an 'irreducible compound'[54] on which 'categories' have once more to be imposed, each thing restored not necessarily to 'the place it had started out', but, ominously, 'the place it deserved to end'.[55] Such social engineering not only parodies and critiques colonial- and apartheid-era town planning but also mimics those attempts at the organization of the seemingly chaotic—or the only ostensibly chaotic.

That Tearle sets 'The Proofreader's Derby' in Alibia, which readers recognize from the first part of the novel as the imaginary place pictured in a mural in the Café Europa, confirms that what is at issue here is a project of restorative nostalgia, an attempt to imagine the recuperation of a lost home. The home lost here is an imaginary one, of course, and one whose composite nature is as much a comment on the heterogeneity of Johannesburg's immigrant communities as it is an indication that no pure point of origin can, in fact, be recuperated. The cityscape combines stereotyped features of European townscapes in which many of Hillbrow's white immigrants might recognize signs of home: 'A Slav would feel just as at home there as a Dutchman.' Alibia also suggests that retaining an investment in an imagined past, 'a generous elsewhere in which the immigrant might find the landmarks he had left behind' (in Tearle's gloss), provides 'a perfect alibi' for not accommodating oneself to the present—or future.[56] So total is Tearle's investment in this elsewhere that the hill towering over Alibia in the mural becomes, for him, a self-consciously 'egocentric' embodiment of his own head, perhaps his own imagination; he can claim on more than one level, then, that his 'head was in the city, a part of it, as solid as the earth beneath [his] feet', except that the earth beneath his feet engages him rather less than his fantasies.[57]

The moving ground that is an escalator functions in one scene to offer another of Vladislavić's allusions to Benjamin's angel. Making his way up an escalator to the Café Europa, Tearle encounters a 'drunkard, a young black man in a shiny suit' attempting to leave by hurling himself down the moving stairs. Tearle's first-person narrative offers the following description of the scene:

> The stairs were going in the other direction, bearing him back ceaselessly to the top, where they should soon have deposited him in the mechanical course of events. But he applied himself to the task of plunging downwards with such maniacal energy that he managed to make headway and bore slowly down upon me. [...] A nightmare. Imagine: me, Aubrey Tearle, stepping calmly backwards, while rising swiftly and effortlessly into the air; and him, the nameless ruffian, panting and crying out in a fury of exertion, while sinking by painful degrees.[58]

However much he delights in learned allusion, Tearle has displayed little interest in philosophy or mysticism and might not be thought likely to intend the allusion I am suggesting: that the black drunkard is borne backwards like Benjamin's angel, propelled in the direction 'to which his back is turned'.[59] Yet, at a further remove, Vladislavić's darkly comic imagining of this scene allows the reader to transpose the angel's feeling of helplessness onto Tearle, whose ascent of the escalator, stepping backwards yet being ferried onwards in a vain attempt to avoid the approaching dark figure, reads as a metaphorical encoding of his unwilling passage through space and time in the throes of change he is powerless to stop. Tearle's very next thought, he tells us, is of a clock owned by an émigré German shopkeeper-acquaintance whose name evokes the vertigo of someone being blasted into a future against their will: the clock's 'hands sped backwards, trying in vain to erase the motto printed across its face: *Manchmal geht alles verkehrt*—which Toppelmann did into English as "On several occasions, everything is going wrong"' (Tearle delights in the quaint formulation). 'Could there be a more disquieting concept,' Tearle wonders, 'one more filled with dreadful fascination, than "anticlockwise".'[60]

The escalator episode appears to Tearle himself to be a significant moment: it is followed by the discovery that he has been shut out of the Café, whose doors have been locked behind the expelled drunkard. Soon afterwards, he feels that his acquaintances are 'ganging up on' him: they accuse him not only of being a 'misanthrope' with 'nauseating' 'affectations', but also reactionary and, worst of all, complicit with the apartheid government because the directories he once proofread might have led security police to dissidents' homes. Such accusations fuel Tearle's self-pity and confirm his fondness for the conspiracy theory—a key narrative device in the restorative nostalgic's worldview, Boym suggests.[61]

Tearle's recuperative nostalgia is clearly a refuge sought as escape from his experience of an acute form of politically determined melancholia. He offers this diagnosis himself, after recalling his pride in a past proofreading project—'the Pentateuch in isiZulu' (even though he had no Zulu). He had made 'only one error', a fact that strikes Tearle in the moment of recollection as unutterably, inexplicably sad, precipitating a 'wave' of what he calls 'melancholic nostalgia'.[62] In the classical and Renaissance traditions, melancholia was attributed to an excess of black bile. Its symptoms, Galen noted, included vertigo, 'much wit', 'heaviness of the heart', 'continuous fear, sorrow, discontent, superfluous cares and anxiety'—all of them arguably descriptions of Tearle's disposition.[63] For Freud, melancholia was pathological, characterized inter alia by 'a profoundly painful depression' and 'a loss of interest in the outside world' (also evident in

Tearle).[64] It appeared instead of mourning in individuals in whom mourning's proper work—that of 'decathecting', of withdrawing emotional investment in what has been lost until the individual is ready to form a new love object, a new object of investment—has been interrupted or short-circuited.[65] And it was not caused only by the death of another person but might also result from the frustration of plans or a loss of ideals (like 'fatherland' or 'freedom'), by multiple 'situations of insult, slight, setback and disappointment through which an opposition of love and hate can be introduced to [a] relationship, or an ambivalence already present can be intensified'.[66] Crucially, in Freud's understanding, melancholia is also often found where the love object has been chosen narcissistically. 'Unlike grief that mourns an impoverished world, in melancholia, the remains of loss of disappointment have come to be negatively identified with a part of the self: the lost object has come to be incorporated into the ego as an agency of wounding criticism.'[67]

There is of course something of the self-reflective critique of white complicity on the author's own part here, exaggerated for effect. Vladislavić himself has also worked as editor and proofreader. Although *The Restless Supermarket* is a sustained satire on Tearle, the reader is invited, too, to sympathize, if only in part, with Tearle's loneliness and lack of self-knowledge,[68] or at least to contemplate the ethics of being drawn into complicity with this grumbling, mean-spirited character. 'I can see the ethical dimension in creating a complex relationship between characters and readers', Vladislavić has remarked.[69] Those likely to be drawn into such complicity are, perhaps, most likely to be white readers of a certain age—as were almost all those who reviewed *The Restless Supermarket* rapturously in the South African press in 2001. Tearle, irascible pedant and racist, is a difficult character to like, even if his incipient friendship with (the implicitly mixed-race) Shirlaine offers a glimpse at the novel's end of someone who might just be able to acknowledge the promise of another life, after apartheid. Questions of complicity, and of the link between restorative and reflective nostalgia, continue to be central to Vladislavić's interest, seen for example in several of the short fictions that comprise *The Exploded View* (2004), and also in aspects of the self that emerge in the memoiristic *Portrait with Keys* (2006).

SCEPTICAL SALVAGE

If Tearle struggles to bring concern for the self and recognition of relational ties, not to mention an identification with the nation, together, this failure makes him representative of a particular kind of (white) South

African in this historical moment, one with his gaze fixed backwards, already disappointed in a future he cannot imagine. He stands as a subject whose work of mourning—here for the loss of a life remembered as comfortable—has not been successful, and has become melancholic by virtue of its narcissism. He is trapped, one might say, in a wishful fantasy of restoration. If this is the case, how, then, might one look back *without* the danger of such pathology? *Portrait with Keys* tries formally and thematically to model an answer to this question. The book's germ was a sequence of short reflections on urban life entitled 'Street addresses, Johannesburg', written in 1998 for the collection *blank_Architecture, apartheid and after* (which Vladislavić co-edited with Hilton Judin), and subsequently augmented. Several sections of the work appeared in other contexts, chiefly catalogues and art books, excerpted and assembled to form linked sequences that can be reconstructed by a reader following a number of 'itineraries'—metaphorical keys—provided at the end of the book, paths through the text linking the 137 numbered passages. The mode of engagement encouraged is consequently metapoetic: just as *Portrait* meditates on how the city is experienced and remembered, so the reader might engage with the numbered sections randomly or by following a route mapped out in advance. Insofar as they appear in no particular order, reading from cover to cover approximates an experience not unlike walking through a city, with its varied sensory stimuli.[70]

Like Benjamin, most especially in the vast unfinished *Arcades Project*, Vladislavić amasses a record of debris, descriptions of curiosities and dream objects, and reflections on affective investments. But where Benjamin looks to a comparatively more remote past, the shopping arcades of nineteenth-century Paris, for traces of the unconscious of the age that had most directly formed his own (that of the post industrial revolution bourgeoisie), Vladislavić's focus is on the relatively recent past whose debris is still visible in the present. Like Benjamin, he is concerned with the small, not the large, 'the rags, the refuse—these I will not inventory but allow, in the only way possible, to come into their own: by making use of them', Benjamin notes in 'Convolute' N of the *Arcades Project*, the section of the quotations and notes dealing with theories of knowledge and of progress.[71] As Susan Buck-Morss explains, a 'construction of history that looks backward, rather than forward, at the destruction of material nature as it *has actually taken place*, provides dialectical contrast to the futurist myth of historical progress (which can only be sustained by forgetting what has happened)'.[72] Elsewhere in the same convolute, Benjamin makes clear his sense of how the present charges past moments with meaning by casting such moments metaphorically in terms of an 'image' that is dialectical, bringing the past into the present with a particular ethical purpose. '[E]ach "now" is the now of a particular recognizability', he writes, one in which 'truth is charged to the bursting point with time'.[73] We should read this reference to truth as an invocation of theological and messianic language directed at conveying a sense of desired—but secular—utopian possibility.

I detect in Vladislavić's insistence on focusing on the inconvenient in *Portrait with Keys*, his tripping over the excrescences of dirty urban life—as he does a piece of packing tape in one of the text's early fragments, comically bleeding wine, rather than blood, from a broken bottle in his rucksack—and his acts of noticing that which is hidden under the surface (rather than eliding such detail), a refusal to submit to the easy narrative of liberation secured that insists that literary representations of South Africa now focus on the present or future, never the past. Vladislavić frequently focuses on signs that mark past events, like the mosaic that marks the place where anti-apartheid activist David Webster was assassinated. Though these are difficult to read, they attest (as does any memorial) to varied interpretations of the past—in Webster's case there are competing stories about what he was doing when he was shot: unloading plants after a trip to a nursery; walking his dogs; returning from a bakery. The unstable nature of markers of and narratives about the past is evident, too, in recurring tropes and motifs involving the destruction of buildings, wall markings that are too easily erased, and the discovery of objects whose original purpose is no longer apparent, which suggest themselves to be puzzling remnants, as if from another civilization.[74] But how might one collect such objects without engaging in restorative nostalgia?

Vladislavić's friend, Jeff, proposes a hypothetical solution, a collaborative public-art project, a 'wall of remembrance' made from brick-sized resin blocks that encase objects donated by everyone on the Greater Johannesburg voters' roll.[75] Vladislavić is momentarily entranced by the idea of this proposed structure, an amalgam of the Crystal Palace and the erstwhile Transvaal Museum in Pretoria that he visited as a child. It could be a superstore of affective investment, 'the Hyperama of Sentimental Value', a latter-day Benjaminian arcade in which one could be 'surrounded on all sides by a peculiarly impenetrable transparency', by objects 'attached by nothing but space to the names of the people who once loved them'.[76] Jeff's project owes much, *Portrait with Keys* makes clear, to South African artist Sue Williamson's *Mementoes of District Six*, which comprised a small hut made from resin blocks encasing salvage from the ruins of the mixed-race Cape Town area infamously demolished under the Group Areas Act.[77] And yet this solution also seems too static, altogether too material and hence prone to a monumentalizing impulse. The desire to gather fragments in one place, to give them shape and comprehend their totality always strikes Vladislavić as dangerous—even as he acknowledges its attractions. Part A of *Portrait* ends with the narrator leaving for a residency in Europe, hoping to see the whole of Johannesburg from the air, but disappointed when the plane banks and his view is obscured. 'Disappointment wells up in me, disproportionate and childishly ominous', he observes, adding—in what might be read as self-deprecating exaggeration—that the 'failure to see Johannesburg whole, for the last time, will cast a pall over the future'.[78] And yet, one suspects, it is this partial view that he always most appreciates.

Art that deals with absence rather than insisting on presence provides a better model, for example Sophie Calle's *The Detachment / Die Entfernung*, which Vladislavić visits at the Johannesburg Art Gallery. It records former East Germans' memories of disappeared objects or demolished buildings by photographing the remaining empty space, replacing 'missing monuments with their memories'.[79] The fragment recounting the visit ends with a dilemma that draws Vladislavić's attention back to the present, away from all artistic projects that dwell on the past: he has to decide whether or not to report the presence of two homeless children, who have entered the gallery and hidden away, moments before closing time, in the men's restroom, hoping to secure a warm place to sleep. He does not report them: the juxtaposition of artwork that records absence, and the very real experience of children with no home in the present, forecloses on the possibility of Vladislavić's own project—his meditation on memory, space, absence—from becoming merely recuperatively nostalgic, that is to say, refusing the demands of the present. Nor is Vladislavić immune from the social consequences of homelessness: another fragment offers a meditation on his collection of his late grandfather's lapel pins, housed in an inlaid wooden box that had belonged to Vladislavić's mother, which is stolen by two boys asking for food or money who take advantage of the open door and Vladislavić's absence in his kitchen fetching food.[80] Access to 'consoling histories', let alone other consolations in the present, to extend Vladislavić's formulation in his 2006 interview with Fred de Vries, remains unequal. There are always, this is to say, other experiences of the present, each with their own contexts and causes, all evidence of the continuing inequalities of postapartheid society. To invoke a sense of home in this place is to occlude—or be defined always in contradistinction to—the unhomed, as much as it is to be attentive to the unhomely. Another recurring motif, the alarmed house, a prison rather than a sanctuary, primed to explode in protest at unwelcome intrusion, confirms this understanding: 'Behind the walls, the houses are ticking like bombs.'[81] The text is preoccupied with crime and the fear of crime that is the cost of the good life still enjoyed by the middle classes: the narrator interrupts a burglary in progress; a (white) friend finds the language of deep-seated racial prejudice erupt when he encounters a (black) man urinating on his front door; liberal hosts must overlook the exploitative labour practices of a security company in order to cater to the anxieties of guests at their party.[82]

The metaphorical juxtaposition of surface and depth evident in a range of polarities (including conscious and unconscious, public and private) is germane here too. While some critics detect an 'aesthetics of flatness' in popular art and culture of the present, reading this as sign of the absence of 'an ontological or topographical model of encountering' a city so fragmented and marked by surface flows (of migrants, of capital),[83] surface also requires depth for self-definition. The city, for instance, is not merely that which is described—the streets, the buildings—but that which is below. Johannesburg is literally undermined: it sits on one of the world's most complex systems of deep-level mining. The very idea of a singular city is metaphorically and structurally undermined by the fact that it continues to be (and to proliferate) a series of unequal spaces. Mining, reliant on the exploitation of black migrant labour restricted to specific zones in the city, financed the city's development from a mining camp on farmland into a metropolis of several million people, the wealthiest city in Africa. It is thus entirely apt that *Portrait with Keys* utilizes, in Sarah Nuttall's formulation, 'a vocabulary of critical and writerly excavation, acts of noticing, and close reading, in order to decipher and bring to light the texture of the city's past and our presence in it'.[84]

Yet direct treatments of these capital flows are rarer in *Portrait* than the occasional representations of precarious lives: the youths who steal the pins or hide in the art gallery; the homeless man known to the narrator as Piet Retief; nameless hawkers, outdoor cobblers and car-guards; the unemployed whose signs implore passers-by for work; the many 'street people [. . .] the tramps, car parkers and urchins'—who store their clothes in the spaces under the iron manhole covers that dot the urban pavements.[85] Vladislavić records the effects of precarious life in *Portrait* even as the text's first-person narrator (who I have been calling Vladislavić) dramatizes his own relative insulation, as a middle-class white subject, from such conditions. During one of *Portrait*'s final scenes, he finds himself outside Johannesburg's central library in the midst of a group of striking security guards. He retreats to the library as riot policemen with tear-gas move in, the white librarians admitting him because he is judged unthreatening, and he wonders whether protestors think of him as a 'cut-off whitey', ignorant of their grievances.[86] It is in moments like these that we might sympathize with Nuttall's critique of the text, that 'what seems missing, to a degree that is surprising, is cross-racial friendship'—in fact, interaction in positions that are not marked by unequal power relations in general: 'This is how it is, the narrator seems to be saying to us.'[87]

In fact, Vladislavić seems to see himself as out of place, marginalized by similar economies that side-line the truly precarious, but also entirely at home. This is not, of course, to suggest equivalence. Although he is a contingent labourer, a contract editor, he is not homeless or hungry. He rummages in junk shops to scavenge for narrative, while others are reduced to hunter-gathering for basic survival.[88] In one vignette he finds himself in 'a bioscope junk shop' (a converted cinema) in Primrose, Johannesburg, holding a second-hand book, sensing the 'sublime disdain' of the cashier, and, despite feeling acutely 'self-conscious', relishing a strange blend of displacement and belonging: 'I should feel utterly out of place, but instead I feel that I belong here. I am given shape. I do not follow but I conclude, as surely as a non sequitur. It's enough to make me laugh.'[89] If restorative nostalgia 'takes itself dead seriously', Boym argues, reflective nostalgia partakes in irony and empathy.[90] Vladislavić—or his first-person persona—is keen to embrace his relationality, to balance an interest in the fragments of the past with an embrace of the contingencies, the uncertainties, of the present.

DOUBLE NEGATIVE: MEMORY, REFERENTIALITY, RELATIONALITY

How to embrace relationality—including to the version of oneself one was in the past (a version of the *autre* I discussed in Chapter 2)—is also a concern of Vladislavić's most recent novel to date, *Double Negative*. Concerned with disappointment, it also asks the reader (and in some cases the collector) to think about the ways in which fiction that involves looking back might work differently from other arts in relation to memorialization and what I have been calling critical nostalgia. The novel has three parts, all sharing a first-person narrator, Neville (Nev) Lister, a commercial photographer in Johannesburg, who reflects from a point in 2009 (the novel's third section) on significant moments in his past. In the first section, 'Available Light', Nev recalls episodes in early 1982 when, as a disaffected university dropout, he spent a day shadowing Saul Auerbach, a friend of the family and famous photographer. The second ('Dead Letters') describes a period following Nev's return to the country in late 1994, from London (he had left the country to avoid military conscription in the mid 1980s): this a 'parenthetical age', immediately following the first elections, marked for him by hauntings and spectral projections of other possible selves.[91] In the novel's third part, 'Small Talk', set in

Johannesburg in April 2009, an enthusiastic young reporter named Janie spends a day with Nev to research a feature about his first solo exhibition as art photographer, a project that bears all the marks of Auerbach's influence, though with significant and instructive differences.

Back in 1982, Nev had accompanied Auerbach and a third man, a visiting British journalist, on an expedition to make photographs directed by chance encounters. Passing through Bez Valley, then a low-income white area east of downtown Johannesburg, they make their way up a hill from which each man selects a suburban roof below (chillingly evoking snipers). Seeking out these houses in turn, they ask the occupants to pose for an Auerbach portrait. At the first house, they find Veronica Setchedi, a black woman living with her children, Joel and Amos, in a shack in the garden of a student commune. In the second, they find Mrs Ditton, a white woman whose son has been paralysed by a landmine in Angola (this being the period of South Africa's dirty war deep inside that country). The third house, Nev's choice, is adjacent to Mrs Ditton's, but goes unexplored as the light fades. The photograph that Nev witnesses Auerbach take of Mrs Ditton (published in his collection '*Accidental Portraits*', we learn) is very—though crucially not entirely—like an image by South Africa's most eminent documentary photographer, David Goldblatt, whose publications over a long and celebrated career include such important collections as *On the Mines* (1973), *Lifetimes: Under Apartheid* (1986), and *South Africa: The Structure of Things Then* (1998). The congruence was made clear when an abridged extract from *Double Negative* appeared in the 'Life*style*' supplement of South Africa's *Sunday Times* on 26 September 2010, illustrated by, amongst other Goldblatt images, one from the series 'Soweto and Hillbrow', first published in 1976.[92] Captioned 'A woman in her parlour, Bezuidenhout Valley, November 1973', it differs only in minor degrees from the photograph described by Nev: the fictional subject of Auerbach's gaze sits, we read, in an 'armchair beside the fireplace. The coffee table had been dragged away—there is no trace of it in the photograph—to expose the floorboards and a corner of the rug'.[93] In Goldblatt's photograph, there is no fireplace and more rug than exposed wooden floor. The photographed cabinet on Goldblatt's subject's left, but on Auerbach's subject's right, is perhaps not quite as grand as the cabinet that looms in Auerbach's, but the armchair in which Goldblatt's woman sits matches closely the description of Mrs Ditton's. There is no curtain, described by Nev, in Goldblatt's image, and no cockatiel, pictured by Goldblatt, in Vladislavić's text: in the gap between image and text, a curtain flies out and a pet bird flies in. The relationship between text and image is suggestive rather than mimetic, Auerbach's name serving here ironically, if so taken, as an allusion to Erich Auerbach, the author of *Mimesis: The Representation of Reality in Western Literature* (1946).[94]

One explanation for the similarities and differences is that Vladislavić's novel is a response to Goldblatt, but was written without particular images in mind; the men agreed, when a collaboration was first discussed in 2005, that the fictional response would be a loose one. However, Vladislavić was very familiar with Goldblatt's photographs (their work had appeared side-by-side before), and his working methods. Goldblatt confirms that the circumstances of Auerbach's photographing of Mrs Ditton echo the making of his 1973 photograph of her Bezuidenhout Valley progenitor.[95] Goldblatt's image is one of the selections in the volume *TJ* (named for the apartheid-era motor vehicle registration prefix for the city), with which *Double Negative* appeared as companion volume in a handsome slip-cased boxed set published by Italian art publisher Contrasto. Vladislavić claims to have been shocked when he realized how close Mrs Ditton was to the Bez Valley woman in the book.[96] Yet the incongruities between Goldblatt's image and Nev's description of Auerbach's points to a more thoroughgoing juxtaposition of photography and fiction, image-making and text in the novel, with implications for understanding Vladislavić's wider engagement with the past—his critical nostalgia—more broadly. 'What I wanted to do', Vladislavić explains, 'was create a field of references to the photographs, to images produced by David or by other photographers, and in so doing to generate in the reader a certain discomfort.'[97] *Double Negative* may have appeared initially to be a companion to Goldblatt's images in *TJ*, but I want to argue rather that, as complement, its textual supplementarity—that which marks its representations of the past as being in excess of that which is captured in images—points us towards a subversive critique of attention to the surface.

Lister being an archaic form for *reader*, Nev Lister might be read as 'new reader', Patrick Flanery suggests in a review of the British and American edition of *Double Negative*. Given Nev's attitude to images (a refusal to read as deeply as the model of the photographer-figure suggested by Goldblatt clearly does), this description is surely as ironic as Nev himself considers the homonym for another version of his name *enlister* (N. Lister), on account of his emigrating to avoid conscription (*enlistment*).[98] At a further remove, this implied critique of Nev, and possibly of Auerbach, operates in Vladislavić's text to validate the kind of work writing might do in relation to the past, work that photography might not be able to do, at least not packaged like Goldblatt's *TJ*, an expensive, collectible art book, to whose images of Johannesburg's past at least some of its purchasers might be expected to respond with variously inflected kinds of nostalgia. The incongruity of media is highlighted (inadvertently, one might wish to argue) by the fact that, in its box-set first edition (in which it is cased with a similarly large-format, slip-covered *TJ*), *Double Negative* is in fact not a large-format book: it is inside a dummy that the novel, a modest paperback, hides. These books are not doubles: their relationship is something other, though whether or not *negative* remains to be seen.

Nev reflects on a complicated splitting of time that he thinks he detects in the moment Auerbach photographs Mrs Ditton in her living room. The image is severed from the object from whose reflected light it is captured in a photographic negative that becomes both a double *and* an inverse, one in which white appears black and vice versa (a metaphorics with obvious resonances in South Africa). The older, narrating Nev re-enacts his younger self's speculation that the photographed subject understands that something magical has happened in this moment of image-making. Mrs Ditton appears stunned, frozen like the image that now waits to be developed on the roll of film. 'Captured and released in the same instant', she is 'unsure of her will'. She has 'two destinies': one she occupies 'still', while 'the other had stepped away from her; it was receding into the past, but with its face turned to the future'.[99] Here there is an inversion—a negative double—of Benjamin's description of the angel of history, a spectre that has been with Nev for some time (he carried a poster of Klee's painting with him from Johannesburg to Britain and back again).[100] The photographic image remains unchanged, but the subject of the representation is never again that subject—in that particular moment, at that age, in that location. What is produced is thus not a so-called true likeness, the recording of a general truth or something (some object, some event) that continues to be as and when it was photographed.[101]

These tensions between original and copy, object and representation, pervade *Double Negative*. In its second part, Nev recalls feeling anxious about how he would be perceived on his return to Johannesburg from a decade abroad, about whether South Africans would think him 'a foreigner', a pale copy of an original.[102] Nev has, in the period since the episode described in part one, become a commercial photographer—not quite a copy of his mentor, for 'Saul Auerbach is an artist. I'm just a photographer', he shrugs.[103] Nev produces stock photographs for advertisements and portfolios; he is a 'frozen moment guy' specializing 'in things falling, spilling, flying apart', an exaggerated doubling of what he understands Auerbach's images do.[104] By part three, Nev has begun to think of himself as an artist. His first solo exhibition, drawn from his project on 'Thresholders', features subjects posing before their properties' enclosing walls, in doorways, or at letterboxes. Their liminality—they are not subjects in their own space, as Auerbach's were—suggests either a critique of Auerbach's practice (consider the presumption of the white male photographer gaining access to spaces, both of which in the first part of the novel belong to women, the second to a black woman) or a suggestion that Nev's own presumption at documentary practice is stymied, held always at a threshold. Certainly, from the moment the reporter Janie arrives to interview Nev, Vladislavić moves into the territory of the reduced copy, with Nev a pale imitation of Auerbach. Janie asks Nev to repeat his greeting for her digital camera but he finds himself unable to do so in the same words; the second time around his language, too, has much less force.[105] Janie's arrival is also an inversion of the earlier 'invasions' of homes by the photographers, in this case a woman of colour penetrating the home of a not entirely willing white man.

While attention to doubling, referentiality, and authenticity is crucial to this novel, what is also at stake is ethics and nostalgia (or, to invoke Benjamin, 'aura' and politics). So, to return to the Benjaminian allusions, the photograph as a category in *Double Negative* can be read usefully against both Benjamin's idea of the dialectical image and his ideas about aura and reproducibility. In the context of the disappointments of his own life and of the fits and starts of the politics of liberation and development in South Africa, Nev's repeated musing on particular moments captured in photographs suggests a reading in which he becomes an aspirant historical materialist, attempting to make connections between moments of past promise and a disappointing present, to revivify moments in which some promise of political or aesthetic freedom seemed nascent. Nev seeks a way to be other than the subject of universal historicism—early in the novel, he feels 'like some object left on the shoreline' waiting for 'History' to 'break over' him.[106] The role of photographs in these moments is crucial: Vladislavić has explained that his interest in photography is 'as a mode of representation that's different' from literature, that can 'condense large amounts of information into an instant'. The instant itself, Vladislavić suggests (in another echo of Benjamin), 'comes to represent so much and gets loaded with so much meaning over the years as it moves away from the moment in which it was made'.[107]

Both the photograph *in general*, and Nev's musings on *particular* photographs, involve something like the constellation of relational temporal nuclei, shocked or blasted out of the flow of time in Benjamin's thought. Construed in the context of Benjamin's Theses, however, the photograph is always an ambivalent object. The older Nev seems unsure about the relationship photographs might have with memory: do they work against it or create false memory, he wonders? Do they not so much freeze a moment in time as make it impossible to remember a moment differently? In the middle section of the novel, thinking back from a point in 1994 to that significant day in 1982 when he accompanied Auerbach around the city, Nev wonders whether it is in fact the case that photographs 'annihilate memory', whether 'they swallow the available light and cast everything around them into shadow'.[108] The question raised here is one of responsibility to the past.

Invoking another of Benjamin's ideas, that of the aura (or absence thereof) of reproducible images, brings into conjunction Benjamin's ambivalence about the loss associated with technology, Vladislavić's scepticism of any pretence to authenticity advanced by claims of originary or final authority (including the rendering ironic of Nev's own narrative voice), and *Double Negative*'s own performance as a reproducible object, a book paired in its first instance of publication with a volume of reproduced images. Benjamin borrows the term *aura* from its use to describe sacred objects in religious ritual. He argues that a work of art has just such a special status, although this was changed definitively by the advent of capitalist mass production, specifically the technological capacity to reproduce works of art. This devalued the concept of the original and altered aesthetic perception itself by detaching 'the reproduced object from the domain of tradition'.[109] In most readings of this argument, Benjamin is thought to be celebrating the democratic impulse inherent in making images widely available to a mass public—for example in his argument that 'the instant the criterion of authenticity ceases to be applicable to artistic production, the total function of art is reversed'; it 'begins to be based on [...] politics' rather than 'ritual'.[110] Diarmuid Costello, however, returns to Benjamin's 1931 'Little History of Photography', in which Benjamin first explored the idea of aura in relation to changes in portraiture during the nineteenth century, to find a different way of reading aura. In his 1931 essay, Benjamin blamed photographers like Atget and Sander for exhibiting merely 'a documentary ambition to record the physiognomy of their historical moment'; 'this intention, and the attitude towards the photographic medium that this intention expresses, rather than the medium *per se*' was 'anti-auratic', Benjamin charged.[111] What emerges from a broad consideration of his thought, then, is both a celebration of and lament for aura, what Costello labels dual 'liquidationist' and 'elegiac' imperatives.[112] Costello suggests further that if aura names 'a general category of experience that is fading as a result of the transformations of our experience of space and time brought about by technological modernity', then what is at stake too is the 'very *possibility* of experiencing—let alone respecting—difference or particularity'.[113] The positive (and mourned) aspect of the auratic, in short, concerns the way in which it compels the recognition of singularity or alterity.[114]

Costello's suggestion for an application of this understanding of aura for a contemporary engagement with photography is to regard particular art photographers' distinctive viewpoints of the world as being what grants their works something like an approach to the auratic about which Benjamin is not wholly dismissive. Thus 'it is not the *sitters* who look back at us from the work of either [Thomas] Ruff or [Rineke] Dijkstra'—Costello's examples—'but, rather, the *artists* themselves'.[115] Applied to a reading of *Double Negative*, Costello's suggestions would endorse the novel's valorization of Auerbach's particular talent (as opposed to Nev's pale imitations thereof). Furthermore, at one remove from the fictional world of the novel, they mitigate any suspicion that it is the subjects of Goldblatt's documentary photography that might attract purchasers of the art book for which Vladislavić's novel was written as companion piece, at least when those images record a version of apartheid-era life that could be regarded with nostalgia by some viewers of the images (those that record an opulence or a supposed simplicity in white life in Johannesburg's past). A reading enabled by Costello's gloss on Benjamin allows for the singularity of Goldblatt's gaze as that which is recorded, and valorized.

Something critical is nonetheless still implied about photography's claims—or about claims made on photography's behalf—by Vladislavić's ironic rendering of Nev's own middle-aged artistic dabbling, about the sense that a photograph grants us access to a particular moment or truth, or even, given the equivocal picture we have of Auerbach, about the singularity of an artist-photographer's gaze. *Double Negative* implies, I am arguing, something about the representation of the past that is at an angle to how one encounters photographic representations of the past—representations that are of necessity made *in* and are therefore *from* the past. The novel implies, in my reading, that to represent the past in a manner that avoids the pitfalls of a reactionary nostalgia might involve a form of re-enactment made possible only in and through the reading of fiction—particularly fiction that dramatizes a non-identity of represented past with the past itself (for the past can never truly be known), that has its eye always on the future, and on future readings. Hence Vladislavić's project of recreating a day which *is* and *is not* a day that happened, and which recounts taking photographs that are *like* but *are not* photographs known to exist in the world, those by David Goldblatt, who is not the same as the man Auerbach (whose name serves as reminder that mimesis always mediates reality). What Vladislavić's text emphasizes is the disjunction between representation and anything that might be called real. Looking down over the rooftops of the suburb before descending to photograph Mrs Ditton, Auerbach had wondered: 'How could you ever do justice to something so rich in detail? You couldn't do it in a novel, let alone a photograph.'[116] Except that one could do it in a novel like Vladislavić's, one that shares with all of his work, fiction and non-fiction alike, an investment in memory work that is critically and not recuperatively nostalgic, that does not seek to offer a representation with an aura of veracity (which would be to range moments from the past against the present), but offers us instead a vision always grounded in and circumscribed by a particular act of reflection, or recollection, always contextualized, ironized, inevitably flawed. Benjamin would have approved. As he wrote in 1932, in a fragment unpublished during his lifetime (and cited as the epigraph to this chapter), 'genuine memory must therefore yield an image of the person who remembers, in the same way a good archaeological report not only informs us about the strata from which its findings originate, but also gives an account of the strata which first had to be broken through'.[117]

5

South Africa, Time or Place?

> In a country where so many homes have been demolished and people moved to strange new places, home temporarily becomes the shared experience of homelessness, the fellow-feeling of loss and the desperate need to regain something. But where, and how? [. . .] Home and exile. [. . .] Roots and rootlessness. [. . .] In between is a void. [. . .] Is a country of so much dislocation a home?
>
> —Njabulo Ndebele, *The Cry of Winnie Mandela* (2003)[1]

In Zoë Wicomb's short story 'Boy in a Jute-Sack Hood' (2007), Grant Fotheringay, a middle-aged expatriate Scot living in Cape Town, asks himself what it means 'to be at a loose end', and in so doing poses a question that echoes the anxiety of a great many subjects in postapartheid South Africa, adrift in the condition of unfulfilled expectation, provisional affiliation, and uncertain commitment to a shared project. Formulating his question, Grant 'thinks images: a rope dangling from a mizzen sail; the frayed edge of fabric, something rough like jute; the forlornness of something or other, and he sighs theatrically at the unfinished that passes itself off as freedom or enticement'.[2] Waiting for the unfinished to come to pass while knowing it may not, feeling the tension between desired ontological condition (freedom, fulfilment) and the frustrated teleology of forestalled futurity—these conditions are comments on the time and place within which Grant muses: the supposedly new South Africa. Notwithstanding that his might be considered a variant of a kind of white experience of loose ends, Grant's question does engage with key concerns of the postapartheid period—and with some of the recurring tropes of recent South African cultural and political discourse that I have been tracking. These include the banality of the provincial, the Gramscian interregnum and its morbid symptoms, the location of home, and the affective and temporal experience of disappointment that is, after all, at the heart of being at a loose end.

Grant's loose end has several causes: he is bored; although he has lived in South Africa since 1984 (he was an unwitting boycott-buster), he is far from his childhood home in Glasgow; he is an unmarried and childless academic, for whom a scholarly monograph stands in place of a 'first-born'—the loose end is therefore also that of a genealogical line.[3] Grant's attention to his emotional state is focused tellingly through Samuel, the eleven-year-old son of Grant's gardener, who reminds him of his own poor childhood. 'Weird', Grant thinks of the connection, and of his own thinking about loose ends; he might as well have used that loaded synonym *queer*, for there is something about the way he engages the child in activities inside his home every Saturday, not to mention his defensiveness in disclaiming ulterior motives ('who cares about proprieties anyway?'), that suggests participation, however unwittingly, in a fetishization of the body of the racial other, here infantilized and of the same sex.[4] Furthermore, Samuel is implicitly associated with a commodity intimately linked to slavery and indenture through his wearing of a 'sugar-sack hood', a 'folded jute sack, the type in which sugar is sold in bulk'.[5] There are dangers in associating Grant too easily with homosexuality on account of his interest in a young male child, of course. Grant is, the text suggests, heterosexual. Yet his platonic affection for Samuel attracts the suspicions of friends, raising the spectre of the association of homosexuality with paedophilia, a significant strand of nationalist homophobic discourse that casts gay men as a threat to the family, and the security of the heteronormative family as essential for the health of the nation. This alone, that is to say Grant's potential queerness in the broadest sense, makes of him a figure of disruption. It also connects him to many characters in Wicomb's fiction who challenge communal or national narratives of memory, authenticity, and belonging.

One need not look far, Brenna Munro has suggested, to find queer characters functioning in postapartheid writing as 'a kind of stock minor character in the pageant of nationhood'.[6] Their appearance in reimaginings of the national family marks a departure from nationalism's traditional investment in the metaphor of the so-called nuclear family that traditionally substitutes 'for both national origins and patriotic futures', linking 'notions of national belonging to biological reproduction and thus heterosexuality', Munro argues. By contrast, queer subjects are traditionally strangers, not family, outsiders not citizens, and so offer apt figures of disruption for a national script under revision.[7] However, Munro shows, quite apart from being allowed to play a potentially positive, transformative role, the queer subject is frequently domesticated in many of the near-canonical novels of the long transition—in works like J.M. Coetzee's *Disgrace* (1999) and Nadine Gordimer's *None to Accompany Me* (1994) they are made to produce or take on responsibility for a child at the narrative's close, as if the script of the family must prevail at all costs. This also occurs at the end of Gordimer's *The House Gun* (1998), although here it is the parents of the bisexual character, Duncan Lindgard, who take responsibility for the child who might—or might not—be his. It is worth noting that *The House Gun* features the metaphor of the loose end, and, as in Wicomb's story, also in relation to disrupted genealogical and ideological affiliations and narratives of belonging: it describes the nature of Duncan's parents' relationship with him, and while Duncan is described as a '[j]agged end' in the narrative itself, the same phrase is used tellingly to imagine South Africa's figural and geographic relation to the rest of the African continent.[8] 'Boy in a Jute-Sack Hood', Wicomb's story's title, also echoes the name of the character Toby Hood in a much earlier Gordimer novel, *A World of Strangers* (1951), which also uses the idea of the loose end: here Hood, a British expatriate, like Grant, embraces the 'freedom of the loose end' that he finds in South Africa, where everyone seems a stranger to everyone else.[9] Zoë Wicomb is, as we shall see, nothing if not alert to literary genealogy and intertextuality.

Since the publication of her first book, *You Can't Get Lost in Cape Town* (1987, a linked-story cycle or novel-in-fragments), Wicomb has repeatedly thematized the politics of gender, the tyranny of the family, and the fraying cords of affiliation that (also) encompass ties to the nation-as-family. Each subsequent work—three novels, *David's Story* (2000), *Playing in the Light* (2006), and *October* (2014); many short stories, some collected as *The One That Got Away* (2008)—has continued to unsettle the presumptions of those discourses that oversimplify the complexities of lived experience in South Africa, whether narratives of the Struggle that subordinated gender liberation to race, or that dismissed any artistic expression not instrumentally social-realist. These have been the concerns, too, of her substantial body of essays, treating ethics and literary form, the politics of coloured identity (especially in relation to discourses of shame), the use of intertextuality, and the relationship between memory and nostalgia. Wicomb's work is also unusually sympathetic to the condition of transnational lives. Grant Fotheringay is from Glasgow, where Wicomb herself has lived for many years. Born in 1948 in Namaqualand, she moved to England in the 1960s, returned briefly to Cape Town in the early 1990s, and taught at the University of Strathclyde from 1994 until her retirement in 2012.

Whether or not South Africa is home, whether South Africa is a time or a place, whether home itself is a place or an affect—these are questions that animate Wicomb's work. In her fictions the domestic is more *unheimlich* than homely, affiliation negotiated and constantly under stress. Wicomb consistently seeks to hold open the possibility of exploring—and enabling—formal, political, and affective uncertainty. This is clearly the case in 'Boy in a Jute-Sack Hood'. Such concerns also animate Wicomb's most recent novel, *October*, which, amongst its many other engagements, offers a significant writing back to Marilynne Robinson's 2008 novel

Home, which Wicomb's protagonist and chief focalizer, Mercia Murray, is reading as she wrestles with her own autobiography. This chapter seeks to take the measure of Wicomb's sustained engagements with disappointment, affiliation, national and ethnic identity, the disjunctive temporalities of postapartheid South Africa, and the potential of the textual as a privileged space within which to hold open the promise of the loose end, its potential to unravel older formations in the social fabric and suggest new narrative threads. It proceeds by assessing a long-running engagement with queer characters in Wicomb's work, figures who serve as emblems of subversion and promise. I turn thereafter to consider the metaphorical queering that Wicomb's bold use of intertextuality and metafiction performs in relation to her project of testing the capacity for contemporary South Africa to serve as home. In short, I argue that, like Winterbach's use of *Cosmopolis* and *Age of Iron*, and Coetzee's conversation with Middle European writers and thinkers, Wicomb's intertextuality constitutes a refusal to cede the revolutionary potential of the transition to monolithic constructions of nation or family (or national family), to a restrictive sense of what it is proper for a 'South African' text to engage. Rather, Wicomb's restless allusiveness suggests a textual equivalent to her characters' displacements (and perhaps her own transnationalism): a refusal to cede ground to any resurgent nationalism.

QUEERING THE NATIONAL FAMILY

Wicomb's use of the figure of the queer South African offers her most sustained and subversive critique of the dangers of hegemonic discourses of the new nationalism that followed apartheid's demise—a nationalism not necessarily black, but often uncompromising in its unwillingness to countenance the subtleties of a culturally, racially, and linguistically heterogeneous country. Wicomb's own background—born to a family that would have been classified Coloured—and her resistance to the revisionism she has seen at work in the politics of this community (eliding the experience of slavery and miscegenation, for instance, in its drive to claim descent instead from autochthonous communities like the !Xam and the Khoi), drives this critique, which finds its formal expression in a deep scepticism of omniscient narration, or of texts that do not reveal their own limitations and inevitable investments. There is much scope for disappointment here: the promise of non-racialism has been eclipsed by a fetishization of ethnicity and origin at which Wicomb's work repeatedly takes aim. I will have more to say on the formal issues in due course. Here let me note that apartheid-era racial classificatory laws used the term Coloured (capitalized) for a broad range of South Africans of mixed-race, slave, and autochthonous heritage, and many South Africans still identify using this term, often in lower-case form to differentiate it from the apartheid-era legal category. Wicomb herself prefers this usage, while rejecting the need to use such terms at all and questioning the continued imbrication of discourses of coloured identity with those of concupiscence and shame.[10]

'In Search of Tommie', a short story published online, in *Wasafiri* magazine, and in an edited collection of short fiction on the theme of contact (all in 2009), showcases a great many of the concerns and strategies I have been describing. TS, whose real name is Tommie but who answers only to the initials, lives in Cape Town's Langa township with his mother, who is from the erstwhile apartheid-era homeland of the Transkei. TS's father, repeatedly described by his mother as a 'university man' and a 'gentleman' from the north, abandoned his family while studying in England, where he is rumoured to have fathered a child with a white woman.[11] TS has a white male lover, Joe, a schoolteacher who lives in Sea Point, and suffers from an unnamed disease; the reader learns that TS has 'bad blood', which might be read as a cipher for HIV/AIDS, though this is not made explicit. Never much of a reader, although more educated than Joe believes, TS has, during his illness, become 'addicted to heading off into stories', and it is in a book by an English writer, Chris Hallam, that he becomes convinced he recognizes a portrait of his long-vanished father.[12] The book is a memoir and the father is Hallam's, too. TS writes to her, though she is understandably unnerved by the unexpected approach and wonders whether TS is a third-world opportunist, 'a fruitcake, or worse, a fraud'.[13] It is only when Hallam accepts an invitation to the Cape Town Book Fair and decides to indulge her curiosity, venturing into the township in a hire car, dowdily dressed and clutching her keys in a plastic packet, that she meets TS, his mother, and (subsequently) Joe. TS produces the only photograph of his father that his mother possessed and Hallam, despite seeing no family resemblance between this man and herself, indeed having never seen a photograph of her own father, declares the two men one and the same. Here the story ends—prematurely, as we imagine will TS's life—with Hallam making her newfound, imagined half-brother promise her that she will not be made to eat 'authentic African offal' by TS's mother.[14] TS ironically likens his mother's belief in her own version of history (that TS's father must have been 'ensnared' by Hallam's mother) and her notions of what is authentic (she calls TS 'a proper black African', while Hallam is his 'coloured sister') to offal, holding up his hands when she begins to reminisce, 'as if to push back down her throat the story that rose like so much poorly digested offal, ready to be spewed'.[15]

TS calls himself 'a bigoted, sexist moffie' (an Afrikaans pejorative for homosexual) who 'has never had anything to do with women'. His disdain for reproduction as 'horrible, the thing that dogs or pigs do', finds a correlation in the text's concern with reproducibility, with likeness and affiliation.[16] Not only is the character TS constructed as gay, but he becomes the centre of an imagined family in a non-genealogical revisioning of affiliation that is suggestive for Wicomb's engagement with the cosmopolitan, figured as the opposite of the homogeneous, parochial, or ethnocentric. This alternative national family complements—if it does not rival—the fantastically alternative 'queer familial soap opera' discerned by Brenna Munro in the manner in which some of the leading figures of South Africa's first decade of democracy figured in the popular imagination: Mandela as 'a warm, indeed *maternal* [. . .] "founding father"', the late 'black singer Brenda Fassie as queer prodigal daughter, the Jewish Afrikaner playwright and cross-dressing personality Pieter-Dirk Uys as "tannie," or aunt "of the nation," and of course, Mandela's now ex-wife, Winnie, as disgraced mother'.[17] In 'In Search of Tommie', Wicomb's version of this queer family comprises a traditional but tolerant Xhosa mother, absent Venda father, queer black son, his gay white lover, and a (conjectural) foreign half-sister, whose name allows her to pass as a man. TS himself alludes to an arguably even more transgressive couple presiding over the whole show: 'that old mincing couple, the bickering faggots, God and his Devil'. The description is prompted by TS wondering whether prayers will be offered to end the incessant rain, given that prayers had been offered for the rain in the first place: 'how, by the way, do you turn prayers round? Would reversing the words not be like praying to the devil?'[18] I draw attention to this camp configuration because it forms part of yet another queer subtext, linked via a circuitous route through the location in which Wicomb stages her alternative national family drama, to a queer subtext legible in the new nation's revivification of tradition more broadly. Untangling this subtext allows us to glimpse some of Wicomb's larger concerns with affiliation and home.

TS and his mother live in a 'respectable part of Langa', one of the oldest residential areas designated for black residents in the Cape Peninsula, established after Ndabeni, a government reserve on the edges of Cape Town, was razed in the wake of the 1918 influenza epidemic.[19] The name commemorates Langalibalele, chief of the Hlubi people of present-day western KwaZulu-Natal, who was tried over a stand-off with the Natal colonial authorities (and subsequently a series of skirmishes in 1873), banished from the colony, and imprisoned on Robben Island, before being released to a farm on the site of the present-day Cape Town suburb of Pinelands (adjacent to what became Langa). Langalibalele was known as a rainmaker, making Langa an appropriate location for TS's reverie on rainmaking. In a fortuitous coincidence, Langa was also the name of the chief of the Mbalu (and brother of the powerful Xhosa chief Gcaleka), in the Zuurveld in the late eighteenth century, who led his people in the first of the conflicts with Dutch colonists on the eastern fringes of the Cape (the so-called Frontier Wars), ending in 1781. The township's name thus evokes banishment, ethnic heritage, and, related to both, the discursive—and real—ramifications of borders, margins, and frontiers.[20]

Rainmaking is an interest shared by Chief Andrew le Fleur in Wicomb's 2000 novel *David's Story*. In a section set in the parched Namaqualand in 1922, he is shown wishing to resurrect the 'lapsed tradition' of the Rain Sisters, who will 'bring back the idea of radical moisture that will drench us through the months of drought'.[21] The occasion of this cultural resurrection is offered in part by David Dirkse (the David of the novel's title), who reconstructs it himself (the fragments are reworked by the novel's narrator-amanuensis) from stories told by his grandmother, Ragel, and augmented by his own suspicions that he is in fact descended from an affair between his great-grandmother Antjie, one of Le Fleur's chosen Rain Sisters, and the Chief himself. The narrator-amanuensis speculates that this was one more of Le Fleur's 'old customs' that were, in fact, not in any way authentically Griqua at all, but rather a 'cultural translation, a severely Calvinised version culled from Eugene Marais's poem' 'Die Dans van die Reën' ('The Dance of the Rain')—'it is one of the many signs of the Chief's confused adoption of a native voice that was in fact produced by a European', she comments.[22]

In the context of *David's Story*, demonstrating the hybrid or syncretic nature of Le Fleur's faux-authentic custom allows the narrator—and Wicomb—to emphasize the absurdity of claims of purity in relation to cultural practice and markers of ethnic identification. This is a running concern of the novel, and indeed of Wicomb's critical project more broadly. 'When you've got "pure blood"? Isn't it replicating the old identities of apartheid?', Wicomb remarks in interview about what she calls 'this business about finding out who you are'.[23] 'What would be the South African tradition?', she retorts, when asked about a South African canon and a national tradition. 'It would, like in any culture, be a mixed bag, with little to hold it together other than geography, precisely because no "nation" is cohesive, and affiliations of gender, race and class will always woof across such national traditions'.[24] The amanuensis's reference in *David's Story* to Marais, a key figure in the Afrikaans literary movement of the early twentieth century, participates, too, in the broader project of cultural questioning and disruption. Intertextuality, Wicomb writes elsewhere (discussing translation and allusion in Coetzee's *Disgrace*), is a 'writing strategy' that has not surprisingly 'become such a staple of postcolonial discourse' because of its 'translative' disruptive possibilities (I will return to this point in due course).[25] Nor is it the only such ironic engagement with the Afrikaans canon. In *Playing in the Light*, Wicomb's 2006 novel, Brenda McKay asks about the decidedly queer representation of coloured boys in poetry by C. Louis Leipoldt: 'what on earth is this wicked stuff doing in the Afrikaans canon?'[26]

But why evoke rainmaking in 'In Search of Tommie', both in TS's meditation on the prayers of 'those up-country preachers on television',[27] and indirectly through the story's setting in a township named for a rain-making chief? Perhaps because rainmaking is associated, in the popular imagination in South Africa, with the Modjadji, the Rain Queen of the Balopedu people in Limpopo, who live not very far from the erstwhile Venda (from whence came TS's father). What makes these traditional leaders particularly relevant for this discussion is that they do not marry male consorts, but are allowed numerous 'wives', women courtiers and assistants whose children are considered the Queen's. The Modjadji is not necessarily lesbian-identified, though she is on a continuum with a broader occurrence of female traditional healers or sangomas, particularly in parts of KwaZulu-Natal and Gauteng, who commonly take 'ancestral wives' in forms of marriage of great variety.[28] Queer characters, queered performances of faux traditions, cultural practices more open to queerness than Bible-thumping or leopard-skin-clad leaders would have us believe, are everywhere, it turns out.

This is an important point to make in relation to contemporary South Africa, in which the promise of cultural openness, the recognition of syncretism, the positive unsettling of binaries promised—and indeed represented—by recognition of the rights of the sexually (supposedly) dissident, as in South Africa's famously inclusive Bill of Rights, is constantly in danger. Traditional leaders and ANC politicians frequently fulminate against the supposedly un-African nature of homosexual relationships; so-called corrective rape is perpetrated on black lesbians with alarming frequency. 'In Search of Tommie' is significant and suggestive because it offers a compendium of queering far in excess of merely including a character labelled a 'moffie'. Aspects of the broader (buried) cultural context are shown to be always already queer, in other words. Furthermore, it is not only TS, but the text itself—the *TS*, or *typescript*—that is rendered queer, that enacts formally the subversiveness it describes.

COSMOPOLITANISM AND CULTURAL TRANSLATION

As I have suggested, Wicomb's impulse to queer the normative, in the context of discourses of gender, ethnicity, and nationalism, is evident from the beginning of her career. But the engagement with the word *queer* is equally apparent. In *You Can't Get Lost in Cape Town*, it is used as an adjective in the sense of its original meaning: 'strange, odd, peculiar, eccentric'.[29] In the title story, the narrator Frieda's white boyfriend Michael has a crooked smile, his teeth forming 'a queer diagonal line above his chin'.[30] In *David's Story*, Andrew le Fleur is described as 'neighing' 'queerly' as he tells a story of release from Robben Island and of the disbelief of the warden at his pardon. At the very end of the narrative, a 'queer message' appears on the narrator-amanuensis's computer: '*this text deletes itself*'.[31] These instances are surely always imbued with a sense of the usage, since the 1890s, to refer to homosexuals; they serve to emphasize the off-kilter, the unsettled or unsettling.[32] It is just this unsettling that the strangeness of the queer subject performs, and that accords with the energies of queer theory as it has developed over the past two decades. Insisting on the term queer 'has the effect of pointing out a wide field of normalization, rather than simple intolerance, as the site of violence', Michael Warner observes.[33] Queer theory is broadly useful and suggestive precisely because it offers a so-called 'subjectless' critique: there is no 'proper subject of or object for the field'; it is potentially widely disruptive.[34]

In Wicomb's fiction, the terms used most often by characters and narrators to refer to subjects who are queer in the sense of being different from heteronormative models are the colloquially derogative 'moffie' or the more clinical 'homosexual'. In *David's Story*, the narrator-amanuensis suggests more than once that David's father regarded his son as a disappointment, weak, too interested in politics, and consequently both a 'windbroek' (wind-trousers, glossed as 'lacking full buttocks. Man without courage or nerve') and a 'moffie' ('an effeminate homosexual man').[35] David is reluctant to meet the narrator at the Rhodes Memorial café on the slopes of Table Mountain on one occasion because he regards it as one of those '[w]hite-middle-class-moffie-wholefood-places'.[36] Here the narrator channels the prejudices if not of David, then of the Griqua and coloured communities. Consider, for example, how the gem 'sodalite' is said to sound to David's wife, Sally, like 'sinful sodomites'; David may not 'mind being called a moffie', we learn, but he is keen to avoid behaviour that his community associates with a certain kind of white cosmopolitanism.[37] Because David's description is reported, which is to say only implicitly David's construction, we might also wonder about the narrator-amanuensis's prejudices. The term 'moffie' also appears in *October*, where it is used by the protagonist's alcoholic brother Jake to dismiss as weak the idea of loyalty being owed to parents: 'That's just moffie talk, girls' stuff'.[38] Again, the queer is cast in relation to genealogy, though here interestingly associated *with* (not against) the family, as well as with sentiment.

In 'Nothing Like the Wind', a story first published in 2004 and subsequently collected in Wicomb's 2008 collection *The One That Got Away*, a similar if more extreme assumed communal disapproval of homosexuality serves to typify one character's sense of the state of South Africa as a whole in the wake of the 1994 elections. The story's chief character and focalizer, Elsie, recalls her father, after the death by natural causes of his mother (Elsie's grandmother) on a farm in the Karoo, citing the constitution's guarantee of freedom from discrimination on the basis of sexual orientation as an example—perhaps even the epitome—of the inversion of the previous order: 'After the years of terrorism, just more of the same, only now of course it's all legal. Even homosexuals. Anyone in his right mind would just pack up, pack in this whole thing and start again in another place, somewhere civilised.'[39] Here Elsie's father's homophobia becomes a correlative for a version of conservative disappointment in the postapartheid order. Starting again in another place is exactly what Elsie's father decides to do, moving the family to Glasgow, where Elsie's sense of displacement is experienced in terms reminiscent of a roaring and buzzing that recurs elsewhere in Wicomb's fictions (more on this shortly).[40] Although her family is said (by her father) to be 'of good Scottish blood', Elsie finds that if they are Scots they are queer ones. They are implicitly coloured, and they find adapting to white working-class Scottish culture difficult. The sign of their difference is visited on them troublingly in the story's suggestion that Elsie's brother Freddie, who, it is suggested, has abused Elsie, either is or is *like* a 'man who did unmentionable things to adolescent boys before he strangled them'.[41] In this curious story, then, queerness is both a marker of anathema, but also something that marks those who are apparently appalled by otherness.

Same-sex sexuality thus has an unsettling aspect in some of Wicomb's fictions, or it is perceived as being other by a particular kind of (almost always diegetic) third-person narrator, as is the case in 'Boy in a Jute-Sack Hood'. In 'In Search of Tommie', TS's queerness likewise has a darker side—or the representation of TS as queer in the most obvious sense does. Here there are a number of ways of understanding the character's ambiguity as a figure whose disruptive potential both endorses (or enacts) and indicts stereotype. In particular, we could consider his encounters with white men, and his illness. Indeed, why should he be afflicted with 'bad blood'? Does this place TS in the territory of Lee Edelman's *No Future*, in which the gay person, but particularly the young gay person, represents a refusal of a future that merely recapitulates the past? '[W]e do not intend a new politics, a better society, a brighter tomorrow, since all these fantasies reproduce the past, through displacement, in the form of the future', Edelman contends, choosing rather to endorse 'irony', the 'queerest of rhetorical devices'.[42]

Such irony, of course, is to be found in the theatricality of Grant's sigh in 'Boy in a Jute-Sack Hood' and the archness of TS's asides. 'Political hope fails queers', according to Edelman (paraphrased here in José Muñoz's critique), because 'it was not originally made for' them; on the contrary, political hope 'resonates only on the level of reproductive futurity'.[43] Perhaps the affirmative choosing of affiliation—on the part of TS and of Hallam (delightfully, TS as typescript chooses its own author)—is sufficient frustration of this reproductive futurity. It certainly proposes an alternative to the heteronormative national family and to the script of the national allegory as both sides might have imagined it during the apartheid period (and period of the anti-apartheid struggle).

TS's illness renders him a virus or parasite lodged in the body politic, one whose presence might be considered positive—he tests the limits of the nation's cosmopolitanism, understood (following Derrida following Kant) as its hospitality without limits.[44] What of TS's encounters with white men, however? Inherent in the description of TS's relationship with Joe is the suggestion if not of exploitation then of the uncomfortable possibility of the exotic appeal of the queer of colour. As Hiram Perez puts it polemically, the 'brown body is a fetish for what the cosmopolitan has lost or forgotten at the other side (the brown underside) of civilization'. A brown sexual partner marks a white man in this context as sharing a 'subject position originating with a white, urban, leisure-class gay male whose desire is cast materially onto the globe at the close of the nineteenth century'.[45] Discussing Cathy Cohen's critiques of the under-interrogated white gaze of queer theory, Andrew Tucker observes in his exploration of the limited spaces for queer visibility in Cape Town's black townships that 'queer only functions for those with the time, money, resources and community that allow for it'.[46] The transgressive subject, in this case the brown queer, is, in other words, always in danger of being overwhelmed by stereotype. Yet Wicomb's 'In Search of Tommie' arguably answers back to white cosmopolitanism's stereotypical constructions of brown queerness by staging TS's—and Wicomb's unsettling, unsettled typescript's—answering back. We might regard her project as in part an exploration or dramatization of the struggle against a particular kind of construction of black queer subjectivity (one might perhaps call it a limited cosmopolitanism) perpetrated by a local community riven by its own prejudices, ones that might in fact be colonial importations. The rain queens might stand as examples of autochthonous queerness that have thus far survived the colonial encounter and the new nation's investment in heritage and authenticity.

In a discussion of J.M. Coetzee's *Disgrace*, Wicomb comments on the 'patently pathological' aspects of cultural translation in that novel, those that emphasize David Lurie's displacement, for instance, or compound the desperation of his daughter Lucy's choice to bear the child of her rapist. Such pathologies, Wicomb suggests, are inevitable in 'the failure of post-apartheid culture' and should 'be read as elements of the untranslatable, the residue of apartheid—an overarching intertext—that continues its vulgar influence on its subjects'.[47] (It is worth recalling the idea of the remainder cited in my discussion of the difficulties of translation in relation to Van Niekerk's *Agaat*.) The unsettling aspects of queerness in 'In Search of Tommie' perform a similar function, working both to exemplify and to endorse the disruptively queer project—positively cosmopolitan, but also critical of a cosmopolitanism that is blind to race, gender, sexuality, and material need—of Wicomb's fiction and criticism more broadly. In what follows, I want to suggest that this queer project extends to Wicomb's attitude towards realism, and that her sophisticated employment of intertexuality is key to this engagement.

ON INTERTEXTUALITY AND RESPONSIBILITY

In 'In Search of Tommie', Joe warns TS that Hallam's narrative is 'a fictionalised autobiography', and there is 'something about its post-modernness' that TS decides accounts 'for the jumping about of the story, the fact that he was not always sure of what was going on'.[48] Even the experience of reading reproduces this subversiveness, as the represented text induces symptoms that are like those of being ill: TS mistakes 'the tingling sense of recognition' he feels when he encounters the portrait of Hallam's fictionalized father 'for a new symptom of his sickness'; the experience of reading causes in TS a 'roaring in the ears'.[49] This is of the same order of interference as the buzzing, whistling, and roaring that intrudes into many of Wicomb's fictions, sounds or sensations that accompany experiences of displacement, whether physical or psychic, and that seem to be occasioned by the breakdown of the unacknowledged fictions by which characters persist in making sense of their lives. In the chapter in *You Can't Get Lost in Cape Town* ironically titled 'Home Sweet Home', for example, the young narrator-protagonist Frieda Shenton attempts to escape the narratives being spun for and about her by her family by walking down to the river, but she continues to hear the sound of their chatter: 'Their words, all their words, buzz like a drove of persistent gnats about my ears.'[50] In *Playing in the Light*, Marion Campbell's sleep is disturbed by 'something' that 'buzzes in her ears, a sense of swarming that grows louder and louder', presaging the unsettling news about her parents' pasts that will revise her own sense of identity.[51]

David's Story is full of references to loud or buzzing noises, often at moments in which fallible memories or constructions put upon the past are at issue. Ouma Ragel's recollections of the start of the 1976 Soweto rising, and also of the 1960 Sharpeville massacre, 'buzz like persistent flies around her head'.[52] The noises made by rain or by running water sometimes drown out speech or threaten the composure of those who hear these sounds. Something roaring functions metaphorically, as in 'the new roar of eugenics' discussed at one point.[53] The buzzing of insects is especially persistent, as when David urges the narrator-amanuensis to see the corruption and dirty tricks at the heart of the revolutionary movement: 'It's only you arty types who think of such problems as something special [...]. Stick to the real world and you'll find the buzz of bluebottles deafening.'[54] This 'buzz' reappears in the narrator-amanuensis's description of David's increasing distress towards the end of the narrative as his determination that she help him tell the story of his fellow liberation movement cadre, Dulcie September (a story he ends up being unable to tell), is redoubled, but also as he is tortured by memories of his father's treatment of him as a child.[55] Most memorably, it appears as the 'rude buzz of bluebottles' that threatens to drown out the narrator-amanuensis's voice in the final descriptions of her garden, which seems to have become the site either of the fantasized appearance of Dulcie's (or indeed Saartje Baartman's) body, 'covered with goggas [insects] crawling and buzzing all over her syrup sweetness', or more prosaically—but no less chillingly—of a shot fired by an unknown assailant that shatters the screen of her computer, destroying the narrative of betrayal and subversion that is buried between the lines of David's halting reminiscences.[56]

These staged sonic interferences mark the very limit of textual veracity and narrative authority in Wicomb's work, and are one of the ways in which her fictions' 'postmodernness' announces itself most clearly. But the postmodernness is not merely playfully meta-; it has a serious ethical imperative, focused on the question of the authority of the writer herself. Hallam is here set in place of the male author, though she is both like a male author (in that she authors her own father) and yet also an author-mother (in her act of generative affiliation, accepting TS as family). Hallam is consequently also a cipher for Wicomb: TS's description of Hallam's 'photograph on the dust jacket' of her book ('a slim woman, with short, frizzy hair and big, strong features') could be of Wicomb; their surnames are each two syllables, ending with a similar phoneme.[57] Hallam is one of many female writer-figures in Wicomb's oeuvre. Aside from David Dirkse, who is unable to bring his text (or texts) to a satisfactory conclusion in *David's Story*, and two characters in stories in *The One That Got Away* (the sympathetically figured Roddy in 'Trompe l'oeil' and the more ambiguously represented Grant Fotheringay in 'Boy in a Jute-Sack Hood'), all of Wicomb's writer-figures (writer-protagonists and, in some cases, implied narrators) are female: Frieda Shenton; the unnamed narrator of *David's Story*; *Playing in the Light*'s Brenda McKay (if it is she who is the implied narrator); and Mercia Murray in *October*. Wicomb's texts—or more significantly, the texts *within* her texts—are thus mothered, not fathered; their affiliation and genealogy is gynocentric, presuming to displace the patriarchal male author and, implicitly, the patriarchal authority presumed by the author of the kind of realism that Wicomb's work consistently undermines.

In 'In Search of Tommie', Chris Hallam's acquiescence in a claim of affiliation—recognizing her unknown father in a photograph only ostensibly of TS's father—is neither more nor less strange than TS claiming a paternal figure actualized only in print. Both acts are fitting for characters bearing the names they do, names that accord with the narrative's preoccupation with affiliation and genealogy, and with authenticity. TS's initials mark him as a typescript and also make of him a character-cipher who draws the reader's attention to the author's metafictional concern to unsettle expectations of an uncomplicated realism. They also, of course, recall T.S. Eliot, an echo that is not lost on schoolteacher Joe, who had seemed so pleased with the name on first meeting Tommie and discovering the moniker that he had intoned 'I grow old, I grow old, Shall I wear the bottoms of my trousers rolled? Dare I eat a peach?'[58] This is a misquotation from 'The Love Song of J. Alfred Prufrock'—lines 120–1 in the original offer a statement of sartorial choice, not a question, and line 122 poses the question about the peach differently. The error suggests yet another act of distancing from an original, precisely what is at issue in a story about absent fathers and narrative provenance.[59] Whose story is this, after all? Who fathers and who *mothers* the narrative? Such questions are at the heart of the story's engagement with its intertexts (something that is also significant in relation to *October*).

TS is clearly connected in Joe's mind with Prufrock, Eliot's exemplary figure of ennui and hesitation and a descendant of the flâneur—which is to say if not an archetypal street-cruiser, then one rendered queer in the broadest sense of the term. This bolsters the story's concern with dissidence and subversion. 'Only a moffie would worry about eating a peach', TS jokes in response to his lover's misquotation.[60] The last question in Joe's Prufrockian aside—'Dare I eat a peach?'—appears in exactly the same misquoted form in Wicomb's 2006 novel, *Playing in the Light*, where Brenda McKay asks the same question. There Brenda credits Eliot, and the allusion functions as a marker of her university education, countering the assumptions about race held by her employer, Marion Campbell; it is also a suggestion, through its relationship with other allusions to Eliot in that novel, of Brenda's identity as an author-narrator, perhaps even of the novel's own text.[61] There are several further allusions to Eliot in *Playing in the Light*: Marion Campbell, unable to sleep one night, sits on her balcony watching the sea 'throw up broken images that she strains to put together', not unlike the narrative voice at the end of *The Waste Land*; later, in London, she is 'mesmerised' by light on a wall that 'conjures first a corner of the frame before the whole trapezium returns in a flash, [. . .] announcing its death by drowning', the final three words another reference to Eliot's long poem.[62] Such intertextual allusions to Eliot might be thought to serve as markers of authority and authenticity, of an ostensibly established literariness, rather as Eliot (or his work) functions in much South African writing and cultural discourse as a marker of an Anglo-American tradition valorized by the New Critical pedagogy that predominated in the country's departments of English for much of the last century. (Compare the use of Eliot in Michiel Heyns's translation of Marlene van Niekerk's *Agaat*, discussed in Chapter 3.) In an essay entitled 'Setting, Intertextuality and the Resurrection of the Post-colonial Author' (2005), Wicomb discusses Toni Morrison's allusions to 'Prufrock' and *The Waste Land* in the novel *Jazz*, observing that these references to 'modernist intertexts' serve 'as a counter-discourse' rather than endorsement. Morrison's engagement with the city—'the site of passion, of freedom of ex-slaves to love, the birthplace of jazz, and the site of black modernity'—is the inverse, Wicomb suggests, of Eliot's 'unreal city of alienation and spiritual sterility'.[63] Allusion can thus be something other than blind validation, and Eliot is a complexly suggestive figure in the work of a writer as concerned as Wicomb with transnational identifications and with the benefits and costs of cosmopolitanism. He is both an attractive and cautionary figure, an American-born Anglophile with European sensibilities whose early cosmopolitanism settled into a reactionary royalist, conservative, Anglo-Catholic proximate Englishness.

'TS' evokes other connections and ambiguities in 'In Search of Tommie'. It 'turned out to be a good name', particularly when Tommie met 'his first lover' on a beach, a man named Richard for whom TS became 'TESS' ('T' and 'Ess') in letters written in the sand.[64] This marks TS as feminized black man, but also suggests an allusion to Thomas Hardy's *Tess of the d'Urbervilles*, a novel that serves as a canonical intertext in a story (or chapter) in Wicomb's *You Can't Get Lost in Cape Town*. In 'A Clearing in the Bush', Frieda struggles to write an essay on 'Fate in Tess' on the day of assassinated Prime Minister H.F. Verwoerd's memorial service at the university college for coloured students that she attends. She has 'always been able to distinguish good from bad' but Hardy's novel is confusing, and her lecture notes unhelpful. She finds herself merely repeating her white lecturer Retief's formulation about Tess: 'Murder is a sin which should outrage all decent and civilised people.'[65] Yet she finds the sentiment complicated by her sympathy for Tess—and in the context of the murder of the hated Prime Minister, architect of many of the most pernicious apartheid laws. Significantly, the moral injunction against murder that damns Tess is delivered second-hand: Retief's lecture is copied from the course notes from the correspondence university to which the college is affiliated, offering simply a paternalistic diktat to be accepted without question. Frieda has to decide for herself what to think and feel, precipitating a clash between politics and affect that she does not yet have the capacity to resolve. She disagrees with the direction to rehearse a sense of outrage in relation to Tess's act, but not—despite the politics of her peers, of her own implicit politics—in relation to Verwoerd. And yet she defers to the views of her teacher and her peers: she uses the pretext of finishing her essay as an excuse not to attend the memorial service, acquiescing by default in the student boycott. And although she begins formulating an essay 'that wantonly moves towards exonerating Tess' (she fears Retief 'will not be pleased'), Frieda finds herself, in her rush to finish it, offering a normative analysis such that Tess, 'branded guilty', is 'betrayed once more on this page'—Frieda's page, but also the page of the book of loosely autobiographical stories that the adult Frieda is said to be about to publish at the end of *You Can't Get Lost in Cape Town*.[66]

Hardy's Wessex stands as embodiment of an England that is an imagined place of escape for Frieda, one presented by Michael, who, trying to convince the pregnant Frieda not to abort their child (in the collection's title story), is 'gripped by the idyll of an English landscape of painted greens' and suggests that they 'get to England and marry'.[67] In the following story, 'Home Sweet Home', the dusty Namaqualand of the Shenton family home is juxtaposed with another such vision of 'the bright green meadows of Hardy's England, a landscape anyone could love'.[68] Hence *Tess* marks a complex nexus of association with place and belonging, and with difficult moral decision-making, making it particularly apt as intertext for 'Home Sweet Home'. In Hardy's novel, Tess Durbeyfield's father's belief that the family is descended from the Norman d'Urbervilles prompts Tess's claim of kinship with the widow d'Urberville, and her ultimately disastrous entanglement with that family—which is in fact not related to Tess's at all.[69] False relatives, assumed names, and the perils of 'claiming kin' make *Tess of the d'Urbervilles* a singularly suggestive intertext for 'In Search of Tommie', too—indeed for Wicomb's recurring concerns to unsettle claims of autochthony, purity, or pre-eminence. Nor is it the only intertextual allusion that suggests the complexity of family and kinship in 'In Search of Tommie', because Chris Hallam's name invariably suggests that of Arthur Henry Hallam, bosom friend of Alfred Tennyson and fiancé of his sister, Emily; each sibling named their sons for Hallam, to whom Tennyson's *In Memoriam A.H.H.* is dedicated.

Wicomb's insistence on foregrounding the textuality of her fictions, the manner in which the reader is often reminded that reading occurs at several removes from reality, reflects an insistence on respecting the bodily experiences of real subjects of the types of discrimination experienced by her fictional characters. That is to say, one is reminded always of the residue in translating trauma to the page. So too, and as a correlative, Wicomb's examination of the situatedness of the implied narrative voice in many of her fictions indexes her concern to be mindful of her own transnational position, her privileged position as one able to come and go. This is not to downplay the psychic and emotional costs of the navigation of affiliations to a place one lives, and to a place that is—in complex ways—always home but no longer where one lives (where others with less choice remain). Many of these negotiations, and those discussed above in relation to what I have been calling Wicomb's project to render queer normative discourses of identity and belonging, continue in ways that are intertextual to a different degree in her most recent novel, *October*.

ON INTERTEXTUALITY AND RETURN TO THE *PAYS NATAL*

Wicomb concludes her essay on intertextuality, place, and postcolonial authorship with an enigmatic but characteristically suggestive reference to her own state of displacement, or, as she puts it, her 'own situation as a writer living in Scotland whose fictions are set in South Africa'. Promising to address the issue, she does so by means of a 'defer[ral] once again'—a digression by way of Mieke Bal and Kaja Silverman that addresses the crucial role of setting in the presentation of narrative. Bal and Silverman, Wicomb notes, each augment Emile Benveniste's assertion that 'the subject is constructed through language'; for Bal, setting serves crucially in the 'concretization and subjectification of space into place', while Silverman adds the conviction that 'the apprehension [by] the subject of his/her ownness' requires an awareness not only of 'mental registration' but of a bodily being, a 'physical feeling' of being *in* one's own skin and, by extension, in a particular place.[70] What this means for Wicomb and her own displacement is suggested rather than asserted. She gestures to Bessie Head's 'difficulties with setting fictions in her new country', Botswana, but notes that it was Head's embrace of a consciousness of bodily blackness that enabled her to transform spatial dislocatedness into a fictional space that could be inhabited. Head credited Robert Sobukwe, Wicomb notes, with giving her 'a comfortable black skin in which to live'. This notion of an inhabitable space 'renders problematic' Homi Bhabha's idea that the postcolonial space par excellence is an 'inbetween' one, Wicomb suggests; Bhabha's fetishization of the interstitial 'denies the postcolonial writer's corporeality in much the same way as does the foreign culture that hosts her invisibility, and thus legitimizes incivility'.[71] Wicomb's impatience with Bhabha's metaphorics is evident elsewhere, too. In what is perhaps her most famous essay, 'Shame and Identity: The Case of the coloured in South Africa', she criticizes his engagement with Gordimer's depiction of coloured characters in *My Son's Story* (1990). Wicomb finds in Bhabha's reliance on 'hybridity', the 'borderline', and the 'inbetween', all terms deployed in *The Location of Culture*, 'echoes of the tragic mode where lived experience is displaced by an aesthetics of theory'.[72]

Wicomb's essay on intertextuality concludes with yet another deft displacement in which space becomes metaphorical once more. 'The writer's envelope of space', Wicomb writes, 'find[s] a ready metaphor in the house of fiction, a structure that occupies a circumscribed place, the setting of which is literally foundational, which is to say that it can be taken for granted'. The '*homeliness*' of this space is what 'allows fictional characters to act and interact in the context of a shared history and a common identity', she concludes.[73] And yet here Bhabha's suggestion that the postcolonial writer finds creativity in 'the unhomely world' strikes Wicomb as a 'brave view' also worth considering, though she doubts the possibility of 'build[ing] such a house of fiction in a foreign world': 'I fear that what cravenly comes to mind is a construction that promises to be none other than a folly'.[74] This ambivalent, even testy treatment of the very possibility of a writer, feeling herself displaced, conveying a sense of belonging in the space in which she feels provisional—even within the space of fiction (in which setting 'can be taken for granted', in Wicomb's formulation)—naturally invites autobiographical interpretation, however suspicious of the impulse to read autobiographically Wicomb warns us to be.[75] She has herself said of Scotland that she has 'a ghost existence' there and that her 'whole intellectual and emotional life is in South Africa'.[76]

It is telling that while episodes in Wicomb's three novels published to date unfold in Scotland, specifically in Glasgow (David Dirkse recalls a trip there on ANC business in *David's Story*; Marion Campbell spends time there in *Playing in the Light*; Mercia Murray in *October* is, like Wicomb, an expatriate South African academic at one of the city's universities), each is set largely in South Africa. Scotland functions less to provide a realistic setting (and certainly not to provide a space within which to construct 'a house of fiction') than as space always already overlaid on the South African landscape. Scottish colonial administrators, engineers, and missionaries had a significant influence on the Cape

Colony in the nineteenth century and Scotland is consequently a place both uncannily familiar for Wicomb's South African characters (David Dirkse finds in Scotland 'the names of places at home: Kelvingrove, Glencoe, Aberdeen, Lyndoch, Sutherland, Fraserburgh, Dundee'), and yet wholly foreign: 'There was no danger of feeling lost in Scotland,' we read of David's experience, 'except that he felt dizzy with the to-ing and fro-ing between rain-sodden place names and the dry, dusty dorps at home.'[77] Scots settled in South Africa, men marrying local women to bequeath family names—*October*'s Murrays, *Playing in the Light*'s Campbells and McKays—that serve not only as markers of respectability to satisfy some coloured families' desire to differentiate themselves from black Africans or from supposedly uncivilized autochthonous peoples, but also as rejoinder to the countervailing (and, since 1994, fashionable) impulse to claim indigeneity, to endorse the kinds of exclusionary discourses of aboriginality and racial purity that Wicomb finds little different from apartheid's classificatory mania, and which additionally elides the significant history of slaves imported to the region from the Indian Ocean rim. Consider David's wife Sally's scathing dismissal of this discourse of purity in *David's Story*: 'I forget, it's the African roots that count. What do you expect to find? Ours are all mixed up and tangled; no chance of us being uprooted, because they're all in a magnificent knot, stuck'.[78]

For *October*'s Mercia Murray, an expatriate South African long resident in Glasgow, the potential for feeling multiply displaced is exacerbated, the idea of home particularly fraught. Mercia finds herself abandoned by her Scottish partner, Craig, and almost simultaneously summoned to South Africa by her brother Jake, apparently to take on his and his wife Sylvie's son Nicky: 'Please come and get the child. You are all he has left', Jake writes.[79] At issue therefore are concerns with the idea of family and the notion of home. 'An older woman is not only left, but left behind', Mercia thinks, supposing this refers also 'to reproduction, as if that is what every woman wants'.[80] She thinks about spawning salmon she had been taken to see by Craig, and thinks it repellent, 'the endless repetition, not only the biological imperative to reproduce, but the need to return to origins, to the very same stream, to make their babies back home'.[81] Her trauma is compounded when Craig's new partner, a Scot like himself, is soon pregnant. Reproduction is connected with the idea of origins, and concomitantly with notions of national or ethnic identity tied up with place.

Returning to Kliprand, the small Namaqualand town of her childhood and youth, Mercia finds Jake a recidivist alcoholic, 'a drunk' who 'wears his drunkenness on his sleeve', and Sylvie resentful and suspicious of her cosmopolitan sister-in-law.[82] It soon emerges that Jake and Mercia's late father, Nicholas, 'pillar of respectability' in the community, a dour and humourless Calvinist and stern disciplinarian in the siblings' childhood (he beat Jake mercilessly), had previously been Sylvie's older lover.[83] Far from having revenged himself on his father through an unsuitable marriage, Jake has in fact taken on the older man's hand-me-down mistress. Mercia, caught between a desire to understand Jake's torment, and frustration at his talent for self-destructive behaviour, must manage both her own sense of disappointment at having been abandoned by Craig and her growing sense of alienation and displacement from any sense of home—either in Glasgow, which 'cannot be her home', or in Kliprand, about which she wonders: '*How could anyone want to live there? Why would anyone stay there?*'[84]

In an attempt to negotiate these contending claims, Mercia begins to write a memoir titled tentatively 'Home' after Marilynne Robinson's novel of the same name, which she has been reading as a distraction from her academic monograph (on 'postcolonial memory').[85] The memoir becomes a form of self-analysis, a therapeutic means of approaching the brother who lies insensate in the next room, and the father who lies dead in the graveyard. Mercia is as sceptical about memoir as Wicomb is herself and feels a twinge of uncertainty about the ethics of her project, about the claim of the real: 'why not rather write a book for real people about real people?', Jake asks, to which she responds, 'a book about people like you? It's been [. . .] done to death'.[86] Mercia wants to think of the memoir as 'private' rather than exploitative, which she feels it would undoubtedly be if published, and yet she 'can't help wondering what Jake would make of being translated into these words'.[87] Cast as a reflection of Wicomb's own authorial concerns (which is not to impute an autobiographical imperative; speculation on intention is not the same as speculation about the author's life), what is at issue here is the claim of real subjects whose lives might mirror those of the fictional Jake's, indeed the idea more broadly of rendering lived experience as aesthetic object. A twin danger is the lure of nostalgia, Mercia senses (and behind her, Wicomb, surely the least nostalgic of South African authors), though for Mercia it would be 'a past that cannot be considered without irony'.[88] Irony, Mercia discovers, is no salve for the absence of a sense of uncomplicated nostalgia.

As one might expect, Mercia's writing project does not go well, as the following passages demonstrate. In the first the danger of generation, and in the second the danger of aestheticizing trauma, is raised, troubling the notion that setting, in the house of fiction, cannot be overdetermined:

> Mercia switches on her computer and stares dolefully at the screen. She wishes herself far away from this place called home. Never again will she complain about the pressures of academic life, the nightmare of trying to write. Being with family is far more stressful. She thinks of the parallel construction, being with child, and winces.[89]

> Mercia stares at the keyboard. This is a father-son story into which she has stumbled, nothing to do with her, and thus not fit for memoir. She cannot find the words; she would have to skirt around their story, around the father, and how then would she avoid the fiction that telling begets? Mercia wants nothing to do with artfulness; besides, having snaked its way into their lives, the thing must be laid to rest. It must not be given the chance to take another shape.[90]

Stories of oedipal anxiety, of challenges to patriarchal authority, have concerned Wicomb before. In 'In Search of Tommie', TS's absent father is called a *vark* (pig). So too is Jake's father: 'Dirty vark. May he squirm in his grave.'[91] What takes shape here is a narrative whose form suggests an uncanny mirroring of Robinson's *Home*, an intertextuality of which Mercia is aware and through which Wicomb engages in a conversation of great subtlety. Mercia thinks to herself that she 'may not be as good as the glorious sister in the novel', Robinson's novel's protagonist Glory (for Gloria), 'but the correspondences are there, including the ironic depiction of home'. As much as 'theirs—Mercia and Jake's story—is from a different continent, a different hemisphere, a different kind of people, a kind so lacking in what is known as western gentility', Mercia muses, the connections are such that when she reaches the end of Robinson's novel, 'she has doubts about her own memoir. Is hers not redundant for the telling?'[92]

The points of comparison with *Home* are many, though of course the differences counter Mercia's fears of redundancy. The chief protagonist of each is the daughter of a religious—in both cases Calvinist—household with Scottish connections.[93] The female protagonist in each novel bears a name reflecting their parents' expectations of a female child's virtue: in *October* Mercy, who renames herself Mercia but thinks of herself as an 'angel of mercy'; in *Home* Glory, whose sisters are Faith, Hope and Grace (or as her brother Jack jokes, '*Fides, Spes, Gratia, Gloria*').[94] Each woman has been an English or literature teacher, each has been expected to return home by her father, each has had traumatic breaks with partners to whom they have not been married.[95] Both novels are deeply concerned with the negotiation of parental disappointment: in *October*, this also becomes the disappointment with the parent, while in *Home*, Glory reflects frequently on her father's 'inexpressible disappointment'.[96] In each novel, it is the prodigal son's dissipation, born of a sense of unease with family and authority (represented by the paterfamilias) and his apparent abnegation of responsibility for a child (a girl born out of wedlock, who dies young, in *Home*; Nicky in *October*), that focuses the childless sister's own conflicted sense of belonging and futurity.[97] The prodigal sons are significantly also both novels' chief voices of engagement with politics, and in each, disappointment with the parent is tied clearly to the previous generation's complicity with reactionary politics—particularly in relation to race. In the case of *Home*, set during 1956, it is news of civil-rights protests that excites debate.[98] In *October*, Jake accuses his father of having been a 'bloody apartheid collaborator', of encouraging his children to be prejudiced against black people and to look down on the ordinary folk of Kliprand.[99] Mercia initially thinks the charges unfair, but is unable to challenge them; Glory merely absents herself from the worst of the quarrels in *Home*.

It is Jake and Mercia's father's insistence on their being better than other coloureds, those who were not 'English-speaking [...] with straight hair', that might be understood to have recast Mercia's ability to relate to the idea of home, and of South Africa as home.[100] A constrained notion of decency and civility replaces location in Nicholas Murray's sense of identity. Kliprand's coloureds are 'uncouth, uneducated people' in his eyes, and while the Murrays might live there, they could not 'think of belonging':

> As long as they could fit in anywhere with decent people, also city people, that was the important thing, that was where they would be at home. [...] Thus the notion of home was revised. Decoupled from location and belonging, and crucially from community, it was shrunk into a prefabricated rectangular structure of walls that could be dropped down anywhere as long as it was surrounded by people who looked like them, people related to them.[101]

In *October*, home also always significantly (and self-consciously) bears the sinister echo of the apartheid government's policy of granting 'citizenship of new Homelands' to black South Africans on the basis of ethnicity.[102]

Mercia struggles with a sense of obligation similar to Glory's in Robinson's novel, questioning, with Glory (more or less precisely, 'here' becoming '*there*' in *October*), 'How could anyone want to live here? [....] Why would anyone stay here?'[103] In *Home*, Glory finds that her return changes her relationship to memory entirely: Gilead, her hometown, had long been 'the subject and scene of nostalgic memory', but 'her returning now, to stay, as her father said, had turned memory portentous' and caused it to 'overrun its bounds' in a manner not to be desired.[104] While Glory returns 'to the *pays natal*' permanently, however much it feels 'like exile', there can, for Wicomb's Mercia, 'be no return to the pays natal' at all.[105] Mercia's is a state of permanent displacement from home as fixed location; she is 'liminal', as her adopted name—for Mercia, the dominant kingdom of Anglo-Saxon Britain that occupied the location of the present-day English Midlands and is derived etymologically from the Old English for *borderers*—suggests.[106] And if South Africa remains home, it is as time or affect rather than space, she discovers. Perhaps it is in language itself, and language in which a relationship is asserted, however temporarily, that she finds a provisional home. Mercia feels closest to belonging in Glasgow when working-class Scots call her 'pal': in these casual moments of contact ('There you are, pal, or, Got the time, pal?') she feels 'named, [...] the warmth of an embrace, a welcome that came close to a sense of belonging'. Though here, as ever, Wicomb's characters cannot but undercut such provisional certainty: 'Whatever that [belonging] was, Mercia was careful to add. And Craig teased, Oops, we mustn't let go of the exilic condition now, must we? But she knew that he knew what she meant.'[107]

FICTION AS HOME-FROM-'HOME'

Where, then, is home? Wicomb's transnationalism is not exceptional, nor is a broad notion of expatriation foreign to South African letters. Indeed, the history of South African literature in English (in particular), can be regarded as always-already a history of expatriation if we expand the idea of expatriation (whether in the sense of having been banished, or being out of country by choice) to texts themselves, in their material instantiations. Much of the earliest published imaginative writing in the Cape Colony was by British expatriates (think of Thomas Pringle, admired by Coleridge). High-Victorian narratives of imperial adventure set in the region by H. Rider Haggard, Bertram Mitford, and others, and more inventive works (from which the country's serious writers have sought to claim descent), like Olive Schreiner's *The Story of an African Farm* (1883), were all published in Britain. This was long the pattern: writers desiring returns, symbolic or material, left—or their works did. Coetzee's works did not, at least initially, wholly conform to this trend: *Dusklands* was published by a small, local, independent press in 1974, and Coetzee succeeded, until the mid 1980s, in fighting to allow it to publish South African editions. He declared in interview in 1978 that he was 'suspicious of lines of division between a European context and a South African context' in relation to literary production, pointing out that the local 'experience' remained 'largely colonial', as evidenced by the fact that the country's 'literary products' were routinely 'flown to the metropolitan centre and re-exported to us from there at a vastly increased price'; this alone, he suggested, 'should give people pause before they start talking about a South African literature'.[108]

Nor is Wicomb's work unusual in representing expatriate South Africans who return. We find similar representations in recent novels by Zakes Mda (*The Heart of Redness*, 2000), Eben Venter (*Horrelpoot*, 2006, translated as *Trencherman* in 2008), Mark Behr (*Kings of the Water*, 2010), Patrick Flanery (*Absolution*, 2012), and Marli Roode (*Call It Dog*, 2013), to name but a few examples. They also appear in poetry like Catherine Taylor's *Apart* (2012), and in a range of creative non-fiction (Rob Nixon's *Dreambirds* and Breyten Breytenbach's *Dog Heart*, both published in 1999). Recall that Marlene van Niekerk's *Agaat* is framed by the thoughts of a South African-born character returning briefly from exile in Canada. In many of these works, relationships with the parent or family who remained are unpicked in scenes of a return amid crisis. S.J. Naudé's *Alfabet van die voëls* (2011), translated by the author as *The Alphabet of Birds* (2015), features several characters that live or have lived abroad. Many of these texts test the generic expectations of narratives of return to a native land, enacting with requisite self-reflexivity an awareness of the difficulties of inhabiting the subject position *native* in a country in which such positions are always overdetermined in relation to the spectres of race and structural privilege. In respect of these writers, we might need, in framing a methodology equal to the complex transnational investments of authors (and likely readers), and in order to take account of the ways literary products are rendered commodities in a marketplace, to pay attention to the multiply suggestive ways of understanding expatriation (escaping the shadow of the fatherland and father-figure; being outside the place with which one continues to feel inextricably, ineluctably bound) in relation to literary representation and also to the fates of the texts in which they are to be found (considering their readers, their publishing contexts, the institutions through which they are marked or marketed, whether or not in relation to categories of national belonging).

Book-historical considerations of the location of publication of texts has not been a principal concern of this study, though I have posed such questions elsewhere.[109] Suffice it to observe that Wicomb's texts have all been published in South Africa—though *You Can't Get Lost in Cape Town* only had a local impression some years after the end of apartheid. Wicomb's work is routinely published in the United States, but she has struggled, since her debut, to find British publishers willing to take chances on writing, by a black woman, which refuses the expectation of social realism or autobiography.[110] What makes Wicomb's work so uniquely engaging in the context of present negotiations of what it means to be at home, I contend, is that it recognizes that if being at home (indeed, in the act of reading, of being present) is only ever a construct (and a function of the text), then the intertextuality with which Wicomb conjures is a textual equivalent of her characters' displacements, and perhaps even of her own restless transnationalism.

Intertextuality marks postcolonial writing in particular, Wicomb claims in her extraordinary essay on Coetzee's *Disgrace*, 'Translations in the Yard of Africa'. Here she revisits a number of theoretical engagements with the idea of intertextuality as translation: George Steiner on what Wicomb calls 'intracultural translation'; Bakhtin's dialogics; Kristeva on intertextuality; Barthes on the 'vast stereophony' of textuality. Summarizing Kristeva—but offering her own gloss, too—Wicomb concludes as follows:

> The function of the author then is both junctive (i.e. ties together narrative and citational utterances) and translative (transfers utterances from one

textual space into another) which changes its ideologemes. It is precisely because of its translative possibilities that intertextuality as writing strategy has become such a staple of postcolonial discourse [. . .].[111]

Foregrounding authorship through metafictional turns, staging displacement, offering the reader writers writing, has more profound resonances in a South African context, however. Wicomb writes about the revelation of the author's intervention at the end of Morrison's *Jazz* that the '[a]bandonment' of the narrator 'foregrounds the artifice': 'Morrison's reader, having reached the end of the narrative, is free to interpret the story and to recycle it, as indeed she, the author, has done'.[112] Wicomb performs a similar act of revelation in *David's Story*, but there does so proleptically in a self-dramatizing 'Preface' in which the unnamed female frame narrator declares that the novel 'is and is not David's Story'.[113] The explosion of the narrator-amanuensis's computer screen at the novel's end seems a more violent progenitor of Mercia's act of deleting the icon for her memoir-project 'Home' in *October*.[114] Wicomb's metafictional layering and her desire to unsettle the occasion of production of narrative can be read as a cautious contextualization (or an insistence of the fictional nature) of the acts of storytelling to which her narratives play host. She gives a sense, in the essay on intertextuality to which I have been returning, of what might be at stake in this operation.

Discussing Ivan Vladislavić's short story 'Kidnapped', she observes that postcolonial texts frequently interrogate 'the notion of authorship and authority', and she cites Gayatri Spivak's distinction between 'metropolitan decentred subject and Rushdie's staging of the author' (in *The Satanic Verses*) as 'representation of decentring the subject, so that Rushdie's is "more like a self-ironic yet self-based modernism than an object coded or subject decentred avant garde"' (here Wicomb quotes Spivak). Wicomb's gloss on Spivak's formulation gestures at the implications of her own staging of storytelling. Such 'foregrounding of the authorial', she writes, is a 'departure from the usual traffic with subjectivity', but in place of 'staging representation, such resurrection of the author is also concerned with asserting an ethics of authorial responsibility in an ostentatious coupling of author and narrator'.[115] Something similar can be said of the many author-narrators in Wicomb's fiction: all become agents of such an ethics. Wicomb's embrace of the metafictional and of intertextuality comprises a queer ethical response to the strange now-time of contemporary South African socialities and imaginaries. It is a textual, but also an ethical, strategy, one that is particularly suited to an oeuvre imbued with a frustration at the inevitability of the disappointment of utopian expectations, wise to the habit nations have of cycling back to the hearth, the heteronormative family, ideas of ethnic purity, abhorrence of the in-between. Wicomb's narrative ethics will have much to say to and about South Africa for some considerable time.

'Unsupported. Stuck. Frustrated. Private security guards outside the Department of Student Affairs after students were evicted from the building during the 2016 #FeesMustFall, #FreeDecolonisedEducation #BringBackOurCadres #End Outsourcingmovement. Steve Biko Students Union Building, University of Cape Town. 4 October 2016.'

Image source: @therealcityofcapetown Instagram contributor @tships (Leanne Brady). Reproduced with permission.

6

Stasis Anxiety

On Contemporary Waithood

South Africa I have loved you all life long
But April 1994 is but a dim dream today.
Twenty years is more than enough.
I can't stand the waiting.

—Sindiwe Magona, from
'The More Things Change' (2011)[1]

Consider the opening lines of two recent novels by young black South African writers, both set in Cape Town in the recent past. In each, first-person narrators—both black men in their late twenties or early thirties—offer accounts, from positions coterminous with their acts of narration (though each includes some retrospection), of their experience of a present characterized by torpor, uncertainty, and disappointment. They speak, largely in the present tense, about an imperfect condition of stasis.

> This is not how things are meant to be. I walk past sickly people in the street. One man's face is charred, with pink lips that have been licked by spirits. He moves like he is dying. A disabled man sits in his wheelchair in front of the Claremont BMW dealership; he looks around absent-mindedly with narrow eyes. I cross Main Road and wait for a taxi a few metres before Edgars. It does not take long for one to stop. [. . .] I sit in the first row facing the front. The dark-brown seats are oily and torn.[2]

> This morning, when I opened my eyes, I found another warm Saturday wrapping itself around the peninsula. Someone had left Cissie's living-room window open again, the one on the east-facing wall [. . .]. Standing there in front of the glass, I couldn't tell you which one of us had left the window open, only that when I heard the wind blowing under the wooden sash again, I felt I was on my own here. There was a blanket of smog stretching itself thick over the rim of the metropolis, and everything looked inflated and exhausted all at once.[3]

In the first extract, from a novel published in 2013, the narrator describes a street scene peopled by an assortment of the sick, disabled, and intoxicated, one that offers objective correlatives for his own state of desperation—and, it will emerge, mental illness. It is as if his environment, even the minibus-taxi he hails (as well as the very fact of his reliance on this mode of transportation: the bus is contrasted with the luxury cars nearby), offers metaphors for his situation: the taxi seats, matching the colour of its passengers, are tired and worn. The taxi journey becomes a metaphor for the protagonist's movements through this stratified postapartheid space, more specifically his entrapment in the role to which he appears to have been consigned: '*This is where I'm supposed to get off. But I just do not know where*'.[4] Anxious, stuck in a cycle of repetitious behaviour, our narrator is alienated from an environment he should be able to navigate: he is a citizen of the new South Africa, after all. The echo of that great novel of post-colonial (African) disappointment and existential anxiety, *The Beautyful Ones Are Not Yet Born*, which we might discern in this opening, confirms a sense that the affective register of the book is very much a part of its political challenge. Armah's 1968 novel also begins with an unnamed passenger in a soiled and rusty bus, one that, like post-independence Ghana, barely functions, moving forward, like the nation, in shudders and jolts, managed by the corrupt and transporting the somnolent to—or from (it matters little which)—a missed appointment with a promised future that has not come to pass.[5] That novel's protagonist, known only as the Man, is both a representative alienated postcolonial native and a particular individual, with family ties, friends, and obligations. The same is true of this alienated, young South African, Mangaliso 'Manga' Zolo, the narrator-protagonist of Songeziwe Mahlangu's debut novel, *Penumbra.*

The second extract is from a novel published in 2014, Masande Ntshanga's *The Reactive.* (The lines in fact begin the novel's first part, which follows a brief prologue.) Here we encounter a similarly stagnant situation in a city that comes, in a variant of the pathetic fallacy, to seem as tired and soiled—as 'inflated and exhausted'—as the narrator and his friends, barely awake from one of the regular sessions with drugs with which they palliate their present disaffection. 'Where I am right now', this protagonist, Nathi Mda, goes on to explain, 'is Newlands', a real, a solidly middle-class suburb, though here also an ironic nod to the *new land* that postapartheid South Africa was meant to become. The 'situation', Nathi continues, is easily explained: he and his friends wake up, take a variety of pills, and 'drift through' the weekend in a haze.[6] In interview in November 2014, Ntshanga explained that his debut novel (as well as a short story, 'Space', which won him the inaugural PEN International New Voices award in 2013) dealt 'with the listlessness of youth', was 'about people living in the vicinity of great trauma, and about people who are waiting for something, but who aren't quite sure of what that thing is'. He speaks of his characters being 'in a suspended state', which is to say in a situation of stasis, a standing still rather than a moving forward.[7] Lauren Berlant would likely call them stuck. Each novel self-consciously explores routes out of impasse in a way that raises questions about the role of enchantment in political life in the present (a point I will elaborate in due course).

The first chapter of this book looked to Ingrid Winterbach's oeuvre for representations of a kind of contemporary stuckness, a postapartheid version of the condition of anxious stasis that Vincent Crapanzano described in *Waiting: The Whites of South Africa* (1985). I suggested that Winterbach's examinations of stasis might be understood with recourse to the idea of a hybrid genre, the situation tragedy, which Berlant outlines in *Cruel Optimism* (2011) in relation to post-1990s fiction and film in Europe and North America, read with the idea of postcolonial tragedy adumbrated by David Scott in *Conscripts of Modernity* (2004) and *Omens of Adversity* (2014). This final chapter considers how a similar condition might extend beyond white experience in the present, and whether a version of that generic hybrid can be observed in work by some of the most engaging of a new generation of young black writers (note Nathi's identification of a 'situation', quoted above). I am interested in how varieties of waiting feature in such writing, and in how this work deals with what I have been discussing as a constellated structure of (bad) feeling(s) in early twenty-first-century South Africa. Individual novels can confirm a shared horizon of expectation, or disaffection, and these texts do precisely that.

BLACK FICTIONS OF THE PRESENT

Over the past decade and a half, a number of important voices have emerged, each concerned to engage with the experience of black urban subjects (in particular), in novels that offer powerful indictments of the promises of the liberation movement—and of the neoliberal consensus that has stymied any real socio-economic revolution in South Africa. Representations of the seeming dead-ends to which many young South Africans have been consigned by the legacies of structural inequalities fostered by apartheid and by the accommodations with local and global capital of the post-liberation government, provide subject matter for work, for example, by Niq Mhlongo, whose *Dog Eat Dog* (2004) and *After Tears* (2007) follow young black men, university dropouts and others, struggling with disaffection and high expectations in the wake of the transition. Kgebetli Moele's first novel, *Room 207* (2006), covered similar territory; it won a number of prizes, but divided critics. The academic Michael

Titlestad, who served that year as a judge in a local literary competition, suggested that Moele's novel had been poorly edited and too hastily published, that local publishers had taken to rushing out books that offered 'seemingly unmediated vision[s] of a gritty post-apartheid reality' without paying due attention to the conditions that explained the tonal and stylistic awkwardness of such work—deficits occasioned by long-running failures of the education system included. As the political emergency of the 1970s and 1980s had subordinated aesthetic experimentation and literary avant-gardism to social realism, so a similar impulse to represent black lives as they were lived was leading to the publication of texts that were 'unfinished'. Titlestad called Moele's novel 'fundamentally unsatisfying' and suggested that it eschewed 'the niceties of novelistic prose and the formal criteria of plot and character development in favour of immediacy. Structurally it sprawls, comprising as it does seemingly random encounters and loosely related narrative lines.'[8]

Such sprawling and limning of loose relations might tell us something about the experiences of the characters represented, their sense of affective and temporal disappointment in the new era, though Titlestad's point was that the novels did not set out to stage awkwardness in service of such a critique—they were simply not well enough written, edited, or copy-edited.[9] Other novels were similarly attuned to post-Truth-and-Reconciliation-Commission South Africa's desire for a multiplicity of new voices, and specifically for representations of black characters negotiating the new order, but many of these struck (largely white) critics as better written. Sifiso Mzobe's *Young Blood* (2010), a fast-paced story of cars, drugs, and the aspirations of inhabitants of the sprawling township of Umlazi, on the fringes of Durban, also did well in the literary prize stakes.[10] *Young Blood* stages conspicuous consumption as trope, and while not necessarily offering a structural critique of that which this might indict, joined novels like K. Sello Duiker's *Thirteen Cents* (2000) in exploring the effects of crime on black subjects—a salutary counter to many (white) South Africans' fascination with crime fiction that often features white subjects, playing on ongoing paranoia amongst the affluent about crime, and offering a surrogate for fantasies of the reimposition of social order by the institutions of state.

Perhaps the most successful of these new voices in the immediate postapartheid period, however, was Kopano Matlwa's debut, *Coconut* (2007), published after the manuscript won a European Union-sponsored competition for unpublished authors. *Coconut* contrasts the lives of two young women from very different social milieus: Ofilwe (Fifi), whose nouveau riche family has moved to a gated community in Johannesburg; and Fikile (Fiks), who lives in poverty with an abusive uncle in the squalor of a township. Fifi's mother struggles with the transition from poverty and a life lived in Sepedi, while Fifi herself encounters racist micro-aggression in the playground and at sleepovers (her brother, Tshepo, invests in pan-Africanist Black Consciousness politics as escape). Fikile, meanwhile, waits on tables at the Silver Spoon Coffee Shop, frequented by Fifi's family.[11] As the title suggests, the novel grapples with similar problematics to those identified by Frantz Fanon in *Black Skin, White Masks*—hierarchies of race, the dilemmas of the black subject co-opted into the structures of privilege associated with whiteness yet required to conform to a different set of rules in order to be regarded as civilized (and so worthy of citizenship), and the psychic violence of such accommodations. This novel, too, shows us an urban South African reality transforming under the conditions of accommodation with global finance, consumer capitalism, and an exacerbation of the divide between rich (still largely, but not entirely white) and poor.

Some of these novels go further than others in locating the nexus of neoliberalism, gender violence, horizontal violence, and infrastructural degradation at which some of the causes of the stagnation of postapartheid South Africa's economic, political, and cultural renovations might be located. All, however, would seem susceptible of the critique contained in Achille Mbembe's observation, in September 2015 (against the background of the student protests that were galvanizing a new activism amongst the generation born during and immediately after the years of transition), that 'tropes of pain and suffering' had come to saturate 'current narratives of selfhood and identity', and especially ('[i]ronically', in Mbembe's analysis) amongst an emergent black middle class. These tropes had, he wrote,

> become the register through which many now represent themselves to themselves and to the world. To give account of who they are, or to explain themselves and their behavior to others, they increasingly tend to frame their life stories in terms of how much they have been injured by the forces of racism, bigotry and patriarchy.

'Often under the pretext that the personal is political', Mbembe continues, 'autobiographical and at times self-indulgent "petit bourgeois" discourse has replaced structural analysis. Personal feelings now suffice. There is no need to mount a proper argument.'[12] Mbembe is not here addressing literary representations specifically, rather a mode of speaking he observes having come to prominence in testimony and statements of protest activism in the public sphere. And yet his analysis offers a useful—and polemical—prompt for the reader of fiction, in particular fiction in which the reader encounters a black first-person narrator, perhaps especially speaking in the present tense, about feelings of personal injury and impasse. It has been a contention of every chapter of this study that the personal *is* political, and that while '[p]ersonal feelings' (especially bad ones) might not 'suffice', affect is a site (a space and a time) for diagnosis and prognostication—for the registering of political possibility. In Pumla Gqola's words, 'South African literature has veered away from a preoccupation with the spectacular contest between dominant and disempowered to a textured exploration of emotion, possibility and entanglement.'[13] I am less interested in whether or not this is a good or a bad thing (Mbembe might certainly be understood to be arguing the latter), than with what we might *do* with such explorations.

I turn to the two novels from which I quoted at the beginning of this chapter, Mahlangu's *Penumbra* and Ntshanga's *The Reactive*, in part because they seem to me a departure from Mhlongo's, Moele's, Matlwa's, and Mzobe's texts, in their formal assuredness, their awareness of intervening in a developing canon, in their self-conscious allusiveness (indeed, their intertextuality—a feature of many of the texts discussed in this book), and in their engagement with the lives of apparently and always precariously middle-class characters, for whom 'petit bourgeois' discourse (of personal freedom, or the logic of the market) constitutes both a measure of achievement and a trap. This is to say that each text succeeds in ways that are new and commendable in registering the affective experience of stasis in contemporary South Africa, a stasis that I seek to understand in relation to Wendy Brown's discussion of the eclipsing of the individual subject of political rights—also the individual capable of collective action in the public sphere—by the neoliberal subject, whose very life is framed by its potential to be understood as capital, alongside Giorgio Agamben's elaboration of the ancient Greek understanding of *stasis* as civil war.

DOWN AND OUT IN NEWLANDS AND OBSERVATORY

Songeziwe Mahlangu's *Penumbra* registers the complexity of urban life in which young black (socially) middle-class characters might be at home equally in jazz bars in Cape Town's student-bohemian Observatory neighbourhood as at township barbeque joints. Set largely in Cape Town, but with short diversions to King William's Town (where Mahlangu himself grew up), the novel is a first-person account by Manga Zolo, a graduate of the University of Cape Town, in his mid-twenties, currently working as an intern at a medical aid company. Here he is given no responsibility (his boss is racist) and is profoundly bored; each day there is 'like detention, just waiting for the day to come to an end'.[14] Manga feels that his 'life is a railway line along which the days drag' and he has 'become the rust-stained stones beside the line'.[15] But Manga's malaise is also psychic and spiritual: he is not sure what precisely he should desire, and everywhere he suspects the hand of sinister forces. The novel follows him around the southern suburbs as he hangs out with a series of acquaintances representing a range of possibilities: his friend Nhlakanipho aspires to wealth with little idea of what might earn it; Mfundo is a credit-card fraudster; Rasun spouts new-age platitudes; Ndlela, a school friend, has embraced corporate culture and is on the fast-track to a business leadership role. Ndlela says things like: 'What we need now are people who can do the job. We need to buckle down and work. It's high time black students excel at university, come top of their class.'[16] He tells Manga he should be able to save money, run a small car, lift himself up, in other words model the 'responsible self-investor and self-provider' demanded by neoliberalism's 'practice of responsibilization' (in Wendy Brown's helpful formulation).[17] Ndlela asks: 'Do you think you are anywhere near your potential?'[18]

But there are other models of potentiality in play (sometimes fascinatingly imbricated). Resigning from his internship, Manga drifts about, looking for answers. He attends a church service with a Mozambican migrant acquaintance and evangelical ministry meetings with an African American family friend, Paul, who criticizes Manga's interests in Malcolm X and communism. Moses, another friend, is 'bitter' and 'aggrieved' about conditions in the townships. Paul is simply despondent, 'does not see any hope' for South Africa, 'even with the upcoming World Cup' (the novel's present unfolds in 2010).[19] With his flatmate, Tongai, a Zimbabwean interning at an ad agency, Manga attends the Cape Town Book Fair, though he is dismissive of what he calls 'Tongai's fascination with African intellectuals'—including Achille Mbembe. 'These guys', Manga suggests, 'keep coming up with verbose theories, whereas circumstances are not changing.'[20] Everywhere, it seems, past promise—and, more specifically, the disappointment of promise—is invoked. In an effort to drown his despair, Manga spends what little money he has left on alcohol, drugs, and sex. 'I am disappearing into a precarious existence', he thinks at one point. He phones his mother and tells her: 'I'm not well'.[21] After an apparent psychotic episode, he is hospitalized and fetched home by his mother. Cape Town, it seems, has defeated him, though the reader infers that a recovery might be possible back in the Eastern Cape. I will have something to say about this return to roots in due course.

Masande Ntshanga's *The Reactive* features another first-person narrator in his late twenties. Nathi Mda, like Mahlangu's Manga, has a mixed history of tertiary education—he dropped out of a journalism degree at the University of Cape Town and completed a science diploma at Peninsula Technikon. The novel is set principally over a few days in 2003, with a coda a couple of months later and flashbacks to earlier periods. Nathi had found work after graduation in Peninsula Technikon's molecular biology department as an HIV lab technician, testing samples for positive reactives (whence the novel's title). After being mugged, an event precipitating a torpor that is also connected to guilt over his complicity in the death of his younger brother, Luthando, ten years earlier, Nathi leaves his job, though not before purposely infecting himself with HIV.[22] He uses his severance pay and medical compensation to buy a treatment plan that pays for anti-retrovirals (ARVs), at this time not widely available or provided by the state. Finding that the HI virus has a very slow effect on him, however, he takes to selling his ARVs in order to buy intoxicants of various kinds, aided and abetted by two friends, whom he meets at an HIV and drug-counselling clinic in Wynberg. Ruan Russell, who works unhappily for his uncle's firm, had been attending the clinic to 'shop for a social issue they could use for their corporate responsibility strategy', while Cecelia (Cissie) Evans works at a day-care centre in Mowbray that has admitted its first HIV-positive child.[23] Together the friends spend their spare time sniffing industrial-strength glue and benzene, popping Ibuprofens, or scoring dagga (cannabis, marijuana). Days pass in a haze, and the reader is offered engaging descriptions of Nathi's experiences of disjunctive temporality: 'I guess this is how everything moves today. It's like riding on the back of a large, dying mammal. It matches the tepid warmth, and I close my eyes against it.'[24] In fact, life itself comes to seem like nothing but a series of periods of waiting for everyone in the novel. Each Sunday, Cissie visits her aunt in a Muizenberg nursing home, a liminal space of waiting (for recovery, or to die), while her own apartment building in Newlands is a converted nursing home.[25] The Wynberg clinic attendees are all waiting, too. One, Olive, has a respiratory obstruction that causes rasping breathing that sounds to Nathi like 'a whistle of the damage she carries inside her, or maybe it's just human wear: the kind we all have, waiting to waylay us'.[26] Cape Town itself is a space marked by disjunctive temporalities—time 'seems to speed up here, and then it stalls, and then it seems to speed up again before it stalls', observes Nathi, 'I guess this is what they mean when they call Cape Town the city of slumber'.[27] The city's pace is exemplified in the slow progress of a container ship that Nathi and friends watch lazily one day from Bloubergstrand, where they imagine, too, all that might have happened in the past at any single spot on the beach.[28]

Finally, entirely appositely for my analysis, Nathi's full name, Lindanathi, means 'wait with us' in isiXhosa, although he observes that '[w]hat I'm meant to be waiting for, or who I'm meant to be waiting with, I was never told'. 'Ever since I could spell its ten letters out, I've been trying to make it shorter, into five', as if trying to speed up time, he notes.[29] Nathi suggests that his decision to infect himself with the HI virus, to become 'a reactive', was an attempt to find a way out of inaction, a way of restaging a reaction in his own body that he should have had in the world: 'I never had the reactions I needed for myself, and I couldn't react to you when you called to me for help, so I gave my own body something it couldn't flee from.'[30] The novel concludes with Nathi's address to his brother (the whole book is addressed to the dead): 'in the end, I guess this is to you, Luthando. This is your older brother, Lindanathi, and I'm ready to react for us.'[31]

Cissie suggests that the condition of waiting in which she and her friends find themselves makes them slaves: 'Maybe it's this whole slavery thing.'[32] Her salutary injunction, only half understood by the character herself, to think about the effects of structural violence is set against the inclination (represented by Ruan) to see a non-political state of existential ennui (just as, in *Penumbra*, Manga comes to find Sartre's *Nausea*, which he reads on Tongai's recommendation, too opaque and non-specific).[33]

> Ruan looks up and says, dude, explain this slavery thing to me. He gets up to take a thin book from the counter and flops himself down on a torn bean-bag. Then he starts reading the book—*A Happy Death* by Camus—from the back, his eyes training the sentences inward, as if the French author had written a Japanese manga.
>
> Cissie just says her word again.
>
> Slavery. [...]
>
> You know what I mean, she says. The three of us, we're basically slaves.[34]

Nathi also does not understand the connection, observing that he and his friends 'each wrote matric in the country's first batch of Model Cs', which is to say were amongst the first pupils in multiracial schools after 1991: 'The three of us aren't slaves.'[35] They are all comparatively middle class, if precariously so: Model C schools were fee-paying (white) government schools whose governing bodies voted to admit students of colour who could pay the fees, or qualify for scholarships (Nathi is black; Cissie is white; Ruan is, it is implied, coloured).[36] To what, then, *are* they slaves, if not their own addictions?

Here the curious middle section of Ntshanga's novel seems to suggest an answer. A strange man enters the characters' lives, a potential client looking to buy all of their ARVs. He deposits money into Ruan's account but then sends them scans of their identity documents: he knows everything about them. Later, he summons them to a house and hypnotizes them from a laptop (they are exhausted, they need sleep, he tells them). It transpires that what he really wants is for them to launder his money (after several days in Ruan's account, it disappears), and to pass cash and counterfeit identity documents to a child who lives in an apartment building near Cissie's. 'We never hear from the ugly man again. I guess there isn't much else to say about him. He's just one of this city's many ciphers, we decide, one of the strange things that happen in the alleyways of the Southern Peninsula.'[37] The plot twists suggest forces beyond the imaginings of ordinary citizens; perhaps this is a version of the situation tragedy overlaid with the speculative fiction genre that has produced so many locally successful South African novels in recent years, many of them set in Cape Town—I am thinking of dystopian work like Lauren Beukes's *Moxyland* (2008), as well as more gently speculative fictions like Henrietta Rose-Innes's *Green Lion* (2015). But so drug-addled are the characters at this point in *The Reactive* that we have no way of knowing whether Nathi really believes any of what he narrates as having happened, or whether it could have happened as he narrates it. If it does, we might read the mysterious man, who is grotesquely disfigured and hides his face behind a mask, as a stand-in for any number of faceless entities who surveil, direct, beguile, swindle, or indebt ordinary South Africans. At this point the novel comes to look like an allegory of the neoliberal capitalization of life, against which no political action seems possible in this exhausted social milieu.

We have a suggestion that this is how we might understand the mysterious man through a game the three friends play while intoxicated. They print out pictures of the faces of three African leaders, turn these into masks, then declare themselves not the historical figures, but the countries themselves. 'Ruan's up first and he tells us we should call him the country of Zimbabwe. [. . .] [H]e has thirteen million people inside of him, and lying down he's four hundred thousand square kilometres wide, and the way his pockets are set up, only seventy per cent of his people live under the breadline.' Next comes Cissie, who gets Liberia's Charles Taylor, then Nathi, with DRC's Joseph Kabila. Nathi reports Cissie's gloss on the implications of this game: 'you know when people say the people? I always think presidents are what they mean when they say the people'.[38] This places the novel suddenly in the realm of debates about the commons and a version of postcolonial tragic modernity. African liberation movements' capacities to revert to authoritarianism and exploitation have been well evidenced. Yet the turn to authoritarianism is not exclusively an African phenomenon, nor one that might be located only in the body of a president: *The Reactive*'s disfigured man is linked by his mask to the figures of the African despots, but he also suggests a conflation of the operations of the market (he is a customer) and of global capital (he moves money effortlessly across borders). Recall here anthropologist Hylton White's observation, referred to in this book's Introduction, that global conditions of what he calls a politics of 'authoritarian post-Fordism' map convincingly onto present South African (and African) conditions.[39]

When Ntshanga's protagonists debate what to do about the strange man, Cissie suggests that the worst outcome would be 'that someone dies, and that's already kind of happened, hasn't it?' (she means that Nathi has HIV).[40] 'It's a scam', Nathi says of the man's promised transaction. Ruan says: 'we should just use the money and then kill ourselves'; this 'could be a life'.[41] *The Reactive* wants, in fact, to suggest that this is *no* kind of life, and a statement that approximates this judgment is given to Nathi's uncle, Bhut'Vuyo, who is presented as voice of moral authority and mediated tradition in the text. (It is he whose message urging Nathi to undergo circumcision precipitates memories of Luthando's death during an initiation retreat years before on which Nathi promised to accompany him but did not; Nathi has consequently not attained the status of adult man, according to Xhosa custom, but is trapped in a version of minor waithood.) Bhut'Vuyo's words are 'That's not living'—although this is, in context, specifically a description of conditions in the township of Khayelitsha. Bhut'Vuyo still thinks Nathi is at university, that he will one day be able 'to change all of this', though adds '[y]ou and your whites' and it is initially not clear whether this is an instance of defeatism, scorn, envy, or of admiration, at his nephew's becoming an approximation of 'white' (whether with a positive or negative connotation), or whether he is being ironic (he laughs and a 'smile stays on his face for a long time'). Bhut'Vuyo builds his family its own toilet, Nathi notes, though it is 'more of a gesture than a necessity'; in fact, Nathi realizes, it constitutes 'a political project'.[42]

Manga's situation, and Nathi's, corresponds well to what Alcinda Honwana (in a 2013 essay) calls 'waithood', a 'twilight' or 'interstitial' zone typically associated with a transition to adulthood—the space in which 'young people are forced to make choices' that 'define their relationships towards work, family, and intimacy, as well as the type of citizens they will become'—but that has become less a period of transition than a replacement for adulthood itself in many parts of the world.[43] Honwana borrows the term from Diane Singerman's work on young adults and marriage customs in the Middle East and also cites the *geração à rascal* (precarious generation) movement in Portugal, and the *indignados* (indignant) movement in Spain, both mobilizing unemployed young people on the left, as evidence of global connections (or at least similarities) amongst popular expressions of disaffection with neoliberalism. Hylton White comments on the widespread sense, in Zuma's South Africa, of 'people who say that freedom of a political sort has been compromised by states of arrested development in personal life, occasioned above all by joblessness'.[44]

The point Mahlangu's and Ntshanga's novels animate is that conditions of waithood or arrested development are not limited to those without employment or (limited) means, those about whom, for instance, Duiker wrote in *Thirteen Cents* (2000) or Phaswane Mpe in *Welcome to Our Hillbrow* (2001). They suggest that such states of impasse are more widespread and associated—as for many of Manga's friends in *Penumbra*—with an investment in conventional global good-life fantasies that have replaced narratives of promised (local) liberation. We continue to invest in such fantasies, even as we understand that they are, in fact, not good for us, that our optimism might in fact be toxic, in Berlant's formulation. 'In scenarios of cruel optimism', she argues, 'we are forced to suspend ordinary notions of repair and flourishing to ask whether the survival scenarios we attach to those affects weren't the problem in the first place.'[45] These scenarios cast the young black citizen as 'responsibilized' subject, whose very conditions of life (like Nathi's ARVs) are economized.

Each novel's dense allusiveness puts it in conversation with representations of precarity and disappointment that extend beyond South Africa's particular conditions. In *Penumbra*, for instance, Tongai is a loyal listener to the popular radio show *This American Life*, which Manga describes as 'a depressing radio programme on Sunday evenings [. . .] about the blandness of lives led by Americans working dry jobs like call-centre agents'.[46] Manga also reads a great deal, and here *Penumbra* departs from the field of comparable novels by showing us characters who quote hip-hop and *kwaito* lyrics alongside Can Themba and J.M. Coetzee, are as interested in sex and money as in Sartre, and as able to share the frustrations of office life as the subjects of *This American Life* (whose work ranges more widely than Manga's description—though conditions of precarity and stasis are frequent points of connection with the world depicted in *Penumbra*).[47]

STASIS AS CIVIL WAR

I have suggested that both *Penumbra* and *The Reactive* offer glimpses of the experiences of subjects of South Africa's neoliberal postcolony and I have already invoked political theorist Wendy Brown to suggest that neoliberalism's responsibilizing practice is at stake in some of the pressures faced by Mahlangu's character, Manga Zolo, in *Penumbra*.[48] Brown is helpful in understanding the effects of a 'neoliberal reason' she identifies as 'ubiquitous today in statecraft and the workplace, in jurisprudence, education, culture, and a vast range of quotidian activity'.[49] In order to consider how literary representations of stasis in the novels under discussion might point to a way *out* of stasis, it is worth following her elaborations a little further. Brown argues in *Undoing the Demos* (2015) that neoliberalism is responsible for nothing less than the conversion of the political 'character, meaning, and operation of democracy's constituent elements into *economic* ones'.[50] Her understanding of this phenomenon is built on a careful reading and revision of Michel Foucault's 1979 Collège de France lectures on biopolitics, which anticipate (she argues) a great deal about a neoliberalism that was not yet named. In Foucault's analysis, neoliberalism arose not from a crisis of capitalist accumulation (as a Marxist analysis would hold), but from crises of 'liberal governmentality'.[51] Rather than the protection of the rights of individuals, of property rights, which is how liberalism is generally understood, neoliberalism instead sets the state to work on behalf of the market, Foucault argues, it 'activates the state on behalf of the economy'.[52] Indeed, neoliberalism reconceptualizes the market itself as 'site of veridiction' for and as means of 'organizing, limiting, measuring, and legitimating' government itself.[53] If neoliberalism is viewed as 'a modality of governance, and an order of reason', then, it is possible to discern a family resemblance in its varied global forms: in Sweden, it includes a strained endorsement of welfarism; in the United States, it intersects with a blend of 'long-established antistatism and new managerialism'; in South Africa, it has not been regarded by the government as antithetical to 'a post-Apartheid expectation of a democratizing and redistributive state', Brown observes.[54] All cases involve a rationality that inculcates consensus about the role of the state in creating conditions conducive to a free market. In Foucault's analysis, 'political integration and consensus replace the atomization and individuation of classical liberalism'.[55]

Neoliberal governing rationality therefore dictates economic policies less than it reconceives the relationships amongst economy, state, and subject entirely, casting all aspects of life susceptible to market valuation: the rise of neoliberalism thus accompanies 'the emergence of biopolitics'.[56] In both *The Reactive* and *Penumbra*, the market is cast as common sense, in each most notably in relation to healthcare (and thus biopolitics): Manga works for a healthcare provider in *Penumbra*; in *The Reactive*, Nathi buys private medical coverage to access ARVs, which he then sells.[57] The government roll-out of ARVs tellingly takes place after the events of the novel: Ntshanga chooses to focus on the anterior moment as if to illustrate how the postapartheid (neoliberal) state licensed individual subjects to behave in a free market. Rather than the 'invisible hand' of liberal governance that, in Adam Smith's (in)famously utopian vision of mercantile capitalism, secures common good out of the self-interested actions of individuals, Nathi is a character of whom Manga's friend Ndlela (in *Penumbra*) might well approve, a citizen 'who appropriately self-invest[s] in a context of macroeconomic vicissitudes and needs that make all of these investments into practices of speculation'.[58]

Nor does the fact of the eventual ARV roll-out, which came in response to unprecedented pressure from civic action groups (who mounted a successful challenge in the Constitutional Court), neutralize the critique implied by Nathi's actions. It amounted merely to one of very few examples of what some observers have called 'tokenistic welfarism', decisions that did little to mitigate the pernicious effects of a nonetheless pervasive neoliberal governing rationality, one whose validation of and through the market has continued.[59] One might say, with Patrick Bond, that such decisions fostered the conditions that enabled the Marikana massacre, the fatal shooting of striking mineworkers at multinational Lonmin's platinum mine near Rustenberg in the North West Province on 16 August 2012, an event that continues to resonate in South African politics and may come to mark a decisive turn in the fortunes of the ANC (at the time of writing, its current Deputy President, Cyril Ramaphosa, is Chairman of a company that owns a significant stake in the mine).[60] At the ANC conference at Mangaung later in the same year, agreement amongst pro-business nationalists and conservative trade unions ensured the election of party leaders who would continue the neoliberal project, Bond observes, a project involving fiscal discipline, levying fees for basic public services (and privatization of companies providing these), liberalizing currency controls, deregulating the financial services industry, removing import tariffs, and emphasizing exports as an economic priority. In an economy in which up to 40 per cent of working-age people are excluded from employment, its effects have been predictable: declining growth rates and growing civil unrest.[61]

Striking mineworkers at Marikana mistakenly believed they could still operate as rights-bearing individuals, free to organize collectively and demand better working conditions in a country whose constitution enshrines such rights. But in the market model that operates under neoliberalism, subjects are configured 'exhaustively as market actors'; they become *homo oeconomicus*, a term whose history Brown charts over the past several centuries, at the expense of *homo politicus*, the subject of individual rights.[62] Lonmin, and the armed forces of the state whose very organizing rationale has become the defence of the conditions for the marketization of all resources, saw only examples of *homo oeconomicus* failing to act as the system required. Rather than the figure Adam Smith regarded as 'propelled by the natural urge to "truck, barter, and exchange"', Brown suggests, 'today's *homo oeconomicus* is an intensely constructed and governed bit of human capital tasked with improving and leveraging its competitive positioning and with enhancing its (monetary and nonmonetary) portfolio value across all of its endeavors and venues'.[63] In a neoliberal world, citizens are 'no longer [. . .] *most importantly* constituent elements of sovereignty, members of publics, or even bearers of rights'.[64] Daniel Magaziner and Sean Jacobs rightly argue that the Marikana tragedy should be interpreted less in the light of South Africa's own past, but as a symptom of its integration into a global community of capitalism and poverty.[65]

What happened at Marikana and the circumstances that adhere in the lives of the characters in Ntshanga and Mahlangu's novels are on a continuum. The turning of its weapons on striking mineworkers is but an extreme instance of the disciplining power of the neoliberal state that disposes over the power to enable markets—a power that is simultaneously, perhaps especially in the postcolony, also one of life and death (the same state that chooses, culpably late, to roll out ARVs[66]). I read *Penumbra* and *The Reactive*, in which not a great deal by way of political activism happens, precisely for their attempt to name and recuperate the *quotidian* as political, to identify and begin to imagine a response to the eclipsing of *homo politicus* by *homo oeconomicus*. This entails seeing something else in their stasis—an incipient energy, as Benjamin might have looked back to moments of earlier revolutionary potential; something like this looking back in fact occurs in *Penumbra*'s recursive form, and might be read in what I have been describing as the turn to the family and tradition, or to other temporalities, in both texts.

Agamben's reminder that, for the ancient Greeks, *stasis* named a condition of civil war, makes it possible to contemplate the energies involved in states of impasse from another angle, one that is powerful for the South African context. Agamben follows Nicole Loraux in suggesting that the relationship between the '*oikos*, the family or the household, and the *polis*, the city' is central to understanding *stasis*, and reads Plato and Thucydides to establish that 'the *stasis* [is] at the border between the household and the city'.[67] The tension between these two realms, *oikos* as the zone of the economic and *polis* of politics, shares a logic with the division between *zōē* and *bios*, which Agamben's analysis of bare life in *Homo Sacer* set out to interrogate. 'In classical Greece', he notes in *Stasis*, looking back to his earlier work, '*zōē*, simple natural life, was excluded from the *polis* and remained confined to the sphere of the *oikos*'. Aristotle makes a clear distinction in *Politics* between the head of an enterprise (*oikonomos*) and of a family (*despótēs*), whose concern is with 'the reproduction and conservation of life, from the statesman', Agamben notes, thus

> when, in a passage that will become canonical in the Western political tradition, he [Aristotle] defines the end of the *polis* as a perfect community, he does so precisely by opposing the simple fact of living (*to zen*) to politically qualified life (*to eu zen*). This opposition between 'life' and 'the good life' is nonetheless at the same time an implication of the first in the second, of the family in the city and of *zōē* in political life.[68]

It is this double implication that is navigated by the tension that pertains between the household and the state, the realms of *oikos* and *polis*, and that keeps the threat of *stasis*, or civil war, at bay at the same time that it proves intermittently inevitable. What belongs in each realm (*oikos* and *polis*) becomes confused in time of civil war, Agamben suggests: politics moves into the household ('the *oikos* is politicised'), and questions of life, as opposed to the 'good life', move into public ('the *polis* is "economised", that is, it is reduced to an *oikos*').[69] *Stasis* does not emerge from the *oikos*, however (it is not a family feud), but is a device not unlike the state of exception Agamben describes in *Homo Sacer*: 'Just as in the state of exception, *zōē*, natural life, is included in the juridico-political order through its exclusion, so analogously the *oikos* is politicised and included in the *polis* through the *stasis*.'[70] Consequently, says Agamben, one ought to think about politics 'as a field of forces whose extremes are the *oikos* and the *polis*': 'between them, civil war marks the threshold through which the unpolitical is politicised and the political is "economised"'.[71]

This maps well onto Brown's understanding of *homo oeconomicus* and *homo politicus*. If for the Greeks economy has to do with the household (as opposed to the public or political life associated with the city), neoliberalism economizes the private sphere, forcing it into the public, so that there is a movement of *homo oeconomicus* into the realm of politics and a forcing of *homo politicus* into the home, an operation not dissimilar from that which Agamben suggests is characteristic of *stasis* understood as civil strife. Thus Agamben's analysis serves in unexpectedly useful ways for my purposes: stasis understood as impasse is in fact a (civil) war amongst ourselves, a kind of horizontal violence in a sense Fanon might recognize, a civil war that neoliberalism forces us to wage as we compete for what should accrue to us by virtue of being specimens of *homo politicus*. Neoliberalism, in other words, thrives on a version of civil strife that is experienced affectively by individual subjects as impasse, *stasis* experienced as stasis. The uprising understood as *stasis* by the Greeks is also a standing still, Agamben points out, a standing firm, and is linked by its etymon (*stasis*, from *histemi*) to an act of standing upright as if to speak a certain truth, to take a stand, to look to the future: '*stasimos* is the point in the tragedy when the chorus stands still and speaks' (recall, here, Scott on postcolonial tragedy, and Berlant on the situation tragedy); '*stas* is the one who swears the oath while standing'.[72] How, I want to ask in the final section of this chapter, do Ntshanga and Mahlangu's novels point to a recuperation of stasis in this potentially affirmative vein?

ANXIETY, REPETITION, PROPHECY

Towards the end of *The Reactive*, Nathi finally decides to attend initiation school. Returning to Cape Town, he stays with extended family in the township, finds a girlfriend, and seems on the verge of accepting this existence as more authentic than the drug-fuelled suburban life described earlier in the book. That there might be some measure of normative judgment here seems likely given moments of moralizing in the novel, like its brief satire on the Michaelis art school graduate Julian, who throws overnight parties, stages protests with his guests ('a half-stoned mass') outside Parliament the next morning, photographs these, and sells them at inflated prices in a commercial Woodstock gallery.[73] The latter is certainly an indictment of the economization of the everyday, but perhaps also an invitation to think about the role of aestheticized representations of waiting more broadly (even as this is also what the novel is in some measure doing itself). If *The Reactive*'s final turn is susceptible of a reactionary reading, however, this is mitigated in part by its queer subplot, for Luthando, whom Nathi had effectively tricked on behalf of unnamed friends and relatives into going to the Eastern Cape to undergo initiation, was gay, and what was intended for him was likely sinister: 'the Mda house came under pressure to make a man out of its cissy son', Nathi recalls, while he 'kept away—I crossed my arms in Cape Town'.[74] He regrets this now, however, appearing to wish for a more accommodating structure of sociality that accommodates queer desire, even as he himself seems ready to embrace marriage, tradition, and township life. His act of self-infection (with HIV) might also be read as the willing embrace of victim status, for whatever complicated reasons: as penance for his complicity in Luthando's death; as positive 'conversion' in a cultural context in which he is not considered fully an adult man.[75] It allows, too, for the discovery of incipient power, as Nathi finds that the virus has few effects on him (which is why he can safely sell his ARVs). A generous reading of Ntshanga's ending is that Nathi's reinvestment in tradition is neither complete, nor without pragmatism or qualification: we leave him in a moment of stasis in which he finds a provisional way of standing up for himself, accounting for his past and figuring out what might come next.

In *Penumbra*, Mahlangu offers something equally if not more complex, in part reflected in the novel's non-linear narrative: Manga is fetched home by his mother after his breakdown at the end of part one; part two offers a flashback to an earlier return, leading to the moment with which part one begins; part three stages the return—this time to Cape Town—from the visit to the Eastern Cape seen at the end of the first part, and ends with a drive to the airport to fly east to the family home once more. This repeated return-to-roots structure might seem similar to the ending of *The Reactive*, but in fact the looping nature of Manga's narrative suggests that the journey to come, after the close of part three, is not likely to be final, that he will have to continue navigating different locations in which he is required to perform variously as Eastern Cape homeboy or Cape Town urbanite, ethnic (rural) Xhosa or aspiring young black professional. Tensions amongst these different identities are in part the cause of Manga's mental illness, which he diagnoses himself as 'intense anxiety',[76] and it is this anxiety that focuses attention on the real political causes of his condition, and which reveals the psychic and structural violence of *stasis* in his stasis.

In *The Forms of the Affects* (2014), Eugenie Brinkema offers a fascinating account of the metaphors by which anxiety as affective state, as bad feeling, has been conceptualized in existential philosophy and psychoanalysis. Kierkegaard, Heidegger, and Freud all held that while fear requires a definite object, anxiety is directed towards nothing in particular.[77] In *The Concept of Anxiety*, Kierkegaard first posited that anxiety's object is precisely nothing—or rather '*a* "something that is nothing"'.[78] In other words, anxiety had to do with plenitude or its lack, which is to say the future and its potential to disappoint our investments in it. In Brinkema's more lyrical formulation, 'anxiety has something to do with the not-yet, and, as such, the nothingness of the future that always has not taken place, but that might, in its not-yet-having-happened dimension, take place, displacing that nothing that it is at the moment it is realized and is therefore no longer, I mean it no longer may be regarded as, the future'.[79] Anxiety may in fact be the only response to a future whose possibilities are radically open; it corresponds therefore to 'the futurity of futurity—in particular, the utterly contingent moment and manner of the self's certain future death, a finitude colored by temporality, what existentialism describes as being's awareness of nonbeing'.[80]

It is psychoanalysis rather than existentialism, however, that here provides more useful conceptual levers. The 'problem of anxiety' was central to Freud's project, 'a nodal point at which the most various and important questions converge, a riddle whose solution would be bound to throw a flood of light on our whole mental existence', he writes in the *Introductory Lectures on Psychoanalysis*.[81] But while, in Freud's earliest discussions of anxiety (in 1895), he envisages its causes in directional terms, imagining that repression is the *source* of anxiety, by 1926 (in *Inhibitions, Symptoms and Anxiety*) anxiety instead arises as a *response* to situations of trauma or threat, precisely those circumstances under which repression is a defence mechanism. Here anxiety leads to repression, not vice versa.[82] In the earlier formulation, anxiety results from 'blockage in the forward progress of energies'; it is 'an interruption to or absolute breach in that system' and is explained through a metaphorics of space.[83] Freud's later thinking turns less on the idea of an interruption imagined spatially than one marked by *temporal* metaphors of intermittency and repetition. Rather than causing a blockage imagined in spatial terms, anxiety instead arises 'from the *failure* or inability to interrupt a system', it is 'linked to pressures squeezing time and choking the possibility for a forward progress that nevertheless persists'.[84] In Freud's words, anxiety comes to bear 'an unmistakable relation to *expectations*: it is anxiety *about* [*vor*; before, in the sense of both facing and prior to] something'.[85] What is desired, then, by the one suffering anxiety, is to introduce a temporal interval, a time that is no-time, that might prevent the further happening of that which is anticipated.

If Freud's earlier understanding of anxiety goes some way to providing a way of understanding Nathi's working through of his earlier repression of complicity in Luthando's death (in *The Reactive*), Freud's later view of anxiety as itself arising from a failure to interrupt systemic structural disadvantage might provide a way of reading Manga's state (in *Penumbra*). Mahlangu's novel's recursive structure, too, replicates the intermittency and repetition associated with Freud's later description of the operations of anxiety in temporal rather than spatial terms. It also helps to make sense of another aspect of the text—those moments in which Manga weighs past instances of forestalled expectation, instances in which the causes of the particular nervous condition identified by Manga as anxiety become visible. Recall that Crapanzano noticed that the kinds of waiting in which white South Africans in the 1980s seemed trapped frequently occasioned investment in apocalyptic discourse of revivalism that gave structure to states of hopeless hopefulness.[86] In *Penumbra*, Manga's attraction to charismatic Christianity and his fear of the demonic suggest the availability of similar palliative narratives, though in very different political circumstances. But it is his invocation of anti-colonial activity, including of prophecy, that requires further comment.

In the midst of the mental breakdown that follows his resignation from his internship, Manga is moved by *kwaito* star Zola's song 'Bhambata'.[87]

This invokes a fated anti-colonial rising, the so-called Bambata Rebellion, in Natal in 1906 (its proximate cause was resistance to the imposition of a poll tax), which was brutally suppressed by colonial forces with the loss of many thousands of lives.[88] Later, Manga observes: 'It would seem we are in a season of mourning. Singers are crying on CD covers. [. . .] They sing many songs bemoaning the loss of our cattle. The cattle will come back in a different way. It will take a spiritual awakening.'[89] The reference is to the infamous Xhosa Cattle Killing episode of 1856, which followed a prophecy, by a young woman called Nongqawuse, that the mass slaughter of the nation's cattle would call forth support from spirit ancestors in the overthrow of the white colonists. A terrible famine ensued and further colonial subjugation followed as survivors were absorbed into the wage economy of the Cape Colony. In each case, a link is intimated (though not clearly drawn by Manga) between his present state of disaffection and disappointment, and past moments that promised liberation from structural violence. Manga's bad feelings, in other words, have historical precedents that confirm them as political: his stasis is linked to *stasis*. Either event might indeed be thought precursor to the massacre at Marikana discussed in the previous section, 'Stasis as Civil War'. Reports that the miners had invoked the protection of ancestors, smeared themselves with fat to ward off bullets, and forbade women journalists from approaching the hilltop lest their invincibility be compromised, connects resistance at Marikana to that, equally futile, offered by any number of participants in millenarian movements, from those who followed Nongqawuse or Bambata, to Isaiah Shembe's Nazarite Baptist Church or, perhaps most notoriously, Enoch Mgijima's Israelite sect, whose occupation of land at Bullhoek, near what is now Whittlesea (outside Queenstown, in the Eastern Cape), ended with a massacre by South African government forces in May 1921.[90]

Jennifer Wenzel has shown how prophecy can be traced through many African and black-diaspora engagements with the desire for, and too frequently the failure of, revolutionary aspirations. In her discussion of Zakes Mda's 2000 novel *The Heart of Redness*, at the centre of which is the cattle-killing prophecy and its aftermath amongst descendants, in the same Eastern Cape village, of those who believed in the prophecy and those who did not, Wenzel suggests that Mda presents prophecy neither as 'failed nor fulfilled, but rather as *unfailed*, alive and partially realized in the present'. This notion of *unfailure*, she suggests, allows for the apprehension of 'the heterogeneity of time, a nonsynchronous multiplicity of pasts and presents in which the incompletion of the past implies the unfinishedness of the present'.[91] Temporality in the postcolony is always layered: one is always already late, out of time entirely, on one's own time (or on another's clock). Achille Mbembe makes this point, too, with the reminder that 'every age, including the postcolony' (for the postcolony is for Mbembe a time as much as a geography), 'is in reality a combination of several temporalities'.[92] The postcolony 'encloses multiple *durées* made up of discontinuities, reversals, inertias, and swings that overlay one another, interpenetrate one another, and envelope one another: an *entanglement*'.[93] 'The cattle killing's vexed temporality', Wenzel observes, 'its entanglement of retrospection and anticipation, and the potential for haunting by its unrealized visions of liberation', provides postapartheid South Africa with a timely model for animating the 'utopian surplus' that lingers amid, or on account of, such temporal entanglement, 'a still dynamic remnant of undischarged anticipation that can be put to work'.[94]

Unfailure describes well what Manga ascribes to art that sees, like a prophecy, beyond the present, art in which the promise of past moments of resistance is kept alive, in which a squeezing of those multi-layered temporalities apprehended by black South Africans like Manga, the time of the village and of the township, of the homestead and the city, the time of the promise of prophecy and that of the experience of present disappointment, might be resisted. During one of his breakdowns, he calls to mind those he describes as 'beautiful artists' blessed with 'a gift of seeing beyond conditions' (notice how the final word stands for so much—impasse, stasis, waiting). These artists are able, Manga muses, to 'draw us to the blackness of uncertainty. That's what art should achieve: point out the other side. Art is not there to unearth any truths, but rather to show the multiplicity of the nature of things'.[95] It is art itself that offers an alternative to stasis in *Penumbra*, then, or that gives shape to its possibility. Manga (like his friend Tongai) is an aspiring writer, too, and *Penumbra* itself is cast as an accounting, a looking back from a period of static now-time, from which Manga might see beyond present conditions precisely by looking to moments of past promise in a manner that accords perfectly with Benjamin's injunction to revivify moments of past revolutionary promise, a looking back that is also a pledge to the future.[96] Art, in this sense, can serve as 'a repository for dissident temporalities' (in Paul Saint-Amour's suggestive phrasing), an archive for memories of futures past, which may yet be reactivated.[97]

*

Whatever kinds of community art can allow to cohere, there are always barriers to such performance in a place like South Africa, however. I give the reader credit and assume that, at this point in the book, I need elaborate no further, although I will offer a final word to counter any appearance that I might be arguing that art is *necessarily* the answer to the everyday experience of structural violence. Lauren Berlant cautions that 'projects of compassionate recognition have enabled a habit of political obfuscation of the differences between emotional and material (legal, economic, institutional) kinds of social reciprocity' (note her careful formulation). Thus, while solidarity is a good thing (it can make 'movements thrive contentiously against all sorts of privilege'), believing that one can make a difference also holds the danger of making small adjustments—through compassionate identifications and any actions that may issue from these—seem like big steps, precisely 'because the theater of compassion is emotionally intense'.[98]

'Recognition', Berlant observes, 'all too often becomes an experiential end in itself',[99] which is not of course to assert that affective identification is never active in the 'social empowerment of minoritized or negated communities' (indeed, 'it *always* is'). Rather, it is to acknowledge that 'the intensities of affective performance' are seldom 'matched in scale' by political or legal transformations.[100] Real justice takes longer. To feel bad, and to read writing that features bad feelings, is not to change the world—although it might lead towards action in that direction. In South Africa *what* action and in *which* direction is anyone's guess. Things happen so quickly, and also so slowly, in that country that there is simply no telling whether present imperfection may yield to more perfect futures, or to imperfect futures replete with the hopes of futures past, richly entangled, ready to be reanimated anew. As we protest, or wait and watch, or write, we can do worse than to read this rich literature of disappointment and of hope with care, alert to all that it might still reveal.

Endnotes

NOTES TO PREFACE

1. Neil Lazarus, 'South African Ideology: The Myth of Exceptionalism, the Idea of Renaissance', *South Atlantic Quarterly* 103.4 (2004), 611.
2. Achille Mbembe, 'Achille Mbembe on The State of South African Political Life', *Africa in Words*, 19 September 2015, http://africasacountry.com/2015/09/achille-mbembe-on-the-state-of-south-african-politics/.
3. 'disappointment, n.', *OED Online*, Oxford University Press, September 2016. Web. 16 November 2016.
4. 'disappoint, v.', *OED Online*, Oxford University Press, September 2016. Web. 16 November The *OED* gives illustrative quotations from 1530 through to 1633, 'So as to put off, and disappoint the day', for this meaning, the last a quotation attributed to Joseph Hall's *A plaine and familiar explication (by way of paraphrase) of all the hard texts of the whole divine Scripture of the Old and New Testament*. Some time after my first draft of a paper that used dis-appointment in this sense, I was pointed to an essay that employs a similar sense of the word to mean 'not living in one's proper time'; see Eric Worby and Shireen Ally, 'The Disappointment of Nostalgia: Conceptualising Cultures of Memory in Contemporary South Africa', *Social Dynamics* 39.3 (2013), 468.

NOTES TO INTRODUCTION

1. Joan Bybee, Revere Perkins, and William Pagliuca, *The Evolution of Grammar: Tense, Aspect, and Modality in the Languages of the World* (Chicago and London: University of Chicago Press, 1994), 126.
2. Nadine Gordimer, *No Time Like the Present* (London: Bloomsbury, 2012), 4.
3. Ibid., 8.
4. Ibid., 126.
5. On the arms-procurement and related scandals, see former ANC Member of Parliament Andrew Feinstein's *After the Party: Corruption, the ANC and South Africa's Uncertain Future* (London and New York: Verso, 2009). For an analysis of economic conditions since the millennium, see Patrick Bond, 'Consolidating the Contradictions: From Mandela to Marikana, 2000–2012', in John S. Saul and Patrick Bond, *South Africa—The Present as History: From Mrs Ples to Mandela and Marikana* (Rochester, NY: James Currey/Boydell & Brewer, 2014).
6. William Gumede, 'Zuma's victory may trigger the break-up of the ANC', *The Guardian*, 19 December 2007, cited in Bond, 'Consolidating the Contradictions', 208–9.

7. See Gordimer, *No Time Like the Present*, 217, 233–4, 249–51. On the UFS case, see Melissa Steyn, '"The Creed of the White Kid": A Diss-Apology', in *The Handbook of Critical Intercultural Communication*, ed. Thomas K. Nakayama and Rona Tamiko Halualani (Malden, MA and Oxford: Blackwell, 2010), 539.
8. Gordimer, *No Time Like the Present*, 327.
9. Ibid., 351.
10. Permanent Secretary, The Swedish Academy, 'Nobel Prize in Literature 1991—Press Release', *Nobelprize.org*, 3 October 1991, http://www.nobelprize.org/nobel_prizes/literature/laureates/1991/press.html (accessed 24 July 2014).
11. Quoted by Justice Malala, 'Nadine Gordimer used last interview to condemn South Africa's secrecy bill', *The Guardian*, 14 July 2014, http://www.theguardian.com/world/2014/jul/14/nadine-gordimer-south-africa-secrecy-bill (accessed 4 July 2014).
12. Gordimer, *No Time Like the Present*, 72.
13. One might observe here that South African English ascribes multiple meanings to adverbial phrases involving the word 'now' that might well be taken to mean precisely the opposite: 'now-now' (modelled on the Afrikaans *nou-nou*) can mean in 'the immediate past' or in 'the immediate future'; similarly, 'just now' (after the Afrikaans *netnou*) can mean either 'after some time' or 'precisely at present'. See 'now-now, adv. phr. Colloq.' and 'just now, adv. phr.', *A Dictionary of South African English on Historical Principles* (Oxford: Oxford University Press, 1996), 511, 338.
14. Nadine Gordimer, 'Gag the mouth and block the ears', *Mail & Guardian*, 18 October 2013, http://mg.co.za/article/2013-10-28-gag-the-mouth-and-block-the-ears (accessed 24 July 2014).
15. Nadine Gordimer, 'Living in the Interregnum', in *The Essential Gesture*, ed. Stephen Clingman (1988; London: Penguin, 1989), 262–3. See also Nadine Gordimer, *July's People* (1981; London: Penguin, 1982), iii. Gordimer cites as her source a 'slightly different translation' in *Selections from the Prison Notebooks of Antonio Gramsci*, ed. and introduced by Quintin Hoare and Geoffrey Nowell Smith (London: Lawrence & Wishart, 1971), 276 ('Living', 263).
16. Nadine Gordimer and Stephen Clingman, 'The Future is Another Country', *Transition* 56, n.s. 2.2 (1992), 139.
17. Ibid., 142.
18. Stephen Clingman, 'Prologue to the Second Edition', in *The Novels of Nadine Gordimer: History from the Inside*, 2nd edn (1992; London: Bloomsbury, 1993), xxxiii.
19. Ibid., xxv.
20. Gordimer, *No Time Like the Present*, 29.
21. Bernard Comrie, *Aspect* (Cambridge: Cambridge University Press, 1976), 23.
22. Bybee, Perkins, and Pagliuca, *The Evolution of Grammar*, 126, 175. These comments are made in a study of semantic development in grammaticization; I acknowledge I am consciously deploying their descriptions for symbolic effect

and am not concerned with the finer points of their analysis. It is worth noting that grammarians are divided on the difference between tense and aspect, although a useful distinction might be that tense concerns the relationship between reference point and speech act, while aspect concerns that between event and reference point. See Robert I. Binnick, ed., 'Introduction', in *The Oxford Handbook of Tense and Aspect* (Oxford: Oxford University Press, 2012), 22.

23. For his description of Klee's *Angelus Novus*, see the ninth thesis in Walter Benjamin, 'On the Concept of History', trans. Harry Zohn, in *Selected Writings: Vol. 4, 1938–1940*, ed. Howard Eiland and Michael W. Jennings (Cambridge, MA: Harvard University Press, 2003), 392. On Cronin's engagement with Benjamin see Andrew van der Vlies, 'An Interview with Jeremy Cronin', *Contemporary Literature* 49.4 (2008), 526–7.
24. Benjamin, 'On the Concept', 395.
25. Walter Benjamin, 'Theses on the Philosophy of History', trans. Harry Zohn, in *Illuminations*, ed. and introduction Hannah Arendt (1968; London: Pimlico, 1999), 253. The translations credited to Zohn in *Illuminations* ('Theses') and in the authoritative *Selected Writings* ('On the Concept') differ in a number of respects; I have used whichever version best suits my purposes.
26. Benjamin, 'Theses', 252–3.
27. Benjamin, 'On the Concept', 397.
28. Ibid., 389, 390. There are many debates about the nature of Benjamin's idea of weak messianism, including Derrida's positing of a *messianicité sans messianisme* (a 'messianicity without messianism') in response. See Jacques Derrida, 'Marx and Sons', trans. Kelly Barry, in *Ghostly Demarcations: A Symposium on Jacques Derrida's Specters of Marx*, ed. Michael Sprinker (London and New York: Verso, 1999), 248–51. On Derrida's differentiation of his utopian thinking from Benjamin's, see Owen Ware, 'Dialectics of the Past/Disjuncture of the Future: Derrida and Benjamin on the Concept of Messianism', *Journal for Cultural and Religious Theory* 5.2 (April 2004), 99–114.
29. Benjamin, 'Theses', 255.
30. On the 'leap' and on 'constellation' see Benjamin, 'On the Concept', 395, 396, and his 'Paralipomena to "On the Concept of History"', trans. Edmund Jephcott and Howard Eiland, in *Selected Writings: Vol. 4, 1938–1940*, 403. Benjamin also uses imagery from spectrum analysis and from crystallography—'thinking is crystallized as a monad' in the moment of constellation: see 'On the Concept', 402, 396.
31. Benjamin, 'Theses', 254.
32. Benjamin, 'On the Concept', 396. The original for 'arrest of happening' is 'Stillstellung des Geschehens'.
33. Benjamin, 'Paralipomena', 402.
34. As exemplar of a critique of the reconceptualization of the National Democratic Revolution in neoliberal terms, see Blade Nzimande, 'What is the National Democratic Revolution?', *Umsebenzi* 5.66 (18 October 2006), http://www.sacp.org.za/main.php?ID=1850#redpen (accessed 21 August

2014). Nzimande was at the time General Secretary of the South African Communist Party (SACP), junior party in the ruling tri-partite alliance (with the ANC and Congress of South African Trade Unions), and *Umsebenzi* the SACP's mouthpiece.

35. Hylton White, 'A Post-Fordist Ethnicity: Insecurity, Authority, and Identity in South Africa', *Anthropological Quarterly* 85.2 (2012), 399. See Brett Neilson and Ned Rossiter, 'Precarity as a Political Concept, or, Fordism as Exception', *Theory, Culture & Society* 25.7–8 (2008), 52.
36. See SAPA, 'EFF launches in Marikana', *The Sowetan*, 14 October 2013, http://www.sowetanlive.co.za/news/2013/10/14/eff-launches-in-marikana (accessed 17 October 2013); Thapelo Lekgowa and Greg Nicolson, 'Marikana: Malema's 2014 battle begins', *The Daily Maverick*, 14 October 2013, http://www.dailymaverick.co.za/article/2013-10-14-marikana-malemas-2014-battle-begins/#.Ul_P5RbIaCQ (accessed 17 October 2013).
37. Much influential queer theory has been concerned with negative affect, often in relation to temporality and political action, most notably Lee Edelman's *No Future* (Durham, NC: Duke University Press, 2004) and Judith (Jack) Halberstam's *The Queer Art of Failure* (Durham, NC: Duke University Press, 2011). For a concise overview of the issues, see Robert L. Caserio et al., 'The Antisocial Thesis in Queer Theory', *PMLA* 121.3 (2006), 819–28. See also Carolyn Dinshaw et al., 'Theorizing Queer Temporalities: A Roundtable', *GLQ* 13.2–3 (2007), 177–95.
38. There are gay and lesbian characters in two of the Winterbach novels I discuss in Chapter 1. Each of Coetzee's fictionalized memoirs, discussed in Chapter 2, stage moments of queer desire or panic: in *Boyhood*, John feels something like desire for the lithe and athletic 'Coloured' boys he sees around Worcester (see my note on the racial term in Chapter 1, n22); in *Youth*, John dismisses his own speculation that he is homosexual, though such speculation is made by his cousins in *Summertime* (I will not discuss these further). There are implicitly queer characters in queer author Van Niekerk's *Agaat* (the subject of Chapter 3), speculations about Aubrey Tearle's sexuality in Vladislavić's *The Restless Supermarket* (discussed in Chapter 4), and references to '*moffies*' (queers) in Wicomb's work (see Chapter 5). In Ntshanga's *The Reactive* (discussed in Chapter 6), the fate of the narrator's younger gay brother is a key motor in the plot's unfolding.
39. See Heather Love, *Feeling Backward: Loss and the Politics of Queer History* (Cambridge, MA: Harvard University Press, 2007), 5, 22–3. Arguments about the need for ongoing struggle are very much more easily made in relation to queer lives elsewhere than North America and Western Europe, of course. In brief, the antisocial thesis might be caricatured thus: queers should refuse the heteronormative family; politics privileges the heteronormative family so should be spurned; queers should embrace failure and shame, owning those feelings labelled non-normative by heteronormative investments in family- and futurity-oriented politics.

40. Love, I think, reads Benjamin's angel of history too instrumentally, too in keeping with her project. For her, his '"angel of history" is a pre-eminently backward figure, an emblem of resistance to the forward march of progress' (147). While Benjamin contrasts his historical materialism to historical narratives of progress, it is the latter's method and conservatism that he rejects, not the possibility of progress per se, achieved through other, revolutionary means.
41. Love, *Feeling Backward*, 146.
42. Elizabeth Freeman, *Time Binds: Queer Temporalities, Queer Histories* (Durham, NC: Duke University Press, 2010), xiii. Freeman cites Eve Kosofsky Sedgwick, 'Paranoid Reading and Reparative Reading; or, You're So Vain, You Probably Think This Introduction Is About You', in *Novel Gazing: Queer Readings in Fiction*, ed. Sedgwick (Durham, NC: Duke University Press, 1997), 8, emphasis in the original.
43. José Esteban Muñoz, *Cruising Utopia: The Then and There of Queer Futurity* (New York: New York University Press, 2009), 12. 'My turn to Bloch, hope, and utopia is a challenge to theoretical insights that have been stunted by [. . .] various romances of negativity and have thus become routine and resoundingly anticritical.'
44. Ann Cvetkovich, *Depression: A Public Feeling* (Durham, NC: Duke University Press, 2012), 190–1. See also Sara Ahmed, *The Promise of Happiness* (Durham, NC: Duke University Press, 2010), 6. Cvetkovich is responding here to Michael Snediker's association of her earlier book, *An Archive of Feelings*, with what Snediker calls 'tropaic gravitation toward negative affect and depersonation'. See Michael D. Snediker, *Queer Optimism: Lyric Personhood and Other Felicitous Persuasions* (Minneapolis: Minnesota University Press, 2009), 4. Despite Cvetkovich's retort, Snediker's critique of Edelman's *No Future*—whose 'egregious militancy', he suggests, 'presents an apogee of [. . .] queer pessimism', or at least 'pessimism in drag'—is perceptive and forthright (ibid., 22). He offers a particularly useful contextualization of the antisocial thesis, tracking the influence of Judith Butler and Leo Bersani. Muñoz is also very critical of Edelman et al., arguing that 'antiutopian theoretical faltering is often nothing more than rote invocation of poststructuralist pieties' (*Cruising Utopia*, 12).
45. A right to freedom of discrimination on grounds of sexual orientation is included in South Africa's 1996 Constitution, the only such guarantee in Africa, and one of very few globally. Brenna Munro's *South Africa and the Dream of Love to Come: Queer Sexuality and the Struggle for Freedom* (Minneapolis: University of Minnesota Press, 2012) offers a comprehensive and nuanced discussion of the queer figure in late twentieth-century and contemporary South African literatures and other media and a perceptive reading of novels in which queer figures are made to fit (back) into a notional national family. I discuss this—and Munro's insights—at greater length in Chapter 5.

46. Gordimer, *No Time Like the Present*, 9.
47. Ibid., 12.
48. Ibid., 51.
49. Ibid., 92, 94, 95.
50. Freeman, *Time Binds*, xiv, and see 3, 5. Freeman draws on sociological and historical engagements with, for example, industrialization and the spread of wage labour, and is indebted in her theorization to Judith Butler's idea of gender performativity and (especially) to Pierre Bourdieu's elaboration of *habitus*, the process by which repeated gestures, behaviours and attitudes come to structure group and societal norms. Freeman's use of Benjamin includes a reading of his notion of 'homogeneous empty time' to refer not only to the bland time of history in which historicist narratives traffic, but many such normative (teleologically driven) narratives, including of 'coming out, consummation, development, domesticity, family, foreplay, genealogy, identity, liberation, modernity, [. . .] all of which take their meanings from, and contribute to, a vision of time as seamless, unified, and forward moving.' Queer temporalities, by contrast, are interruptive, resistant, and 'propose other possibilities for living in relation to indeterminately past, present and future others' (*Time Binds*, xxii).
51. Freeman, *Time Binds*, xiv.
52. Jane Elliott, *Popular Feminist Fiction as American Allegory: Representing National Time* (London: Palgrave, 2008); Jennifer Wenzel, *Bulletproof: Afterlives of Anticolonial Prophecy in South Africa and Beyond* (Chicago: University of Chicago Press, 2009).
53. Muñoz, *Cruising Utopia*, 1. Bloch engages directly with Benjamin's language of exploding constellations that bring together present and past (specifically a moment of revolutionary potential rescued from the past) in his essay 'On the Present in Literature,' trans. Jack Zipes and Frank Mecklenburg, in *Literary Essays*, trans. Andrew Joron and others (Stanford: Stanford University Press, 1998), 130.
54. See Neville Plaice, 'Translators' Introduction', in Ernst Bloch, *The Principle of Hope* (1959), vol. 1, trans. Neville Plaice, Stephen Plaice, Paul Knight (Cambridge, MA: MIT Press, 1986), xxvii. Muñoz makes much of his ideas of the not-yet-here and the no-longer-conscious (*Cruising Utopia*, 12), the surplus (7), indeterminacy (3), and the front along which the future arrives; all are ideas key to Bloch's *Principle of Hope*.
55. Bloch, 'On the Present in Literature', 133.
56. Bloch, 'Can Hope Be Disappointed?' (1961), trans. Andrew Joron, in Bloch, *Literary Essays*, 342.
57. Ibid., 341. See Ruth Levitas, 'Educated Hope: Ernst Bloch on Abstract and Concrete Utopia', in *Not Yet: Reconsidering Ernst Bloch*, ed. Jamie Owen Daniel and Tom Moylan (London and New York: Verso, 1997), 70. Amongst scholars of South African writing, Russell Samolsky has utilized Bloch's futural thinking in a productively polemical reading of the afterlife of Coetzee's *Waiting for the Barbarians*; see *Apocalyptic Futures* (New York: Fordham University Press, 2011), ch. 3.

58. Hirokazu Miyazaki, *The Method of Hope: Anthropology, Philosophy, and Fijian Knowledge* (Stanford: Stanford University Press, 2004), 5, 2.
59. Ibid., 23, my emphases.
60. David Scott, *Omens of Adversity: Tragedy, Time, Memory, Justice* (Durham, NC: Duke University Press, 2014), 5.
61. Ibid., 2.
62. Hannah Arendt, *On Revolution* (New York: Viking, 1963), 21, cited by Scott, *Omens*, 3.
63. Scott, *Omens*, 5.
64. See further Love, *Feeling Backward*, 12, 150; Cvetkovich, *Depression*, 108; Scott, *Omens*, 99–101.
65. Scott, *Omens*, 2.
66. See ibid., 35–6; Raymond Williams, *Modern Tragedy* (London: Chatto & Windus, 1966), 76, 82.
67. Scott, *Omens*, 62.
68. Gordimer, *No Time Like the Present*, 4.
69. Brenna Munro observes that Madikizela-Mandela has served as 'tragic figure'; 'Nelson, Winnie, and the Politics of Gender', in *The Cambridge Companion to Nelson Mandela*, ed. Rita Barnard (Cambridge: Cambridge University Press, 2014), 92.
70. Gordimer, *No Time Like the Present*, 216–17.
71. Ibid., 218.
72. A reading with Bloch might make more of Steve's turn to the classics to encounter the utopian potential of a dwelling on the present. See Bloch, 'On the Present in Literature', 127, and *The Principle of Hope*.
73. Elliott, *Popular Feminist Fiction*, 22.
74. Ibid., 27. If 'it is the coalescence of goal and conclusion that creates the temporal form of narrative [. . .] the narrative time of history must cease when we reach the goal *of* that narrative.'
75. Elliott, *Popular Feminist Fiction*, 33.
76. Lauren Berlant, *Cruel Optimism* (Durham, NC: Duke University Press, 2011), 27.
77. Cvetkovich, *Depression*, 110.
78. Lauren Berlant and Michael Hardt, '"On the risk of a new relationality": An Interview with Lauren Berlant and Michael Hardt', *Reviews in Cultural Theory* 3.2 (2012), 24.
79. Cvetkovich, *Depression*, 6, 7. She might have turned to Bloch for a language of sedimented utopian hopes—indeed she does develop an argument for the 'utopia of ordinary habit' (191). Sianne Ngai makes a slightly different case for negative affects, especially those that 'often seem to be the psychic fuel on which capitalist society runs'. Their ambivalence, she argues, allows them 'to resist, on the one hand, their reduction to mere expressions of class *ressentiment*, and on the other, their counter-valorization as therapeutic "solutions" to the problems they highlight and condense'. See Sianne Ngai, *Ugly Feelings* (Cambridge, MA: Harvard University Press, 2005), 3.

80. See especially Berlant, *Cruel Optimism*, 176.
81. Ngai, *Ugly Feelings*, 1. Ngai's archive ranges from fiction by Herman Melville, Samuel Beckett, and Nella Larsen, to films by Alfred Hitchcock and Michelangelo Antonioni. She is interested, too, in tropes deployed by philosophers including Martin Heidegger, to whom she is indebted for her treatment of tone and mood, about which I will have more to say in Chapter 2.
82. Ngai, *Ugly Feelings*, 2. Ngai notes that if Adorno's *Aesthetic Theory* suggests that bourgeois art's sense of aesthetic autonomy (from the world of 'empirical society') 'ironically coincides with its growing awareness of its inability to significantly change that society—a powerlessness that then becomes the privileged object of the newly autonomous art's "guilty" self-reflection,' such art's concern with its own lack of power 'is precisely what makes it capable of theorizing social powerlessness in a manner unrivalled by other forms of cultural praxis' (ibid.).
83. See Raymond Williams, *Marxism and Literature* (Oxford: Oxford University Press, 1977), especially 128–33. Williams is widely invoked as methodological model, for example by Cvetkovich (*Depression*, 13), Love (*Feeling Backward*, 11), and Ngai (*Ugly Feelings*, 24).
84. Love, *Feeling Backward*, 11.
85. Wenzel, *Bulletproof*, 162.
86. Susan Stewart, *On Longing: Narratives of the Miniature, the Gigantic, the Souvenir, the Collection* (1984; Durham, NC: Duke University Press, 1993), ix–x.
87. Scott, *Omens*, 69, quoting Ricoeur, *Time and Narrative*, 1:6; and 1:3.
88. See Paul Ricoeur, 'Narrative Time', in *On Narrative*, ed. W.J.T. Mitchell (Chicago: University of Chicago Press, 1981), 173, and Frank Kermode, *The Sense of an Ending* (New York: Oxford University Press, 1967).
89. Peter Brooks, *Reading for the Plot: Design and Intention in Narrative* (New York: Knopf, 1984), 23; see Wenzel, *Bulletproof*, 160.
90. John J. Su, 'Epic of Failure: Disappointment as Utopian Fantasy in *Midnight's Children*', *Twentieth-Century Literature* 47.4 (2001), 546.
91. György Lukács, *The Theory of the Novel: A Historico-Philosophical Essay on the Forms of Great Epic Literature* (1916), trans. Anna Bostock (Cambridge, MA: MIT Press, 1971), 126.
92. Su, 'Epic of Failure', 546.
93. Wenzel, *Bulletproof*, 235, 236 (Wenzel is here paraphrasing an insight from Dipesh Chakrabarty).
94. Elleke Boehmer, 'Endings and New Beginning: South African Literature in Transition', in *Writing South Africa: Literature, Apartheid, and Democracy, 1970–1995*, ed. Derek Attridge and Rosemary Jolly (Cambridge: Cambridge University Press, 1998), 43–56.
95. Elleke Boehmer, 'Permanent Risk: When Crisis Defines a Nation's Writing', in *Trauma, Memory, and Narrative in the Contemporary South African Novel: Essays*, ed. Ewald Mengel and Michela Borzaga (Amsterdam: Rodopi, 2012), 35, 35, 39.

96. Ibid., 35.
97. Cvetkovich, *Depression*, 4.
98. Ibid.
99. Eugenie Brinkema, *The Forms of the Affects* (Durham, NC: Duke University Press, 2014), xiii. Brinkema observes that the turn to affect is 'part of a larger reawakening of interest in problematics of embodiment and materiality in the wake of twentieth-century Western theory that, for many, was all semiotics and no sense, all structure and no stuff' (xi).
100. Ibid., xiv. Italics original.
101. Ibid., see also xv.
102. I am thinking of long-running debates about the ending of Gordimer's *July's People*, for instance. For an engagement with temporality, experimental form, and black subjectivity, see David Attwell, *Rewriting Modernity: Studies in Black South African Literary History* (Athens, OH: Ohio University Press, 2005), in which he issues a call for South African literary historiography to shift from concern with how one might write about difference, to a concern with temporality, ibid., 8.

NOTES TO CHAPTER 1

1. Wopko Jensma, 'Spanner in the What? Works', in *I Must Show You My Clippings* (Johannesburg: Ravan Press, 1977), 6–9.
2. Born Ingrid Gerda Winterbach in Johannesburg in 1948, though known too by her married name, Ingrid Gouws, she published her first five novels under the alias Lettie Viljoen.
3. Ingrid Winterbach, *It Might Get Loud*, trans. Michiel Heyns (Cape Town: Human & Rousseau, 2015), 33. Originally published as *Die aanspraak van lewende wesens* (Cape Town: Human & Rousseau, 2012), quotations from the English text hereafter are from Heyns's translation, unless indicated.
4. Winterbach, *It Might Get Loud*, 34.
5. Ibid., 37.
6. Ibid., 43.
7. Their Afrikaans titles might be rendered literally as 'The book of happenstance and expectation' and 'The underworld', respectively. Winterbach's other novels to date are: as Lettie Viljoen, *Klaaglied vir Koos* (1984, Elegy for Koos), *Erf* (1986; both the verb *to inherit* and a unit of land or property), *Belemmering* (1990, hindrance), *Karolina Ferreira* (1993; the proper name of the lead character yielded to *The Elusive Moth*, object of entomologist Karolina's quest, when the translation appeared under Winterbach's name in 2003), and *Landskap met vroue en slang* (1996; landscape with women and snake); and as Winterbach, *Buller se plan* (1999; Buller's plan), *Niggie* (2002; *niggie* means either niece or cousin, but the novel was published in English as *To Hell With Cronjé* in 2007), the three already mentioned, and *Vlakwater* (shallow or stagnant water), published in Afrikaans in 2015.

8. Ingrid Winterbach, *The Road of Excess*, trans. Leon de Kock (Cape Town: Human & Rousseau, 2014), 36. Originally published as *Die benederyk* (Cape Town: Human & Rousseau, 2010). Quotations from the English translation are from De Kock's translation.
9. Winterbach, *The Road of Excess*, 9.
10. Ibid., 247; see also 166.
11. See Lauren Berlant, *The Queen of America Goes to Washington City: Essays on Sex and Citizenship* (Durham, NC: Duke University Press, 1997), 15. In *Cruel Optimism*, Berlant makes clear the relation of recent work to her longer engagement with 'U.S. aesthetics, erotics, and politics over the last two centuries' (specifically in what she called her 'national sentimental trilogy'—*The Anatomy of National Fantasy*, *The Female Complaint*, and *The Queen of America*), reiterating her central concerns with 'the affective components of citizenship and the public sphere,' especially with 'how intimate publics work in proximity to normative modes of love and the law.' See Lauren Berlant, *Cruel Optimism* (Durham, NC: Duke University Press, 2011), 2–3.
12. Berlant, *Cruel Optimism*, 3.
13. Ibid., 259.
14. Ibid., 49.
15. Ibid., 15–16.
16. Ibid., 16. My emphasis.
17. Ibid., 6–7.
18. Ibid., 5.
19. Ibid., 195.
20. Ibid., 176.
21. See Loren Kruger, *The Drama of South Africa: Plays, Pageants and Publics since 1910* (New York: Routledge, 1999), 86–91, and Lewis Nkosi, *Home and Exile and Other Selections* (London: Longman, 1983), 139.
22. This term, distinct from the word 'Colored' in United States English usage, signifies in a particular way in South Africa, whose fraught history of racial classification regrettably makes it unavoidable to continue to use such terms. The editors of the *Cambridge History of South African Literature* offer this useful gloss:

    > The terms 'black' and 'African' are used to refer to the indigenous Bantu language speakers and their descendants, 'white' to European immigrants and their descendants, and 'coloured' (without capitalisation or quotation marks) to what the apartheid legislators called 'Coloured' or 'mixed-race' peoples. [...] In opposition to the official vocabulary of apartheid, '"coloured"' in quotation marks and 'so-called coloured' were widely used, but the term can now be employed without any stigma.

    See 'Note on racial nomenclature and languages', in *The Cambridge History of South African Literature*, ed. David Attwell and Derek Attridge (Cambridge: Cambridge University Press, 2012), xvii. I take issue with the final statement, given that many intellectuals and writers who might once have been expected to self-identify in this way refuse the term. I use coloured throughout, where it seems unavoidable to do so, and Coloured where I refer to the apartheid-era classificatory term.

23. Jensma, 'Spanner in the What? Works', 9. An artist and author of three volumes of poetry, Jensma was educated there and in Pretoria. He married Lydia Thabede, a black woman whom he met in Mozambique, in Swaziland in 1967, which meant that they could not live together in South Africa (due to the notorious Immorality and Mixed Marriages Acts). Jensma suffered mental-health problems and, after the collapse of his marriage, left his family and lived an itinerant life in South Africa. See Peter McDonald, *The Literature Police: Apartheid Censorship and its Cultural Consequences* (Oxford: Oxford University Press, 2009), 297–302; Michael Gardiner, 'Wopko Jensma', in *Wopko Jensma: Possessing Tools/Professing Artistry* (Johannesburg: Gallery AOP, 2013), 19–20. I am grateful to Hedley Twidle for reminding me of the valences of 'situation' in Nkosi's and Jensma's work.
24. *Die boek van toeval en toeverlaat* did particularly well, winning the W.A. Hofmeyr Prize, M-Net award in the Afrikaans category, University of Johannesburg Prize, and C.L. Engelbrecht Prize, while the translation won the SALA Prize for translation in 2010. Other prizes include: the Hofmeyr for *Die aanspraak van lewende wesens* (2013) and *Buller se plan* (2000); the Hertzog for *Die aanspraak* (2013) and *Niggie* (2004); the M-Net prize in Afrikaans for *Die aanspraak* (2013), *Die benederyk* (2011), and *Karolina Ferreira* (1994). *Die aanspraak* also won the University of Johannesburg Prize (2013) and *Karolina Ferreira* the Old Mutual literature prize (1994).
25. Helize van Vuuren, '"Alles vloei en niks hou stand": 'n Verkenning van Ingrid Winterbach se *Die boek van toeval en toeverlaat*', *Stilet* 20.1 (2008), 171–2, my translations.
26. On the library, see Ingrid Winterbach, *The Book of Happenstance*, trans. Dirk and Ingrid Winterbach (2008; Rochester, NY: Open Letter, 2011), chapter 7, and on black optimism, consider the unusually 'irrepressible optimism' ascribed to Nathi Gule, the museum's dreadlocked 'geologist in training' (176). Originally published as *Die boek van toeval en toeverlaat* (Cape Town: Human & Rousseau, 2006), quotations are from the English translation.
27. Winterbach, *Book of Happenstance*, 87.
28. See Van Vuuren, 'Alles vloei en niks hou stand', 164.
29. Winterbach, *Book of Happenstance*, 76.
30. Ibid., 96.
31. Ibid., 74; see also 7–8. Sof's surname, Benade, is symbolic and allusive too; readers of Marlene van Niekerk's *Triomf*, discussed briefly in Chapter 3, will recognize the surname from that novel of transition-era trauma.
32. Winterbach, *Book of Happenstance*, 104.
33. Ibid., 62.
34. Berlant, *Cruel Optimism*, 185–6.
35. Ibid., 185.
36. Ibid. See also Sara Ahmed, *The Promise of Happiness* (Durham, NC: Duke University Press, 2010).

37. Winterbach, *Book of Happenstance*, 31, 56. Regarding Verwey, in that his name suggests the decline of religious belief (*theo* for god; *ver-* a prefix indicating past action), the absence of explanation is entirely appropriate. Names in the novel are frequently suggestive of existential dilemmas or the inadequacy of apparent responses to them. Sof's name may suggest wisdom but she is erratic and eccentric; Frans, Helena's lover, has a name (meaning 'France', historically an abbreviation of *Fransman*, 'Frenchman') gesturing backwards (to many Afrikaners' French Huguenot ancestry) and forwards (to emigration), but in both cases not engaging with the present. I suggest below that Freek van As may represent death. As in other Winterbach novels, the reader is also tempted to unpick a host of biblical names (Ruth, Judith, etc.).
38. See J.M. Coetzee, 'Alex La Guma and the Responsibilities of the South African Writer', *Journal of the New African Literature and the Arts* 9–10 (September 1971), 5–11. This was later revised as 'Man's Fate in the Novels of Alex La Guma (1974)', in *Doubling the Point: Essays and Interviews*, ed. David Attwell (Cambridge, MA: Harvard University Press, 1992), 344–60. For a discussion of Coetzee's assessment, and its development, see Andrew van der Vlies, *South African Textual Cultures: White, Black, Read All Over* (Manchester: Manchester University Press, 2007), 124–6.
39. Winterbach, *Book of Happenstance*, 66.
40. See ibid., 160, 168.
41. Ibid., 104, 144. There is a parallel to Helena's sexual abuse in Sailor's memory of his father abusing his brother (115), and Hugo Hattingh having 'a taste for child pornography' (34).
42. Winterbach, *Book of Happenstance*, 109, my emphasis. Sailor is also shown to be unstable, and there is at least a suggestion that he may have been responsible for stealing Helena's shells (he wears the same Hugo Boss aftershave that the police detective notices in Helena's garden flat after the theft, for instance; see 7, 221).
43. Ibid., 26.
44. Ibid., 42.
45. See ibid., 183.
46. Helena selects works by many of these Afrikaans writers from books being de-accessioned by the Durban library. There are repeated references to Van den Heever (ibid., 21, 124), and there is a silent quotation from Leipoldt's much-loved poem 'Oktobermaand' ('The Month October'), in translation as 'October is the loveliest month' (200). For references to Kafka (45), Joyce (55, 140), Stevens (14–15, 124), and Stoppard (152), see the pages referenced parenthetically here.
47. For a discussion of the novel's setting and chronology, see Andrew van der Vlies, '"[*From*] whom this writing then?": Politics, Aesthetics and the Personal in Coetzee's *Age of Iron*', in *Approaches to Teaching Coetzee's* Disgrace *and Other Works*, ed. Laura Wright, Elleke Boehmer, and Jane Poyner (New York: MLA, 2014), 96–104.

48. Winterbach, *Happenstance*, 129. See J.M. Coetzee, *Age of Iron* (1990; London: Penguin, 1991), 16.
49. All Winterbach, *Happenstance*, 117, see also 249.
50. Coetzee, *Age of Iron*, 6, 85. The morbid symptoms are exemplified in Coetzee's text by Mrs Curren's cancer, on which more follows.
51. Winterbach, *Book of Happenstance*, 235.
52. Ibid., 249.
53. Ibid., 235.
54. See ibid., 12, 16, 17, 186–8.
55. See Joseph M. Conte, 'Conclusion: Writing Amid the Ruins: 9/11 and *Cosmopolis*', in *The Cambridge Companion to Don DeLillo*, ed. John N. Duvall (Cambridge: Cambridge University Press, 2008), 181; and Jerry A. Varsava, 'The "Saturated Self": Don DeLillo on the Problem of Rogue Capitalism', *Contemporary Literature* 46.1 (2005), 83–4.
56. See Don DeLillo, *Cosmopolis* (London: Picador, 2003), 77–107, for Kinski and the anti-capitalist demonstrations; see also Varsava, 'The "Saturated Self"', 90–1.
57. See Nathan Geffen, *Debunking Delusions: The Inside Story of the Treatment Action Campaign* (Auckland Park: Jacana Media, 2010), Mandisa Mbali, *South African AIDS Activism and Global Health Politics* (New York: Palgrave Macmillan, 2013), and Mark Gevisser, *A Legacy of Liberation: Thabo Mbeki and the Future of the South African Dream* (New York: Palgrave Macmillan, 2009), especially 276–96.
58. On the detective plot in DeLillo, see Philipp Schweighauser and Adrian S. Wisnicki, 'The End of Resolution? Reflections on the Ethics of Closure in Don DeLillo's Detective Plots', in *Terrorism, Media, and the Ethics of Fiction: Transatlantic Perspectives on Don DeLillo*, ed. Peter Schneck and Philipp Schweighauser (London: Bloomsbury, 2012), 158–70. It is worth noting that the arcane ways of the stock market (referenced in *Cosmopolis*) fit as easily into the category of knowledge systems whose attractions DeLillo is keen to hold up to scrutiny as does Islamic fundamentalism (most obviously in *Falling Man*, 2007, though also in *Mao II*). In general, on DeLillo's engagement with postmodernism, consumption, and belief, see Mark Osteen, *American Magic and Dread: Don DeLillo's Dialogue with Culture* (Philadelphia: University of Pennsylvania Press, 2000).
59. Etienne Leroux was the pseudonym of Stephanus Petrus Daniël Le Roux (1922–89). The *Sestigers* were a movement of avant-garde Afrikaans poets and novelists who came to prominence in the 1960s, and whose number included Breyten Breytenbach, Jan Rabie, and André Brink. Leroux's most celebrated novel is *Sewe dae by die Silbersteins* (1962), translated as *Seven Days at the Silbersteins* by Charles Eglington (1964). This appeared alongside *The Third Eye* (1966; *Die Derde Oog*, 1966) and *One for the Devil* (1968; *Een vir Azazel*, 1964) in a single volume: *To a Dubious Salvation: A Trilogy of Fantastical Novels*, published by Penguin in 1972. Ronél Johl observes that Brink had popularized new theories of temporality for Afrikaans readers

(Einstein, Planck, Heisenborg, Bergson, Proust, amongst others) in his 1967 *Aspekte van die nuwe prosa* (aspects of the new prose), a textbook much in use in university classrooms that had a significant impact on a generation of writers (not only the *Sestigers*, but also their successors, like Winterbach). See Ronél Johl's 'Oor eindes en beginne: Tyd en ruimte in Ingrid Winterbach se *Die boek van toeval en toeverlaat*', *Stilet* 20.1 (2008), 144.

60. Don DeLillo, 'In the Ruins of the Future: Reflections on Terror and Loss in the Shadow of September', *Harper's Magazine* (December 2001), 33.
61. Ibid.
62. Ibid., 37, 34.
63. Adam Thurschwell, 'Writing and Terror: Don DeLillo on the Task of Literature After 9/11', *Law and Literature* 19.2 (2007), 289.
64. Don DeLillo, *Falling Man* (New York: Scribner, 2007), 12. See Linda S. Kauffman, 'Bodies in Rest and Motion in *Falling Man*', in *Don DeLillo:* Mao II/Underworld/Falling Man, ed. Stacey Olster (London and New York: Continuum, 2011), 147. It is worth observing that *The Body Artist* also features the unexplained death of a man, protagonist Lauren Hartke's husband (echoed, perhaps, in the death of Theo Verwey), and also the appearance of a stranger in her house (like, though also quite unlike, Vercueil in *Age of Iron*).
65. DeLillo, 'In the Ruins of the Future', 39.
66. Thurschwell develops these points by putting into conversation DeLillo's desire for a narrative to counter the 'competing destructive "world narratives" of cyber-capitalism and terror' (identified in his *Harper's* essay), and Maurice Blanchot's characterization of literature *itself* as a kind of terror. For Blanchot (in 'Literature and the Right to Death'), and for Jean Paulhan before him (Thurschwell notes that the idea was proposed by Paulhan, for whom those who challenge literary convention are 'Terrorists' as opposed to 'Rhetoricians', who merely work within conventions), writing negates the entire world in order to offer the reader, in its place, a substitute fictional world. If representation replaces the object represented, this argument goes, then insofar as the representation is literary *and* constitutes an act of mourning, it is *like* terrorism on two counts: in the manner of Blanchot and Paulhan's metaphoric description of the force of the truly (original) literary act, *and* because it stands in for something annihilated (see Thurschwell, 'Writing and Terror', 281–4). At the same time, Thurschwell continues (291), if the work of artistic production is susceptible to commodification, it *doubly* annihilates that which it is meant to represent. On the whole, this argument has suggestive force, although to agree entirely with his comparisons one would have to imagine that the representation *intends* to replace the object mourned (which seems, for this reader at least, a step too far). The difference, Thurschwell argues, 'between the death inflicted in Blanchot's account of terror in literature and the death mourned in DeLillo's depiction of the artist-in-mourning', which resides in 'the difference between murder and mortality' (terrorism kills; but everyone dies in the absence of terror—or murder—

anyway), means that representation that is self-consciously memorialization leaves room for love 'alongside of'—thus overriding—'the annihilating idealization that (Blanchot teaches us) constitutes the essence of every signifying act' (291–2).

67. Though there are strong echoes of *Underworld* in *It Might Get Loud* too, for example in the similarities between the disused military installations in which the respective mage-like artist figures set up their transformative workshops in both novels: Klara-Sax's airbase out in the desert (*Underworld*), and Josias Brandt's military storage depots in the mountainside in Tamboerskloof (Winterbach, *It Might Get Loud*, 257–68). *Cosmopolis* is also invoked in *The Road of Excess*.
68. Winterbach, *It Might Get Loud*, 80.
69. Winterbach, *Die aanspraak van lewende wesens*, 88. Here *research* and *installation*, like the italicized *vast*, are also rendered in English.
70. Winterbach, *It Might Get Loud*, 141.
71. Winterbach, *The Road of Excess*, 11. Aaron wonders, too, whether the young artists who have replaced him in his gallerist's esteem are sent to him as guides (66, 150).
72. Winterbach, *It Might Get Loud*, 105. The Afrikaans original attempts to give the flavour of *Kaaps*, the form of Afrikaans spoken by coloured first-language speakers in the Western Cape, which is nearly impossible to convey in English.
73. See Winterbach, *It Might Get Loud*, 107–15.
74. Ibid., 250.
75. Winterbach, *The Road of Excess*, 98.
76. See Vincent Crapanzano, *Waiting: The Whites of South Africa* (1985; London: Paladin, 1986), x, 43–7, and on religion in particular, 70, 99, 219–33. In *Imaginative Horizons: An Essay in Literary-Philosophical Anthropology* (Chicago: University of Chicago Press, 2010), Crapanzano reflects on white South Africans' 'waiting-induced paralysis' in the 1980s, and remembers their 'end-of-the world fantasies' (115). The location of Crapanzano's fieldwork is nowhere named, but is clearly Franschhoek.
77. Crapanzano, *Waiting*, 43.
78. Crapanzano, *Imaginative Horizons*, 115.
79. Ibid., 114.
80. Several characters in *The Road of Excess* and *It Might Get Loud* strongly resemble producers of the kinds of art much in favour with the most powerful commercial galleries. In the former, Jimmy Harris is a white working-class Afrikaner video artist, while the work of Moeketsi Mosekedi, a sculptor, suggests that of Nicholas Hlobo. Like Hlobo, Mosekedi works 'with just about any waste material he could lay his hands on,' which is 'transformed into something astonishingly ingenious' (50). In *It Might Get Loud*, the black artist whose visit to Brandt's farm is recounted in a letter to Maria is not unlike Nandipha Mntambo, 'princess of Swaziland and Sheba. She works in cowhide and bronze' (295).

81. Winterbach, *The Road of Excess*, 94.
82. Though Aaron later finds that Beuys and other post-war German artists seem too enmeshed in a cult of personality to offer the selfless models he finds in certain Renaissance artists (ibid., 152).
83. Winterbach, *The Road of Excess*, 137.
84. Ibid., 13.
85. Ibid.
86. Ibid., 54–5.
87. See ibid., 152.
88. See for example Emmanuel Levinas, 'Ethics and the Face', in *Totality and Infinity* (1961), trans. Alphonso Lingis (1969; Dordrecht: Kluwer, 1991), 194–219.
89. Emmanuel Levinas, 'Is Ontology Fundamental?' in *Basic Philosophical Writings*, ed. Adriaan T. Peperzak, Simon Critchley, and Robert Bernasconi (Bloomington: Indiana University Press, 1996), 1–10; 9. Judith Butler discusses Levinas's idea of the face of the other/Other in *Precarious Life: The Powers of Mourning and Violence* (2004; London and New York: Verso, 2006), 131–40.
90. Winterbach, *The Road of Excess*, 146, 302.
91. Sigmund Freud, 'Mourning, and Melancholia' (1917), trans. Shaun Whiteside, in *On Murder, Mourning and Melancholia* (London: Penguin, 2005), 204–5. See also Ian Craib, *The Importance of Disappointment* (London and New York: Routledge, 1994), 17. Judith Butler notes, however, that Freud would suggest later, in *The Ego and the Id* (1922), 'that incorporation, originally associated with melancholia, was essential to the task of mourning' (*Precarious Life*, 20–1). I engage further with melancholia in relation to nostalgia in Chapter 4.
92. Winterbach, *The Road of Excess*, 98 (also 167); 197.
93. Wilhelm Reich, *Reich Speaks of Freud*, ed. Mary Higgins and Chester M. Raphael (New York: Farrar, Straus and Giroux, 1967), 6. Reich is referring here in interview to his previous work, in *The Cancer Biopathy* (New York: Orgone Institute Press, 1948), and applying it to Freud. Susan Sontag, *Illness as Metaphor* (1977), reprinted in *Illness as Metaphor* and *AIDS and Its Metaphors* (London: Penguin, 1991), 23.
94. Coetzee, *Age of Iron*, 142, 132. See Siddharta Mukherjee, *The Emperor of All Maladies: A Biography of Cancer* (2010; London: Fourth Estate, 2011), 48.
95. Butler, *Precarious Life*, 22 (and see 20–1). 'Is this not another way of imagining community, one in which we are alike only in having this condition separately and so having in common a condition that cannot be thought without difference?' she asks (27).
96. Ibid., 30.
97. Berlant, *Cruel Optimism*, 182.
98. Ibid.
99. Winterbach, *The Road of Excess*, 11, 163.
100. Berlant, *Cruel Optimism*, 176, and see 5.

101. David Scott, 'Tragedy's Future: Postemancipation Futures Past and Present', in *Rethinking Tragedy*, ed. Rita Felski (Baltimore: Johns Hopkins University Press, 2008), 209, 213. See also 204–5.
102. Ibid., 213. Scott's formulation is: 'the conceptual languages bequeathed by colonial enlightenment'. Scott explores this analysis at greater length in his earlier monograph, *Conscripts of Modernity: The Tragedy of Colonial Enlightenment* (Durham, NC: Duke University Press, 2004), and develops them in *Omens of Adversity*, cited in the Introduction to this study.
103. Scott, 'Tragedy's Future', 200.
104. Ibid., 215. I return to the idea of 'attunement' in Chapter 2 below.
105. Crapanzano, *Waiting*, x.

NOTES TO CHAPTER 2

1. J.M. Coetzee, 'Erasmus: Madness and Rivalry', *Giving Offense: Essays on Censorship* (Chicago: University of Chicago Press, 1996), 83. The essay first appeared in print in *Neophilologus* 76.1 (January 1992), 1–18.
2. John Ashbery, 'Grand Galop', in *Self-Portrait in a Convex Mirror* (New York: Viking, 1975), 14 (lines 11–13). Photocopied pages in box 94.1 (Research Materials, Adorno-Augustine, 1934–89), Coetzee papers, Harry Ransom Humanities Research Center, University of Texas at Austin (hereafter HRC).
3. Vincent Crapanzano, *Waiting: The Whites of South Africa* (1985; London: Paladin, 1986), 44.
4. J.M. Coetzee, *Life & Times of Michael K* (1983; London: Vintage, 2004), 151, 152. Invoking Elizabeth Freeman's *Time Binds: Queer Temporalities, Queer Histories* (Durham, NC: Duke University Press, 2010), we might say K refuses 'chrononormativity' (xiv).
5. J.M. Coetzee, *Age of Iron* (1990; London: Penguin, 1991), 6 (and see 85); 164.
6. Ibid., 132. I discuss Gordimer's use of Gramsci's diagnosis in this book's Introduction. *Age of Iron* engages with the kind of activism imagined by some of Gordimer's female characters in moments of crisis; *July's People* (1981) and *The Late Bourgeois World* (1966) are key intertexts. See Andrew van der Vlies, '"[*From*] whom this writing then?": Politics, Aesthetics and the Personal in Coetzee's *Age of Iron*', in *Approaches to Teaching Coetzee's* Disgrace *and Other Works*, ed. Laura Wright, Elleke Boehmer, and Jane Poyner (New York: MLA, 2014), 102–3.
7. Timothy Bewes, *The Event of Postcolonial Shame* (Princeton: Princeton University Press, 2011), 153 (citing Alain Badiou's *The Century*, trans. Alberto Toscano [2007], 65); 138; 153.
8. This served as subtitle for *Boyhood*; absent from *Youth*, it was used again for *Summertime*, and as title for the single volume comprising all three: J.M. Coetzee, *Scenes from Provincial Life* (London: Harvill Secker, 2011).

9. J.M. Coetzee, 'SA authors must learn modesty', *Die Vaderland*, 1 May 1981, 16. David Lurie describes South Africa as being 'in the margins of history' in *Disgrace* (London: Secker & Warburg, 1999), 167.
10. J.M. Coetzee, *Doubling the Point: Essays and Interviews*, ed. David Attwell (Cambridge, MA: Harvard University Press, 1992), 391; see 394.
11. J.M. Coetzee, *Truth in Autobiography* (Cape Town: University of Cape Town Press, 1984), 5. In general, see Sue Kossew, '*Scenes from Provincial Life* (1997–2009)', in *A Companion to the Works of J.M. Coetzee*, ed. Tim Mehigan (Rochester, NY: Camden House, 2011), 9–22.
12. Coetzee, *Doubling the Point*, 18.
13. J.M. Coetzee, 'All Autobiography is *Autre*-biography' (Interview), in *Selves in Question: Interviews on Southern African Auto/Biography*, ed. Judith Lütge Coullie, Stephan Meyer, Thengani Ngwenya, and Thomas Olver (Honolulu: University of Hawai'i Press, 2006), 214–15.
14. J.M. Coetzee and Arabella Kurtz, *The Good Story: Exchanges on Truth, Fiction and Psychotherapy* (London: Harvill Secker, 2015), 3. Coetzee continues: 'The claim here is not that autobiography is free, in the sense that we can make up our life-story as we wish. Rather, the claim is that in making up our autobiography we exercise the same freedom that we have in dreams, where we impose a narrative form that is our own, even if influenced by forces that are obscure to us, on elements of a remembered reality.'
15. J.M. Coetzee and Arabella Kurtz, '"Nevertheless, My Sympathies Are With The Karamazovs": An Email Correspondence: May-December 2008', *Salmagundi* 166/167 (2010), 46.
16. Margaret Lenta, in one of the most insightful early discussions of Coetzee's *autre*biographical practice, notes that Coetzee at times extends free-indirect discourse to allow 'the author/narrator not only to offer access to the perceptions and reactions of his protagonist, but also to summarise descriptions of events known to the boy/youth and incorporate the commentary of others'. Lenta also cites Shlomit Rimmon-Kenan, whose 1983 narratology textbook was widely used in South African universities, observing how free-indirect discourse, 'enhances the bivocality or polyvocality of the text by bringing into play a plurality of speakers and attitudes'. See Margaret Lenta, '*Autre*biography: J.M. Coetzee's *Boyhood* and *Youth*', *English in Africa* 30.1 (2003), 164.
17. Coetzee, *Doubling the Point*, 391; Coetzee, 'All Autobiography', 214–15.
18. David Attwell, *J.M. Coetzee and the Life of Writing: Face to Face with Time* (Oxford: Oxford University Press, 2015), 26, see 30.
19. See ibid., 180–1, on the elision of married life from *Summertime*. In the text, there is much speculation amongst John's cousins that he might be gay, a '*moffie*'. See J.M. Coetzee, *Summertime* (London: Harvill Secker, 2009), 101, 114.
20. Coetzee, *Summertime*, 63. Coetzee's work has frequently engaged with the comic, broadly construed. I am reminded of Elizabeth Costello's observation to Paul Rayment in *Slow Man*, a text in which the Croatian family's name, Jokič, thematizes the joke: 'Jokes may indeed have a relation to the unconscious. But

also: sometimes a joke is just a joke. [. . .] Directed against you. Whom else? The man who doesn't laugh. The man who can't take a joke'. J.M. Coetzee, *Slow Man* (2005; London: Vintage, 2006), 259.

21. Sianne Ngai, *Ugly Feelings* (Cambridge, MA: Harvard University Press, 2005), 29 (citing Steve Evans, 'The Dynamics of Literary Change', *Impercipient Lecture Series* 1.1 [February 1997], 8), and see 43.
22. Lars Svendsen, *A Philosophy of Boredom* (1999), trans. John Irons (London: Reaktion, 2005), 114. (*How* is his emphasis, *be* is mine.)
23. Ibid., quoting from Heidegger's *Nietzsche, Erster Band* (Pfullingen, 1989), 119. Emphasis mine.
24. Victor Biceaga, 'Temporality and Boredom', *Continental Philosophy Review* 39 (2006), 144. Biceaga gives a useful account of Heidegger's engagement with boredom in his *Fundamental Concepts of Metaphysics.* Here Heidegger elaborates on three typologies of boredom, 'the superficial *being-bored-by* (*das Gelangweiltwerden von . . .*), the deeper *being-bored-with* (*das Sichlangweilen bei/mit . . .*) and the profound or genuine boredom expressed by the impersonal phrase *it is boring for one* (*es ist einem langweilich*)' (ibid.). The latter, Biceaga explains, is 'attainable through the deepening of ordinary boredom', and involves the indistinguishable intermingling of 'subjective and objective components of mood' (146). See also Svendsen, *Philosophy of Boredom*, 116.
25. 'Idleness in SA 1982', folder in box 64.1 (Short Works: Typescript early works, 1981–82), Coetzee Papers, HRC.
26. J.M. Coetzee, *Diary of a Bad Year* (London: Harvill Secker, 2007), 217, 219, 220.
27. Quoted by Ngai, *Ugly Feelings*, 269.
28. Kant and the sublime features in a significant scene of the negotiation of reason and feeling in a key intertext for *Boyhood* and *Youth*, Robert Musil's *The Confusions of Young Törless.*
29. Coetzee and Kurtz, 'Nevertheless, My Sympathies Are With The Karamazovs', 66.
30. See Ann Cvetkovich, *Depression: A Public Feeling* (Durham, NC: Duke University Press, 2012), 85–6. Cassian's volume was *De Institutis de Coenobiorum.* Cvetkovich also notes how *acedia* served in the Renaissance and Romantic periods as negative (religious) counterpart to melancholia, where the latter was cast as potential source of creativity or inspiration (89).
31. Roland Barthes, *How to Live Together: Novelistic Simulations of Some Everyday Spaces. Notes for a Lecture Course and Seminar at the Collège de France (1976–1977)* (2002 as *Comment vivre ensemble*), trans. Kate Briggs (New York: Columbia University Press, 2013), 21. The course was animated (he explains) by a fantasy of idiorrhythmy, an attempt to balance the individual's 'rhythm' with the community's (see 6–9).
32. J.M. Coetzee, *Boyhood: Scenes from Provincial Life* (London: Secker & Warburg, 1997), 162.
33. Ibid., 34. We might assume from J.C. Kannemeyer's detailed biography that, by and large, these movements track the 'real' Coetzee's own—although

Kannemeyer himself relied heavily on *Boyhood* as a source for his biography. I am not interested here in precise correlation between representation and 'truth': where there is fictionalization it is itself an autobiographical act, if we follow Coetzee's logic, and we can therefore ask what aesthetic 'truth' any representation of disaffection might convey without undue concern about its veracity.

34. Coetzee, *Boyhood*, 108, 70. Heroes referenced range from the (white) South African folk hero Wolraad Woltemade, to those from myth, legend, and imperial adventure, whom John invokes: Leonidas at Thermopylae, Horatius defending the bridge across the Tiber from the Etruscans, 'Roland holding the pass against the Saracens' (24–5), and Scott of the Antarctic (46–7). Even the Russians (26–7) serve as romantic (anti-)heroes, chosen because everyone else likes the Americans.
35. J.M. Coetzee, *Youth* (London: Secker & Warburg, 2002), 104.
36. Ibid., 41.
37. Ibid., 37.
38. Ibid., 165.
39. Ibid., 80.
40. A number of scholars have written illuminatingly on Coetzee's debts to Beckett. See for example Chris Ackerley, 'Style: Coetzee and Beckett', in Mehigan, ed., *A Companion to the Works of J.M. Coetzee*, 26–30. Coetzee has also said, however: 'Let us not overestimate my involvement with Beckett. There are writers who have meant more to me than he has.' Lawrence Rainey, David Attwell, and Benjamin Madden, 'An Interview with J.M. Coetzee', *Modernism/Modernity* 18.4 (2012), 847.
41. Coetzee, *Youth*, 65, 117.
42. J.M. Coetzee, 'Homage', *The Threepenny Review* 53 (Spring 1993), 5. On Eliot and his significance for (proto-)postcolonial modernists, see Matthew Hart, *Nations of Nothing But Poetry: Modernism, Transnationalism, and Synthetic Vernacular Writing* (New York: Oxford University Press, 2010), ch. 4.
43. Attwell, *J.M. Coetzee and the Life of Writing*, 33, citing Eliot's 'Tradition and the Individual Talent' (1919), in *Selected Essays* (London: Faber, 1932), 21.
44. Coetzee, *Youth*, 136.
45. Ibid., 138.
46. Ibid., iii. Rita Barnard suggests that Coetzee's use of the epigraph from Goethe for *Youth* might be read not only as 'motto of the aspirant author, John', who has followed his poetic mentors' footsteps to London, but also as 'guidance to Coetzee's readers': 'despite his rejection of the designation "South African writer," his fiction has to be understood in some sort of relation to his native country'. Rita Barnard, *Apartheid and Beyond: South African Writers and the Politics of Place* (New York: Oxford University Press, 2007), 15.
47. Paul Sheehan, 'The Disasters of *Youth*: Coetzee and Geomodernism', *Twentieth-Century Literature* 57.1 (Spring 2011), 29.

48. Coetzee, *Summertime*, 7 (and see 205).
49. Ibid., 23.
50. Ibid., 111.
51. Ibid., 209.
52. Coetzee, 'SA authors must learn modesty', 16.
53. The speech was delivered on 9 November 1987 at the Weekly Mail Book Week literary fair in Johannesburg, and published the following year as J. M. Coetzee, 'The Novel Today', *Upstream* 6.1 (Summer 1988), see 2.
54. 'Russian literature of the age of Dostoevsky and Tolstoy is provincial and major', Coetzee noted. 'SA authors must learn modesty', 16.
55. Saikat Majumdar, *Prose of the World: Modernism and the Banality of Empire* (New York: Columbia University Press, 2013), 35.
56. Ibid., 176. One is reminded, in the South African context, of Njabulo Ndebele's call for the 'rediscovery of the ordinary', which Majumdar references.
57. Majumdar, *Prose of the World*, 5.
58. Anna Snaith, *Modernist Voyages: Colonial Women Writers in London, 1890–1945* (New York: Cambridge University Press, 2014), 7; David James and Urmila Seshagiri, 'Metamodernism: Narratives of Continuity and Revolution', *PMLA* 129.1 (2014), 90. In Douglas Mao and Rebecca L. Walkowitz's formulation, the new modernist 'rubric encompasses at least two significant enterprises: one that reconsiders the definitions, locations, and producers of "modernism" and another that applies new approaches and methodologies to "modernist" works'. See their 'Introduction: Modernisms Bad and New', in their (eds), *Bad Modernisms* (Durham, NC: Duke University Press, 2006), 1. For other seminal work on the new modernism, see Susan Stanford Friedman, 'Periodizing Modernism: Postcolonial Modernities and the Space/Time Borders of Modernist Studies', *Modernism/Modernity* 13.3 (2006), 425–43, and 'Planetarity: Musing Modernist Studies', *Modernism/Modernity* 17.3 (2010), 471–99; and Jessica Berman, *Modernist Commitments: Ethics, Politics, and Transnational Modernism* (New York: Columbia University Press, 2011).
59. James and Seshagiri, 'Metamodernism', 88, 89, 88; see 91.
60. As David James has argued elsewhere about the oeuvre in general, citing Coetzee's own assessment of the lesson of Beckett's work (the refusal of 'style as consolation, style as redemption', in *Doubling the Point*, 47). See his '*Dusklands* (1974)', in Mehigan, ed., *A Companion to the Works of J. M. Coetzee*, 52.
61. Coetzee, *Youth*, 48–9, 68–76, 91.
62. See Fredric Jameson, *A Singular Modernity: Essay on the Ontology of the Present* (London: Verso, 2002), especially 198–9.
63. See Franco Moretti, *The Way of the World: The* Bildungsroman *in European Culture* (1987), trans. Albert Spragia (London and New York: Verso, 2000), 5. See also David Scott, *Omens of Adversity* (Durham, NC: Duke University Press, 2014), 73.

64. Jed Esty, *Unseasonable Youth: Modernism, Colonialism, and the Fiction of Development* (New York: Oxford University Press, 2012), 5 (quoting Bakhtin's 'The Bildungsroman and Its Significance in the History of Realism'), 3.
65. Ibid., 21, 5.
66. Coetzee, *Slow Man*, 114.
67. Arne De Boever, *States of Exception in the Contemporary Novel: Martel, Eugenides, Coetzee, Sebald* (New York and London: Continuum, 2012), 144; see 145.
68. Joseph Slaughter, *Human Rights, Inc.* (New York: Fordham University Press, 2007), 123.
69. Coetzee, *Boyhood*, 140.
70. Ibid., 165, 108, 17.
71. Ibid., 29.
72. Ibid., 13.
73. Ibid., 161. Coetzee repeats almost precisely this phrasing in an exchange with Arabella Kurtz about the relationship between storytelling and therapy: 'The Wordsworthian term "intimations" seems to me about as far as one can go: for an instant the veil opens and one has a flash of insight; then it closes again.' Coetzee and Kurtz, 'Nevertheless, My Sympathies Are With The Karamazovs', 58.
74. Coetzee, *Summertime*, 32, 44.
75. Ibid., 193 (and for Margot, see 88, 91, 119, 137).
76. Ibid., 193.
77. Coetzee, 'Erasmus: Madness and Rivalry', 83.
78. Ibid., 84.
79. Ibid., 103.
80. Coetzee, *Diary of a Bad Year*, 136, 142.
81. Ibid., 151.
82. Ibid., 127.
83. David Attwell, 'Mastering Authority: J.M. Coetzee's *Diary of a Bad Year*', *Social Dynamics* 36.1 (March 2010), 219.
84. Johan Geertsema, 'Coetzee's *Diary of a Bad Year*, Politics, and the Problem of Position', *Twentieth-Century Literature* 57.1 (Spring 2011), 75.
85. J.M. Coetzee, handwritten notes for a reading in Reykjavik on 12 September 2007, 'Iceland' folder, box 62.4 (Long Works: *Diary of a Bad Year*, printouts for public readings, 2007), Coetzee papers, HRC, 1, deletion Coetzee's own. On the second page, he calls *Diary* 'a work of mixed genre, essay and narrative. The mixture of forms allows me to frame the opinions it contains'.
86. See variously Lenta, '*Autre*biography', 158–60; Hermione Lee, 'Uneasy Guest', *London Review of Books* 24.13 (11 July 2002), 14–15; Derek Attridge, *J.M. Coetzee and the Ethics of Reading: Literature in the Event* (Chicago: University of Chicago Press, 2004), 141; Kossew, '*Scenes from Provincial Life*', 22.
87. Derek Attridge, 'Introduction', in *Inner Workings: Literary Essays 2000–2005* by J.M. Coetzee (New York: Viking, 2007), xi.

88. Márai's origins were in Kaschau (Kassa in Hungarian), which became Košice in the new state of Czechoslovakia after 1919. Though Musil (a key influence on Coetzee, he claims in 'Homage') also lived at times in Germany and Switzerland, where he died in exile after fleeing Nazi Austria, his chief context is Austro-Hungarian (the school that provided the model for *The Confusions of Young Törless* was in Moravia; Musil lived for long stretches in Vienna). Roth was born in Austro-Hungarian Galicia, a province of Austro-Hungary that largely reverted to Poland after World War I and was absorbed into Ukraine in 1939. Schulz was also born in Galicia (he died under the Nazi occupation). Aaron Ettore Schmitz, for whom Svevo was a pseudonym, was born in Austro-Hungarian Trieste. See variously, J.M. Coetzee, *Inner Workings: Literary Essays 2000–2005* (New York: Viking, 2007), 1–14, 30–9, 65–113, for essays on these authors.
89. See Coetzee, *Inner Workings*, 114. See also J.M. Coetzee, *Stranger Shores: Essays, 1986–1999* (London: Secker & Warburg, 2001), 71–122, and 212–18.
90. Coetzee, *Youth*, 41, see 86.
91. Coetzee, *Summertime*, 69.
92. See ibid., 41, 48, 53. In further references to this part of the larger Habsburg Empire, *Slow Man* features the Croatian Jokič family (see 34, 43, 174). Kiš also echoes Danilo Kiš, the Serbian writer with whom Coetzee engages in *Giving Offense*.
93. Dubyl/du Biel met his wife, Anna Brecher, daughter of Moravian missionaries, in German South West Africa, now Namibia. The couple proselytized in the Midwestern United States for some years before returning to Southern Africa to raise their children, one of whom, Louisa, was mother of Coetzee's mother, Vera Wehmeyer. See Attwell, *J.M. Coetzee and the Life of Writing*, 37, 40. In *Boyhood*, John tries to read Du Biel's memoir, but finds it 'boring' (118).
94. Coetzee glosses the ethnic composition of the empire in *Inner Workings*, 79.
95. Ibid., 35.
96. Ibid., 80.
97. Mabel van der Horst, a character in William Plomer's *Turbott Wolfe* (London: Hogarth, 1925), exclaims of South Africa, 'My good man, there is no native question. It isn't a question. It's an answer' (122). The 'question' was much in the air in the international press in the 1920s. See for instance Anon., '"Solving" the South African Native Problem', *The New Statesman* 30.789 (9 June 1928), 282–4.
98. Gregor von Rezzori, *Memoiren eines Antisemiten* (München: Verlag Steinhausen GmbH, 1979); see 'Memoirs of an Anti-Semite', *The New Yorker*, 26 April 1969, 42–83.
99. André A. Aciman, 'Family Fictions', Review of *The Snows of Yesteryear*, *Salmagundi* 90/91 (1991), 35. The extent of the autobiography is clear by comparing the text to Rezzori's reminiscences, *The Snows of Yesteryear*, trans. H.F. Broch de Rothermann (New York: Knopf, 1989).
100. Gregor von Rezzori, *Memoirs of an Anti-Semite*, trans. Joachim Neugroschel and Gregor von Rezzori (1981; New York: New York Review of Books, 2008), 9, 1.

101. Coetzee, *Boyhood*, 22. See the young John's casual racism towards the children looking in on him through the window of the café where he celebrates his birthday: 'It is quite normal to chase beggar children away' (72). On the usage coloured, see Chapter 1, n22.
102. Coetzee's judgment on romantic attachments to the land (and the idleness this cultivates amongst the master-class) had been made known in advance of *Boyhood*, of course, in his 1988 monograph about the pastoral tradition in South African letters, *White Writing*, and in his 1987 'Jerusalem Prize Acceptance Speech', collected in *Doubling the Point*.
103. John's mother says 'Jews are exploiters', but she also 'prefers Jewish doctors because they know what they are doing'. We learn that 'the stories that Norman and Lance and his mother tell' feature 'the figures of Jews, comic, sly, but also cunning and heartless, like jackals'; they persuade farmers (their father included) to abandon wool farming for ostriches, then take over the farms when the ostrich-feather market crashes. 'That is how the Jews operate, says Norman: you must never trust a Jew.' See Coetzee, *Boyhood*, 37, 22.
104. Rezzori, *Memoirs*, 60; Coetzee, *Boyhood*, 119.
105. Rezzori, *Memoirs*, 72.
106. Ibid., 71.
107. See, for example, the prostitute who gives Rezzori's protagonist 'crabs' (81). His relationship with an older Jewish woman bears comparison with John's relationship with Jacqueline Laurier in the first chapter of *Youth*.
108. On Coetzee's relation to Afrikaans, see Rita Barnard, 'Coetzee in/and Afrikaans', *Journal of Literary Studies* 25.4 (December 2009), 84–105.
109. Coetzee, *Summertime*, 25.
110. Ibid., 54.
111. Coetzee, *Boyhood*, 24.
112. Rezzori, *Memoirs*, 194.
113. Ibid., 224.
114. Ibid., 246, 252–3. This story features the death of a son (249), something shared by Coetzee, though not explicitly by the John Coetzee of any of the *autre*biographical texts. There is an innocent childhood crush on a female cousin, as with John and Margot in *Summertime*.
115. Coetzee, *Summertime*, 228–9.
116. Ibid., 12. As an aside: we might notice here that the challenge of outliving the death of a character sharing his name is staged by *Summertime*, in which the author John Coetzee is dead; and also that the challenge of being outside politics, staged by John Coetzee in relation to Jesus, comes in a book that immediately precedes J.M. Coetzee's enigmatically titled *The Childhood of Jesus* (2013).
117. Coetzee, *Summertime*, 230.
118. Ibid., 229.
119. Ibid., 240.
120. Photocopied page from Anthony Arblaster, *The Rise and Decline of Western Liberalism* (Oxford: Basil Blackwell, 1984), 300, box 94.1 (Research Materials, Adorno-Augustine, 1934–89), Coetzee papers, HRC.

121. Richard Rorty, *Contingency, Irony, and Solidarity* (Cambridge: Cambridge University Press, 1989), 187.
122. Mark Sanders, *Ambiguities of Witnessing: Law and Literature in the Time of a Truth Commission* (Stanford: Stanford University Press, 2007), 6. Geertsema, in 'Coetzee's *Diary of a Bad Year*, also discusses irony (as parabasis).

NOTES TO CHAPTER 3

1. Lauren Berlant, *The Queen of America Goes to Washington City: Essays on Sex and Citizenship* (Durham, NC: Duke University Press, 1997), 4.
2. J.M. Coetzee, 'The Great South African Novel', *Leadership SA* 2.4 (1983), 79.
3. Marlene van Niekerk, *Triomf*, trans. Leon de Kock (London: Abacus, 2000), 150. Quotations are from this edition. For the original Afrikaans, see *Triomf* (Cape Town: Queillerie, 1994). Earlier works included poetry collections *Sprokkelster* (1977) and *Groenstaar* (1983), and the short-story collection *Die vrou wat haar verkyker vergeet het* (1992), none translated.
4. Van Niekerk, *Triomf*, 493. Lambert, tellingly, cannot identify her as mixed-race.
5. Marlene van Niekerk, *Agaat*, trans. Michiel Heyns (Jeppestown: Jonathan Ball, Cape Town: Tafelberg, 2006), 235. Quotations are from this translation. References to the novel's Afrikaans text—Marlene van Niekerk, *Agaat* (Cape Town: Tafelberg, 2004)—are indicated [A]. On my use of coloured, see Chapter 1, n22.
6. Mark Sanders also makes this point, in his 'Miscegenations: Race Culture, Phantasy', *Journal of the Association for the Study of Australian Literature* (2008), 27.
7. Van Niekerk, *Triomf*, 35. On Sophiatown as site of early and mid-twentieth century black modernity, see Ian Baucom, 'Township Modernism', in *Geomodernism: Race, Modernism, Modernity*, ed. Laura Doyle and Laura Winkiel (Bloomington: Indiana University Press, 2005), 227–45.
8. Van Niekerk, *Triomf*, 212.
9. Ibid., 166; see 378.
10. Ibid., 395, 174, 393.
11. See ibid., 359. Mokaba's infamous slogan 'One settler, one bullet' is also to be found as graffiti on a shipping container (279). Later, hearing Terre'-Blanche on the radio, Treppie makes up a song about the multiple colours of the right-wing AWB leader's underpants (476).
12. Ibid., 386. See Willie Burger, '"Om kommunikasie op gang te kry": Die begin en einde van Marlene van Niekerk se oeuvre', *Journal of Literary Studies/Tydskrif vir Literatuurwetenskap* 25.3 (2009), 11.
13. See Van Niekerk, *Triomf*, 368–9. I omit discussion of dogs and fridges, other key metaphors in the novel.
14. Ibid., 20; 31 (and see 33).

15. See variously ibid., 6, 389.
16. Ibid., 199, 201.
17. Sonja Loots, 'Nog in die kielsog', *Rapport, Perspektief,* 28 November 2004, IV. Van Niekerk told Loots she intended *Agaat* 'to record the Afrikaans language, to archive the language, bits of it that are no longer heard' (my translations).
18. See Chapter 1, n22, on this usage.
19. See Patrick Denman Flanery, 'At Grandmother's Ford', *Times Literary Supplement*, 7 December 2007, 19–20.
20. Van Niekerk describes this strand in interview as 'a court of conscience'. See Leon de Kock, 'Intimate Enemies: A Discussion with Marlene van Niekerk and Michiel Heyns about *Agaat* and its Translation into English', *Journal of Literary Studies* 25.3 (2009), 143.
21. This is made clear early in the novel; see, for example, the passage 'She'd already marked the bit she wants to read tonight, the corner of the page emphatically dog-eared'. Van Niekerk, *Agaat,* 9.
22. Matthee's novel *Fiela se Kind* was popularized in its 1988 film adaptation by Katinka Heyns.
23. See Carol J. Singley, *Adopting America: Childhood, Kinship, and National Identity in Literature* (New York: Oxford University Press, 2011), 5, see 3.
24. Ibid., 119. *Our Nig* was 'rediscovered' by Henry Louis Gates, Jr in 1982; it is considered the first novel by an African American woman.
25. Jak calls her a 'hanshotnosmeid', which the English text renders 'a cast-off kitchen-goffel'. See Van Niekerk, *Agaat,* 229; *Agaat* [A], 239.
26. On tragedy, see Van Niekerk, *Agaat,* 304, 546, 666; on soap opera, 606.
27. See variously ibid., 95–100, 284, 330.
28. Ibid., 415, 546, 416.
29. Ibid., 599. Note that this quotation from the South African English translation retains accents for emphasis, as in the Afrikaans; the diacritics were dropped in the British edition: Marlene van Niekerk, *The Way of the Women*, trans. Michiel Heyns (London: Little, Brown, 2007). See also the longer italicized quotation that follows.
30. Van Niekerk, *Agaat,* 692. English in the original ([A] 718).
31. Van Niekerk, *Agaat,* 582 ([A] 603).
32. Van Niekerk, *Agaat,* 487.
33. Ibid., 528 (and see 469).
34. Ibid., 688–9. This is but one of Agaat's many versions of her life experience; she also offers Jakkie a nursery-tale version (365; [A] 379) and Milla a marching song (407; [A] 422–3).
35. Van Niekerk, *Agaat* [A], 716.
36. Van Niekerk, *Agaat,* 136 (compare [A] 142).
37. Ibid., 478.
38. As evidence of this anxiety, notice how, during Jakkie's twenty-fifth birthday party in August 1985, Milla 'realize[s] for the first time' that neighbouring farmers, 'the sallow Dieners of Vreugdevol with their smooth blue-black

hair', are likely 'pure Malay' '[p]ass[ing] for white, whatever that might mean'. Van Niekerk, *Agaat*, 605.

39. Milla, planning to move Agaat into a servant's room, lists them as necessities in her diary on 12 May 1960 (Van Niekerk, *Agaat*, 52, compare [A] 55), and meditates on their relevance as she unpacks them on 4 July (74–5, cf. [A] 78–9). In chapter 16, in the section set on 13 December 1996, Milla notices that Agaat has piled all three volumes on the dressing table as if 'Exhibits' (449, cf. [A] 464). Van Niekerk speaks in interview about happening on *Borduur só*: 'I thought, bingo! Because the term itself lends itself to allegorisation, *borduur*, and then, you know, the whole idea of improvisation in the figurative meaning of the word "embroidery" and so on also could be used in self-reflecting on the novel'. See De Kock, 'Intimate Enemies', 148. There is a rare anachronistic slip (or intended curiosity) here, however, in that *Borduur só* was published in 1966, which means that Milla could not have purchased it in 1960.
40. Elizabeth Freeman, *Time Binds: Queer Temporalities, Queer Histories* (Durham, NC: Duke University Press, 2010), 3, 5.
41. The now classic discussion of the dilemma of black labour in the Afrikaans-language farm novel is to be found in J.M. Coetzee, *White Writing: On the Culture of Letters in South Africa* (New Haven: Yale University Press, 1988); see 5–6, 11.
42. As described in the second 'voices' of chapters 3–5, in which Jak derides Milla's enlightened vision of rotation farming and careful soil conservation, and achieves—but only initially—enormous yields with modern methods that soon deplete the land.
43. Van Niekerk, *Agaat*, v. This is Heyns's translation, my emphases; for '*adopt* it as their own', the original has 'as eie aanneem' ([A] iii).
44. Van Niekerk, *Agaat*, 554.
45. Brian Massumi, 'Perception Attack: The Force to Own Time', in *Theory After 'Theory'*, ed. Jane Elliott and Derek Attridge (Abingdon: Routledge, 2011), 76, and citing Søren Kierkegaard, *Fear and Trembling, and Repetition*, trans. H.V. and E.H. Hong (Princeton: Princeton University Press, 1983), 131.
46. Van Niekerk, *Agaat*, 682; see 2–3, 242. In a wonderful intertextual allusion to *Agaat*, Fanie Naudé's short story, 'VNLS', features a South African composer-performer-musicologist, Ondine, who recalls hearing Jakkie de Wet, 'an exiled South African ethnomusicologist', give a paper titled 'Numbing the Ear: The Afrikaans Folk Music Project (1948–1994) and the Construction of an Aural Past' at a conference in London. S.J. Naudé, *The Alphabet of Birds* (2011; London: And Other Stories, 2015), 199.
47. In interview, Van Niekerk comments: 'I give everybody a mirror: I give Agaat a cracked mirror or a broken one; I give Jak a full-wall one; and I give Milla one with wings that can be adjusted by somebody else; and a broken middle pane that had been broken at some point that reflects differently.' See De Kock, 'Intimate Enemies', 149.
48. Homi K. Bhabha, *The Location of Culture* (London and New York: Routledge, 1994), ch. 4.

49. Van Niekerk, *Agaat*, 3.
50. Ibid., 677.
51. Donna Haraway, 'A Manifesto for Cyborgs: Science, Technology, and Socialist Feminism in the 1980s (An Ironic Dream of a Common Language for Women in the Integrated Circuit)' (1985), in *The Norton Anthology of Theory and Criticism*, 2nd edn, ed. Vincent B. Leitch et al. (New York: WW Norton, 2010), 2199.
52. Ibid., 2215; 2199.
53. See Van Niekerk, *Agaat*, 594–5, 167–8.
54. Marlene van Niekerk, 'So it is a risk, this business of writing', Interview with Hans Pienaar, *LitNet*, 2 June 2005, http://www.oulitnet.co.za/nosecret/van_niekerk_pienaar.asp (accessed 25 November 2013).
55. Haraway herself suggests that the 'three crucial boundary breakdowns' she is most interested in exploring are those between 'human and animal', 'animal-human (organism) and machine', and 'physical and non-physical' ('Manifesto for Cyborgs', 2192–4). 'A cyborg is a cybernetic organism, a hybrid of machine and organism, a creature of social reality', she notes—'as well as a creature of fiction' (2190). For more on how Haraway anticipated cybernetics, see N. Katherine Hayles, 'Unfinished Work: From Cyborg to Cognisphere', *Theory, Culture & Society* 23.7–8 (2006), 159–66.
56. Haraway, 'Manifesto for Cyborgs', 2192.
57. Ibid., 2195.
58. 'The tragic Greek understanding of technics [. . .] composes *topoi* that are constitutive of mortality, being at mortality's limits: on the one hand, immortal, on the other hand, living without knowledge of death (animality); in the gap between these two is technical life—that is, dying'. Bernard Stiegler, *Technics and Time 1: The Fault of Epimetheus* (orig. *La technique et le temps 1. La faute d'Epiméthée*, 1994), trans. Richard Beardsworth and George Collins (Stanford: Stanford University Press, 1998), 186.
59. Bernard Stiegler, *Technics and Time 2: Disorientation* (orig. *La technique et le temps 2. La désorientation*, 1996), trans. Stephen Barker (Stanford: Stanford University Press, 2009), 5; see 4–5, and see also Stiegler, *Technics and Time 1*, 216–18.
60. Stiegler, *Technics and Time 2*, 4.
61. '[W]e must think of cinema and writing within a more vast process, which I call "grammatization." And this is truly what is at stake in *Technics and Time 3*.' Marcel O'Gorman, 'Bernard Stiegler's *Pharmacy*: A Conversation', *Configurations* 18 (2010), 464.
62. Stiegler, *Technics and Time 2*, 4.
63. Including, for example, a book, or more precisely a particular edition of a book. See Bernard Stiegler, *Technics and Time 3: Cinematic Time and the Question of Malaise* (orig. *La technique et le temps 3. Le temps du cinéma et la question du mal-être*, 2001), trans. Stephen Barker (Stanford: Stanford University Press, 2011), 16.
64. O'Gorman, 'Bernard Stiegler's *Pharmacy*', 461–2.

65. Stiegler, *Technics and Time 1*, 219.
66. Stiegler, *Technics and Time 3*, 37–40, 60–1, and *passim*. 'The chief characteristic of temporal objects is that their flux coincides "point-by-point" with the stream of consciousness of which it is the object—which means that consciousness of a temporal object adopts the object's time' (33).
67. Stiegler, *Technics and Time 3*, 99. Although, he argues, '[t]his adoption process works only if it is concealed: it can *take place*, says Ernest Renan, only if it is forgotten' (89).
68. Ibid., 90–1.
69. Ibid., 89. Italics in the original.
70. Stiegler, *Technics and Time 2*, 186.
71. Ibid.
72. Van Niekerk, *Agaat*, 3; in the original Afrikaans, 'MêME OP STERWE STOP BEVESTIG KOMS STOP LIEFDE AGAAT' ([A] 3).
73. 'meme, n.,' OED Online, September 2013 (first included in the OED's Additions Series, volume 3, 1997), Oxford University Press (accessed 24 September 2013).
74. Van Niekerk, *Agaat*, 202.
75. Emily Apter explains that, in a paper delivered in Toronto in the early 1980s, Derrida refers to '"suicide by translation" to talk about cases like "I am speaking in French" that are enunciated in English. Here, the original, in his words, "lets itself be destroyed almost without remainder, without apparent remainder *inside* the corpus".' Emily Apter, *Against World Literature: On the Politics of Untranslatability* (London: Verso, 2013), 242.
76. Writing in 2008, Lawrence Venuti argued that whereas British and American traditions of translation had long been 'dominated by domesticating theories that recommend fluent translating,' the production of a resistant translation could perform an ethical role, constituting what he called 'a strategic cultural intervention [. . .] pitched against the hegemonic English-language nations and the unequal cultural exchanges in which they engage their global others'. See Venuti, *The Translator's Invisibility: A History of Translation*, 2nd edn (Abingdon: Routledge, 2008), 16.
77. Heyns's translation has been justly praised, winning the South African *Sunday Times* fiction prize for author *and* translator, and the South African English Academy's Sol Plaatje prize for translation. In Britain, the translation (published as *The Way of the Women* in 2007) was shortlisted for the *Independent* Foreign Fiction Prize, and in the United States, where it was published in 2010 under its original title, it was named as one of *Publishers Weekly*'s top 100 Best Books, a *Booklist* Editor's Choice List for 2010, and was shortlisted for translation awards.
78. Leon de Kock, 'Cracking the Code: Translation as Transgression in *Triomf*', *Journal of Literary Studies* 25.3 (2009), 22.
79. Leon de Kock, 'Found in translation', *Sunday Times,* 28 January 2007, *Lifestyle* supplement, 18.

80. For an extended discussion of these issues, see Andrew van der Vlies, '"MêME DYING STOP CONFIRM ARRIVAL STOP": Provincial Literatures in Global Time: The Case of Marlene van Niekerk's *Agaat*', in *Institutions of World Literature: Writing, Translation, Markets*, ed. Pieter Vermeulen and Stefan Helgesson (London and New York: Routledge, 2015), 191–208.
81. Michiel Heyns, translator's note, Van Niekerk, *Agaat*, iii.
82. Van Niekerk, *Agaat* [A], 564.
83. See D.J. Opperman, ed., *Groot Verseboek: 'n Bloemlesing uit die Afrikaanse Poësie* (Kaapstad, Bloemfontein, Johannesburg: Nasionale Boekhandel, 1951), 147. South African singers Valiant Swart and Randall Wicomb have both offered versions set to music.
84. Van Niekerk, *Agaat*, 545. See *W.H. Auden: Collected Poems*, ed. Edward Mendelson (New York: Vintage, 1991), 133–5. The quotation is credited in a general note in the acknowledgements at the end of the translation (696).
85. Heyns, translator's note, Van Niekerk, *Agaat*, iii. My emphasis.
86. Van Niekerk, *Agaat*, 74. The line is 'Tears idle tears I know not what they mean'. The corresponding entry in the Afrikaans original ends with the preceding observation: 'must be the hormones that are mixed up'; in the original Afrikaans, 'seker maar die hormone wat deurmekaar is' ([A] 77).
87. The Swedish reads: 'vara hormonerna som spökar. Tårar tomma tårar jag vet inte vad de betyder.' See Marlene van Niekerk, *Agaat*, trans. Niclas Hval (Stockholm: Svante Weyler, 2012), 84. This translation is hereafter [S].
88. Niclas Hval, 'Om översättningen' [On the Translation], *Agaat* [S], 716.
89. Marlene van Niekerk, *Agaat*, trans. Riet de Jong-Goossens (2006; Amsterdam: Querido, 2010).
90. Van Niekerk, *Agaat*, 46.
91. Van Niekerk, *Agaat* [A], 213.
92. Van Niekerk, *Agaat*, 46, [A] 48.
93. Van Niekerk, *Agaat*, 14, [A] 14. The Swedish translation follows Heyns, but translates *all* English *and* Afrikaans titles *except* for the *Oxford Collected Poems* and *Northanger Abbey*. The Dutch translation repeats the Afrikaans exactly.
94. Frank England, 'Imposing Eliot: On Translating *Agaat* by Marlene van Niekerk', *Journal of Literary Studies* 29.1 (2013), 16.
95. Ibid., 6.
96. Michiel Heyns, 'Irreparable Loss and Exorbitant Gain: On Translating *Agaat*', *Journal of Literary Studies* 25.3 (2009), 132.
97. Ibid.
98. De Kock, 'Intimate Enemies', 138 (my emphasis).
99. De Kock, 'Cracking the Code', 23, 24.
100. Ibid., 26.
101. David Damrosch, *What is World Literature?* (Princeton: Princeton University Press, 2003), 4–5; Rebecca L. Walkowitz, 'Unimagineable Largeness: Kazuo Ishiguro, Translation, and the New World Literature', *Novel: A Forum on Fiction* 40.3 (2007), 217.

102. J.M. Coetzee, 'SA authors must learn modesty', *Die Vaderland*, 1 May 1981, 16.
103. Apter, *Against World Literature*, 3.
104. Ibid., 326.
105. Ibid., 20.
106. 'homœopathy, n.,' OED Online, September 2013 (entry not updated since 1899), Oxford University Press (accessed 25 November 2013).
107. Chris Holmes, 'What the World Leaves Behind: Ready-Made Translations and the "Closed Book" in the Postcolonial Novel', in *Literature, Geography, Translation: Studies in World Writing*, ed. Cecelia Alvstad, Stefan Helgesson, and David Watson (Newcastle upon Tyne: Cambridge Scholars Publishing, 2011), 42.
108. De Kock, 'Cracking the Code', 18. See further: 'recasting perceived and reimagined experience about others and otherness in a language other than that in which it arose—across different value systems, incommensurably divergent cultures, unevenly aligned epistemologies, opposing cosmologies and inconsistent worldviews, has historically been the core matter of the writing project itself' (17–18).
109. Apter, *Against World Literature,* 329.

NOTES TO CHAPTER 4

1. Walter Benjamin, 'Excavation and Memory' (*c.*1932), trans. Rodney Livingstone, in *Selected Writings: Volume 2, Part 2 (1931–1934)*, ed. Michael W. Jennings, Howard Eiland, and Gary Smith (Cambridge, MA: Belknap Press of Harvard University Press, 1999), 576.
2. Eric Worby and Shireen Ally, 'The Disappointment of Nostalgia: Conceptualising Cultures of Memory in Contemporary South Africa', *Social Dynamics* 39.3 (2013), 457–80.
3. David Medalie, 'The Uses of Nostalgia', *English Studies in Africa* 53.1 (May 2010), 36, 37.
4. See Denis Hirson, *I Remember King Kong (the Boxer)* (Johannesburg: Jacana, 2004). Hirson explains his indebtedness to Perec in *White Scars: On Reading and Rites of Passage* (Johannesburg: Jacana, 2006), 131–57.
5. Trevor Romain, *Random Kak I Remember about Growing Up in South Africa* (Johannesburg: Penguin South Africa, 2013). Romain's use of *kak* (Afrikaans for *crap,* idiomatically perhaps also *stuff*, thus the title might be rendered *Random Shit I Remember*) seems calculated to speak to a particular kind of white readership, perhaps a white male reader over forty who served in the South African army—the publisher's promotional blurb asks readers to remember 'when there were call-up papers in the mailbox' and the title's language mixing recalls colourful military terms like *afkak* (shitting or being shat on) and *bosbefok (bush-befucked,* suffering from PTSD). See J.H. Thompson, *An Unpopular War: From Afkak to Bosbefok, Voices of South African National Servicemen* (Cape Town: Zebra, 2006).

6. Svetlana Boym, *The Future of Nostalgia* (2002; New York: Basic Books, 2002), 41. See also Heidi Grunebaum, *Memorializing the Past: Everyday Life after the Truth and Reconciliation Commission* (New Brunswick: Transaction, 2011), 12.
7. Mark Gevisser, *Lost and Found in Johannesburg: A Memoir* (New York: Farrar, Straus and Giroux, 2014), 22. This title served as subtitle, after *Dispatcher*, for the first British edition, published by Granta in 2014.
8. Four if one includes *The Exploded View* (2004), a collection of four narratives set in Johannesburg.
9. Fred de Vries, 'Joburg's Ambiguity Mirrored in *Portrait*', Interview with Ivan Vladislavić, *The Weekender*, Weekend Review supplement, 9–10 September 2006, 11.
10. Ivan Vladislavić, *Willem Boshoff* (Houghton: David Krut, 2005), 88. See Ivan Vladislavić, *Double Negative* (Rome: Contrasto, 2010), 90.
11. Ivan Vladislavić, *The Loss Library and Other Unfinished Stories* (London, New York, Calcutta: Seagull Books, 2012), 2.
12. Francis Fukuyama, *The End of History and the Last Man* (1992; London: Penguin, 2012), xi. Fukuyama later troubled this characterization of his thesis as an over-simplification. The negotiated settlement in South Africa served at various points for Fukuyama as example.
13. Ivan Vladislavić, 'Propaganda by Monuments', in *Propaganda by Monuments and Other Stories* (Cape Town and Johannesburg: David Philip, 1996), 17.
14. She takes it more broadly, too, as an invitation to construe the implications of post-communist reflections on Marxism for postcolonial theory; see Monica Popescu, *South African Literature Beyond the Cold War* (New York: Palgrave Macmillan, 2010), 113.
15. Vladislavić, 'Propaganda by Monuments', 25, 26. Vladislavić cites its translation in the journal *International Literature* No. 5, in 1935, in the acknowledgements, but I have thus far been unable to confirm whether or not this is a fabrication. Anatoly Vasilyevich Lunacharski (1875–1933) was the first Soviet People's Commissar of Enlightenment (October 1917–September 1929), before serving as the Soviet Ambassador to Spain.
16. Vladislavić, 'Propaganda by Monuments', 27–8.
17. Ibid., 36.
18. Strijdom Square Monument consisted of a large partial dome over a bust of the former Prime Minister and a statue of horses on a column. The bust and dome collapsed; the horse statue was undamaged.
19. Vladislavić, 'Propaganda by Monuments', 28, 25.
20. Ibid., 24.
21. Ibid., 23.
22. Ibid., 13, see 29. Popescu uses the acts of translation to make an argument about the ambiguities that render 'the relationship between the original and the translated text fuzzy', such fuzziness being 'a result of the cultural debris, the obliterated footnotes, the palimpsest of traces of history that is overwritten in the new context' (*South African Literature Beyond the Cold War*, 116).
23. Vladislavić, 'Propaganda by Monuments', 15.

24. Ibid., 23.
25. Boym, *The Future of Nostalgia*, xiii. As she puts it, nostalgia can also be 'prospective': 'Fantasies of the past determined by needs of the present have a direct impact on realities of the future' (xvi).
26. Vladislavić, 'Propaganda by Monuments', 38.
27. Ibid., 36.
28. Catherine Taylor, *Apart* (Brooklyn, NY: Ugly Duckling Press, 2012), 13, 31; see 63, 95.
29. J.M. Coetzee, *Age of Iron* (1990; London: Penguin, 1991), 13, 153, 160.
30. Sam Durrant, *Postcolonial Narrative and the Work of Mourning: J.M. Coetzee, Wilson Harris, and Toni Morrison* (Albany, NY: SUNY Press, 2004), 30, quoting Coetzee in *Doubling the Point: Essays and Interviews*, ed. David Attwell (Cambridge, MA: Harvard University Press, 1992), 248.
31. Walter Benjamin, 'On the Concept of History', trans. Harry Zohn, in *Selected Writings, Vol. 4 (1938–1940)*, ed. Howard Eiland and Michael W. Jennings (Cambridge, MA: Harvard University Press, 2003), 392. The more familiar 1968 English translation by Zohn, titled 'Theses on the Philosophy of History'—in the collection *Illuminations*, ed. and introduction Hannah Arendt (1968; London: Pimlico, 1999)—reads very slightly differently (see 249).
32. Bronwyn Law-Viljoen, 'Make-believe is Easier to Catch than Truth-telling', *Art South Africa* 9.2 (Summer 2010), 69.
33. Rolf Tiedemann, 'Historical Materialism or Political Messianism? An Interpretation of the Theses "On the Concept of History"', in *Benjamin: Philosophy, Aesthetics, History*, ed. Gary Smith (Chicago: University of Chicago Press, 1989), 180.
34. Benjamin, 'On the Concept', 397 (Thesis A). Benjamin offers equally enigmatic yet also useful glosses on this idea of the 'constellation' in discussing the nature of what he calls the dialectical image, in Convolute N of the *Arcades Project*, where in fragment [N2a, 3] he explains that 'image is that wherein what has been comes together in a flash with the now to form a constellation'; it is 'dialectics at a standstill. For while the relation of the present to the past is a purely temporal, continuous one, the relation of what-has-been to the now is dialectical: is not progression but image, suddenly emergent.' See Walter Benjamin, *The Arcades Project*, trans. Howard Eiland and Kevin McLaughlin (Cambridge, MA: Harvard University Press, 1999), 462.
35. Benjamin, 'On the Concept', 390 (Thesis II).
36. Bronwyn Law-Viljoen, 'Interview with David Goldblatt and Ivan Vladislavić', in *Marginal Spaces: Reading Ivan Vladislavić*, ed. Gerald Gaylard (Johannesburg: Wits University Press, 2011), 346–7.
37. Christopher Warnes, 'Interview with Ivan Vladislavić', *MFS: Modern Fiction Studies* 45.1 (Spring 2000), 279.
38. Ibid., 279–80.
39. Ivan Vladislavić, *Portrait with Keys: The City of Johannesburg Unlocked* (London: Portobello, 2006), 186.

40. Ivan Vladislavić, 'Frieze', in *The Loss Library*, 52.
41. Ibid., 52–3.
42. Ibid., 54.
43. Ivan Vladislavić, *The Restless Supermarket* (Cape Town: David Philip, 2001), 62, 80.
44. Ibid., 260, 15, 41, 58.
45. Ibid., 127, 174.
46. Carrol Clarkson, 'Visible and Invisible: What Surfaces in Recent Johannesburg Novels?' *Moving Worlds* 5.1 (2005), 86, quoting Alan Morris, *Bleakness and Light: Inner-City Transition in Hillbrow, Johannesburg* (Johannesburg: Witwatersrand University Press, 1999), 3.
47. Vladislavić, *Restless Supermarket*, 130, 129.
48. Ibid., 81, 260.
49. Ibid., 170. 'CODESA this and CODESA that', Tearle complains, South Africa is 'disappearing behind a cloud of acronyms' (12).
50. Ibid., 97. Several critics have elaborated this connection. See: Mike Marais, 'Visions of Excess: Closure, Irony, and the Thought of Community in Ivan Vladislavić's *The Restless Supermarket*', *English in Africa* 29.2 (October 2002), 101–17; Shane Graham, 'Memory, Memorialization, and the Transformation of Johannesburg: Ivan Vladislavić's *The Restless Supermarket* and *Propaganda by Monuments*', *MFS: Modern Fiction Studies* 53.1 (2007), 80; Popescu, *South African Literature Beyond the Cold War*, 130.
51. Vladislavić, *Restless Supermarket*, 61.
52. This section, Vladislavić told interviewers, grew in much the way Tearle suggests that *he* has compiled it from scraps collected over many years. Originally full of errors, he explained, he corrected it for fear of a forty-page, error-ridden text taxing readers too severely; see Mike Marais and Carita Backström, 'An Interview with Ivan Vladislavić', *English in Africa* 29.2 (October 2002), 123. See also J.C. Peters, 'The Missng [sic] "i": Corrigenda in Ivan Vladislavić's Second Edition of *The Restless Supermarket*', *English in Africa* 36.2 (2009), 45–62. Peters notes that a later edition of the novel, published in 2006, introduces multiple errors throughout the narrative, and speculates that this was intentional.
53. Vladislavić, *Restless Supermarket*, 83–4. It is based, Vladislavić told a reviewer, on a real place he saw 'in Twist Street in the early 1980s. It really appealed to me—I took people to see it. It was an extraordinary image, a ready-made accidental metaphor for how things work.' Charlotte Bauer, 'Up close and impersonal', *Sunday Times*, *Lifestyle* supplement, 23 September 2001, 12.
54. Vladislavić, *Restless Supermarket*, 221–2.
55. Ibid., 227.
56. Ibid., 19.
57. Ibid., 20, 152.
58. Ibid., 141.
59. Benjamin, 'On the Concept', 392.
60. Vladislavić, *Restless Supermarket*, 141.
61. Ibid., 259–60; Boym, *The Future of Nostalgia*, 43.

62. Vladislavić, *Restless Supermarket*, 296.
63. Quoted in Boym, *The Future of Nostalgia*, 5.
64. Sigmund Freud, 'Mourning, and Melancholia' (1917), trans. Shaun Whiteside, in *On Murder, Mourning and Melancholia* (London: Penguin, 2005), 204.
65. Ibid., 203.
66. Ibid., 203, 211. Ross Truscott offers a nuanced discussion of the development of Freud's speculation about melancholia in relation to national identifications (including that it 'may be the precondition for mourning, rather than its opposite or failure'), in his analysis of Afrikaner youth culture: 'National Melancholia and Afrikaner Self-parody in Post-apartheid South Africa', *Psychoanalysis, Culture & Society* 16.1 (2011), 90–106.
67. David Scott, *Omens of Adversity* (Durham, NC: Duke University Press, 2014), 101; see Freud, 'Mourning, and Melancholia', 210.
68. There are clues that Tearle might be read as a repressed homosexual. Not only does he seem attracted to Spilkin, but other characters tease him about being 'bent' (Vladislavić, *Restless Supermarket*, 256). In the ambulance with Floyd and Shirlaine, he sees his 'crooked reflection' in a reflective surface and muses on being 'bent', '[t]wisted in the wrong place. [. . .] I needed straightening out' (280–1).
69. Marais and Backström, 'An Interview with Ivan Vladislavić', 122.
70. See Vladislavić, *Portrait with Keys*, 191–5. See Ivan Vladislavić, 'Street addresses, Johannesburg', in Ivan Vladislavić and Judin, eds, *blank_Architecture, apartheid and after* (Rotterdam: Netherlands Art Institute, 1998), E11.
71. Benjamin, *The Arcades Project*, 460 [fragment N1a, 8].
72. Susan Buck-Morss, *The Dialectics of Seeing: Walter Benjamin and the Arcades Project* (Cambridge, MA: MIT Press, 1989), 95. Buck-Morss argues that 'Benjamin attempted to construct a counter-discourse by unearthing buried markers that expose "progress" as the fetishization of modern temporality, which is an endless repetition of the "new" as the "always-the-same"' (56).
73. Benjamin, *The Arcades Project*, 463 [fragment N3, 1].
74. See variously Vladislavić, *Portrait with Keys*, 55 (which deals with Vladislavić's partner Minky's brother Alan's alarm that their childhood home has been demolished), and 82–3 (Vladislavić's own childhood home). The most evocative of the fragments relating to walls involve that of the house across from Vladislavić's, which its owners employ a woman to paint with an Ndebele design that seems to Vladislavić a wonderful 'metaphor' for South Africa's transformation (24). When it is painted over some years later (56–7), he regrets not having photographed its emergence; it joins the roster of obliterated, remembered things. This and many other murals spur meditations on the palimpsestic nature of writing and memory.
75. Vladislavić, *Portrait with Keys*, 43.
76. Ibid., 45.
77. Ibid., 77.
78. Ibid., 99.
79. Ibid., 28.
80. Ibid., 74–6.

81. Ibid., 50; see also 11.
82. See ibid., 127–31; 29–30; 114–16. See also Patrick Lenta, '"Everyday Abnormality": Crime and In/security in Ivan Vladislavić's *Portrait with Keys*', *Journal of Commonwealth Literature* 44.1 (2009), 117–33.
83. See David Bunn, 'Art Johannesburg and Its Objects', in *Johannesburg: The Elusive Metropolis*, ed. Sarah Nuttall and Achille Mbembe (Durham, NC: Duke University Press, 2008), 162.
84. Sarah Nuttall, 'The Invisible City: Surface and Underneath in *Portrait with Keys*', in Gaylard, ed., *Marginal Spaces*, 333.
85. Vladislavić, *Portrait with Keys*, 46; see also 141–2, 18, 32–4, 110, 70.
86. Ibid., 175, see 178.
87. Nuttall, 'The Invisible City', 335.
88. The narrator's friend, Dave, suggests that 'the hunter-gatherer is in the ascendancy' in 'African cities', 'filled' as they are 'with roamers, intent on survival, plucking what they can at the roadside', an opinion saved from being racist only because he contends that 'we were all hunter-gatherers' now. Vladislavić, *Portrait with Keys*, 35.
89. Ibid., 80.
90. Boym, *The Future of Nostalgia*, 49–50.
91. Vladislavić, *Double Negative*, 90. I quote from the first English-language edition (Contrasto, 2010); it was republished as a separate volume in South Africa (Cape Town: Umuzi) in 2011, and for the world English market, excluding South Africa, in 2013 (London and New York: And Other Stories).
92. Ivan Vladislavić and David Goldblatt, 'Posers', *Sunday Times*, 26 September 2010, Life*style*/Culture, 12–13. The abridged extract (compare *Double Negative*, 64–7) appears on page 12 of the *Sunday Times* feature. Goldblatt's images appear on pages 12–13 and on the supplement's cover. Goldblatt's photograph can be easily found online.
93. Vladislavić, *Double Negative*, 65–6.
94. The allusion serves ironically, too, though differently so, if we are made to think of the painter, Frank Auerbach (b. 1931), well known for his heavily worked paintings and for requiring multiple sittings from his subjects.
95. David Goldblatt, Ivan Vladislavić, and Marlene van Niekerk, 'Double Exposure', *British Journal of Photography* (May 2011), 46. One of the early sequences that would find a home in *Portrait with Keys* first appeared in the catalogue for a retrospective of Goldblatt's work, *fifty-one years: David Goldblatt* (Barcelona: Museu d'Art Contemporani de Barcelona, 2001), while in 2008 reflections in a similar genre ('Modderfontein Road') closed the catalogue for a commercial gallery's exhibition of contemporary South African art in London that also included recent photographs by Goldblatt: see *Home Lands—Land Marks: Contemporary Art from South Africa*, ed. Tamar Garb (London: Haunch of Venison, 2008), 154–61.
96. Ivan Vladislavić, in conversation with Neel Mukherjee and Patrick Flanery, 'Camera Obscura: A View of South Africa', Diorama Arts Studio, London, 25 June 2014.

97. Law-Viljoen, 'Interview with David Goldblatt and Ivan Vladislavić', 352.
98. Patrick Flanery, 'Eyes Wide Shut', *The Guardian*, Review supplement, 9 November 2013, 14. See Vladislavić, *Double Negative*, 157.
99. Vladislavić, *Double Negative*, 67.
100. Ibid., 162. There are other references to the angel: Earlier, Nev suggests that he was shadowed by an invisible 'Benjamin's Angel' at the start of his day with Auerbach; he imagines it leaning against the car 'beside me with his wings folded across the bonnet' (37). In the novel's third part, one of Nev's photographic subjects, Antoine, a refugee from the Democratic Republic of the Congo who has been a victim of xenophobic violence in South Africa, reminds him of Benjamin's angel, transfixed by disaster (162).
101. Derrida's thoughts on the split temporality occasioned by the photograph are germane here, though also so obvious as not to require quotation as authority. Jacques Derrida, 'Copy, Archive, Signature: A Conversation on Photography' (2000 in German), translated by Jeff Fort, in Derrida, *Copy, Archive, Signature: A Conversation on Photography*, ed. Gerhard Richter (Stanford: Stanford University Press, 2010), 4.
102. Vladislavić, *Double Negative*, 77.
103. Ibid., 146.
104. Ibid., 78, 78–9.
105. Ibid., 140.
106. Ibid., 37.
107. Tymon Smith, 'Double Positive', *Sunday Times* Lifestyle, 12 June 2011, 33.
108. Vladislavić, *Double Negative*, 87.
109. Walter Benjamin, 'The Work of Art in the Age of Mechanical Reproduction', trans. Harry Zohn, in *Illuminations*, ed. Hannah Arendt (1968; London: Pimlico, 1999), 215.
110. Ibid., 218.
111. Diarmuid Costello, 'Aura, Face, Photography: Re-reading Benjamin Today', in *Walter Benjamin and Art*, ed. Andrew E. Benjamin (London and New York, 2005), 171–2.
112. Ibid., 178, see also 165.
113. Ibid., 177.
114. Ibid., 180.
115. Ibid., 184.
116. Vladislavić, *Double Negative*, 45.
117. Benjamin, 'Excavation and Memory', 576.

NOTES TO CHAPTER 5

1. Njabulo Ndebele, *The Cry of Winnie Mandela* (2003; Banbury: Ayebia Clarke, 2004), 82.
2. Zoë Wicomb, 'Boy in a Jute-Sack Hood', *Antigonish Review* (Summer 2007), 17. Reproduced in Wicomb's *The One That Got Away* (Roggebaai: Umuzi, 2008), 9–21.

3. Wicomb, 'Boy in a Jute-Sack Hood', 18.
4. Ibid., 17, 24.
5. Ibid., 20, 19.
6. Brenna Munro, 'Queer Family Romance: Writing the "New" South Africa in the 1990s', *GLQ: A Journal of Lesbian and Gay Studies* 15.3 (2009), 398.
7. Ibid., 405.
8. Nadine Gordimer, *The House Gun* (1998; London: Bloomsbury, 1999), 278, 279; see 51. Note that David Lurie, in J.M. Coetzee's *Disgrace* (London: Secker & Warburg, 1999), also talks of himself being 'at a loose end' (52, 165).
9. See Nadine Gordimer, *A World of Strangers* (1951; London: Bloomsbury, 2012), 168. One might, incidentally, also hear in Grant's surname an allusion to the Fothering*h*ays in William Plomer's decidedly queer *Turbott Wolfe,* characters who, 'although they had spent nearly all their lives in Africa', 'had barely begun to think' of it at all, certainly not as home. William Plomer, *Turbott Wolfe* (London: Hogarth, 1925), 89.
10. Her most considered critique of this continuing entanglement is to be found in Zoë Wicomb, 'Shame and Identity: The Case of the coloured in South Africa', in *Writing South Africa: Literature, Apartheid, and Democracy, 1970–1995*, ed. Derek Attridge and Rosemary Jolly (Cambridge: Cambridge University Press, 1998), 91–107. See also Chapter 1 n22.
11. Zoë Wicomb, 'In Search of Tommie', *Wasafiri* 24.3 (2009), 52. The story also appears on the *Untitled Books* website, dated 7 September 2009, and in *Touch: Stories of Contact by South African Writers*, ed. Karina Magdalena Szczurek (Cape Town: Zebra Press, 2009), 67–80.
12. Wicomb, 'In Search of Tommie', 51.
13. Ibid., 54.
14. Ibid., 55.
15. Ibid., 52, 55, 54, 53.
16. Ibid., 52.
17. Munro, 'Queer Family Romance', 407. As source of the description of Uys as 'tannie of the nation' Munro cites Calvin Trillin's essay 'Gadfly: The Satirist Pieter-Dirk Uys Adjusts to the New South Africa' in the *New Yorker,* 10 May 2004, 78.
18. Wicomb, 'In Search of Tommie', 51.
19. Ibid., 54. See Monica Hunter and Archie Mafeje, *Langa: A Study of Social Groups in an African Township* (Cape Town: Oxford University Press, 1963), 3–4, 6.
20. See John Lambert, 'Chiefship in Early Colonial Natal, 1843–1879', *Journal of Southern African Studies* 21.2 (1995), 280. Bishop Colenso's riposte to the semi-official published proceedings of the trials against Langalibalele and his family and retinue mentions—without contesting—the chief's description in official papers as a 'rain-doctor'. See John William Colenso, *Langalibalele and the AmaHlubi Tribe* (London: Spottiswoode & Co., 1874), 1. On the Mbalu link, see Noël Mostert, *Frontiers: The Epic of South Africa's Creation and the Tragedy of the Xhosa People* (London: Pimlico, 1993), 244–7.

21. Zoë Wicomb, *David's Story* (New York: Feminist Press at CUNY, 2000), 153.
22. Ibid., 153, 159. Wicomb cites from Jack Cope's 1968 translation of the 1921 (revised 1959) poem.
23. Zoë Wicomb, 'Interview: Zoë Wicomb in Conversation with Hein Willemse', *Research in African Literatures* 33.1 (Spring 2002), 147, 145.
24. Stephan Meyer and Thomas Olver, 'Zoë Wicomb Interviewed on Writing and Nation', *Journal of Literary Studies* 18.1 (2002), 189.
25. Zoë Wicomb, 'Translations in the Yard of Africa', *Journal of Literary Studies* 18.3 (2002), 218.
26. Zoë Wicomb, *Playing in the Light* (New York: New Press, 2006), 86.
27. Wicomb, 'In Search of Tommie', 51.
28. The Modjadji procreates with men chosen by a royal council, but they do not become consorts. See Zethu Matebeni, 'Blissful Complexities: Black Lesbians Reflect on Same-sex Marriage and the Civil Union Act', in *To Have and to Hold: The Making of Same-sex Marriage in South Africa*, ed. Melanie Judge, Anthony Manion, and Shaun de Waal (Auckland Park: Fanele, 2008), 254–5.
29. The *Oxford English Dictionary* cites historical examples back to 1513. See 'queer, adj.1.' *OED Online*. Oxford University Press, September 2014. Web. 13 October 2014 (from the third edition, December 2007).
30. Zoë Wicomb, *You Can't Get Lost in Cape Town* (London: Virago Press, 1987), 76.
31. Wicomb, *David's Story*, 62, 212.
32. See *queer*, n.2. *OED* (third edition, December 2007), online.
33. Michael Warner, ed., 'Introduction', in *Fear of a Queer Planet: Queer Politics and Social Theory* (Minneapolis: University of Minnesota Press, 1993), xxvi.
34. On '"subjectless" critique', see David L. Eng, Judith Halberstam, and José Esteban Muñoz, eds, 'Introduction: What's Queer about Queer Studies Now?' *Social Text* 23.3–4 (2005), 3.
35. Wicomb, *David's Story*, 20, 277, 275.
36. Ibid., 185.
37. Ibid., 175, 176.
38. Zoë Wicomb, *October* (New York: New Press, 2014), 82.
39. Wicomb, *The One That Got Away*, 140.
40. Ibid., 144, 135.
41. Ibid., 140, 143.
42. Lee Edelman, *No Future: Queer Theory and the Death Drive* (Durham, NC: Duke University Press, 2004), 31, 23.
43. José Esteban Muñoz, *Cruising Utopia: The Then and There of Queer Futurity* (New York: New York University Press, 2009), 91.
44. See Jacques Derrida, 'On Cosmopolitanism', in *On Cosmopolitanism and Forgiveness*, trans. Mark Dooley (New York: Routledge, 2001), 20.
45. Hiram Perez, 'You Can Have My Brown Body and Eat It, Too!', *Social Text* 23.3–4 (2005), 185, 176.

46. Andrew Tucker, *Queer Visibilities: Space, Identity and Interaction in Cape Town* (Malden, MA and Oxford: Wiley-Blackwell, 2009), 16.
47. Wicomb, 'Translations in the Yard of Africa', 221.
48. Wicomb, 'In Search of Tommie', 53.
49. Ibid., 52, 51.
50. Wicomb, *You Can't Get Lost*, 103.
51. Wicomb, *Playing in the Light*, 2.
52. Wicomb, *David's Story*, 208.
53. Ibid., 41; see also 144, 154, 162.
54. Ibid., 196.
55. Ibid., 204.
56. Ibid., 213, 212.
57. Wicomb, 'In Search of Tommie', 52. Wicomb's own analysis of *Slow Man* suggests her willingness to countenance such connections, as she traces phonetic links between COETZEE and COSTELLO. See Zoë Wicomb, '*Slow Man* and the Real: A Lesson in Reading and Writing', *Journal of Literary Studies* 25.4 (2009), 13.
58. Wicomb, 'In Search of Tommie', 52.
59. See T.S. Eliot, 'The Love Song of J. Alfred Prufrock', in *Collected Poems 1909–1962* (1963; London: Faber and Faber, 1974), 17.
60. Wicomb, 'In Search of Tommie', 53.
61. Wicomb, *Playing in the Light*, 100. On Brenda as narrator, see Andrew van der Vlies, 'The Archive, the Spectral, and Narrative Responsibility in Zoë Wicomb's *Playing in the Light*', *Journal of Southern African Studies* 36.3 (2010), 593–6.
62. Wicomb, *Playing in the Light*, 185, 192.
63. Zoë Wicomb, 'Setting, Intertextuality and the Resurrection of the Postcolonial Author', *Journal of Postcolonial Writing* 41.2 (2005), 150.
64. Wicomb, 'In Search of Tommie', 52.
65. Wicomb, *You Can't Get Lost*, 42.
66. Ibid., 49, 56. I have discussed this story in detail elsewhere: Andrew van der Vlies, '"I'm only grateful that it's not a Cape Town book", or Zoë Wicomb, Textuality, Propriety, and the Proprietary', *Journal of Commonwealth Literature* 48.1 (2013), 9–25.
67. Wicomb, *You Can't Get Lost*, 74.
68. Ibid., 90.
69. Thomas Hardy, *Tess of the d'Urbervilles* (1891; Oxford: Oxford University Press, 2008), 44.
70. Wicomb, 'Setting, Intertextuality', 152.
71. Ibid., 153.
72. See Wicomb, 'Shame and Identity', 101, quoting Bhabha, *The Location of Culture* (London and New York: Routledge, 1994), 13. In similar vein, in her essay on translation, intertextuality, and verbal aspect in Coetzee's *Disgrace*, Wicomb charges that 'the question of agency' is 'omitted in Bhabha's description' of translation; see Wicomb, 'Translations in the Yard of Africa', 211.

73. Wicomb, 'Setting, Intertextuality', 153, emphasis mine.
74. Ibid., 153, quoting Bhabha's *Location of Culture*, 18.
75. Addressing the tendency of Western readers to approach fiction by black women from the third world as necessarily autobiographical, Wicomb remarked in the mid 1990s, tongue firmly in cheek, 'whether written in first or third person, we produce social documents that speak of our personal experiences and grievances and which therefore are primarily of social and anthropological value'. Zoë Wicomb, 'To Hear the Variety of Discourses', *Current Writing* 2 (1990), 42.
76. David Robinson, 'Under the Skin of Lies', *The Scotsman*, 27 May 2006 (Saturday Critique), 20. Wicomb claims to need to leave Glasgow in order to write (private conversation with the author, Glasgow, 13 April 2014).
77. Wicomb, *David's Story*, 188. See also Derek Attridge, 'Zoë Wicomb's Home Truths', *Journal of Postcolonial Writing* 41.2 (2005), 158.
78. Wicomb, *David's Story*, 27.
79. Wicomb, *October*, 14.
80. Ibid., 27.
81. Ibid., 124.
82. Ibid., 3.
83. Ibid., and see 184.
84. Ibid., 14.
85. Ibid., 9.
86. Ibid., 46; see 8–9.
87. Ibid., 171.
88. Ibid.
89. Ibid., 45.
90. Ibid., 214.
91. Ibid., 183.
92. Ibid., 12–13.
93. In *Home*, the Reverend Robert Boughton's grandmother had emigrated from Scotland; his daughter jokes about the family's Presbyterianism that Scottishness might be 'another name for predestination. It explains everything, more or less'. See Marilynne Robinson, *Home* (London: Virago, 2008), 141. In *October*, we learn that '[t]he Murrays were of old Scottish stock, people who had settled before the Europeans were corrupted by Africa' (138). *Home* features a Presbyterian minister, while Nicholas Theophilus Murray is a deacon in the Sendingkerk, the coloured mission branch of the Dutch Reformed Church.
94. Wicomb, *October*, 28; Robinson, *Home*, 194.
95. In *Home* (unlike *October*) the father is alive and the letter from the drunkard brother (John Ames, called Jack) announces his own return after a twenty-year absence. *Home*'s Glory's supposed former fiancé shares with *October*'s Craig the habit of keeping track of the money given him by his female partner, and in both cases, the women have abandoned any hope of repayment. Compare Wicomb, *October*, 202–3, 226–7, and Robinson, *Home*, 22–3, 201.

96. Robinson, *Home*, 25; see 220, 251, 245.
97. Robinson's novel closes with Glory learning that Jack has another child, Robert, to whose mother, Della, he is in fact married, though he has not been able to tell his family about this as Della—Glory learns when the woman comes looking for her husband—is African American (see 332–6). Jake's withdrawal into his 'fetid, darkened room' (173) in *October* echoes Jack's to his 'dark little room' in the barn, a makeshift retreat under canvas sheeting, in *Home* (297). There are differences of degree and tone: where Jack tries unsuccessfully to commit suicide, Jake succeeds in drinking himself to death. A scene of emotional climax in *Home*, in which Glory washes the filthy Jack on the morning of his attempted suicide, becomes in *October* a bathetic scene in which Mercia hoses Jake down with dishwashing liquid. See Robinson, *Home*, 256–61; Wicomb, *October*, 176.
98. Where Jack is sympathetic to the protestors, his father thinks the law ought to be enforced strictly, that African American Civil Rights protestors are 'creating problems and obstacles for themselves with all this—commotion' (Robinson, *Home*, 163). By the novel's final pages, Jack's outrage at this remark, in particular, becomes poignant: Glory meets Jack's African American partner and their son, Robert, who have driven to Gilead with Della's sister but must make it back to Missouri 'to escape the dangers of nightfall' (337).
99. Wicomb, *October*, 80.
100. Ibid., 81. Note that the United States edition of *October* (published by the New Press) uses the spelling 'colored' throughout, technically incorrect in the South African context (the South African edition, published by Umuzi, uses 'coloured'), but which offers an unconscious paralleling of the term used for African Americans in *Home*.
101. Wicomb, *October*, 81.
102. Ibid., 14.
103. Robinson, *Home*, 293. Compare Wicomb, *October*, 14.
104. Robinson, *Home*, 7–8.
105. Ibid., 294; Wicomb, *October*, 16.
106. Wicomb, *October*, 27. The *OED* (third edition, 2001) records the etymology for Mercian, from the Old English *Merce, Mierce, Mirce* or *Myrce*, which becomes *Mercianus* in late seventh-century post-classical Latin sources. See 'Mercian, n. and adj.' *OED Online*. Oxford University Press, September 2014. Web. 19 October 2014. For three centuries, after 600 CE, Mercia dominated the Anglo-Saxon kingdoms south of the Humber and east of the Welsh borders. Its invocation in *October* is appropriate on a number of counts: Mercia was pagan, but converted to Christianity in the late seventh century, and it occupied what is now the English Midlands. The name thus invokes many of those tropes of the in-between that Wicomb finds both productive and troubling (as, for example, in her readings of Bhabha).
107. Wicomb, *October*, 67.

108. J.M. Coetzee, 'Speaking J.M. Coetzee', interview by Stephen Watson, *Speak* 1.3 (1978), 21–4, quoted in Stephen Watson, 'Colonialism and the Novels of J.M. Coetzee', *Research in African Literatures* 17.3 (Autumn 1986), 370.
109. Andrew van der Vlies, *South African Textual Cultures* (Manchester: Manchester University Press, 2007).
110. See Van der Vlies, 'I'm only grateful that it's not a Cape Town book', 17–21.
111. Wicomb, 'Translations in the Yard of Africa', 217–18.
112. Wicomb, 'Setting, Intertextuality', 151.
113. Wicomb, *David's Story*, 1.
114. Wicomb, *October*, 237; compare *David's Story*, 212–13.
115. Wicomb, 'Setting, Intertextuality', 150.

NOTES TO CHAPTER 6

1. Sindiwe Magona, 'The More Things Change', in *Letter to South Africa: Poets Calling the State to Order* (Cape Town: Umuzi, 2011), 101.
2. Songeziwe Mahlangu, *Penumbra* (Cape Town: Kwela, 2013), 9.
3. Masande Ntshanga, *The Reactive* (Cape Town: Umuzi, 2014), 13.
4. Mahlangu, *Penumbra*, 10.
5. Ayi Kwei Armah, *The Beautyful Ones Are Not Yet Born* (1968; Oxford: Heinemann, 1988), 1. The bus, whose 'confused rattle had given place to an endless spastic shudder, as if its pieces were held together by too much rust ever to fall completely apart', famously transports a furtive (and corrupt) conductor, and a dribbling, sleeping passenger.
6. Ntshanga, *The Reactive*, 13–14.
7. Nick Mulgrew, 'Getting under the skin of the new SA with Masande Ntshanga', *Mail & Guardian*, 21 November 2014, http://mg.co.za/article/2014-11-21-under-the-skin-of-the-new-sa.
8. See Michael Titlestad, 'The pitfalls of the literary debut', *Sunday Times*, 25 March 2007, 37. *Room 207* won several local literary prizes and was shortlisted in the Africa (debut) category for the Commonwealth Writer's Prize.
9. There were many responses to Titlestad's critique, including from the publisher responsible for *Room 207*: see Nèlleke de Jager, 'What every critic should know', *Mail & Guardian*, 4 March 2011, http://mg.co.za/article/2011-03-04-what-every-critic-should-know (accessed 4 September 2014).
10. On this and other township novels, see Megan Jones, 'Conspicuous Destruction, Aspiration and Motion in the South African Township', *Safundi: The Journal of South African and American Studies* 14.2 (2013), 209–24, and 'Township Textualities', *Alternation* 20.1 (2013), 26–51.

11. On *Coconut*, see Lynda Spencer, 'Young, Black and Female in Post-apartheid South Africa: Identity Politics in Kopano Matlwa's *Coconut*', *Scrutiny2: Issues in English Studies in Southern Africa* 14.1 (2009), 66–78.
12. Achille Mbembe, 'Achille Mbembe on The State of South African Political Life', *Africa in Words*, 19 September 2015, http://africasacountry.com/2015/09/achille-mbembe-on-the-state-of-south-african-politics/.
13. Pumla Dineo Gqola, '"The difficult task of normalizing freedom": Spectacular Masculinities, Ndebele's Literary Cultural Commentary and Post-Apartheid Life', *English in Africa* 36.1 (2009), 62.
14. Mahlangu, *Penumbra*, 35.
15. Ibid., 120.
16. Ibid., 130.
17. Wendy Brown, *Undoing the Demos: Neoliberalism's Stealth Revolution* (New York: Zone Books, 2015), 84, citing Ronen Shamir, 'The Age of Responsibilization: On Market-Embedded Morality', *Economy and Society* 37.1 (2008), 1–19.
18. Mahlangu, *Penumbra*, 131.
19. Ibid., 88.
20. Ibid., 143.
21. Ibid., 13, 17.
22. Ntshanga, *The Reactive*, 144. From clues in the text (see 5, 174), we can deduce that Nathi is about twenty-nine at the moment of narration, which Ntshanga confirms in interview is 2003 (Mulgrew, 'Getting under the skin'). The national government's Antiretroviral Treatment Plan, announced as the novel's narrated events end, took place in November 2003 (the roll-out itself began in April 2004). See *Operational plan for comprehensive HIV and AIDS care, management and treatment for South Africa* (Pretoria: National Department of Health, 2003), http://www.info.gov.za/issues/hiv/careplan.htm.
23. Ntshanga, *The Reactive*, 33; see 32, 55, 67, 151.
24. Ibid., 16–17.
25. Ibid., 23, see also 68.
26. Ibid., 44.
27. Ibid., 55–6.
28. Ibid., 60–2.
29. Ibid., 21.
30. Ibid., 174.
31. Ibid., 198.
32. Ibid., 22.
33. 'The feelings of the meaninglessness of everything seem stale.' Mahlangu, *Penumbra*, 47.
34. Ntshanga, *The Reactive*, 24–5.
35. Ibid., 25.
36. See Roger Southall, *The New Black Middle Class in South Africa* (Johannesburg: Jacana, 2016), 97–108.
37. Ntshanga, *The Reactive*, 157.

38. Ibid., 113–14. Cissie also says of Mandela: 'I get it, but that isn't my point. I think my point is more like, on a physical and cultural basis, we were all him, you know, we were all this one man from the island' (115).
39. Hylton White, 'A Post-Fordist Ethnicity: Insecurity, Authority, and Identity in South Africa', *Anthropological Quarterly* 85.2 (2012), 399.
40. Ntshanga, *The Reactive*, 93.
41. Ibid., 107.
42. Ibid., 184.
43. Alcinda Honwana, 'Youth, Waithood, and Protest Movements in Africa' (International African Institute Lugard Lecture, 2013), *African Arguments*, 12 August 2013, http://africanarguments.org/2013/08/12/youth-waithood-and-protest-movements-in-africa-by-alcinda-honwana/.
44. White, 'A Post-Fordist Ethnicity', 406. Honwana, adds that 'young South Africans speak about "just getting by"' ('Youth, Waithood').
45. Lauren Berlant, *Cruel Optimism* (Durham, NC: Duke University Press, 2011), 49; see 259.
46. Mahlangu, *Penumbra*, 106.
47. A range of texts is referenced in *Penumbra*: Manga buys a second-hand copy of *Hard Times* from a bookshop on Long Street; later, he reads Coetzee's *Summertime* and Can Themba's *The Will to Die*; on Tongai's recommendation, he attempts Jean-Paul Sartre's *Nausea* and Thomas Wolfe's essay 'God's Lonely Man'. There is mention of Dambudzo Marechera, and there are copies of the literary journal *Chimurenga* in Manga and Tongai's apartment.
48. Brown, *Undoing the Demos*, 84.
49. Ibid., 17.
50. Ibid.
51. Ibid., 59, citing Foucault, *The Birth of Biopolitics: Lectures at the Collège de France, 1978–79*, trans. Graham Burchell, ed. Michel Senellart (New York: Picador, 2004), 69–70. See also Brown, *Undoing the Demos*, 49–50.
52. Brown, *Undoing the Demos*, 62.
53. Ibid., 58, citing Foucault, *The Birth of Biopolitics*, 37, 63–4. As 'economic principles become the model for state conduct, the economy becomes the primary object of state concern and policy, and the marketization of domains and conduct is what the state seeks to disseminate everywhere' (Brown, *Undoing the Demos*, 62).
54. Brown, *Undoing the Demos*, 20.
55. Foucault, *The Birth of Biopolitics*, 85; see Brown, *Undoing the Demos*, 68, 62.
56. Brown, *Undoing the Demos*, 58, citing Foucault, *The Birth of Biopolitics*, 63–4.
57. Mahlangu, *Penumbra*, 35; Ntshanga, *The Reactive*, 22.
58. Brown, *Undoing the Demos*, 84, quoting Adam Smith, *The Wealth of Nations* (Chicago: University of Chicago Press, 1976), 477.
59. Patrick Bond, 'Consolidating the Contradictions: From Mandela to Marikana, 2000–2012', in John S. Saul and Patrick Bond, *South Africa—The Present as History: From Mrs Ples to Mandela and Marikana* (Rochester, NY:

James Currey/Boydell & Brewer, 2014), 176, and on the Treatment Action Campaign's Constitutional Court challenge, see 190–4.

60. Heidi Swart, 'Platinum wealth holds no shine for people left in the dust', *Mail & Guardian*, 28 June 2012, http://mg.co.za/article/2012-06-28-platinum-wealth-holds-no-shine-for-people-left-living-in-the-dust (accessed 22 August 2012). For my analysis of the events at Marikana see Andrew van der Vlies, 'Response: The People, the Multitude and the Costs of Privacy in South Africa's Postcolony', *Cultural Studies* 27.3 (2013), 508–11.
61. Bond, 'Consolidating the Contradictions', 176–9. On the precarious nature of middle-class aspiration and the effects of the 'credit crunch' in South Africa, see Deborah James, *Money from Nothing: Indebtedness and Aspiration in South Africa* (Stanford: Stanford University Press, 2015).
62. Brown, *Undoing the Demos*, 31.
63. Ibid., 10.
64. Ibid., 110.
65. Daniel Magaziner and Sean Jacobs, 'The End of South African Exceptionalism', *The Atlantic*, 27 August 2012, http://www.theatlantic.com/international/archive/2012/08/the-end-of-south-african-exceptionalism/261591/ (accessed 27 August 2012).
66. See Nathan Geffen, 'Justice After AIDS Denialism: Should There Be Prosecutions and Compensation?', *Journal of Acquired Immune Deficiency Syndrome* 51.4 (2009), 454–5.
67. Giorgio Agamben, *Stasis: Civil War as a Political Paradigm*, trans. Nicholas Herron (Edinburgh: Edinburgh University Press, 2015), 4, 11. Agamben's larger project in the text is to suggest that we need a *theory* of civil war, and to counter Hannah Arendt's argument in *On Revolution* that this political event was the only one that faces us with the question of the beginning. He restricts himself to two moments in Western political thought: the idea of civil strife in Greek city-states, and Hobbes's *Leviathan*. These 'represent the two faces, so to speak, of a single political paradigm, which manifests itself, on the one hand, through the assertion of the necessity of civil war, and on the other, through the assertion of the necessity of its exclusion. That the paradigm is, in truth, single, means that the two opposed necessities maintain a secret solidarity between them' (3).
68. Ibid., 9.
69. Ibid., 12. Agamben concludes thus: '*in the system of Greek politics civil war functions as a threshold of politicisation and depoliticisation, through which the house is exceeded in the city and the city is depoliticised in the family*' (ibid., italics original).
70. Ibid., 16.
71. Ibid., 17.
72. Ibid., 10.
73. Ntshanga, *The Reactive*, 86.
74. Ibid., 174.
75. Even if *The Reactive* is not suggesting it overtly, there is something to be said about a comparatively privileged black character's sense that becoming HIV-

positive might allow him to know what it feels like to have to struggle, to approximate the conditions faced by more precariously placed black South African: 'I gave my own body something it couldn't flee from' (174). Nathi's self-infection is not unlike that prevalent in certain barebacking subcultures—explored by Tim Dean's *Unlimited Intimacy* (Chicago: University of Chicago Press, 2009)—in which gay men (known as 'bug-chasers') actively seek to acquire HIV from so-called 'gift-givers'. Despite some of its proponents' confused ethical rationales and the very obvious public health dangers it poses, Leo Bersani and Adam Phillips note, the practice shares similarities with a kind of mystical self-denial that seeks alternative forms of intimacy and relationality. 'Interpreted as a mode of ascetic spirituality, bug-chasing and gift-giving among barebackers are implicit critiques of [. . .] multiple forms of ego-driven intimacy', they observe; '[i]t is as if barebacking gang-bangs were laboratories in which impulses and fantasies condemned by ego-censorship as nonviable were being tested for, precisely, their social viability'. See their *Intimacies* (Chicago: University of Chicago Press, 2008), 55; 43–4.

76. Mahlangu, *Penumbra*, 17.
77. For Heidegger, it was 'something "completely indefinite"', Brinkema notes, citing *Being and Time*. See Eugenie Brinkema, *The Forms of the Affects* (Durham, NC: Duke University Press, 2014), 184.
78. '*Angst*, in Kierkegaard's famous formulation, is "freedom's disclosure to itself in possibility."' Søren Kierkegaard, *The Concept of Anxiety: A Simple Psychologically Orienting Deliberation on the Dogmatic Issue of Hereditary Sin* (1844), ed. and trans. Reidar Thomte (Princeton: Princeton University Press, 1980), 61, cited in Brinkema, *The Forms of the Affects*, 183.
79. Brinkema, *The Forms of the Affects*, 184.
80. Ibid.
81. Ibid., 192, quoting Sigmund Freud, 'Lecture XXV: Anxiety', in *Introductory Lectures on Psychoanalysis*, trans. and ed. James Strachey (New York: Norton, 1960), 393.
82. Brinkema, *The Forms of the Affects*, 192–3.
83. Ibid., 193, 196.
84. Ibid., 196, 194. It is as if Freud's changed thinking reflects modernism's own turn to metaphors of time from those of space, Brinkema observes.
85. Ibid., 192, quoting Sigmund Freud, *Inhibitions, Symptoms and Anxiety*, trans. James Strachey (New York: Norton 1960), 100, cited in Brinkema, *The Forms of the Affects*, 194.
86. See Vincent Crapanzano, *Waiting: The Whites of South Africa* (1985; London: Paladin, 1986), x, 43–7, and on religion in particular, 70, 99, 219–33. See Chapter 1 n76.
87. Mahlangu, *Penumbra*, 32.
88. Bambata, sometimes rendered Bhambatha, Bhambata, Bambatha, was the chief of the amaZondi Zulu clan held responsible by colonial administrators for the popular uprising. On the broader contexts of the resistance, see Benedict Carton, *Blood from Your Children: The Colonial Origins of*

Generational Conflict in South Africa (Charlottesville: University Press of Virginia, 2000).

89. Mahlangu, *Penumbra*, 205.
90. For another comparison between Marikana and Bullhoek, see Bongani Madondo, 'Go tell it on the mountain', *Mail & Guardian*, 23 August 2012, http://mg.co.za/article/2012-08-23-deep-read-go-tell-it-on-the-mountain (accessed 23 August 2012).
91. Jennifer Wenzel, *Bulletproof: Afterlives of Anticolonial Prophecy in South Africa and Beyond* (Chicago: University of Chicago Press, 2009), 163.
92. Achille Mbembe, *On the Postcolony* (Berkeley: University of California Press, 2001), 15.
93. Ibid., 14. Sarah Nuttall has enlarged on Mbembe's keyword in her own discussion of the entangled destinies of contemporary South Africans, particularly in Johannesburg; see her *Entanglement: Literary and Cultural Reflections on Post-Apartheid* (Johannesburg: Wits University Press, 2009).
94. Wenzel, *Bulletproof*, 189.
95. Mahlangu, *Penumbra*, 205.
96. Here I also have in mind Agamben's reminder that the '*stas* is the one who swears the oath while standing' (*Stasis*, 10). For Wenzel's engagement with Benjamin, see *Bulletproof*, 189–90.
97. Paul K. Saint-Amour, *Tense Future: Modernism, Total War, Encyclopedic Form* (Oxford: Oxford University Press, 2015), 31, referencing Reinhart Koselleck, *Futures Past: On the Semantics of Historical Time*, trans. Keith Tribe (Cambridge, MA: MIT Press, 1985), 259. Saint-Amour refers to David Scott's musing on failed revolutions: 'For Scott, our capacity to imagine more habitable political futures relies on how we narrate not just the past generally but futures-past specifically. The living, he argues, need to be able to renarrate futures-past so as not to be constrained by now-obsolete emplotments of those futures by earlier generations' (31).
98. Berlant, *Cruel Optimism*, 182.
99. Ibid.
100. Ibid., 292 n25.

Bibliography

ARCHIVAL SOURCES

Harry Ransom Center, The University of Texas at Austin
J.M. Coetzee Papers

DIGITAL RESOURCES

OED Online, Oxford University Press
<www.oed.com>

PUBLISHED SOURCES

Aciman, André A. 'Family Fictions', *Salmagundi* 90/91 (1991), 33–44.

Ackerley, Chris. 'Style: Coetzee and Beckett', in Mehigan, ed. *A Companion to the Works of J.M. Coetzee.*

Agamben, Giorgio. *Stasis: Civil War as a Political Paradigm*, trans. Nicholas Herron (Edinburgh: Edinburgh University Press, 2015).

Ahmed, Sara. *The Promise of Happiness* (Durham, NC: Duke University Press, 2010).

Apter, Emily. *Against World Literature: On the Politics of Untranslatability* (London: Verso, 2013).

Arendt, Hannah. *On Revolution* (New York: Viking, 1963).

Armah, Ayi Kwei. *The Beautyful Ones Are Not Yet Born* (1968; Oxford: Heinemann, 1988).

Ashbery, John. *Self Portrait in a Convex Mirror* (New York: Viking, 1975).

Attridge, Derek. *J.M. Coetzee and the Ethics of Reading: Literature in the Event* (Chicago: University of Chicago Press, 2004).

Attridge, Derek. 'Zoe Wicomb's Home Truths', *Journal of Postcolonial Writing* 41.2 (2005), 156–65.

Attridge, Derek. 'Introduction', in J.M. Coetzee, *Inner Workings: Literary Essays 2000–2005*, ix–xiv.

Attridge, Derek, and Rosemary Jolly, eds, *Writing South Africa: Literature, Apartheid, and Democracy, 1970–1995* (Cambridge: Cambridge University Press, 1998).

Attwell, David. *Rewriting Modernity: Studies in Black South African Literary History* (Athens, OH: Ohio University Press, 2005).

Attwell, David. 'Mastering Authority: J.M. Coetzee's *Diary of a Bad Year*', *Social Dynamics* 36.1 (March 2010), 214–21.

Attwell, David. *J.M. Coetzee and the Life of Writing: Face to Face with Time* (Oxford: Oxford University Press, 2015).

Auden, W.H. *W.H. Auden: Collected Poems*, ed. Edward Mendelson (New York: Vintage, 1991).

Barnard, Rita. *Apartheid and Beyond: South African Writers and the Politics of Place* (New York: Oxford University Press, 2007).

Barnard, Rita. 'Coetzee in/and Afrikaans', *Journal of Literary Studies* 25.4 (December 2009), 84–105.

Barthes, Roland. *How to Live Together: Novelistic Simulations of Some Everyday Spaces. Notes for a Lecture Course and Seminar at the Collège de France (1976–1977)*, trans. Kate Briggs (New York: Columbia University Press, 2013).

Baucom, Ian. 'Township Modernism', in *Geomodernism: Race, Modernism, Modernity*, ed. Laura Doyle and Laura Winkiel (Bloomington: Indiana University Press, 2005), 227–45.

Bauer, Charlotte. 'Up close and impersonal', *Sunday Times*, *Lifestyle* supplement, 23 September 2001, 12.

Benjamin, Walter. *The Arcades Project*, trans. Howard Eiland and Kevin McLaughlin (Cambridge, MA: Harvard University Press, 1999).

Benjamin, Walter. 'Excavation and Memory', trans. Rodney Livingstone, in *Selected Writings: Vol. 2, Part 2 (1931–1934)*, ed. Michael W. Jennings, Howard Eiland, and Gary Smith (Cambridge, MA: Harvard University Press, 1999), 576.

Benjamin, Walter. *Illuminations*, ed. and intro. Hannah Arendt (1968; London: Pimlico, 1999).

Benjamin, Walter. *Selected Writings: Vol. 4, 1938–1940*, ed. Howard Eiland and Michael W. Jennings (Cambridge, MA: Harvard University Press, 2003).

Benjamin, Walter. 'On the Concept of History', trans. Harry Zohn, in *Selected Writings: Vol. 4*, 389–400.

Benjamin, Walter. 'Paralipomena to "On the Concept of History"', trans. Edmund Jephcott and Howard Eiland, in *Selected Writings: Vol. 4*, 401–11.

Benjamin, Walter. 'Theses on the Philosophy of History', trans. Harry Zohn, in *Illuminations*, 245–55.

Benjamin, Walter. 'The Work of Art in the Age of Mechanical Reproduction', trans. Harry Zohn, in *Illuminations*, 211–44.

Berlant, Lauren. *The Queen of America Goes to Washington City: Essays on Sex and Citizenship* (Durham, NC: Duke University Press, 1997).

Berlant, Lauren. *Cruel Optimism* (Durham, NC: Duke University Press, 2011).

Berlant, Lauren, and Michael Hardt. '"On the risk of a new relationality": An Interview with Lauren Berlant and Michael Hardt', *Reviews in Cultural Theory* 3.2 (2012), 7–27.

Berman, Jessica. *Modernist Commitments: Ethics, Politics, and Transnational Modernism* (New York: Columbia University Press, 2011).

Bersani, Leo, and Adam Phillips. *Intimacies* (Chicago: University of Chicago Press, 2008).

Bewes, Timothy. *The Event of Postcolonial Shame* (Princeton: Princeton University Press, 2011).

Bhabha, Homi K. *The Location of Culture* (London and New York: Routledge, 1994).

Biceaga, Victor. 'Temporality and Boredom', *Continental Philosophy Review* 39 (2006), 135–53.

Binnick, Robert I., ed., 'Introduction', in *The Oxford Handbook of Tense and Aspect* (Oxford: Oxford University Press, 2012), 3–56.

Bloch, Ernst. *The Principle of Hope*, trans. Neville Plaice, Stephen Plaice, Paul Knight (1959; Cambridge, MA: MIT Press, 1986).

Bloch, Ernst. *Literary Essays* (Stanford: Stanford University Press, 1998).

Bloch, Ernst. 'Can Hope Be Disappointed?' (1961), trans. Andrew Joron, in *Literary Essays*, 339–45.

Bloch, Ernst. 'On the Present in Literature', trans. Jack Zipes and Frank Mecklenburg, in *Literary Essays*, 119–35.

Boehmer, Elleke. 'Permanent Risk: When Crisis Defines a Nation's Writing', in *Trauma, Memory, and Narrative in the Contemporary South African Novel: Essays*, ed. Ewald Mengel and Michela Borzaga (Amsterdam: Rodopi, 2012), 29–46.

Boehmer, Elleke. 'Endings and New Beginning: South African Literature in Transition', in Attridge and Jolly, eds, *Writing South Africa*, 43–56.

Bond, Patrick. 'Consolidating the Contradictions: From Mandela to Marikana, 2000–2012', in John S. Saul and Patrick Bond, *South Africa—The Present as History: From Mrs Ples to Mandela and Marikana* (Rochester, NY: James Currey/Boydell & Brewer, 2014), 176–210.

Boym, Svetlana. *The Future of Nostalgia* (2002; New York: Basic Books, 2002).

Brinkema, Eugenie. *The Forms of the Affects* (Durham, NC: Duke University Press, 2014).

Brooks, Peter. *Reading for the Plot: Design and Intention in Narrative* (New York: Knopf, 1984).

Brown, Wendy. *Undoing the Demos: Neoliberalism's Stealth Revolution* (New York: Zone Books, 2015).

Buck-Morss, Susan. *The Dialectics of Seeing: Walter Benjamin and the Arcades Project* (Cambridge, MA: MIT Press, 1989).

Bunn, David. 'Art Johannesburg and Its Objects', in *Johannesburg: The Elusive Metropolis*, ed. Sarah Nuttall and Achille Mbembe (Durham, NC: Duke University Press, 2008), 137–69.

Burger, Willie. '"Om kommunikasie op gang te kry": Die begin en einde van Marlene van Niekerk se oeuvre', *Journal of Literary Studies* 25.3 (2009), 1–15.

Butler, Judith. *Precarious Life: The Powers of Mourning and Violence* (2004; London and New York: Verso, 2006).

Bybee, Joan, Revere Perkins, and William Pagliuca. *The Evolution of Grammar: Tense, Aspect, and Modality in the Languages of the World* (Chicago and London: University of Chicago Press, 1994).

Carton, Benedict. *Blood from Your Children: The Colonial Origins of Generational Conflict in South Africa* (Charlottesville: University Press of Virginia, 2000).

Caserio, Robert L., Lee Edelman, Judith Halberstam, José Esteban Muñoz, and Tim Dean. 'The Antisocial Thesis in Queer Theory', *PMLA* 121.3 (2006), 819–28.

Clarkson, Carrol. 'Visible and Invisible: What Surfaces in Recent Johannesburg Novels?' *Moving Worlds* 5.1 (2005), 84–97.

Clingman, Stephen. *The Novels of Nadine Gordimer: History from the Inside*, 2nd edn (1992; London: Bloomsbury, 1993).

Coetzee, J.M. 'Alex La Guma and the Responsibilities of the South African Writer', *Journal of the New African Literature and the Arts* 9–10 (September 1971), 5–11.

Coetzee, J.M. 'Speaking J.M. Coetzee', interview by Stephen Watson, *Speak* 1.3 (1978), 21–4.

Coetzee, J.M. 'SA authors must learn modesty', *Die Vaderland*, 1 May 1981, 16.

Coetzee, J.M. 'The Great South African Novel', *Leadership SA* 2.4 (1983), 74–9.

Coetzee, J.M. 'The Novel Today', *Upstream* 6.1 (Summer 1988), 2–5.

Coetzee, J.M. *White Writing: On the Culture of Letters in South Africa* (New Haven: Yale University Press, 1988).

Coetzee, J.M. *Age of Iron* (1990; London: Penguin, 1991).

Coetzee, J.M. *Doubling the Point: Essays and Interviews*, ed. David Attwell (Cambridge, MA: Harvard University Press, 1992).

Coetzee, J.M. 'Homage', *The Threepenny Review* 53 (Spring 1993), 5–7.

Coetzee, J.M. 'Erasmus: Madness and Rivalry', in *Giving Offense: Essays on Censorship* (Chicago: University of Chicago Press, 1996), 83–103.

Coetzee, J.M. *Boyhood: Scenes from Provincial Life* (London: Secker & Warburg, 1997).

Coetzee, J.M. *Disgrace* (London: Secker & Warburg, 1999).

Coetzee, J.M. *Stranger Shores: Essays, 1986–1999* (London: Secker & Warburg, 2001).

Coetzee, J.M. *Youth* (London: Secker & Warburg, 2002).

Coetzee, J.M. *Life & Times of Michael K* (1983; London: Vintage, 2004).

Coetzee, J.M. 'All Autobiography is *Autre*-biography' (2002), Interview with David Attwell, in *Selves in Question: Interviews on Southern African Auto/Biography*, ed. Judith Lütge Coullie, Stephan Meyer, Thengani Ngwenya, and Thomas Olver (Honolulu: University of Hawai'i Press, 2006), 213–17.

Coetzee, J.M. *Slow Man* (2005; London: Vintage, 2006).

Coetzee, J.M. *Diary of a Bad Year* (London: Harvill Secker, 2007).

Coetzee, J.M. *Inner Workings: Literary Essays 2000–2005* (New York: Viking, 2007).

Coetzee, J.M. *Summertime* (London: Harvill Secker, 2009).

Coetzee, J.M. *Scenes from Provincial Life* (London: Harvill Secker, 2011).

Coetzee, J.M. 'Man's Fate in the Novels of Alex La Guma (1974)', in *Doubling the Point*, 344–60.

Coetzee, J.M., and Arabella Kurtz. '"Nevertheless, My Sympathies Are With The Karamazovs": An Email Correspondence: May–December 2008', *Salmagundi* 166/167 (2010), 39–72.

Coetzee, J.M., and Arabella Kurtz. *The Good Story: Exchanges on Truth, Fiction and Psychotherapy* (London: Harvill Secker, 2015).

Colenso, John William. *Langalibalele and the AmaHlubi Tribe. Being Remarks upon the Official Record of the Trials of the Chief, his Sons and Induna, and Other*

Members of the amaHlubi Tribe. By the Bishop of Natal (London: Spottiswoode & Co., 1874).

Comrie, Bernard. *Aspect* (Cambridge: Cambridge University Press, 1976).

Conte, Joseph M. 'Conclusion: Writing Amid the Ruins: 9/11 and *Cosmopolis*', in *The Cambridge Companion to Don DeLillo*, ed. John N. Duvall (Cambridge: Cambridge University Press, 2008), 179–92.

Costello, Diarmuid. 'Aura, Face, Photography: Re-reading Benjamin Today', in *Walter Benjamin and Art*, ed. Andrew E. Benjamin (London and New York: Continuum, 2005), 164–84.

Craib, Ian. *The Importance of Disappointment* (London and New York: Routledge, 1994).

Crapanzano, Vincent. *Waiting: The Whites of South Africa* (1985; London: Paladin, 1986).

Crapanzano, Vincent. *Imaginative Horizons: An Essay in Literary-Philosophical Anthropology* (Chicago: University of Chicago Press, 2010).

Cvetkovich, Ann. *Depression: A Public Feeling* (Durham, NC: Duke University Press, 2012).

Damrosch, David. *What is World Literature?* (Princeton: Princeton University Press, 2003).

De Boever, Arne. *States of Exception in the Contemporary Novel: Martel, Eugenides, Coetzee, Sebald* (New York and London: Continuum, 2012).

De Jager, Nèlleke. 'What every critic should know', *Mail & Guardian*, 4 March 2011, <http://mg.co.za/article/2011-03-04-what-every-critic-should-know>.

De Kock, Leon. 'Found in translation', *Sunday Times*, 28 January 2007, *Lifestyle* supplement, 18.

De Kock, Leon. 'Cracking the Code: Translation as Transgression in *Triomf*', *Journal of Literary Studies* 25.3 (2009), 16–38.

De Kock, Leon. 'Intimate Enemies: A Discussion with Marlene van Niekerk and Michiel Heyns about *Agaat* and its Translation into English', *Journal of Literary Studies* 25.3 (2009), 136–51.

De Vries, Fred. 'Joburg's Ambiguity Mirrored in *Portrait*', Interview with Ivan Vladislavić, *The Weekender*, Weekend Review supplement, 9–10 September 2006, 11.

Dean, Tim. *Unlimited Intimacy: Reflections on the Subculture of Barebacking* (Chicago: University of Chicago Press, 2009).

DeLillo, Don. 'In the Ruins of the Future: Reflections on Terror and Loss in the Shadow of September', *Harper's Magazine* (December 2001), 33–40.

DeLillo, Don. *Cosmopolis* (London: Picador, 2003).

DeLillo, Don. *Falling Man* (New York: Scribner, 2007).

Derrida, Jacques. 'Marx and Sons', trans. Kelly Barry, in *Ghostly Demarcations: A Symposium on Jacques Derrida's Specters of Marx*, ed. Michael Sprinker (London and New York: Verso, 1999), 213–69.

Derrida, Jacques. 'On Cosmopolitanism', trans. Mark Dooley, in *On Cosmopolitanism and Forgiveness* (New York: Routledge, 2001), 3–24.

Derrida, Jacques. *Copy, Archive, Signature: A Conversation on Photography*, trans. Jeff Fort, ed. Gerhard Richter (Stanford: Stanford University Press, 2010).

A Dictionary of South African English on Historical Principles, ed. and compiled Penny Silva and others (Oxford: Oxford University Press, 1996).

Dinshaw, Carolyn, Lee Edelman, Roderick A. Ferguson, Carla Freccero, Elizabeth Freeman, Judith A. Halberstam, Annamarie Jagose, Christopher Nealon, and Nguyen Tan Hoang. 'Theorizing Queer Temporalities: A Roundtable', *GLQ* 13.2–3 (2007), 177–95.

Durrant, Sam. *Postcolonial Narrative and the Work of Mourning: J.M. Coetzee, Wilson Harris, and Toni Morrison* (Albany, NY: SUNY Press, 2004).

Edelman, Lee. *No Future: Queer Theory and the Death Drive* (Durham, NC: Duke University Press, 2004).

Eliot, T.S. *Selected Essays* (London: Faber & Faber, 1932).

Eliot, T.S. *Collected Poems 1909–1962* (1963; London: Faber & Faber, 1974).

Elliott, Jane. *Popular Feminist Fiction as American Allegory: Representing National Time* (London: Palgrave, 2008).

Eng, David L., Judith Halberstam, and José Esteban Muñoz, eds, 'Introduction: What's Queer about Queer Studies Now?' *Social Text* 23.3–4 (2005), 1–17.

England, Frank. 'Imposing Eliot: On Translating *Agaat* by Marlene van Niekerk', *Journal of Literary Studies* 29.1 (2013), 1–19.

Esty, Jed. *Unseasonable Youth: Modernism, Colonialism, and the Fiction of Development* (New York: Oxford University Press, 2012).

Feinstein, Andrew. *After the Party: Corruption, the ANC and South Africa's Uncertain Future* (London and New York: Verso, 2009).

Flanery, Patrick [Denman]. 'At Grandmother's Ford', *Times Literary Supplement*, 7 December 2007, 19–20.

Flanery, Patrick [Denman]. 'Eyes Wide Shut', *The Guardian*, Review supplement, 9 November 2013, 14.

Foucault, Michel. *The Birth of Biopolitics: Lectures at the Collège de France, 1978–79,* trans. Graham Burchell, ed. Michel Senellart (New York: Picador, 2004).

Freeman, Elizabeth. *Time Binds: Queer Temporalities, Queer Histories* (Durham, NC: Duke University Press, 2010).

Freud, Sigmund. *Inhibitions, Symptoms and Anxiety*, trans. James Strachey (New York: Norton 1960).

Freud, Sigmund. *Introductory Lectures on Psychoanalysis*, trans. and ed. James Strachey (New York: Norton, 1960).

Freud, Sigmund. 'Mourning, and Melancholia' (1917), trans. Shaun Whiteside, in *On Murder, Mourning and Melancholia* (London: Penguin, 2005), 201–18.

Friedman. Susan Stanford. 'Periodizing Modernism: Postcolonial Modernities and the Space/Time Borders of Modernist Studies', *Modernism/Modernity* 13.3 (2006), 425–43.

Friedman, Susan Stanford. 'Planetarity: Musing Modernist Studies', *Modernism/Modernity* 17.3 (2010), 471–99.

Fukuyama, Francis. *The End of History and the Last Man* (1992; London: Penguin, 2012).

Gardiner, Michael. 'Wopko Jensma', in *Wopko Jensma: Possessing Tools/Professing Artistry* (Johannesburg: Gallery AOP, 2013), 19–20.

Gaylard, Gerald, ed., *Marginal Spaces: Reading Ivan Vladislavić* (Johannesburg: Wits University Press, 2011).

Geertsema, Johan. 'Coetzee's *Diary of a Bad Year*, Politics, and the Problem of Position', *Twentieth-Century Literature* 57.1 (Spring 2011), 70–85.

Geffen, Nathan. 'Justice After AIDS Denialism: Should There Be Prosecutions and Compensation?', *Journal of Acquired Immune Deficiency Syndrome* 51.4 (2009), 454–5.

Geffen, Nathan. *Debunking Delusions: The Inside Story of the Treatment Action Campaign* (Auckland Park: Jacana Media, 2010).

Gevisser, Mark. *A Legacy of Liberation: Thabo Mbeki and the Future of the South African Dream* (New York: Palgrave Macmillan, 2009).

Gevisser, Mark. *Lost and Found in Johannesburg: A Memoir* (New York: Farrar, Straus and Giroux, 2014).

Goldblatt, David, Ivan Vladislavić, and Marlene van Niekerk. 'Double Exposure', *British Journal of Photography* (May 2011), 44–9.

Gordimer, Nadine. *July's People* (1981; London: Penguin, 1982).

Gordimer, Nadine. *The Essential Gesture*, ed. Stephen Clingman (1988; London: Penguin, 1989).

Gordimer, Nadine. *The House Gun* (1998; London: Bloomsbury, 1999).

Gordimer, Nadine. *No Time Like the Present* (London: Bloomsbury, 2012).

Gordimer, Nadine. *A World of Strangers* (1951; London: Bloomsbury, 2012).

Gordimer, Nadine. 'Gag the mouth and block the ears', *Mail & Guardian*, 18 October 2013 <http://mg.co.za/article/2013-10-28-gag-the-mouth-and-block-the-ears>, accessed 24 July 2014.

Gordimer, Nadine. 'Living in the Interregnum', in *The Essential Gesture*, 261–84.

Gordimer, Nadine, and Stephen Clingman. 'The Future is Another Country', *Transition* 56 (1992), 132–50.

Gqola, Pumla Dineo. '"The difficult task of normalizing freedom": Spectacular Masculinities, Ndebele's Literary Cultural Commentary and Post-Apartheid Life', *English in Africa* 36.1 (2009), 61–76.

Graham, Shane. 'Memory, Memorialization, and the Transformation of Johannesburg: Ivan Vladislavić's *The Restless Supermarket* and *Propaganda by Monuments*', *MFS: Modern Fiction Studies* 53.1 (2007), 71–96.

Grunebaum, Heidi. *Memorializing the Past: Everyday Life after the Truth and Reconciliation Commission* (New Brunswick, NJ: Transaction, 2011).

Halberstam, Judith [Jack]. *The Queer Art of Failure* (Durham, NC: Duke University Press, 2011).

Haraway, Donna. 'A Manifesto for Cyborgs: Science, Technology, and Socialist Feminism in the 1980s (An Ironic Dream of a Common Language for Women in the Integrated Circuit)' (1985), in *The Norton Anthology of Theory and Criticism*, 2nd edn, ed. Vincent B. Leitch et al. (New York: WW Norton, 2010), 2190 220.

Hardy, Thomas. *Tess of the d'Urbervilles* (1891; Oxford: Oxford University Press, 2008).

Hart, Matthew. *Nations of Nothing But Poetry: Modernism, Transnationalism, and Synthetic Vernacular Writing* (New York: Oxford University Press, 2010).

Hayles, N. Katherine. 'Unfinished Work: From Cyborg to Cognisphere', *Theory, Culture & Society* 23.7–8 (2006), 159–66.

Heyns, Michiel. 'Irreparable Loss and Exorbitant Gain: On Translating *Agaat*', *Journal of Literary Studies* 25.3 (2009), 124–35.

Hirson, Denis. *I Remember King Kong (the Boxer)* (Johannesburg: Jacana, 2004).

Hirson, Denis. *White Scars: On Reading and Rites of Passage* (Johannesburg: Jacana, 2006).

Holmes, Chris. 'What the World Leaves Behind: Ready-Made Translations and the "Closed Book" in the Postcolonial Novel', in *Literature, Geography, Translation: Studies in World Writing*, ed. Cecelia Alvstad, Stefan Helgesson, and David Watson (Newcastle upon Tyne: Cambridge Scholars Publishing, 2011), 40–53.

Honwana, Alcinda. 'Youth, Waithood, and Protest Movements in Africa' (International African Institute Lugard Lecture, 2013), *African Arguments*, 12 August 2013 <http://africanarguments.org/2013/08/12/youth-waithood-and-protest-movements-in-africa-by-alcinda-honwana/>.

Hunter, Monica, and Archie Mafeje. *Langa: A Study of Social Groups in an African Township* (Cape Town: Oxford University Press, 1963).

James, David. '*Dusklands* (1974)', in Mehigan, ed., *A Companion to the Works of J.M. Coetzee*, 39–55.

James, David, and Urmila Seshagiri. 'Metamodernism: Narratives of Continuity and Revolution', *PMLA* 129.1 (2014), 87–100.

James, Deborah. *Money from Nothing: Indebtedness and Aspiration in South Africa* (Stanford: Stanford University Press, 2015).

Jameson, Fredric. *A Singular Modernity: Essay on the Ontology of the Present* (London: Verso, 2002).

Jensma, Wopko. *I Must Show You My Clippings* (Johannesburg: Ravan Press, 1977).

Johl, Ronél. 'Oor eindes en beginne: Tyd en ruimte in Ingrid Winterbach se *Die boek van toeval en toeverlaat*', *Stilet* 20.1 (2008), 142–62.

Jones, Megan. 'Conspicuous Destruction, Aspiration and Motion in the South African Township', *Safundi: The Journal of South African and American Studies* 14.2 (2013), 209–24.

Jones, Megan. 'Township Textualities', *Alternation* 20.1 (2013), 26–51.

Kauffman, Linda S. 'Bodies in Rest and Motion in *Falling Man*', in *Don DeLillo:* Mao II/Underworld/Falling Man, ed. Stacey Olster (London and New York: Continuum, 2011), 135–51.

Kermode, Frank. *The Sense of an Ending* (New York: Oxford University Press, 1967).

Kierkegaard, Søren. *The Concept of Anxiety: A Simple Psychologically Orienting Deliberation on the Dogmatic Issue of Hereditary Sin* (1844), ed. and trans. Reidar Thomte (Princeton: Princeton University Press, 1980).

Kierkegaard, Søren. *Fear and Trembling, and Repetition*, trans. H.V. and E.H. Hong (Princeton: Princeton University Press, 1983).

Kossew, Sue. '*Scenes from Provincial Life* (1997–2009)', in Mehigan, ed., *A Companion to the Works of J.M. Coetzee*, 9–22.

Kruger, Loren. *The Drama of South Africa: Plays, Pageants and Publics since 1910* (New York: Routledge, 1999).

Lambert, John. 'Chiefship in Early Colonial Natal, 1843–1879', *Journal of Southern African Studies* 21.2 (1995), 269–85.

Law-Viljoen, Bronwyn. 'Make-believe is Easier to Catch than Truth-telling', *Art South Africa* 9.2 (Summer 2010), 69.

Law-Viljoen, Bronwyn. 'Interview with David Goldblatt and Ivan Vladislavić', in Gaylard, ed., *Marginal Spaces*, 340–57.

Lazarus, Neil. 'South African Ideology: The Myth of Exceptionalism, the Idea of Renaissance', *South Atlantic Quarterly* 103.4 (2004), 607–28.

Lekgowa, Thapelo, and Greg Nicolson. 'Marikana: Malema's 2014 battle begins', *The Daily Maverick*, 14 October 2013 <http://www.dailymaverick.co.za/article/2013-10-14-marikana-malemas-2014-battle-begins/#.Ul_P5RbIaCQ>, accessed 17 October 2013.

Lenta, Margaret. '*Autre*biography: J.M. Coetzee's *Boyhood* and *Youth*', *English in Africa* 30.1 (2003), 157–69.

Lenta, Patrick. '"Everyday Abnormality": Crime and In/security in Ivan Vladislavić's *Portrait with Keys*', *Journal of Commonwealth Literature* 44.1 (2009), 117–33.

Levinas, Emmanuel. *Totality and Infinity* (1961), trans. Alphonso Lingis (1969; Dordrecht: Kluwer, 1991).

Levinas, Emmanuel. 'Is Ontology Fundamental?' in *Basic Philosophical Writings*, ed. Adriaan T. Peperzak, Simon Critchley, and Robert Bernasconi (Bloomington: Indiana University Press, 1996), 1–10.

Levitas, Ruth. 'Educated Hope: Ernst Bloch on Abstract and Concrete Utopia', in *Not Yet: Reconsidering Ernst Bloch*, ed. Jamie Owen Daniel and Tom Moylan (London and New York: Verso, 1997), 65–79.

Loots, Sonja. 'Nog in die kielsog', *Rapport, Perspektief*, 28 November 2004, IV.

Love, Heather. *Feeling Backward: Loss and the Politics of Queer History* (Cambridge, MA: Harvard University Press, 2007).

Lukács, György. *The Theory of the Novel: A Historico-Philosophical Essay on the Forms of Great Epic Literature* (1916), trans. Anna Bostock (Cambridge, MA: MIT Press, 1971).

Magaziner, Daniel, and Sean Jacobs. 'The End of South African Exceptionalism', *The Atlantic*, 27 August 2012 <http://www.theatlantic.com/international/archive/2012/08/the-end-of-south-african-exceptionalism/261591/>.

Magona, Sindiwe. 'The More Things Change', in *Letter to South Africa: Poets Calling the State to Order* (Cape Town: Umuzi, 2011), 101–4.

Mahlangu, Songeziwe. *Penumbra* (Cape Town: Kwela, 2013).

Majumdar, Saikat. *Prose of the World: Modernism and the Banality of Empire* (New York: Columbia University Press, 2013).

Malala, Justice. 'Nadine Gordimer used last interview to condemn South Africa's secrecy bill', *The Guardian*, 14 July 2014, <http://www.theguardian.com/

world/2014/jul/14/nadine-gordimer-south-africa-secrecy-bill>, accessed 4 July 2014.

Mao, Douglas, and Rebecca L. Walkowitz, eds, 'Introduction: Modernisms Bad and New', *Bad Modernisms* (Durham, NC: Duke University Press, 2006), 1–18.

Marais, Mike. 'Visions of Excess: Closure, Irony, and the Thought of Community in Ivan Vladislavić's *The Restless Supermarket*', *English in Africa* 29.2 (October 2002), 101–17.

Marais, Mike, and Carita Backström. 'An Interview with Ivan Vladislavić', *English in Africa* 29.2 (October 2002), 119–28.

Massumi, Brian. 'Perception Attack: The Force to Own Time', in *Theory After 'Theory'*, ed. Jane Elliott and Derek Attridge (Abingdon: Routledge, 2011), 75–89.

Matebeni, Zethu. 'Blissful Complexities: Black Lesbians Reflect on Same-sex Marriage and the Civil Union Act', in *To Have and to Hold: The Making of Same-sex Marriage in South Africa*, ed. Melanie Judge, Anthony Manion, and Shaun de Waal (Auckland Park: Fanele, 2008), 249–57.

Mbali, Mandisa. *South African AIDS Activism and Global Health Politics* (New York: Palgrave Macmillan, 2013).

Mbembe, Achille. *On the Postcolony* (Berkeley, Los Angeles, London: University of California Press, 2001).

Mbembe, Achille, 'Achille Mbembe on The State of South African Political Life', *Africa in Words*, 19 September 2015, <http://africasacountry.com/2015/09/achille-mbembe-on-the-state-of-south-african-politics/>, accessed 1 May 2016.

McDonald, Peter D. *The Literature Police: Apartheid Censorship and its Cultural Consequences* (Oxford: Oxford University Press, 2009).

Medalie, David. 'The Uses of Nostalgia', *English Studies in Africa* 53.1 (May 2010), 35–44.

Mehigan, Tim, ed., *A Companion to the Works of J.M. Coetzee* (Rochester, NY: Boydell & Brewer, 2011).

Meyer, Stephan, and Thomas Olver. 'Zoë Wicomb Interviewed on Writing and Nation', *Journal of Literary Studies* 18.1 (2002), 182–98.

Miyazaki, Hirokazu. *The Method of Hope: Anthropology, Philosophy, and Fijian Knowledge* (Stanford: Stanford University Press, 2004).

Moretti, Franco. *The Way of the World: The* Bildungsroman *in European Culture* (1987), trans. Albert Spragia (London and New York: Verso, 2000).

Mukherjee, Siddharta. *The Emperor of All Maladies: A Biography of Cancer* (2010; London: Fourth Estate, 2011).

Mulgrew, Nick. 'Getting under the skin of the new SA with Masande Ntshanga', *Mail & Guardian*, 21 November 2014 <http://mg.co.za/article/2014-11-21-under-the-skin-of-the-new-sa>.

Muñoz, José Esteban. *Cruising Utopia: The Then and There of Queer Futurity* (New York: New York University Press, 2009).

Munro, Brenna. 'Queer Family Romance: Writing the "New" South Africa in the 1990s', *GLQ: A Journal of Lesbian and Gay Studies* 15.3 (2009), 397–439.

Munro, Brenna. *South Africa and the Dream of Love to Come: Queer Sexuality and the Struggle for Freedom* (Minneapolis: University of Minnesota Press, 2012).

Munro, Brenna. 'Nelson, Winnie, and the Politics of Gender', in *The Cambridge Companion to Nelson Mandela*, ed. Rita Barnard (Cambridge: Cambridge University Press, 2014), 92–112.

Naudé, S.J. *The Alphabet of Birds* (2011; London: And Other Stories, 2015).

Ndebele, Njabulo. *The Cry of Winnie Mandela* (2003; Banbury: Ayebia Clarke, 2004).

Neilson, Brett, and Ned Rossiter. 'Precarity as a Political Concept, or, Fordism as Exception', *Theory, Culture & Society* 25.7–8 (2008), 51–72.

Ngai, Sianne. *Ugly Feelings* (Cambridge, MA: Harvard University Press, 2005).

Nkosi, Lewis. *Home and Exile and Other Selections* (London: Longman, 1983).

Ntshanga, Masande. *The Reactive* (Cape Town: Umuzi, 2014).

Nuttall, Sarah. *Entanglement: Literary and Cultural Reflections on Post-Apartheid* (Johannesburg: Wits University Press, 2009).

Nuttall, Sarah. 'The Invisible City: Surface and Underneath in *Portrait with Keys*', in Gaylard, ed., *Marginal Spaces*, 327–37.

Nzimande, Blade. 'What is the National Democratic Revolution?', *Umsebenzi* 5.66 (18 October 2006) <http://www.sacp.org.za/main.php?ID=1850#redpen>, accessed 21 August 2014.

O'Gorman, Marcel. 'Bernard Stiegler's *Pharmacy*: A Conversation', *Configurations* 18 (2010), 459–76.

Opperman, D.J., ed., *Groot Verseboek: 'n Bloemlesing uit die Afrikaanse Poësie* (Kaapstad, Bloemfontein, Johannesburg: Nasionale Boekhandel, 1951).

Osteen, Mark. *American Magic and Dread: Don DeLillo's Dialogue with Culture* (Philadelphia: University of Pennsylvania Press, 2000).

Perez, Hiram. 'You Can Have My Brown Body and Eat It, Too!', *Social Text* 23.3–4 (2005), 171–91.

Permanent Secretary, The Swedish Academy, 'Nobel Prize in Literature 1991—Press Release', *Nobelprize.org*, 3 October 1991 <http://www.nobelprize.org/nobel_prizes/literature/laureates/1991/press.html>, accessed 24 July 2014.

Peters, J.C. 'The Missng [sic] "i": Corrigenda in Ivan Vladislavić's Second Edition of *The Restless Supermarket*', *English in Africa* 36.2 (2009), 45–62.

Plaice, Neville. 'Translators' Introduction', in Ernst Bloch, *The Principle of Hope*, xix–xxxii.

Plomer, William. *Turbott Wolfe* (London: Hogarth, 1925).

Popescu, Monica. *South African Literature Beyond the Cold War* (New York: Palgrave Macmillan, 2010).

Rainey, Lawrence, David Attwell, and Benjamin Madden, 'An Interview with J.M. Coetzee', *Modernism/Modernity* 18.4 (2012), 847–53.

Reich, Wilhelm. *Reich Speaks of Freud*, ed. Mary Higgins and Chester M. Raphael (New York: Farrar, Straus and Giroux, 1967).

Rezzori, Gregor von. 'Memoirs of an Anti Semite', *The New Yorker*, 26 April 1969, 42–83.

Rezzori, Gregor von. *Memoiren eines Antisemiten* (München: Verlag Steinhausen GmbH, 1979).

Rezzori, Gregor von. *The Snows of Yesteryear*, trans. H.F. Broch de Rothermann (New York: Knopf, 1989).

Rezzori, Gregor von. *Memoirs of an Anti-Semite*, trans. Joachim Neugroschel and Gregor von Rezzori (1981; New York: New York Review of Books, 2008).

Ricoeur, Paul. 'Narrative Time', in *On Narrative*, ed. W.J.T. Mitchell (Chicago: University of Chicago Press, 1981), 165–86.

Robinson, David. 'Under the Skin of Lies', *The Scotsman*, Saturday Critique, 27 May 2006, 20.

Robinson, Marilynne. *Home* (London: Virago, 2008).

Romain, Trevor. *Random Kak I Remember about Growing Up in South Africa* (Johannesburg: Penguin South Africa, 2013).

Rorty, Richard. *Contingency, Irony, and Solidarity* (Cambridge: Cambridge University Press, 1989).

Saint-Amour, Paul K. *Tense Future: Modernism, Total War, Encyclopedic Form* (Oxford: Oxford University Press, 2015).

Samolsky, Russell. *Apocalyptic Futures: Marked Bodies and the Violence of the Text in Kafka, Conrad, and Coetzee* (New York: Fordham University Press, 2011).

Sanders, Mark. *Ambiguities of Witnessing: Law and Literature in the Time of a Truth Commission* (Stanford: Stanford University Press, 2007).

Sanders, Mark. 'Miscegenations: Race, Culture, Phantasy', *Journal of the Association for the Study of Australian Literature* (2008), 10–36.

SAPA. 'EFF launches in Marikana', *The Sowetan*, 14 October 2013 <http://www.sowetanlive.co.za/news/2013/10/14/eff-launches-in-marikana>, accessed 17 October 2013.

Schweighauser, Philipp, and Adrian S. Wisnicki. 'The End of Resolution? Reflections on the Ethics of Closure in Don DeLillo's Detective Plots', in *Terrorism, Media, and the Ethics of Fiction: Transatlantic Perspectives on Don DeLillo*, ed. Peter Schneck and Philipp Schweighauser (London: Bloomsbury, 2012), 158–70.

Scott, David. *Conscripts of Modernity: The Tragedy of Colonial Enlightenment* (Durham, NC: Duke University Press, 2004).

Scott, David. 'Tragedy's Future: Postemancipation Futures Past and Present', in *Rethinking Tragedy*, ed. Rita Felski (Baltimore: Johns Hopkins University Press, 2008), 199–217.

Scott, David. *Omens of Adversity: Tragedy, Time, Memory, Justice* (Durham, NC: Duke University Press, 2014).

Sedgwick, Eve Kosofsky. 'Paranoid Reading and Reparative Reading; or, You're So Vain, You Probably Think This Introduction Is About You', in *Novel Gazing: Queer Readings in Fiction*, ed. Eve Kosofsky Sedgwick (Durham, NC: Duke University Press, 1997), 1–37.

Sheehan, Paul. 'The Disasters of *Youth*: Coetzee and Geomodernism', *Twentieth-Century Literature* 57.1 (Spring 2011), 20–33.

Singley, Carol J. *Adopting America: Childhood, Kinship, and National Identity in Literature* (New York: Oxford University Press, 2011).

Slaughter, Joseph. *Human Rights, Inc.* (New York: Fordham University Press, 2007).

Smith, Tymon. 'Double Positive', *Sunday Times*, Lifestyle, 12 June 2011, 33.

Snaith, Anna. *Modernist Voyages: Colonial Women Writers in London, 1890–1945* (New York: Cambridge University Press, 2014).

Snediker, Michael D. *Queer Optimism: Lyric Personhood and Other Felicitous Persuasions* (Minneapolis: University of Minnesota Press, 2009).

Sontag, Susan. *Illness as Metaphor* (1977), reprinted in *Illness as Metaphor* and *AIDS and Its Metaphors* (London: Penguin, 1991), 1–87.

Southall, Roger. *The New Black Middle Class in South Africa* (Johannesburg: Jacana, 2016).

Spencer, Lynda. 'Young, Black and Female in Post-apartheid South Africa: Identity Politics in Kopano Matlwa's *Coconut*', *Scrutiny2: Issues in English Studies in Southern Africa* 14.1 (2009), 66–78.

Stewart, Susan. *On Longing: Narratives of the Miniature, the Gigantic, the Souvenir, the Collection* (1984; Durham, NC: Duke University Press, 1993).

Steyn, Melissa. '"The Creed of the White Kid": A Diss-Apology,' in *The Handbook of Critical Intercultural Communication*, ed. Thomas K. Nakayama and Rona Tamiko Halualani (Malden, MA and Oxford: Blackwell, 2010), 534–48.

Stiegler, Bernard. *Technics and Time 1: The Fault of Epimetheus* (1994), trans. Richard Beardsworth and George Collins (Stanford: Stanford University Press, 1998).

Stiegler, Bernard. *Technics and Time 2: Disorientation* (1996), trans. Stephen Barker (Stanford: Stanford University Press, 2009).

Stiegler, Bernard. *Technics and Time 3: Cinematic Time and the Question of Malaise* (2001), trans. Stephen Barker (Stanford: Stanford University Press, 2011).

Su, John J. 'Epic of Failure: Disappointment as Utopian Fantasy in *Midnight's Children*', *Twentieth Century Literature* 47.4 (2001), 545–68.

Svendsen, Lars. *A Philosophy of Boredom* (1999), trans. John Irons (London: Reaktion, 2005).

Swart, Heidi. 'Platinum wealth holds no shine for people left in the dust', *Mail & Guardian*, 28 June 2012 <http://mg.co.za/article/2012-06-28-platinum-wealth-holds-no-shine-for-people-left-living-in-the-dust>.

Taylor, Catherine. *Apart* (Brooklyn: Ugly Duckling Press, 2012).

Thurschwell, Adam. 'Writing and Terror: Don DeLillo on the Task of Literature After 9/11', *Law and Literature* 19.2 (2007), 277–302.

Tiedemann, Rolf. 'Historical Materialism or Political Messianism? An Interpretation of the Theses "On the Concept of History"', in *Benjamin: Philosophy, Aesthetics, History*, ed. Gary Smith (Chicago: University of Chicago Press, 1989), 175–209.

Titlestad, Michael. 'The pitfalls of the literary debut', *Sunday Times*, 25 March 2007, 37.

Truscott, Ross. 'National Melancholia and Afrikaner Self-parody in Post-apartheid South Africa', *Psychoanalysis, Culture & Society* 16.1 (2011), 90–106.

Tucker, Andrew. *Queer Visibilities: Space, Identity and Interaction in Cape Town* (Malden, MA and Oxford: Wiley-Blackwell, 2009).

Van der Vlies, Andrew. *South African Textual Cultures: White, Black, Read All Over* (Manchester: Manchester University Press, 2007).

Van der Vlies, Andrew. 'An Interview with Jeremy Cronin', *Contemporary Literature* 49.4 (2008), 514–39.

Van der Vlies, Andrew. 'The Archive, the Spectral, and Narrative Responsibility in Zoë Wicomb's *Playing in the Light*', *Journal of Southern African Studies* 36.3 (2010), 583–98.

Van der Vlies, Andrew. '"I'm only grateful that it's not a Cape Town book", or Zoë Wicomb, Textuality, Propriety, and the Proprietary', *Journal of Commonwealth Literature* 48.1 (2013), 9–25.

Van der Vlies, Andrew. 'Response: The People, the Multitude and the Costs of Privacy in South Africa's Postcolony', *Cultural Studies* 27.3 (2013), 496–518.

Van der Vlies, Andrew. '"[*From*] whom this writing then?": Politics, Aesthetics and the Personal in Coetzee's *Age of Iron*', in *Approaches to Teaching Coetzee's* Disgrace *and Other Works*, ed. Laura Wright, Elleke Boehmer, and Jane Poyner (New York: MLA, 2014), 96–104.

Van der Vlies, Andrew. '"MêME DYING STOP CONFIRM ARRIVAL STOP": Provincial Literatures in Global Time: The Case of Marlene van Niekerk's *Agaat*', in *Institutions of World Literature: Writing, Translation, Markets,* ed. Pieter Vermeulen and Stefan Helgesson (London and New York: Routledge, 2015), 191–208.

Van Niekerk, Marlene. *Triomf* (Cape Town: Queillerie, 1994).

Van Niekerk, Marlene. *Triomf*, trans. Leon de Kock (1999; London: Abacus, 2000).

Van Niekerk, Marlene. *Agaat* (Cape Town: Tafelberg, 2004).

Van Niekerk, Marlene. *Agaat*, trans. Michiel Heyns (Jeppestown: Jonathan Ball, Cape Town: Tafelberg, 2006).

Van Niekerk, Marlene. *The Way of the Women*, trans. Michiel Heyns (London: Little, Brown, 2007).

Van Niekerk, Marlene. *Agaat*, trans. Riet de Jong-Goossens (2006; Amsterdam: Querido, 2010).

Van Niekerk, Marlene. *Agaat*, trans. Niclas Hval (Stockholm: Svante Weyler, 2012).

Van Vuuren, Helize. '"Alles vloei en niks hou stand": 'n Verkenning van Ingrid Winterbach se *Die boek van toeval en toeverlaat*', *Stilet* 20.1 (2008), 163–76.

Varsava, Jerry A. 'The "Saturated Self": Don DeLillo on the Problem of Rogue Capitalism', *Contemporary Literature* 46.1 (2005), 78–107.

Venuti, Lawrence. *The Translator's Invisibility: A History of Translation*, 2nd edn (Abingdon: Routledge, 2008).

Vladislavić, Ivan. 'Propaganda by Monuments', in *Propaganda by Monuments and Other Stories* (Cape Town and Johannesburg: David Philip, 1996), 13–38.

Vladislavić, Ivan. 'Street addresses, Johannesburg', in *blank_Architecture, apartheid and after*, ed. Ivan Vladislavić and Hilton Judin (Rotterdam: Netherlands Art Institute, 1998), E11.

Vladislavić, Ivan. 'An Accidental Island (Street Addresses, Johannesburg, Second Cycle)', in David Goldblatt, *fifty-one years* (Barcelona: Museu d'Art Contemporani de Barcelona, 2001), 383–405.

Vladislavić, Ivan. *The Restless Supermarket* (Cape Town: David Philip, 2001).

Vladislavić, Ivan. *Willem Boshoff* (Houghton: David Krut, 2005).

Vladislavić, Ivan. *Portrait with Keys: The City of Johannesburg Unlocked* (London: Portobello, 2006).

Vladislavić, Ivan. 'Modderfontein Road', *Home Lands—Land Marks: Contemporary Art from South Africa*, ed. Tamar Garb (London: Haunch of Venison, 2008), 154–61.

Vladislavić, Ivan. *Double Negative* (Rome: Contrasto, 2010).

Vladislavić, Ivan. *The Loss Library and Other Unfinished Stories* (London, New York, Calcutta: Seagull Books, 2012).

Vladislavić, Ivan, and David Goldblatt. 'Posers', *Sunday Times*, Life*style*/Culture, 26 September 2010, 12–13.

Walkowitz, Rebecca L. 'Unimagineable Largeness: Kazuo Ishiguro, Translation, and the New World Literature', *Novel: A Forum on Fiction* 40.3 (2007), 216–39.

Ware, Owen. 'Dialectics of the Past/Disjuncture of the Future: Derrida and Benjamin on the Concept of Messianism', *Journal for Cultural and Religious Theory* 5.2 (April 2004), 99–114.

Warner, Michael, ed., 'Introduction', in *Fear of a Queer Planet: Queer Politics and Social Theory* (Minneapolis: University of Minnesota Press, 1993), vii–xxxi.

Warnes, Christopher. 'Interview with Ivan Vladislavić', *MFS: Modern Fiction Studies* 45.1 (Spring 2000), 273–81.

Watson, Stephen. 'Colonialism and the Novels of J.M. Coetzee', *Research in African Literatures* 17.3 (Autumn 1986), 370–92.

Wenzel, Jennifer. *Bulletproof: Afterlives of Anticolonial Prophecy in South Africa and Beyond* (Chicago: University of Chicago Press, 2009).

White, Hylton. 'A Post-Fordist Ethnicity: Insecurity, Authority, and Identity in South Africa', *Anthropological Quarterly* 85.2 (2012), 397–428.

Wicomb, Zoë. *You Can't Get Lost in Cape Town* (London: Virago Press, 1987).

Wicomb, Zoë. 'To Hear the Variety of Discourses', *Current Writing* 2 (1990), 35–44.

Wicomb, Zoë. *David's Story* (New York: Feminist Press at CUNY, 2000).

Wicomb, Zoë. 'Interview: Zoë Wicomb in Conversation with Hein Willemse', *Research in African Literatures* 33.1 (Spring 2002), 144–52.

Wicomb, Zoë. 'Translations in the Yard of Africa', *Journal of Literary Studies* 18.3 (2002), 209–23.

Wicomb, Zoë. 'Setting, Intertextuality and the Resurrection of the Postcolonial Author', *Journal of Postcolonial Writing* 41.2 (2005), 144–55.

Wicomb, Zoë. *Playing in the Light* (New York: New Press, 2006).

Wicomb, Zoë. 'Boy in a Jute-Sack Hood', *Antigonish Review* (Summer 2007), 17–25.

Wicomb, Zoë. *The One That Got Away* (Roggebaai: Umuzi, 2008).

Wicomb, Zoë. 'In Search of Tommie', *Wasafiri* 24.3 (2009), 51–5.

Wicomb, Zoë. '*Slow Man* and the Real: A Lesson in Reading and Writing', *Journal of Literary Studies* 25.4 (2009), 7–24.

Wicomb, Zoë. *October* (New York: New Press, 2014).

Wicomb, Zoë. 'Shame and Identity: The Case of the coloured in South Africa', in Attridge and Jolly, eds, *Writing South Africa*, 91–107.

Williams, Raymond. *Modern Tragedy* (London: Chatto & Windus, 1966).

Williams, Raymond. *Marxism and Literature* (Oxford: Oxford University Press, 1977).

Winterbach, Ingrid. *Die boek van toeval en toeverlaat* (Cape Town: Human & Rousseau, 2006).

Winterbach, Ingrid. *Die benederyk* (Cape Town: Human & Rousseau, 2010).

Winterbach, Ingrid. *The Book of Happenstance*, trans. Dirk and Ingrid Winterbach (2008; Rochester, NY: Open Letter, 2011).

Winterbach, Ingrid. *Die aanspraak van lewende wesens* (Cape Town: Human & Rousseau, 2012).

Winterbach, Ingrid. *The Road of Excess*, trans. Leon de Kock (Cape Town: Human & Rousseau, 2014).

Winterbach, Ingrid. *It Might Get Loud*, trans. Michiel Heyns (Cape Town: Human & Rousseau, 2015).

Worby, Eric, and Shireen Ally. 'The Disappointment of Nostalgia: Conceptualising Cultures of Memory in Contemporary South Africa', *Social Dynamics* 39.3 (2013), 457–80.

Index